C000109321

PAUL MICHAEL GARRETT

WELFARE WORDS

CRITICAL SOCIAL WORK & SOCIAL POLICY

Los Angeles | London | New Delhi
Singapore | Washington DC | Melbourne

Los Angeles | London | New Delhi
Singapore | Washington DC | Melbourne

SAGE Publications Ltd
1 Oliver's Yard
55 City Road
London EC1Y 1SP

SAGE Publications Inc.
2455 Teller Road
Thousand Oaks, California 91320

SAGE Publications India Pvt Ltd
B 1/I 1 Mohan Cooperative Industrial Area
Mathura Road
New Delhi 110 044

SAGE Publications Asia-Pacific Pte Ltd
3 Church Street
#10-04 Samsung Hub
Singapore 049483

Editor: Natalie Aguilera
Editorial assistant: Delayna Spencer
Production editor: Katherine Haw
Copyeditor: Elaine Leek
Indexer: Charmian Parkin
Marketing manager: Susheel Gokarakonda
Cover design: Tristan Tutak
Typeset by: C&M Digitals (P) Ltd, Chennai, India
Printed in the UK

© Paul Michael Garrett 2018

First published 2018

Apart from any fair dealing for the purposes of research or private study, or criticism or review, as permitted under the Copyright, Designs and Patents Act, 1988, this publication may be reproduced, stored or transmitted in any form, or by any means, only with the prior permission in writing of the publishers, or in the case of reprographic reproduction, in accordance with the terms of licences issued by the Copyright Licensing Agency. Enquiries concerning reproduction outside those terms should be sent to the publishers.

Library of Congress Control Number: 2017940490

British Library Cataloguing in Publication data

A catalogue record for this book is available from the British Library

ISBN 978-1-4739-6896-7
ISBN 978-1-4739-6897-4 (pbk)

At SAGE we take sustainability seriously. Most of our products are printed in the UK using FSC papers and boards. When we print overseas we ensure sustainable papers are used as measured by the PREPS grading system. We undertake an annual audit to monitor our sustainability.

CONTENTS

'Rigorous, meticulously researched and edgy, Garrett's new book seeks to understand the ideology underlying welfare words and by doing so, exposes the power and oppression operating through them. Read this book; it is the antidote to those who say that social work cannot be both a deeply intellectual and social justice-engaged endeavour'.

Donna Baines, University of Sydney, Australia

'This is an engaging and engaged revisiting of the cultural excavation of "keywords" pioneered by Raymond Williams. Garrett presents an impassioned and thorough dissection of some of the most important "keywords" of our time, the highly coded lexicon of so-called welfare reform. What you will learn about the histories of containment and struggle sedimented within each term will enrage and energise – get reading, get angry, get ready'.

Gargi Bhattacharyya, University of East London, England

'Paul Michael Garrett's important new book highlights the power of language when it comes to social welfare. Focusing on some of the most crucial keywords of welfare discourse in the neoliberal era, he plots their politics, illuminating their complicity in enacting disciplinary practices of client subordination, but also how their incompleteness leaves an opening for resistance and revision. His politically engaged linguistic interventions help us think about how to take steps toward less oppressive and more affirmative forms of service provision. This is a must read for social workers and social theorists alike, especially if they are interested in moving beyond the strictures of neoliberalism's oppressive disciplinary regime'.

Sanford F. Schram, Hunter College, City University of New York (CUNY), United States

'Paul Michael Garrett's *Welfare Words* takes a modern, fresh look at the language of welfare. He calls upon the reader to re-visit the impact of language upon welfare choices and interventions and in doing so makes an accessible and relevant call to arms to challenge inequality and social exclusion. This book will be the go-to text for students of social work and social policy for many years to come. It is an outstanding text and highly recommended'.

Lel Meleyal, University of Sussex, England

'A must-read for critical social policy theorists but also for anyone alarmed at how neoliberal capitalism has stigmatized every aspect of social rights. Garrett's lens of analysis of welfare keywords – dependency, underclass, social exclusion, resilience – brings out sharply how neoliberal language stereotypes and marginalizes working class people and steers deep social problems into the woefully inadequate channels of individualism. *Welfare Words* provides a timely counter-voice to the neoliberal policies which have devastated our post-austerity world'.

Marnie Holborow, Dublin City University, Republic of Ireland

'This is an original and insightful book, which offers us a fresh perspective on some of the key themes and challenges in social work. It will prompt new thinking and provide practitioners with important critical tools to support their interventions'.

Roger S. Smith, University of Durham, England

'Paul Michael Garrett provides an illuminating analysis of key terms that proliferate within contemporary welfare and political discourse. He examines each term in detail, exploring the origins, meanings and contradictions of each and perceptively shows the way they are used, and misused, within today's political and welfare system. This book is essential reading for those wishing to understand the complexities behind terms that are not only ubiquitous within the political realm but which have also entered common discourse'.

Ken McLaughlin, Senior Lecturer, Manchester Metropolitan University, England

'Garrett's book offers a comprehensive approach to the study of Social policy in social work, encouraging readers to think critically about key words in their wider historical, political and cultural context. Drawing on an innovative conceptual lens in which to view social welfare, this is a key text for critical social work and social policy'.

Karen Roscoe, Senior Lecturer, University of Wolverhampton, England

ABOUT THE AUTHOR

For several years, Paul Michael Garrett has been a member of the *Critical Social Policy* collective and the editorial board of the *European Journal of Social Work*. His interventions have appeared in academic journals across a range of disciplines and he is the author of the acclaimed *Social Work and Social Theory* (Policy Press, 2013) which was also published in Chinese translation. In addition, he wrote three books mapping facets of social work with children and families during the period of New Labour (1997–2010) in the UK: *Remaking Social Work with Children and Families* (Routledge, 2003); *Social Work with Irish Children and Families in Britain* (Policy Press, 2004); *'Transforming' Children's Services? Social Work, Neoliberalism and the 'Modern' World* (Open University/McGraw Hill, 2009). He is also one of the founders of the Social Work Action Network (SWAN) Ireland.

ACKNOWLEDGEMENTS

I am very grateful to a number people who helped me bring this book to fruition. All the anonymous peer reviewers made very helpful suggestions. Doubtless squeezed on top of all the other – frequently unnecessary – demands which scholars have to respond to within neoliberal university settings, their time-consuming reading of the draft manuscript was scrupulously diligent and critically insightful. This is my first book project for SAGE, and Delayna Spencer was always swiftly responsive to my queries and it was lovely to work with her. I am also grateful to Natalie Aguilera, Katherine Haw, Elaine Leek and Susheel Gokarakonda.

A number of ideas featured in *Welfare Words* were initially tested out at international conferences. My engagement with the work of Raymond Williams was shaped in keynote papers I presented at conferences at Ghent University and the University of Chester in 2015. I thank Rudi Roose and Griet Roets and Karen Roscoe for issuing the invitations. In 2016, a paper I was asked to contribute on social work and neoliberalism at the University of Trondheim in Norway also aided me in grappling with some of the book's core concerns and thematic preoccupations. In this context, Edgar Marthinsen, Anne Juberg and Nina Schiøll Skjefstad deserve my thanks. Chapter 9, on child adoption, is mostly derived from the keynote address I gave at the annual TiSSA conference in Ghent in 2016 and here again I would like to thank Rudi and Griet and also Jochen Devlieghere. At all of these conferences, I found the contributions from conference participants, on some of my emerging thoughts, very helpful. Thank you.

As this project neared completion, I became involved in fascinating discussions in relation to the book's themes with Chinese academic colleagues and students. This followed my being invited to lead a series of workshops and give a keynote paper at a symposium on Social Work and Social Theory at the East China University of Science and Technology in Shanghai. I am grateful to Professor He Xuesong for inviting me and for being, along with many others, so hospitable. In summer 2017, Nino Žganec, Robert Bergougnan and Teresa Bertotti asked me to contribute a plenary paper, on 'social work education, disruptive thinking and welfare words', at the European Association of Schools of Social Work (EASSW) conference at the Paris Descartes University. Pervaded by a sense of sorrow and anger following the Grenfell

Tower fire occurring days before, this was still a remarkably successful event and it helped to generate more European conversations on the topic of 'welfare words'.

Closer to home, particular individuals were constantly supportive even though some of them probably do not realise how supportive they actually are. Escaping the icy waters of egotistical calculation, friends on the SIPTU Stewards' Committee at NUI Galway and those associated with the Social Work Action Network (SWAN) sustain vital enclaves of solidarity. As with my other books, Paddy McDonagh provided much of the soundtrack for writing. As well as this, and much more importantly, he formed a key part of the mass movement opposing privatisation and the imposition of water charges in Ireland. Important too are the 'keepers of the castle' at the NUI Galway: Liam Frehan, Frank Darcy, Brian Bredin, Gerry Thornton, Mary Gleeson, Ray Conlon, Martin Maloney, Sinead McGee and Paraic Cahill. I am, of course, also grateful to all the students participating in the courses I have taught that relate to some of the preoccupations in *Welfare Words*. *Go raibh maith agat.*

My main thanks I extend to Valeria Ballarotti who read the manuscript in various forms and suggested a range of changes to aid clarity. I am entirely responsible for any incoherence, errors or outbreaks of rampant foolishness.

Paul Michael Garrett
Galway, July 2017

CHAPTER 1

INTRODUCTION

INTRODUCTION

In late 2016, the Irish Health Services Executive (HSE) issued a memo advising nursing staff to remove 'trespassing' patients who refused to surrender their beds from overcrowded and crisis-ridden hospitals (Cullen, 2016). The movement from 'patient' to 'trespasser' provided an example of not only a discursive shift, in that HSE legal advisors stated that nurses could deploy 'minimum force' in such instances to remove a 'trespasser' refusing to leave a bed once deemed clinically well enough to do so. The nursing unions refused to comply with this new protocol, there was public consternation and the senior managers were compelled to apologise for the controversial memo.

The incident highlights the significance of the use of words within social and health care and the differing practices that they often seek to trigger, promote and embed. This book will specifically examine what I am choosing to call 'welfare words'. Stretching beyond issues simply relating to income maintenance, these are 'welfare dependency', 'underclass', 'social exclusion', 'early intervention', 'resilience', 'care' and 'adoption'[1]. This project is partly rooted in a course I have taught for a number of years and my perspective has been enhanced by having the opportunity to engage with students located in social work, sociology, social policy and politics. Some of the words to be explored are also commonplace on a range of other courses, including those concerned with criminal justice, urban policy, education, health and health promotion etc. As well as the general reader, I hope *Welfare Words* might also attract final year undergraduate and postgraduate students in a range of other spheres and disciplines. In this context, I include a short 'Further Reading' section at the culmination of the first nine chapters. Influenced by my conversation-driven pedagogy, I also insert a series of 'Reflection and Talk Boxes' which, across nine chapters, have twenty questions. The aim of this device (which can be skipped if it is not to the taste of particular readers) is to stimulate critical conversations and debates on key facets of the preceding chapter in class and, for some readers, in fieldwork or workplace settings.

Welfare Words will articulate and discuss how the specific words and phrases analysed may *fit* within the wider economic and cultural patterning so riven with gross social inequalities and complex forms of social marginality. Thinking more deeply, critically and *politically* about the incessant deployment of particular words within prevailing discourses and daily social work encounters may also lead to questioning what such words 'assume about a social totality or infrastructure, or the presumed characteristics of social actors' (Barrett, 1992: 202). Far from being an exercise in 'political correctness', the aspiration will be to delve deeper into how power relations operate through the language and culture of neoliberal capitalism (Philpot, 1999; Fairclough, 2003).

WELFARE WORDS, CRITICAL SOCIAL WORK AND SOCIAL POLICY

Words change meaning over time and are never encountered in isolation. Our engagement with words invariably occurs 'within the flows of our socio-cultural practices' with meaning 'at least in part tied to the social world we inhabit' (Grimwood, 2016: 15). Yet, as Noel Timms, a psychiatric social worker and author, observed in the late 1960s, it is 'surprising' that his profession, 'largely dependent on language, should have paid so little attention to words and what it means to speak a language' (in Gregory and Holloway, 2005: 38). The usage of words shapes the way the profession communicates to itself, how it coalesces, marks out and sustains a distinctive rationality. Through language, social work is able to construct and maintain the domain with words serving as the 'glue' helping it to stick into place. For example, keywords (such as 'assessment', 'risk' and 'supervision') are integral to the training of social workers who learn to *think* within the conceptual parameters of the profession and to *talk the talk* (see also Wilson, 2016). This mimetic dimension – learning the *right* language, perceptions and dispositions – contributes to producing a certain social work identity and *style* (Chiapello and Fairclough, 2002). This is part of the process Pierre Bourdieu (1930–2002) refers to as attaining the 'feel for the game'. The game is acquired through experience and the 'good player, who is so to speak the game incarnate, does at every moment what the game requires' (Bourdieu, 1994: 63). This 'feel' is partly inculcated through prevailing names and descriptions helping to constitute the dominant forms of reasoning which become, in time, 'turned into second nature' (Bourdieu, 1994: 65).

This can also be connected to the ways in which people engaging with social workers are classified. Bowker and Star (1999: 10) maintain that a 'classification system' is a 'set of boxes (metaphorical or literal) into which things can be put to then do some kind of work – bureaucratic or knowledge production'. Such systems have, of course, been central to social work since its inception (Woodroofe, 1962). In the past, this was reflected in the naming practices and types of descriptive language used in depicting and 'fixing' a person in a 'case' file (Foucault, 1991 [1977]).

In more recent times, this form of activity is more likely to be undertaken using electronic templates (Garrett, 2005).

For social work to be operational, some forms of categorisation are inevitable if the day-to-day work is to be rendered *doable*. Yet the verbal categories that social workers use can promote 'symbolic violence' (Bourdieu, 2000; see also Chapter 2). 'Labels', as Schram (1995: 23) avows, 'operate as sources of power that serve to frame identities and interests. They predispose actors to treat the subjects in question in certain ways.' For example, the words 'client' or 'service user' are apt to connote and convey vague, even suppressed, notions of inferior, tainted or spoiled person-hood. Moreover, there may be instances when categories and classifications used by practitioners – often situated within a matrix of ideas associated with particular forms of ostensibly 'scientific' and neutral 'expertise' – can result in oppressive ramifications for those targeted for intervention (Mayes and Horwitz, 2005). An example of how this process can occur is reflected in historical responses to 'unmarried mothers' in Ireland and elsewhere (Garrett, 2015a, 2017). Experts, often straddling the boundaries between the applied social sciences and clerical or pastoral guidance, performed vital 'definitional labour' (Goffman, 1971 [1959]) and charted what was deemed to be the most appropriate forms of intervention. Felix Biestek (1957: 25), an American Jesuit and one of the primary definers of what constituted the philosophical foundation for social work, observed that caseworkers 'have differed in their evaluation of the capacity of "unmarried mothers", as a group, to make sound decisions. Some feel that unmarried mothers are so damaged emotionally that they are incapable of arriving at a good decision themselves' (see also Shahid and Jha, 2014).

Language is not simply the means by which the social work task is 'described and constructed in different ways at different historical junctures', it is also the 'cornerstone of intervention, the lifeline through which all communication between individuals engaged in the process takes place' (Gregory and Holloway, 2005: 49). Given the increasing privatisation of social work services, practitioners' communication skills and ability to use the *appropriate* language is also a commodity and source of potential profit for businesses (Garrett, 2010).

Gregory and Holloway (2005) chart the history of social work in England and identify how the profession has evolved discursively. For example, in the early 1950s the terminology used to describe the subjects of intervention included 'poor', 'needy', 'imbecile', 'problem family' and 'crippled family' (Gregory and Holloway, 2005: 42). As the decade moved on, however, the emphasis on a more clinical orientation and the influence of psychodynamic approaches gave rise to shifting characterizations such as the 'person', the 'client' (Gregory and Holloway, 2005: 42). Somewhat surprisingly, military metaphors – such as officers and duty – have continued to symbolically represent aspects of social workers' day-to-day engagement with the users of services (Beckett, 2003; see also Newberry-Koroluk, 2014). Chris Beckett (2003) proposes that the 'spoken language' of social work is a combination flowing from the dynamic interplay of three identifiable types: the 'sacred language' (reflected in the aspirational language embedded in the profession's codes of ethics and so on); the 'official language' (revealed in the language of the bureaucracy); the 'colloquial' language (used by practitioners in the everyday, more informal interactions with one another).

Within mainstream professional exchanges, 'social worker' and 'client'/'service user' are usually perceived as fixed and discrete categories despite the fact that during a singular lifetime an individual may find themselves passing from one to the other or simultaneously inhabiting both categories. More generally, how the users of services are identified has been a continuing source of debate (Tropp, 1974; Heffernan, 2006; McLaughlin, 2009). Indeed, within social work there is sometimes a 'certain naiveté about the extent to which changing the names of things (using anti-oppressive language for example) can change the world itself' (Beckett, 2003: 627). Nevertheless, critical thinking and engagement remains 'incomplete without a significant element of language critique' because 'discourse, and in particular language' appears to carry considerable 'weight in the constitution and reproduction of the emergent form of global capitalism' (Fairclough and Graham, 2002: 187). Moreover, given we 'socially inherit linguistic use, our "unthinking" engagement in language can often appear to accept uncritically its ideological meanings' (Holborow, 2015: 4).

Mindful as to how language is one of the key mediums through which ideology is generated and potentially transformed, Stuart Hall (1996: 27) stresses that it is important to analyse the 'concepts and the languages of practical thought which stabilise a particular form of power and domination; or which reconcile and accommodate the mass of the people to their subordinate place in the social formation'. For example, in terms of workplaces, there have been sustained cultural and discursive interventions aimed at cajoling *and* coercing workers into altering their values and remaking their identities in ways more conducive to the market. This development has been particularly apparent within public services, such as state social work. Central to the ideological project of neoliberalism, in fact, are strategies to inculcate 'employees into new ways of working and new identities corresponding to them, partly through attempts to get them to not only use but "own" new discourses' (Fairclough, 2003: 20). Such discourses are apt to focus on, and promote a certain idea as to how – to use one of Raymond Williams' own keywords – a 'modern' service should be assembled and what core competencies and attributes compliant staff should possess and exhibit (see also Williams, 1983: 208; Garrett, 2008).

WELFARE WORDS AND KEYWORDS

Keywords: A Vocabulary of Culture and Society by Raymond Williams (1921–1988) is one of the main inspirations for this book. Initially published in 1976, Williams' 'slim, strangely addictive' volume included 110 'micro essays' on words that he perceived as significant in the mid-1970s and into the following decade (Beckett, 2014: 19). These included, for example, charity, communication, community, consumer, family, modern, society, technology, unemployment, welfare and work. These represented, for him, 'binding' words, 'significant, indicative words in certain forms of thought' (Williams, 1983: 15). Hence, they functioned, singularly and collectively, as the 'linguistic-ideological hubs of his time' (Holborow, 2015: 71; see also Fritsch et al., 2016a). The book was subsequently republished, during the period of the Thatcher governments (1979–1990), with an additional 21 words being added in 1983 (Williams, 1983). In 2014, a third edition was published coinciding with the *Keywords: Art, Culture and Society in 1980s Britain* exhibition at the Tate Gallery.

The underlying orientation in Williams' *Keywords* is one maintaining that there is a need to analyse keywords in the social conditions in which they arise, circulate and are then apt to alter or have their meaning culturally and politically re-calibrated. Thus, Williams tended to place 'special emphasis on adversarial uses, as in the repeated phrase "there is then both controversy and complexity in the term"' (Durant, 2006: 12). In his perspective, words can be viewed as 'artillery to be purposefully aimed' (Durant, 2006: 12; see also McGuigan and Moran, 2014). Marie Moran (2015: 4), in her fascinating exploration of one particular keyword – identity – defines a keyword as 'not merely an important or fashionable word, but a key element of a wider social transformation, capturing, embodying and expressing new, historically and socially specific ways of thinking and acting'. Hence, to understand their meaningfulness and social weight, keywords cannot be 'separated from the cultural political economy of the capitalist societies in which they came to prominence' (Moran, 2015: 4). For example, terms such as welfare and welfare state are 'involved in drawing and redrawing the boundaries of state intervention' (Béland and Petersen, 2014: 3). These, and other words and phrases we will examine, change over time 'as newer terms replace or supplement older ones' (Béland and Petersen, 2014: 3).

This focus on keywords is 'traceable back to late nineteenth-century semantics' (Durant, 2006: 5), but Williams injected a quizzical leftist approach into his own project (see also Williams, 1973; Eagleton, 1976; Ferrara, 1989; Hall, 1989). As a Marxist, he also voiced 'reservations about semantic and lexicographical work as a force for change' (Durant, 2006: 16–17). Whilst Williams' work was foundational to the field of 'cultural studies', he remained a cultural *materialist* in that he believed meaningful social and economic change could never be prompted by words alone. This position anticipates, in some sense, later comments by Bourdieu (2000: 2), who chides those placing 'excessive confidence in the power of language'. For the French sociologist, this was a 'typical illusion' of many contemporary academics who regarded an 'academic commentary as a political act or the critique of texts as a feat of resistance, and experience revolutions in the order of words as radical revolutions in the order of things' (Bourdieu, 2000: 2).

Williams acknowledged, however, the power of ideas and culture in consolidating, or rendering more vulnerable to change, a given social order. Expressed somewhat differently, it would be wrong to reduce issues relating to social change to either materialist accounts laying emphasis on structures and the brute forces of history or to entirely idealist explanations stressing the determining importance of ideas, agency and intentions.

'CH-CH-CH-CH-CHANGES': KEYWORDS NOW

> Ch-ch-ch-ch-changes
> (Turn and face the strange)
> Ch-ch-changes
>
> (David Bowie, 1971)

David Bowie's single 'Changes', along with the first edition of Williams' book, appeared in the 1970s. Since then, the economic, political and cultural context has been radically transformed. In 1976, when *Keywords* was initially published, Abba enjoyed weeks at the 'top of the charts' with their shimmering pop classic 'Dancing Queen'. However, a note of cultural discord was struck, in October of that year, when The Damned released what is often regarded as the first 'punk rock' single, 'New Rose'. In December, The Sex Pistols infamously scattered swearwords on Bill Grundy's live television programme and in doing so drew further attention to their new single, 'Anarchy in the UK', released the previous week. In 1976 Harold Wilson unexpectedly resigned as prime minister and was succeeded by James Callaghan. For the first half of the year a 'Cod War', involving British and Icelandic ships, took place. During the summer, the country experienced a heat wave which contributed to the worst drought since the early eighteenth century. Following an upsurge in violence, 'direct rule' was imposed on Northern Ireland in March. The year ended with the Chancellor, Denis Healey, announcing he had negotiated a loan from the International Monetary Fund (IMF) on condition that billions of pounds were cut from the public expenditure budget (Beckett, 2009).

In geopolitical terms, since the 1970s, the implosion of the USSR and the liquidation of degenerated workers' states in other parts of the 'Eastern Bloc' have contributed to the global solidification of capitalism (Becker, 2016). In China, beginning in the late 1990s, sectors associated with safeguarding the 'quality of life of the common people – housing, health, education – became increasingly marketized' (Ngai, 2016: 14). In the West, and elsewhere, there have been substantial sociological transformations connected to changing ideas and practices relating to the family, gender roles, sexualities and ethnicities (Lawler, 2014; Moran, 2015). The Apple Corporation was only founded in 1976 with Microsoft having been established the previous year. Since this time there has been a rapid expansion in information and communication technology (ICT) with the internet and various forms of social media becoming pervasively influential (see also Tarnoff, 2016). Much of this was unimaginable in the 1970s and these are some of the developments which Tony Bennett and his colleagues endeavoured to encompass in a collection called *New Keywords: A Revised Vocabulary of Culture and Society* (Bennett et al., 2005).

Since the mid-1970s, and an earlier round of austerity measures, neoliberal economics and wider cultural processes of neoliberalisation have been dominant. Although publicly 'championed by Thatcher and Reagan, it was applied only gradually and unevenly in the First World. In the Third, by contrast, neoliberalization was imposed at the gunpoint of debt, as an enforced program of "social adjustment" which overturned all the central tenets of developmentalism and compelled postcolonial states to divest their assets, open their markets, and slash social spending' (Fraser, 2013: 218). However, these processes gradually displaced the 'embedded liberalism' which had been widespread across much of Western Europe since the end of the Second World War. During this period, 'market processes and entrepreneurial and corporate activities were surrounded by a web of social and political constraints and a regulatory environment that sometimes restrained … economic and industrial strategy' (Harvey, 2005: 11).

The word neoliberalism is frequently used in a casual way as 'shorthand for a prevailing dystopian zeitgeist' (Venugopal, 2015: 168). However, underpinning this exploration of welfare words is an understanding that neoliberalism is an historically specific form of capital accumulation endeavouring to engineer a 'counter-revolution against welfare capitalism' (Fairclough and Graham, 2002: 221). Relatedly, we are *witnessing*, *feeling* and *experiencing* the wholesale 'extension of a basic feature of capitalist power relations present from the beginning: class domination' (Fleming, 2015: 29). Reflecting neoliberalism's ascendancy as a financial and cultural force, 'social activity and exchange becomes judged on their degree of conformity to market culture' with 'business thinking migrating to all social activities' (Holborow, 2015: 34, 35). Within social work in Ireland, for example, this tendency is discursively reflected in practitioners being compelled to use a 'business model' electronic template when assessing children and families. Neoliberal ways of perceiving the world are also instantiated in a bye-law introduced in 2011 which includes a section stipulating that social workers have to 'use limited resources efficiently' and this should inform decision-making relating to the duty of care owed to service users (Irish Statute Book, 2011).

Restructuring and reorganizing capital, to the disadvantage of the majority of the world's inhabitants, neoliberalism has produced an enormous cleavage between the super-rich and the rest. In 2016, according to Oxfam America (2016: 1):

> The gap between rich and poor is reaching new extremes. The richest 1% have accumulated more wealth than the rest of the world put together. Meanwhile, the wealth owned by the bottom half of humanity has fallen by a trillion dollars in the past five years. Just 62 individuals now have the same wealth as 3.6 billion people – half of humanity.

TABLE 1.1   CHARACTERISTICS OF NEOLIBERALIZATION[2]

Characteristic	Defining feature
Breaking with 'embedded' liberalism	No longer adheres to the post WWII socio-economic settlement aiming to achieve full employment and maintain the 'welfare state'. Injection of market competition into all sectors
Remaking the State	The State is not 'rolled-back', as some argued, but is *reshaped* and *reconfigured* to better serve the demands of capital through the installation of 'workfare' regimes where the unemployed (rebranded as 'jobseekers') are corralled into low-waged employment. Evolution of a 'Surveillance State' (Jameson, 2002)
Being pragmatic	Tends to depart from theoretical purity ('textbook neoliberalism'). In practice, neoliberalism is versatile, malleable and incorporates a 'dogged dynamism' (Peck, 2010)
Accumulating by dispossessing	Takes from an increasingly indebted working class and unemployed poor to give to the rich and super-rich
Injecting precariousness into lives	Deploys the rhetoric of 'flexibility' and 'innovation' whilst injecting uncertainty into lives in, and beyond the workplace (Mahmud, 2012)
Imprisoning	Greater use of imprisonment and forms of quasi confinement for marginalised groups
Articulating nationally	Having an affective as well as material dimension, neoliberalism *looks*, *feels* and *sounds* different in different national and local settings

The following year, Oxfam (2017) reported that the concentration in wealth had continued with the world's eight richest billionaires now controlling the same wealth between them as the poorest half of the earth's population. Moreover, the 'world's 10 biggest corporations – a list that includes Wal-Mart, Shell and Apple – have a combined revenue greater than the government revenue of 180 "poorest" countries combined' (Oxfam, 2017: 16).

More pervasively, the remaking of state apparatuses involves a 'dramatic shift in government commitments from securing the welfare of citizens to facilitating the flow of global capital' with this 'accomplished through a depoliticizing discourse of deficits, competitiveness, and balanced budgets, surrounded by an aura of technocratic neutrality' (Bakker, 2003: 70). A fresh and reinvigorated emphasis on competition has been injected into all levels of society, including those areas of life and social interaction previously perceived as *beyond* the reach of competition and commodification (Cooper, 2008; Brown, 2015; Gough, 2015) (see also Table 1.1).

Building on Foucault's analysis, Wendy Brown (2015: 10) lucidly amplifies that neoliberalism

> transmogrifies every human domain and endeavour, along with humans themselves according to a specific image of the economic. All conduct is economic conduct; all spheres of existence are framed and measured in economic terms and metrics, even when those spheres are not directly

monetized. In neoliberal reason and in domains governed by it, we are only and everywhere ... an intensely constructed and governed bit of human capital tasked with improving and leveraging its competitive positioning and enhancing its (monetary and nonmonetary) portfolio value across all its endeavors and venues.

For example, within the university sector and driven by a new 'comprador class' (Byrne, 2017: 113) of CEO-style chancellors and presidents, this results in constant competition relating to world league tables, research funding, securing the 'best' academics, erecting state-of-the-art buildings and so on (Holborow, 2015: 110).

Nevertheless, irrespective of the sheer scale of change, there is a need to remain attentive to what remains mostly unchanged. Underlying the 1970s transition from 'embedded liberalism' to neoliberalism, is the enduring, vampiric ability of capitalism to absorb what lies beyond it, economically, politically and culturally. The aim is, in the words of the Martini drinks advertising campaign of the late-1970s, to create private profit 'any time, any place, anywhere'. This dynamic logic continuing, during the period of neoliberalism, 'monetizes and commodifies every aspect of our lives, making every thing, person and interaction subject to the value that can be realized in exchange' (Skeggs, 2014: 2). Furthermore, as Eve Chiapello and Norman Fairclough (2002: 187) summarise, the capitalist system has the capacity to take on 'highly variable historical forms' whilst continuing to be capitalist because of the 'continuity of a number of central features (wage labour, competition, private property, orientation to capital accumulation, technical progress, the rampant commodification of all social activities)'. Financialization has resulted in an enormous increase in indebtedness with, at the 'end of 2008, 70 percent of U.S. families held credit cards, with the total credit card debt reaching $972.73 trillion. The turn to debt is linked with the decline in savings triggered by the decline in wages' (Mahmud, 2012: 476) [3].

However, despite the attacks on welfare that have occurred, the data on spending reveals a complex picture. In short, there has been no withering away of the welfare state (Eagleton-Pierce, 2016: 191). While the discrepancy between the neoliberal rhetoric and actual spending patterns may appear 'puzzling' (Eagleton-Pierce, 2016: 178), there is a need to note that wholesale welfare retrenchment is difficult to achieve because drastic public spending cuts are likely to be counterproductive and risk generating unmanageable political opposition and resistance. In terms of the social administration of welfare provision, previous 'political and legal legacies can "lock-in" current government spending patterns' limiting the room for control and manoeuvre' (Eagleton-Pierce, 2016: 178). More fundamentally, capitalism requires substantial state financial outlays, not only to maintain a measure of stability and social harmony, but to help pacify and engineer the smooth social reproduction of the workforce (Offe, 1984).

Relatively high levels of expenditure on welfare throughout the neoliberal period illuminates the fact that actual spending on welfare may not be the most interesting or revealing indicator of what is actually taking place. For example, the patterns of expenditure allocated to so-called jobseekers reveals little about the injection of social authoritarianism and enhanced surveillance evolving in recent years. Jobseekers are increasingly subject to coercive measures and forms of 'psycho-compulsion' aiming to insert them into low-wage and precarious niches within the labour market (Friedli and Stearn, 2015). However, metrics of government expenditure data may actually mask substantial shifts occurring in 'policy, purpose, access conditions' and 'forms of delivery' (Clarke, 2004: 16).

In recent years, some of Williams' keywords have become less significant, whereas others have been reactivated or had their meanings significantly re-worked (see also Eagleton-Pierce, 2016). Many have been deployed by the political right to try and win consent for socially retrogressive policies (Garrett, 2009, 2013a, 2014a, 2016b). Writing prior to the economic crash beginning in 2007, Boltanski and Chiapello (2005) refer to a 'new spirit' of capitalism more inclined to encompass the themes of well-being and social justice. Post-crash, such a tendency has become even more marked and this is exemplified by the startlingly cynical speech made by Theresa May on becoming UK prime minister in July 2016. Having been part of an administration presiding over relentless austerity measures, she proudly declared her intention to 'fight against ... burning injustice' (see also Reflection and Talk Box 2).

Even before Prime Minister May's intervention, other leading Conservatives had strategically committed themselves to tackling social injustice, as evinced by a number of the publications from the Centre for Social Justice (CSJ). Partly driven by the desire to claim some of the terrain historically inhabited by the social democratic centre-left, the phrase, by now emptied of its progressive meaning, has been harnessed to the project of levering people into work. More expansively, under the 'interchangeable rubrics of "modernization", "reform", "democracy", "the West", "the international community", "human rights", "secularism", "globalization", and various others, we find nothing but an historical attempt at an unprecedented regression' (Badiou, 2012: 4). In this context, powerful organisations, such as the Organisation for Economic Co-operation and Development (OECD), continue to play a pivotal role. Moreover, often completely 'disregarding local traditions and cultures', the language used seeks to create 'super-uniformity' amongst nation-states (Holborow, 2015: 106; see also Chapter 4).

Underpinning the exploration in this book, therefore, will be an attentiveness to how, aligned with neoliberal rationality, there is an intense, yet often stealthy, endeavour to adjust or recalibrate the 'semantic order of things' (Brown, 2015: 27). As the late Doreen Massey (2015: 24) stated, this development impacts on the quotidian and mundane social interactions given that on 'trains and buses, and sometimes in hospitals and universities too', we have become customers, not passengers, patients or students. In all these instances, a 'specific activity and relationship is erased by a general relationship of buying and selling that is given precedence over it' (Massey, 2015: 24).

Although still embedded in Article 22 of the United Nations (1948) Universal Declaration of Human Rights, today the phrase 'social security' is rarely uttered in social policy politics in the UK. In a debate on 'welfare reform' in the House of Lords in 2011 Baroness Hollis remarked: 'Until recently, when we introduced a bill like this it would not have been a welfare reform bill, it would have been a social security bill. The gap between social security and welfare is precisely the gap between entitlement and stigma' (in Williams, 2013). Perhaps surprisingly, the unsuccessful challenger to Jeremy Corbyn's leadership of the UK Labour Party attempted to resuscitate 'social security' in a campaign speech in July 2016. Referring to the Department for Work and Pensions having become a 'byword for cruelty and insecurity', Owen Smith pledged to replace it with a manly 'muscular Ministry for Labour and a dedicated Department for Social Security' (Smith, 2016).

More generally, security tends to be mostly embedded in discourses and practices intent on combating terrorism and, across the Atlantic, this is symbolised by the US government's designation of the department of 'Homeland Security' (see also Neocleous, 2008). However, on occasions there is a conflation of themes as illustrated by one tabloid front page headline: 'Terror Family on UK Benefits', *Daily Star Sunday*, 2015, 11 January: 1). Crudely and skilfully merging two, seemingly, different themes promotes a socially authoritarian and xenophobic worldview at a time when there is the 'largest refugee crisis since the Second World War, with more the 22 million people forcibly displaced from their countries by war and persecution' (Legrain, 2016: 7).

The current 'refugees crisis' has contributed to a rise in 'welfare chauvinism' (Keskinen et al., 2016). This refers to the ways in which neo-nationalist and culturally racist parties make use of the welfare state and welfare benefits to draw 'the distinction between "us" and "them" – the natives that are perceived to deserve the benefits and the racialized "others" who are portrayed as undeserving and even exploiting the welfare system at the cost of the "rightful" citizens' (Keskinen et al., 2016: 322). Clearly linked to the material hardships prompted by the imposition of austerity measures, 'new forms of hostility' towards migrants and ethnic minorities, observable in many parts of Europe, 'build on and gain their power from the exclusionary nationalist and racialising ideologies, policies and practices that are part of European history' (Keskinen et al., 2016: 326). As Gargi Bhattacharya (2015: 38) laments, there often seems to be 'discernible enthusiasm for monstering others… when few opportunities to mark superiority are available'.

This development might also be connected to the rise of Marine Le Pen and the Front National in France and the UK Independence Party (UKIP). It can also be interpreted as intertwined, in complex ways, with the Brexit 'no' vote in the summer of 2016. It is echoed in the Nordic countries by political formations such as the (True) Finn Party, the Danish People's Party and the Sweden Democrats. Part of the appeal of such parties is that they position themselves as defenders of welfare for 'hardworking' 'native' people under threat from 'unregulated' migration and the implicit, associated danger of terrorism. In Sweden, an assortment of neo-Nazis and extreme nationalist fringe parties has amalgamated to form the Sweden Democrats, now posing as the true champions and reliable safeguards of the *folkhem* – the historically rooted Swedish concept of welfare (Norocel, 2016; see also Andersson, 2009). Often amplified by corporate media outlets, the popularity of such parties strengthens the 'selective logic' distinguishing between 'desired' and 'undesired' migrants with a new emphasis being placed on 'migrants' presumed '"utility"' [or otherwise] to the nation and its welfare' (Keskinen et al., 2016: 324). In Denmark, for example, this logic results in potential immigrants being sifted, and their worth calibrated, by the state having regard to whether or not they obtained a degree from a university with a high 'world ranking'. It is, therefore, 'no longer a question of whether or not welfare chauvinism is present in the Danish policy frames. Now it is a question of what kind of welfare chauvinism is articulated in the various political party programmes, proposals and debates' (Jørgensen and Thomsen, 2016: 346). To differing degrees, such ideological currents and toxic analytics are now lodged within the political mainstream and they cannot solely be discussed in terms of the 'fringe' parties on the political right.

In the UK, this dimension was illustrated by the Labour Party's production of the notorious 'Controls On Immigration' mug in the period leading up to the 2015 General Election (Sommers, 2015). Such moves undermine the ethic of social solidarity underpinning the construction of the welfare state. Moreover, they can be interpreted as integral to the neoliberal project of welfare retrenchment within which 'the "immigrant" is a particular model of undeservingness' (Guentner et al., 2016: 106).

WELFARE WORDS AND ME: THE AIMS OF THE BOOK

Whilst acknowledging that welfare is configured differently in different national settings, I define welfare words as those words and phrases used by 'primary definers' (Hall et al., 1978) to steer debates on welfare in favour of a neoliberal political, economic and cultural agenda. The circulation of such words and phrases potentially helps, therefore, to sustain and propel the social logic of capitalism in its current form (Boltanski and Chiapello, 2005). Although not always neoliberal in origin, these words are frequently pivotal in neoliberal narratives of social marginality. Gendered and racialised as well as classed, welfare words tend to predominantly concern groups lacking in economic capital or holding significant stocks of 'negative symbolic capital' (Bourdieu in Bourdieu et al., 2002: 185).

The usage of welfare words might be conceptualised in terms of what Antonio Gramsci (1891–1937) refers to as the struggle to maintain hegemony and they are circulated and promoted by figures located within the state and/or particular fields of 'expertise'. The media play a significant role in amplifying, popularising and socially embedding them. Nestled within wider 'common sense' understandings, welfare words might also be interpreted as forming parts of a wider, politically distracting 'screen discourse' (Bourdieu and Wacquant, 2001: 4), deflecting attention from issues related to capitalism, economic exploitation and a differential distribution of power. These words reflect – or mask – how the dominant order is constructed contributing to its constitution and consolidation. However, each word can also, to varying degrees, be perceived as a repository into which 'different sets of actors can pour multifarious meanings, from the hegemonic to the counter-hegemonic' (Eagleton-Pierce, 2016: 144). (If, for some readers, many of the phrases and concepts appearing in the last two paragraphs appear too dense and clunkily alienating, I hope that things will become clearer in the following chapter and as we get deeper into the book.)

Throughout *Welfare Words*, discourse refers to a constellation of interconnected statements, explanations and lines of reasoning functioning to define a given situation at particular historical junctures. Discourses operate within what Bourdieu calls 'fields' – such as social work – determining implicit rules of engagement and restricting what can be legitimately and 'appropriately' represented, said and done. Coupling this understanding to the work of Gramsci, it can be perceived how a pervasive plethora of powerful and dominating discourses, whilst fluid and failing to extinguish the possibility of countervailing alternative ways of sense-making and re-ordering, contribute to the maintenance of neoliberal hegemony, bolstering the solidity of the ruling class (see also Chapter 2)[4].

This book is, of course, not news from nowhere. Its aspiration and intent is, in part, reflective of my specific situatedness. All of us are, as Gramsci observed, products of personal and wider historical processes that deposit 'an infinity of traces' (in Forgacs, 1988: 326). The 'traces', likely to influence my own perceptions on welfare words, include failing the 11+ examination which tested the 'intelligence' of school children to allocate them a place within a new tripartite system of secondary education (see also Ball, 2015: 823). As a result, I became part and product of the English secondary modern school system (Willis, 1977). Now living on the edge of Europe in the west of Ireland, this cultural, political and economic location also impacts on my interpretation of the welfare words examined.

Referring back to Williams, his *Keywords* can be also viewed as a product of his 'habitus' and, despite his working-class origins, his being a Cambridge don and prominent member of the left intelligentsia (Bourdieu, 2002). With him, I share a gender and a commitment to left politics, but my location in social space is clearly very different. Born almost half a century after Williams, I am of a different generation. Williams was Welsh and I am a complex amalgam of Irish and English (see also Williams, 1979; Williams and Eagleton, 1989). Following a lengthy period of unemployment, I worked as a welfare rights worker in a trade union centre. I am now employed – as was Williams – in a university, but one bereft of the 'symbolic capital' attached to the University of Cambridge (see also Eagleton, 1998). These factors aside, Williams was also a pipe smoker and was much more erudite and smarter than I will ever be.

I have an autobiographical and experiential engagement with some of our welfare words and, even if this is not rendered explicit, it might fruitfully contribute to my interpretation and analysis. At the same time, my generational location and habitus may mean that I will fail to grasp and that I am inadequately attuned to the significance and trajectory of emergent words, phrases and practices. Given my membership of the *Critical Social Policy* editorial collective over a number of years, my readings will be viewed through what might be loosely, and unsurprisingly, termed a critical social policy lens. Such a viewpoint entails recognising that the 'power to name a social problem has vast implications for the policies considered suitable to address it' (Silver, 1994: 533). Hence, it is vital that we try to interrogate and question how issues and 'social problems' emerge and become the focus of social, cultural and political contestation (see also Garrett, 2007a).

Because of my class origins and generation, I recollect times when some of the words we will look at may have meant something different; for example, within official discourse, welfare was not – although never socially neutral – always uttered with a sneer, so saturated in stigmatising connotations and wedded to dependency (see also Chapter 3). In a more general historical sense, whilst not seeking to promote a 'golden age' narrative around the welfare state, it is still important to acknowledge that 'after 1945, social programmes in the advanced-capitalist countries brought a limited redistribution of wealth and higher standards of living for major sectors of the working class, especially where trade unions were strong' (Iglesias, 2015: 7). As Nancy Fraser (2016: 109) asserts:

> it was above all the working classes—both women and men—who spear-headed the struggle for public provision ... In effect, they were voting for family, country and lifeworld against factory, system and machine ... [The] state-capitalist settlement resulted from a class compromise and represented a democratic advance.

The welfare state was a complex, somewhat contradictory, form of achievement secured by the working class and, in this sense, an element of nostalgia can be intellectually and politically generative (see also Boym, 2001). There are, in fact, many varieties of nostalgia, 'kinds that are fetishes in the bad sense, genuine blockages, and kinds that are weapons' which can be directed at those seeking to re-appropriate and re-privatise the social gains derived from the struggles of the past (Berlant in Helms et al., 2010: 5). The latter will colour the perspective of *Welfare Words*.

At no point should we embark on the politically, and existentially, forlorn task of trying to re-install anachronistic meanings of particular words. Some older meanings and practices are, of course, pernicious and should not be restored. This applies, for example, to child adoption, which the current government in the UK is seeking to reassemble to mirror, in many ways, the oppressive practices and attitudes of the 1950s (see also Chapter 9). Indeed, this book will be characterised by recognition that there is a need to create a different kind of state to that which evolved as part of the social and economic settlement emerging at the end of the Second World War (Newman and Clarke, 2015).

More broadly, shunning a 'golden age' interpretation, it is acknowledged that the welfare state was implicated in gendered and racialised forms of order making and exclusion (Clarke, 2004; Newman and Clarke, 2015; see also Chapter 3). As Bourdieu confided at the beginning of the century, we are 'paradoxically led to defend what is not entirely defensible' (Bourdieu in Grass and Bourdieu, 2002: 71). Even more critically, it has been argued that the 'idealised post-war welfare state and the Marshallian model of social citizenship ... are in some respects little more than comforting phantoms' produced by a yearning for a 'political imaginary whose efficacy has long since passed' (Pitcher, 2006: 61). In this context, as we know, forms of citizenship take meaning from the 'implication that there is an outside, a space of non-citizenship where such rights and entitlements do not apply' (Bhattacharyya, 2015: 28). The continuing targeting and demonization of migrants in the UK and elsewhere reinforces this understanding.

No attempt will be made in in this book to replicate Williams' *Keywords*. The format is very different with a lengthier focus and investigation of themes associated with far fewer words and phrases. This book will not, therefore, furnish a comprehensive lexicon of words that are central to social work and social policy (see, for example, Timms and Timms, 1982; Davies, 2000; Greve, 2014). Moreover, the aim is not to determine what are 'good' and 'bad' words or what is the decontaminated, 'real' or 'authentic' meaning of the particular words examined. Meriting quoting at length, Marnie Holborow (2015: 121) lucidly articulates that the prime critical purpose should be to:

> unpick the ideological content of any language emanating from the ruling class of a society, it is necessary to identify the link between the language and the specific social world it seeks to represent, including its distortions of reality which have the potential to undermine its hegemony. To grasp how ideology is condensed in certain expressions, it is necessary to see language not as a discursive practice within its own constraints – an 'order of discourse' – but as an utterance which responds to a social order and is fragilely suspended at a social conjuncture.

Some of the words are polysemous, connoting a multiplicity of meanings, and are suggestive of a range of different interpretations. Words, as Terry Eagleton maintains, are 'pulled this way and that by competing social interests, inscribed from within with a multiplicity of ideological accents' (in Holborow, 2015: 128). The key point to recognise is that each of the words and phrases to be discussed can be perceived as focal to a struggle for meaning, where dominant forces seek to embed certain hegemonic understandings to serve their class interests. This is clearly the case with a word, mostly used in a pejorative way – such as underclass – but also with a seemingly, more socially neutral word such as care (see Chapter 4 and Chapter 8).

I will not have recourse to electronic search techniques, drawing on a large corpus of data which tracks and quantifies usage. Whilst not entirely relying on this approach, Arun Kundnani (2012) has used this method to good effect in his critical exploration of the word 'radicalisation' and I acknowledge the advantages. Before electronic searching, tracking and quantifying became more sophisticated and purportedly encompassing, Deborah Cameron (1998) cautioned against too uncritical reliance on such methods. Her main concerns were that 'corpus-based lexicography' tended to embark on a 'flight from history' and was insufficiently alert to the historical evolution of particular words and phrases (Cameron, 1998: 40). Moreover a 'troubling characteristic' of electronic corpora was that it often focused on large quantities of 'very easy to tag and collect' text derived from the narrow spectrum of British newspapers (Cameron, 1998: 41–2). Frequently situated within a positivist discourse, such methods risked entirely failing to recognise, with sufficient critically analytical rigour, the potency of the 'sign as a site of ideological struggle' (Cameron, 1998: 42).

In terms of the investigatory approach adopted, this book will not theorise about language *per se* and is not rooted in applied–linguistic scholarship. Rather, the focus will be on a far from exhaustive list of welfare words and phrases, in an attempt to understand why, and how, they are presently significant in social work and social policy. A disruptive and inquisitive exploration of such words enables us to gain insight into the 'analytical schema or grid of intelligibility' of the social formation in which these words are prevalent (Foucault, 2008: 243). As Chapter 2 makes plain, the book will draw on and utilise concepts and ideas formulated by a number of critical thinkers broadly connected to the disciplines of sociology, social work, social policy and politics.

Welfare Words will not encompass the field of visual sociology (Rose, 2016). However, it is recognised that images are, of course, highly significant. For example, Janet Fink's archival explorations (2008), and especially her detailed analysis of the photographs and captions in the Year Books of the National Children's Home (NCH) charity, illuminates how pictures can help us grasp the historical evolution of particular services. Similarly, the political and cultural landscape of neoliberalism is continually projected via a kaleidoscopic constellation of images. Capital not 'only produces flows of goods and monies but also flows of signs'. An analysis of television 'legitimation' adverts indicates that these 'seem designed to represent corporations as good citizens and ethical actors: environmentally concerned, responsible neighbors supporting local communities' (Goldman and Papson, 2011: 11). Relentlessly light and positive in tone, they 'depict capitalist relations not only as they are, not even as they have been, but as they might be – full of openness, hope, and possibility' (Goldman and Papson, 2011: 17).

In terms of social policy documents, what may appear initially as merely the 'inclusion (or not) of simple illustrations to liven up or improve the appeal of a text heavy document, is imbued with particular latent meanings' tending to favour dominant narratives and interpretations (Wiggan, 2012: 394–5). In short, the visual plays a key role conveying potent agendas and meanings and, despite our focal concern being on words, it is still recognised that neoliberal *remaking* practices are also transmitted through visual presentation (Strangleman, 2008). For example, I will suggest later that the imagery associated with neuroscience, now so central to the whole notion of early intervention, is a vital element serving to amplify the argument that such interventions into the lives of children and families are essential.

THE ORGANISATION OF THE BOOK

As Durant (2008: 123) concedes, in his discussion on Williams' choices, the issue of 'selection, inclusion and exclusion of candidate "keywords" ... is as delicate, or awkward, now as it was then'. As to the particular words and phrases discussed, the choice is largely driven by my own interests and those of my students. My own mode of selection is subjective in that the book is inevitably informed by my political and personal inclinations and many will, of course, detect glaring oversights and omissions. Having said this, all the welfare words and phrases included in the book are ubiquitous within social work and related fields and their usage provides insights into economic and cultural tensions and wider contextual 'social changes' (Voloshinov, 1973: 19).

Although I will focus on a number of specific words and phrases, there will be occasions where I will wander off to explore satellite words moving, so to speak, in the same lexical orbit. For example, in analysing welfare dependency (Chapter 3), it is impossible not to refer to the underclass featured in a different chapter. On other occasions there will be a need to briefly address particular words or phrases, although not the focus of entire chapters, still warranting exploration: it is impossible, for instance, to discuss the underclass without referring to the so-called problem family. Certain words and phrases also seem to almost blend into each other and it may, in fact, be the intention of those propagating them to assemble a deeply ideological mosaic of interconnected themes. Indeed, such a patterning helps to constitute wider, 'common sense' narratives (see also our discussion on Gramsci in Chapter 2).

Chapter 2 provides conceptual insights enabling a better comprehension of some of the welfare words discussed. More specifically, this chapter will explore the work of European thinkers in dialogue with Marx: Antonio Gramsci, Pierre Bourdieu, Loïc Wacquant, the Autonomist Marxist tradition and Jacques Rancière. My perception is that each of them, using different analytical optics, furnishes conceptualisations helping us to account for the prominence of particular welfare words. They alert us to the more encompassing economic, political and cultural context which facilitates the *flow* of these words. Clearly, all are white, male authors and they might be charged with according insufficient analytical attention to questions of intersectionality[5]. I will, however, also seek to draw on writings located within different frameworks sensitive to questions of gender, 'race' and ethnicity. This is not to argue that the theorists selected deploy crude single-axis frameworks and are entirely unattuned to overlapping structures of domination. Some welfare words cannot be critically explored without referring to ideas relating to gender and mothering (e.g. underclass, early intervention, care and adoption) and 'race' and racialisation (e.g. underclass and adoption) as well as class. Many of the welfare words also touch on issues related to age and generation: for example, care is connected to the notion that there is a crisis attributable to an 'ageing population'; a lacuna is present in discourses on child adoption in that the voices of children themselves rarely feature.

Chapter 3 focuses on welfare dependency. We begin here because particular constructions of welfare and its contemporary thematic twin – dependency – also inflect the meanings of a number of the other words examined later. Welfare 'dependency' is also prone to infiltrate many of the exchanges that are central to social work and related fields. This chapter also introduces the format to be used in later chapters, starting with the online Oxford English Dictionary definition of the particular welfare word as a 'take-off' point for a more wide-ranging, perhaps even at times unruly, critical exploration of the term and key associated themes.

Sustained by a 'whole journalistic paraphernalia of menacing alterity' (Badiou, 2002: 27), the underclass has been to the fore in debates on the future of welfare and this word will be the focal concern of Chapter 4. Here, it will be maintained that there are a range of other derogatory labels that have been used, throughout history, to label and regulate the poor and the marginalised. For example, the latest, and most prominent, addition would seem to be Troubled Families. Chapter 5 focuses on social exclusion and dwells on problems with this conceptualisation. It will also look at the situation of the Roma community in the Republic of Ireland to try to discern whether this well-worn phrase may or may not be useful in triggering meaningful changes to address the plight of this group (see also McGarry, 2017). Early intervention 'carries such an overwhelming, *a priori* correctness' (Featherstone et al., 2014: 1737) that it appears beyond question. However, key questions are posed in Chapter 6 investigating the current and seemingly omnipresent fixation with this phrase and practice: What may be the assumptions underpinning early intervention? What roles are mothers particularly expected to play within a conceptual framework in which early intervention is increasingly to the fore?

Resilience is now a prominent welfare word, but it will be argued in Chapter 7 that there is still a need to resist 'resilience talk' becoming uncritically incorporated into the 'common sense' of professions such as social work. Chapter 8 explores care and amplifies the argument that the present strains on care have 'deep systemic roots in the structure of our social order' (Fraser, 2016: 100). The following chapter focuses on child adoption. Finally, the short Conclusion brings together a number of the themes explored in the context of apparent shifts taking place with the introduction of what I term 'rhetorically recalibrated neoliberalism'.

In what follows, I am mindful of the fact that some readers might find my references to social work and social policy in England and – less frequently – Ireland as rather narrow and limiting. Perceptions, policies and practices, relating to welfare words, may differ across the 'devolved entities' of Scotland, Wales and Northern Ireland. Scotland, for example, provides a very different – and often more socially progressive – national framing for some of the issues we will examine and allude to in this book (Mooney and Scott, 2015). The devolved Welsh administration is also at odds with the policies of the Conservative government (Drakeford, 2012). Nationalist opposition to the implementation of the Welfare Reform Act 2012 in Northern Ireland threatened the viability of the 'peace process' and risked collapsing the Northern Ireland Executive. Relating to Chapter 3, Mike Tomlinson (2016: 106) notes the 'narrative of dependency' is apt to shift from 'the social pathology of individuals to the economic and political pathology' of Northern Ireland as a whole.

There may also be a risk that this exploration is insufficiently attentive to what Connell (2007) dubs 'southern theory' with undue weight being given to the preoccupations of northern Europe and the United States. Indeed, it is conceded that those located elsewhere may need to decipher some of the welfare words explored, and others not featured, in their own specific national and cultural contexts. This is because 'welfare arrangements' will appear different in different locations (Pfau-Effinger, 2005: 4). Hence, some readers may feel they need to taper themes and issues featured in the 'Reflection and Talk Boxes' to fit local and particular circumstances.

REFLECTION AND TALK BOX 1

I. The list of welfare words and phrases to be discussed is, of course, far from exhaustive. Having read this chapter, therefore, you may feel that certain significant welfare words and phrases are absent. What are these? Why are they important and why do you think they merit insertion into a book such as this?

FURTHER READING

Readers are encouraged to look at Williams' (1983) *Keywords*. Two recent books, both influenced by Williams, are those produced by Eagleton-Pierce (2016) and Fritsch et al. (2016a). One written in the UK and the other in North America, both locate their exploration of keywords within the economic and social fabric of neoliberalism. Bourdieu and Wacquant's (2001), short, accessible – and scathing – article also chimes with the themes explored in *Welfare Words*. Similarly, Wendy Brown's (2015) intervention is an invaluable accompanying resource. A very useful glossary of some of the conceptualisations featured in what follows is provided by Nick Crossley's (2005) *Key Concepts in Critical Social Theory*. More generally, there is much to be gained by noting how, on an on-going basis, the words and phrases used in *Welfare Words* feature in the media.

CHAPTER 2

THE CONCEPTUAL LENS

INTRODUCTION

Whilst Raymond Williams' *Keywords* provides the starting point for the book, a number of other theorists contribute to its conceptual approach. In Chapter 8, for example, the perspective of Michel Foucault and Wendy Brown will be central in understanding human capital and resilience. Authors such as Nancy Fraser and Stuart Hall (1932–2014) will also occasionally take part in this conversation on welfare words. However, in what follows, the particular focus will be on Gramsci and Bourdieu. In addition, reference will be made to Wacquant, those associated with the Autonomist Marxist tradition and Jacques Rancière. Each of these theorists are likely to disagree with the others on fundamental points and none of them provides neat and tidy lines of reasoning which can be mechanistically applied to interpret a particular welfare word. Collectively, however, they inject a potentially critical incisiveness into the exploration of some of the book's main preoccupations.

ANTONIO GRAMSCI: WELFARE WORDS, HEGEMONY AND COMMON SENSE

HEGEMONY

Williams' focus on the 'controversy' connected to particular words and their changing usage is related to the concept of 'hegemony' (see Williams, 1973, 1977, 1983). Derived from *hegemon*, literally meaning leader, hegemony signifies a combination of authority, leadership and domination. Now associated with Antonio Gramsci, hegemony refers to 'something more substantial and more flexible than any abstract *imposed* ideology' (Williams, 1973: 10, emphasis added). Those attentive to the construction of hegemonic projects dwell on how a dominant class has to organise, persuade and *maintain* the consent of the subjugated by ensuring that its own ideas constitute the core perceptions and 'common sense' within a particular society or social formation (Crehan, 2011). Key themes for analyses influenced by the concept of hegemony are movement, instability and flux since it is 'a process, not a state of being. No victories are final. Hegemony has constantly to be "worked on", maintained, renewed and revised' (Hall, 2011: 727–8).

In this fluid context, welfare words, and the narratives in which they are lodged, fulfil a vital role in bolstering hegemony. Welfare words often need, for example, to be interpreted as part of a more encompassing polity stressing the centrality of paid employment within societies structured to service the needs of capital. As Williams (1977: 110) argued, if an hegemonic project is successful, it can result in a

> saturation of the whole process of living – not only of political and activity, not only more manifest social activity, but the whole substance of lived identities and relationships, to such a depth that the pressures and limits of what can ultimately be seen as a specific economic, political, and cultural system seem to most of us to be the pressures and limits of simple experience and common sense.

Hence, hegemony is 'not to be understood at the level of mere opinion or mere manipulation. It is a whole body of practices and expectations' (Williams, 1973: 9). Part of the political skill integral to such an endeavour is the ability to co-opt and nullify 'alternative meanings and values' (Williams, 1973: 10).

Hegemonic projects do not simply seek to win over people to a particular worldview. Rather, they can be perceived as aspiring to neutralise and render passive competing perspectives 'while recruiting small but strategically significant populations and class fractions into active support' (Gilbert, 2015: 31). What Hall (2011: 727–8) refers to as the excluded 'social forces, whose consent has not been won, whose interests have not been taken into account, form the basis of counter movements, resistance, alternative strategies and visions'. Such resistance involves a tactical 'war of position' being constantly waged to try to strategically destabilise dominant hegemonies (Gramsci in Forgacs, 1988: 233). It can be perceived as an art of politics encompassing an array of interventions, even including the lampooning, satirising and ridiculing of officialdom and its accompanying discourse and practices: ways of seeking to undermine hegemony which Mikhail Bakhtin (1895–1975) terms 'carnivalisation' and 'discrowning' (Brandist, 1996)[1].

Compliant academics are often significant in helping to sustain hegemony. Marnie Holborow (2015), for example, highlights how neoliberal economics have found key supporters within the universities, increasingly modelled on corporate businesses. Affirming the values of the market, academic institutions are apt to amplify and mimic private sector practices underpinned by notions of performance, customer, enterprise and entrepreneurship (Holborow, 2015: Ch. 6). Added to pepper the neoliberal semantic soup is a scattering of upbeat 'hooray words', such as creative, participation and empowerment (Cook in Holborow, 2015: 103).

What counts is what *penetrates*, what *sticks* and what achieves some degree of explanatory power in terms of our experience of the world. Hegemony presupposes an 'active and practical involvement of the hegemonised groups, quite unlike the static, totalizing and passive subordination implied in the dominant ideology concept' (Forgacs, 1988: 424). Nevertheless, there is no guarantee that the dominant narratives of the ruling class will succeed in convincing people. For example, consent relating to processes of neoliberalisation is conditional and grudging, rather than enthusiastic (Clarke and Newman, 2012: 315). However, given their incessant and repetitious deployment, socially regressive hegemonic discourses relating to some of our welfare words – such as welfare dependency – do appear to 'shape the attitudes and language of people experiencing poverty' (Pemberton et al., 2016: 22; see also Chapter 3). Clearly, these discourses can be rejected and resisted by those who are the targets, yet their sheer psychological heft is undeniable.

Hegemonic power does 'not flow automatically from the economic position of the dominated group', rather it has to be 'constructed and negotiated' (Joseph, 2006: 52). As Wendy Brown (2015: 81) insists, even when an explanation of a political event, social crisis – or even dominant interpretation of one particular welfare word – becomes 'hegemonic, it carves itself against a range of other possibilities – tacitly arguing with them, keeping them at bay, or subordinating them'. This can involve tactical positioning to maintain and renew dominance: a strategy illuminated by former UK Chancellor George Osborne, who aimed to 'weaponise' policy on welfare in an attempt to wrong-foot his political adversaries (in Jensen and Tyler, 2015: 478). A somewhat different approach was to be taken by Theresa May (2016a, 2016b) in her comments on becoming prime minister (see also Reflection and Talk Box 2).

Any class that aspires to dominate or hold sway within a particular social formation has to move beyond its own narrow interests and make strategic alliances and compromises with a variety of forces. The maintenance of consent, or the calculated dispensing with consent, is 'dependent upon an incessant repositioning of the relationship between rulers and the ruled' (Jones, 2006: 3). This becomes especially important at specific historical 'conjunctures' (Hall and Massey, 2015). Located within a broadly Gramscian framework, the notion of conjuncture refers to the emergence of social, political, and economic and ideological contradictions at a particular historical moment. Here different 'levels of society, the economy, politics, ideology, common sense, etc, come together or "fuse"' (Hall in Hall and Massey, 2010: 59). Thus, a 'conjuncture' is a 'critical turning point or rupture in a political structure, primarily signifying a crisis in class relations' (Rustin, 2009: 18). Such a multifaceted crisis in the present order – such as a major economic crisis, outbreak of war or an event such as the recent decision to leave the EU by British voters – represents a potential opportunity to construct a new hegemonic settlement which may be socially progressive or retrogressive depending on the political bloc emerging as dominant.

Hegemonic orders are also imbued with specific national characteristics and Sean Phelan (2007) has provided an insightful discussion on the key rhetorical strategies structuring the articulation of elite neoliberal discourses in Ireland before the economic 'crash' (see also Allen, 2012). Throughout Europe, following the near-collapse of capitalism, ruling elites used slogans and sound bites to try to install dominant perceptions and narratives articulating how the crisis was being addressed. During David Cameron's term as the UK prime minister (2010–2016), this tended to circulate around the banal trope 'we're all in this together'. The idea that the UK is a 'broken society' was also deployed by leading Conservatives in the Coalition administration (2010–2015) and subsequently as they became the sole party of government (Cameron, 2010; see also Slater, 2012). Theresa May (2016b) added a dash of surrealism to her wobbly government's binding post-Brexit narrative given her assertion that her party is 'truly' the 'party of the workers'. Indeed, in a remarkable speech to the Conservative Party in October 2016 conference she referred to 'workers' or 'working class' on fifteen occasions. Part of a potentially hegemonic, and nationally chauvinistic, project to chart a 'new centre ground' in British politics, such tactics are prompted by the challenge of Corbynism – heightened since the General Election result in May 2017 – and by post-Brexit economic uncertainty.

Bhattacharyya (2015: 11) argues that since the 'crash', beginning in 2007, the need to gain consent from electorates has become less important. Now that the 'only speakable political project is the one assessing how best to enable markets to "work", the intensive cultural work of the later twentieth century is less necessary' (2015: 12). More emphatically, what is 'distinctive' about the political strategy of austerity is that it is structured to 'tell us, again and again, that it does not matter what we think' (2015: 11). As a 'hegemonic project', this is 'quite a different mode of operation' from, for example, that of Thatcherism in the UK which despite being 'highly divisive...nevertheless elicited the consent of many who lost out materially' (2015: 11). Indeed, the analysis that we have entered a 'post-consent' period (2015: 11) is arguably bolstered by evolution of anti-democratic practices used across Europe. For example, in November 2011, a new Italian government was assembled without any elections taking place. Mostly comprised of technocrats, Mario Monti's government was entirely unencumbered by the inconvenience of electoral democracy and the need to win consent (Garrett and Bertotti, 2017). In Greece, after a 'no' vote in the July 2015 referendum rejecting an EU austerity package, the beleaguered Syriza administration simply disregarded it (see also Pentaraki, 2013; Stavrakakis, 2013).

However, irrespective of these developments, it is difficult to envisage that any form of rule could exist without some measure of consent. As Gramsci recognised, hegemonic powers have to seek and maintain the 'consent given by the great masses of the population to the general direction imposed' (Gramsci in Hoare and Nowell Smith, 2005: 12). However, the 'apparatus of state coercive power' is empowered to 'legally' enforce 'discipline on those groups' failing to render active or passive consent (2005: 12). Importantly, continues Gramsci, this latter apparatus is 'constituted for the whole of society in anticipation of moments of crisis of command and direction when spontaneous consent has failed' (2005: 12). In this way, coercive power is held in reserve for those times and places when the means of generating sufficient consent *fails* (see also Smith, 2011). Ordinarily, the mass of people would not directly be targeted or experience such a deployment of coercive power. However, some population segments – perhaps impoverished minority ethnic populations – or those pariah groups Wacquant (2009: 4) terms 'castaway categories' – regularly encounter the presence of the state's coercive edge in the form of interventions by uniformed and militarised police. Given that the state has more forceful ways to foster compliance and acquiescence, hegemony does not play out merely at the level of culture and it is not simply discursively maintained (Anderson, 1976).

A clear coercive component has, of course, been witnessed in places such as Greece as greater numbers of people have gone on to the streets to resist austerity diktats (Pentaraki, 2016). Over the past few decades in the UK, laws have also been enacted to legally restrict and curtail the capacity of trade unions to collectively combat opposition to neoliberalism. Moreover, at the level of everyday interactions in workplaces, it can also seem that 'punishment will be forthcoming if we express our dissatisfaction' or hint at 'expressions of critique, amusement, or dissent' (Bhattacharyya, 2015: 28).

COMMON SENSE

It has been argued that the whole idea of 'common sense' has become a 'cultural studies joke', a term 'hauled out to cover much too much while explaining all too little' (Bhattacharyya, 2015: 25). This is correct in so far as analyses attached to theorising 'common sense' have to be careful not to become vapid or, indeed, patronising toward those who, in turbulent times, find solace in dominant and popular 'explanations' and mooted 'solutions' to individual and social problems.

Articulating Gramsci's theorisation of 'common sense', Peter Ives (2004: 74) maintains that, unlike in English, the 'Italian notion of common sense (*senso comune*) does not so much mean good, sound, practical sense, rather it means normal or average understanding'. Gramsci himself explained that it is the

> conception of the world which is uncritically absorbed … Common sense is not a single unique conception, identical in time and space [and] it takes countless different forms. Its most fundamental characteristic is that it is a conception which…is fragmentary, incoherent. (Gramsci in Hoare and Nowell Smith, 2005: 419)

For him, therefore, 'common sense' is a 'chaotic aggregate of disparate conceptions, and one can find there anything there one likes' (2005: 422). Tending to fear anything new, it is 'crudely neophobe and conservative' (Gramsci in Hoare and Nowell Smith, 2005: 423). However, this 'does not mean that there are no truths in common sense. It means rather that common sense is an ambiguous, contradictory and multiform concept' (2005: 423).

Often omitted in accounts of Gramsci's conception is his assertion that within common sense is situated 'good sense' (*buon senso*), which is more than a mere reflection of the ideas of the ruling class and its cadre of compliant intellectuals. Far from conformist, it 'necessarily includes elements expressing the people's genuine experiences and interests' (Snir, 2016: 271). Gramsci also suggests that the sheer monotony of capitalist work processes might spark thoughts that are generally subversive. For example, in his interrogation of Americanism and Fordism, he argues that the fact that a worker often 'gets no immediate satisfaction from his [*sic*] work and realises that they are trying to reduce him to a trained gorilla, can lead ... into a train of thought that is far from conformist' (Gramsci in Hoare and Nowell Smith, 2005: 310).

Gaining currency through language, many elements in common sense contribute, however, to 'people's subordination by making situations of inequality and oppression appear to them as natural and unchangeable' (Forgacs, 1988: 421). Hall and O'Shea (2015: 52–3) elaborate on this facet of 'common sense', arguing that it is

> a form of 'everyday thinking' which offers us frameworks of meaning with which to make sense of the world. It is a form of easily-available knowledge which contains no complicated ideas, requires no sophisticated argument and does not depend on deep thought or wide reading. It works intuitively, without forethought or reflection ... Typically, it expresses itself in the vernacular, the familiar language of the street, the home, the pub, the workplace and the terraces.

Here we could add, of course, that social media now also fulfils a significant role in forming popular views and opinions. 'Common sense' provides, therefore, a blurred, hazy and defective lens through which to view the world because it incorporates information which is objectively inaccurate or crucially incomplete. Hence it can gel with the tendency of ruling elites to 'manufacture ignorance' to justify the way society is hierarchised and regulated (Slater, 2012). In the United States, we might also use this body of theory to comprehend the rise of the so-called 'alt-right' and its deployment of 'alternative facts' to try and create a new socially toxic hegemony (see also Crehan, 2016).

USING GRAMSCI

A number of fascinating studies have analysed how hegemonic projects have been assembled in specific historical and national contexts. India, for example, possesses a rich tradition of Gramscian analysis (Guha, 1997; Anderson, 2016). Specifically in relation to social work and having regard to concepts such as hegemony and common sense, Mohd Shahid and Manoj K. Jha (2014) provide a valuable critical perspective on Felix Biestek's (1975) social work ethics theorisation. More well known, Hall and his colleagues mapped how the New Right in the UK appeared to engineer consent for its, initially marginalised, political project in the early 1970s

(Hall et al., 1978). One of the key facets of this analysis was an attentiveness to how particular words and phrases came into popular usage and became installed as 'common sense' (Hall et al., 1978: 152). Their main keyword, the racialised 'mugging', came to trigger and 'connote a whole complex of social themes', meanings and associations (1978: 19). Central here was the work of 'primary definers' who shaped the contours of the 'crisis' (1978: 221). These figures, who Marx (2000: 25) had in an earlier era dubbed the 'interpreters' and 'mouthpieces' of the ruling order, worked to win over the 'silent majority' to the increasingly coercive measures on the part of the state. Influenced by this analysis by Hall and his colleagues, a number of writers later conceptualised 'Thatcherism' to explain the apparent solidity of UK Conservative administrations of the 1980s (Hall and Jacques, 1989).

Although they do not operate from a specifically Gramscian perspective, it has been suggested that Boltanski and Chiapello's *The New Spirit of Capitalism* provides a 'classic analysis of the mechanics by which hegemony is exercised' (Couldry et al., 2010: 110; see also Garrett, 2014a). To simplify a complex and lengthy analysis, their main preoccupation is how the social order is legitimised and what motivates people to participate in the 'spirit of capitalism'. This is the ideology that justifies engagement in capitalism through a series of 'moral justifications' which *bind* people to it. These justifications must be based on arguments that are sufficiently strong to be accepted as self-evident by enough people to overcome 'the despair or nihilism which the capitalist order … constantly induces – not only in those whom it oppresses but also … in those who have responsibility for maintaining it and, via education, transmitting its values' (Boltanski and Chiapello, 2005: 10).

One of the 'difficulties capitalism faces in getting itself accepted is that it addresses itself to people who are by no means ready to sacrifice everything' to the process of capital accumulation (Boltanski and Chiapello, 2005: 487). People are not 'wholly identified with this regime, and have experience of different ones – for example, family attachments, civic solidarity, intellectual or religious life and so on': in fact a 'plurality of value orders' (2005: 487). Nobody can 'be set to work and kept working by force' and so a measure of freedom needs to be 'embedded in capitalism and [this economic system] would negate itself were it to rely exclusively on forcibly enlisting people' (2005: 485). According to this analysis, management discourse fulfils a vital role since today it 'constitutes the form *par excellence* in which the [new] spirit of capitalism is incorporated and received' (2005: 14). Perhaps controversially, Nancy Fraser (2013: 220, 224) argues that second-wave feminism 'may have unwittingly provided a key ingredient of the new spirit of neoliberalism': a 'subterranean elective affinity' serving to unite feminism and neoliberalism may, she suggests, relate to the shared critique of traditional authority.

Although he does not use a Marxist optic, Charles Taylor (2002: 106) addresses 'social imaginaries' which he refers to as the 'ways in which people imagine their social existence, how they fit together with others, how things go on between them and their fellows, the expectations that are normally met, and the deeper normative notions and images that underlie these expectations'. This concept evokes, therefore, how we imagine our social surroundings. Rarely expressed in theoretical terms, imaginaries are carried in images and stories and are 'shared by large groups of people, if not the whole society ... the social imaginary is that common understanding that makes possible common practices and a widely shared sense of legitimacy' (2002: 106; see also Newman and Clarke, 2015). Social imaginaries, the 'largely unstructured and inarticulate understanding of our whole situation', help us to make sense of how we 'fit' with others in a common enterprise or practice and incorporate our grasp of the 'background' (2002: 107). A social imaginary cannot be 'adequately expressed in the form of explicit doctrines', but will include 'an implicit map of social space, of what kinds of people we can associate with, in what ways, and under what circumstances' (Taylor, 2002: 107). An 'important part of this wider background is...a sense of moral order' (p. 109).

Post-Marxists have also drawn on Gramsci (Laclau and Mouffe, 1985; see also Snir, 2016). Whilst perhaps still having their work informed by the Italian communist, some of these theorists stress, for example, how the unconscious can powerfully impact on our perceptions. From a Lacanian perspective, ostensibly purely political discourses frequently tap into or are bolstered by 'a hidden fantasy structure' (Smith, 1998: 75). Hence, they can become 'compelling not just because of what they explicitly say, but also because of their 'concealed responses to our unspeakable desires' (Smith, 1998: 75). In the United States, for example, it has been suggested that an apparently 'neutral technocratic discourse about government budgetary restraint...might be supported by racial and sexual fantasies that are either concealed or referred to in heavily coded ways' (p. 75). Within popular culture, the dreamlike ambience of cinema has exploited and fed the hidden fantasies of audiences in particularly powerful ways. In Frank Capra's 1946 classic *It's a Wonderful Life*, for instance, the liberal town of Bedford Falls only appears decent and dull when contrasted with the cruel, sexually alluring and savage capitalism of Pottersville. Thinking about neoliberal hegemony in this way might contribute to our better interpreting the swirl of ideas and dominant representations, often hinting at procreation and 'deviant' sexuality, welfare dependency and the underclass (see also Chapters 3 and 4). John Macnicol (2015: 4–5), for example, has identified a 'prurient gaze at the alleged sexual profligacy of the underclass, involving ... "the eroticisation of social problems"...in which fears of black male sexuality are interwoven with condemnatory accounts of the alleged sexual profligacy of welfare mothers, all wrapped in apprehensions over miscegenation'. More generally, a persuasive case has been made that when 'linkages between apparently "legitimate" beliefs and unspeakable fantasies are solidified, an extremely influential political force is set in motion' (Smith, 1998: 75). According to this reading, counter-discourses need, therefore, to attend to this 'underlying phantasmatic structure' (1998: 75).

PIERRE BOURDIEU: WELFARE WORDS, THE STATE AND SYMBOLIC VIOLENCE

Perhaps especially in his later work, Pierre Bourdieu was concerned with how neo-liberalism is discursively framed and amplified – *put into words*. Central in his theorisation is the fact that this form of capitalism is trumpeted as 'new', 'modern' and 'radical'. For Bourdieu, in fact, it is a 'characteristic of *conservative revolutions* ... that they present restorations as revolutions' (Bourdieu, 2001: 35, original emphasis). As will become clear, a number of the welfare words to be discussed later – such as welfare and underclass – appear to partly owe their prominence to US-driven discourses. Relatedly, a core concern of Bourdieu is that if free-market orientated US ideas continue to take root, Europe risks being transformed in the same way as a number of US cities where 'public authority has turned into a war machine against the poor' (Wacquant in Bourdieu et al., 2002: 137–8).

The later contributions of Foucault (2008), recovering the German origins of neoliberalism, function as a useful addition to Bourdieu's analysis. However, here the main reason to draw on Bourdieu's theorisation is that, whilst urging us not to overinflate the importance of mere words in a search for meaningful social change, he illuminates how welfare words become embedded. That is to say, like Williams, Bourdieu may be sceptical, but he remains, none the less, alert to the role words play in sustaining or reshaping the world we inhabit. To grasp Bourdieu's relevance to the book's line of analysis, we will, therefore, briefly look at some of the conceptual tools he uses to decipher the workings of the social world (see also Garrett, 2013a: Ch. 7).

HABITUS, FIELD AND CAPITAL

Ideas associated with habitus, field and capital are central to Bourdieu's theoretical architecture. Habitus is 'the constraint of social conditions and conditionings, *right in the very heart* of the "subject"' (Bourdieu, 1994: 15, emphasis added): it constitutes a person's 'whole manner of being' (in Bourdieu et al., 2002: 510). Importantly, given our focus on words, habitus is comprised, in part, of 'specifically communicative dispositions' reflected in the 'form of accent, a way of pronouncing words, a grammatical construction' (Hayward, 2003: 7). However, the acquisition of the 'primary habitus within the family is very far from being a mechanical process of simply inculcation' (Bourdieu, 2000: 164). The same applies to the acquisition of the specific habitus demanded by any 'field' we may subsequently enter, including, for example, those of higher education and social work.

In brief, a 'field' or *champ* is 'a structured social space, a field of forces' (Bourdieu, 1998: 40). Fields constitute 'normative matrices that define socially valued ends and standards and that circulate goods (such as money, awards, prestige, positions, or degrees) accordingly' (Hayward, 2003: 10). They can be interpreted as having at least three key characteristics which are important within Bourdieu's conceptual paradigm. First, the field (or particular fields) are crucial in terms of the evolution of the habitus of those located or positioned there. Second, a field seeks to maintain its autonomy. So, for Bourdieu, maintaining the autonomy of the fields of cultural and scientific production was to become increasingly important, indeed urgent, as the forces of neoliberalism attempt to penetrate them and undermine their relative autonomy. Connected to this, a third characteristic of fields is the competition that takes place within them. In this context, the position of an agent within a given field is determined by the volume and type of capital she/he is able to deploy. The 'right to speak, *legitimacy*, is invested in those agents recognised by the field as powerful possessors of capital' (Moi, 1991: 1022, original emphasis). Bourdieu (1991: 230) argues further that the different 'kinds of capital, like trumps in a game of cards, are powers which define the chances of profit in a given field (in fact, to every field or sub-field there corresponds a particular kind of capital, which is current, as a power or stake in that field)'.

Bourdieu identifies three main forms of capital. First, economic capital, which refers to material and financial assets, ownership of stocks and shares etc. Second, cultural capital which can be viewed as 'scarce symbolic goods, skills and titles' (1998: 221). He believed that educational credentials and familiarity with bourgeois culture, and being at ease in amplifying it, was 'becoming a major determinant of life chances and that, under the cloak of individual talent and academic meritocracy, its unequal distribution was helping to conserve social hierarchy' (1998: 216). A third form of capital, social capital, can be understood as resources or contacts 'accrued by virtue of membership of a particular group' or network (Wacquant, 1998: 221). Symbolic capital can be viewed as different to the three other forms of capital in so far as it can be *any* of these forms. As expressed by Bourdieu (1991: 230), 'symbolic capital, commonly called prestige, reputation, fame, etc … is the form assumed by these different kinds of capital when they are perceived and recognised as legitimate'. What Bourdieu refers to as 'negative symbolic capital' can be interpreted as referring to instances and processes in which individuals and groups, located in particular 'fields', are entirely bereft of any relevant capital. Worse still, they are perceived as possessing negative attributes handicapping their ability to take part in the 'game'. For example, this can be related to the situation of impoverished people having to enter or traverse 'fields' in which the affluent – and their cultural attitudes and dispositions – are recognised or even demanded: for example, the legal 'field', and especially court settings, requiring a certain stilted formality which many – such as parents involved in child care cases – are likely to find intimidating and entirely at odds with their experience of the world. In historical terms, 'unmarried mothers', situated in societies where births within the context of marriage were perceived as the only 'legitimate' form of births, were burdened with 'negative symbolic capital' and associated feelings of socially induced shame (Garrett, 2016a).

In a way that aids the focus on welfare words, Bourdieu uses his overarching theoretical framework and main conceptual tools to dwell on questions of naming, classification and categorization (Bourdieu, 1991). Symbolic capital is brought into play in the 'symbolic struggle for the production of common sense or, more precisely, for the *monopoly of legitimate naming* as the official – i.e. explicit and public – imposition of the legitimate vision of the social world' (1991: 239, emphasis added). Expressed in more simple terms, this means that, on account of their stock of symbolic capital, the powerful have the capacity to describe and define. Conversely, particular groups, lacking in symbolic capital, are often those named, diagnosed and defined by 'experts' within prestigious 'fields' such as medicine and the social sciences (see also Mayes and Horwitz, 2005).

WHAT'S THE PROBLEM? THE STATE AND THE POWER TO NAME

At the university where I work, I am invited to teach a couple of lectures as part of a module called 'Social Issues and Policy Responses'. Through a Bourdieusian lens, this title is conceptually problematic in that it implies that 'social issues' are simply manifest, merely awaiting appropriate 'responses'. Perhaps also integral to the module's framing is the notion that the State, the mechanism responsible for coordinating the 'responses', constitutes a 'neutral delivery system' (Feldman, 2002: 418). What the module's title perhaps insufficiently acknowledges is that the State and its phalanx of 'experts' help to constitute and characterise these 'issues' in the context of the prevailing ordering of economic and political priorities. Indeed, this critical perception will inform the engagement with the welfare words explored in this book. These words are, in fact, integral to the construction and amplification of a plethora of 'social issues' or 'problems' (see also Bacchi, 1999). In this context, ten key questions, or lines of interrogation, might include:

- How does something evolve into a 'social issue'?

- Why does something become a 'social issue' now rather than then?

- Who are the determining forces making the 'social issue'?

- Who are the 'targets' of proposed 'responses'?

- How are the 'target population' imagined, described, rendered knowable?

- How are issues pertaining to class, gender and 'race' generation and (dis)ability being framed and assembled?

- Are the voices and views of the 'targets' heard as part of the discourse defining 'social issues' and policy 'responses'?

- Who is not a target?

- How does the 'social issue' relate to a wider constellation of other connected 'social issues'?

- Given the way the 'social issue' is being assembled, articulated and amplified, can we detect what type of 'solution' is implied and likely to be mooted by 'experts'?

According to Bourdieu (1991: 236), the State is crucial to this 'labour of categorization' and the delineation of 'social issues'. This process is reflected in the neoliberal rebranding of the 'unemployed' into activated 'jobseeker'. Similarly, it is the State, and its agents, imposing the 'legal and administrative categories of "asylum seekers", "refugee" and "economic migrant"' which confer different rights and entitlements' (Loyal, 2003: 83; see also Garrett, 2016b).

Deriving 'reinforcement from the "august apparel" that it deploys, especially through the juridical apparatus', the State relies on the obedient and 'docile dispositions that it inculcates through the very order that it establishes (and also, more specifically, through schooling)' (Bourdieu, 2000: 168). In this sense, the State can be viewed as functioning as a type of engine generating conformism and nurturing – what we have seen Gramsci refer to as – 'common sense'.

Engaging critically with Bourdieu, there is a need to recognise that this 'engine' may *misfire* in that people also awaken and display an ability to discern that they are being manipulated and wilfully misled by the State. His theorisation of the State perhaps also fails to adequately encompass other organisational forms of material and symbolic power lying outside the State. For example, it would be impossible to fully grasp the societal dynamics in Ireland, without taking into account how, historically, the Roman Catholic Church has been empowered to impose its own definitions and interpretations on social relations (Garrett, 2012a, 2013b, 2016a, 2017). Nevertheless, Bourdieu is certainly correct to identify the State as *the* powerful entity largely responsible for naming and classifying. The State also acts as the main mechanism for planning and navigating its own withdrawal from various fields of operation, as services are cut or privatised. Once rendered absent, it still hovers and exerts control by putting in place regimes of regulation and inspection which require that new private and quasi-private agencies provide performance metrics. In this sense, the State is enabled to act as an omnipresent and powerful lever altering and reconfiguring the ways in which social and welfare services are both described and delivered. Andrea Muehlebach (2012) furnishes a good example of how, in Italy, the State constantly promotes the idea that volunteering and filling gaps in formerly publicly funded social work, social care and health provision is vital to the functioning of a civil society imbued with virtue. This has been achieved not only through the creation of a new legal framework, but also through the exhortation and the valorisation of the figure of the volunteer. In this context, the aspiration has been to produce a 'compassionate citizenry' willing to substitute for the absence of the neoliberal State and the dilution of public welfare (Muehlebach, 2012: 110).

SYMBOLIC VIOLENCE

> The people I grew up with were afraid.
> They were alone too long in waiting rooms,
> in dispensaries and in offices whose functions
> they did not understand

These words, featured in the collection *Waiting for the Sky to Fall* by the Irish poet Michael Gorman (1984), incisively evoke what Bourdieu may be trying to convey with his concept of 'symbolic violence'[2]. Living in the west of Ireland in the late 1950s and 1960s, his 'people' felt inferior and ambiguously ill-at-ease in the places that were not meant for the likes of them. These were locations inhabited and governed by petty bourgeois professionals, haughty and confident in their ways of being and fluent with their own vocabularies. Perhaps too they regarded disparagingly those from the lower orders, queuing in their waiting rooms, and spoke about them, and to them, in a condescending manner?

According to Bourdieu, symbolic violence helps us to get a sense of how people respond to descriptions or labels attached to them by the powerful. Symbolic violence, unlike physical violence, it is not a thump on the head or a kick in the stomach, leaving a body crumpled on the floor. Nevertheless, this form of violence *hurts* and degrades and it does so by insidiously imposing the sheer naturalness of a particular worldview reflecting an unequal social order and an asymmetrical distribution of power. As a form of diminishment and disparagement, symbolic violence is not simply confined to language, utterances and verbal exchanges, but tends to infuse *all* forms of engagement involving interactions between the dominant and the dominated. In this regard, Bourdieu's conceptualisation illuminates the 'mundane nature of suffering' which takes the form of petty, daily humiliations and 'routinized types of misery' (McNay, 2014: 34–5). For example, the way that the queuing bodies of claimants – in the neoliberal lexicon 'customers' – are corralled, choreographed and managed as they await 'signing on' in welfare benefit offices.

Often inseparable from enforced material poverty, symbolic violence is not so much an 'identifiable event or specific injury but rather a diffuse and persistent background state of affairs' (McNay, 2014: 34). Impinging on everyday life it gnaws and can prompt in the victims 'feelings of shame, boredom, hopelessness' (2014: 29). It colours the social world and embeds, what Williams (1977) terms 'structures of feelings' and entrenched psychological dispositions. The social suffering generated by symbolic violence also shapes the bodies and comportments of its victims, as illustrated in Simon Charlesworth's (2000) ethnography of life in parts of post-industrial Rotherham in Yorkshire. His respondents, and those he observed around him, were surplus to capital's requirements; casualties, 'people so vulnerable and atomized that they carry the marks of their impoverishment in their bodies as oddity and illness' (2000: 9).

Although it does not preclude the use of physical violence, symbolic violence is a form of ideological violence, which, stigmatising and devaluing an individual or group, is often viewed as legitimate by those subjected to it, because of previous patterns of socialisation. Hence, it can be interpreted as an 'internalized domination that renders individuals complicit with their own oppression' (McNay, 2014: 37). Bourdieu (2000: 169) stresses that this form of violence is 'all the more powerful because it is, for the most part, exercised invisibly and insidiously through familiarization ... and prolonged experience of interactions informed by the structures of domination'. In this context, habitus is the 'dormant force, from which symbolic violence...derives its mysterious efficiency' (2000: 169).

Although he does not use Bourdieu's conceptualisation, US novelist James Baldwin movingly conveyed the feelings of diminishment that symbolic violence generates in subaltern groups in a letter written to his nephew on the one hundredth anniversary of slave emancipation in 1963[3]. Using the still prevalent language of the early 1960s, Baldwin observes that his own father was 'defeated long before he died because at the bottom of his heart, he really believed what white people said about him ...You can only be destroyed by believing that you really are what the white world calls a *nigger*' (original emphasis). Mindful of the character of the pre-civil rights era in the United States, he continues:

> You were born into a society which spelled out with brutal clarity, and in as many ways as possible, that you were a worthless human being. You were not expected to aspire to excellence; you were expected to make your peace with mediocrity. Wherever you turned, James, in your short time on earth, you have been told where you could go and what you could do (and *how* you could do it) and where you could live and who you could marry ...it was intended that you should perish by never being allowed to go behind the white man's definitions. (Baldwin, 1993 [1963]: 8–9, original emphasis)

Arguably, this provides a good evocation of how symbolic violence operates: how it bled into the lives and minds of African-Americans during a period of continuing white supremacy in the early 1960s (see also Reflection and Talk Box 2). In England, and again illuminating the idea of symbolic violence, the writer Lynsey Hanley (2016: xii) similarly observes how working class people are encouraged to become 'stuck in ruts that don't look like ruts: you can be yourself, but only in so far as "being yourself" stays within well-defined social parameters'.

Relating these ideas back to our earlier discussion on Gramsci, it can be argued that, in many ways, hegemony relies on symbolic violence:

> This takes a number of forms ... texts perform symbolic violence in the exclusions they perform and the silences they impose on outsider groups. But symbolic violence also takes the form of taste judgements, where outsiders are marginalized and shamed; of physical behaviour and 'ways of living' where some feel confident and others feel awkward. (Jones, 2006: 52)

Like Gramsci, Bourdieu allows for the 'existence of strategies of resistance, individual, or collective, ordinary or extraordinary' (Bourdieu, 2000: 173). Nevertheless, he criticises the Marxist tradition for allegedly 'ignoring the extraordinary inertia which results from the inscription of social structures in bodies' (2000: 173). Wacquant (2014) has been keen to counteract interpretations of his late colleague's work which, for him, lay too great an emphasis on habitus being a frozen, static and entirely compliant disposition. However, as mentioned earlier, it is still tempting to question whether the State, via schools and a myriad of mechanisms, is always so successful in inculcating the type of 'docile dispositions' identified by Bourdieu. Fairclough (2003: 25–6), for example, refers 'to a stage short of inculcation at which people may acquiesce to new discourses without accepting them – they may mouth them rhetorically, for strategic and instrumental purposes.'

Globally, it is apparent that those who are able to generate and sustain their own counter-hegemonic vocabularies and ways of seeing, do *resist* the State and its agents. As Beverley Skeggs (2014: 16) reminds her sociology colleagues, if we 'can only see from within the blinkers of capital's logic we will never understand or recognize the values ... the gaps, the un-captured and better ways of being and doing' actively present with capitalism. Such tendencies and acts of resistance are instantiated in uprisings, rebellions and riots (Badiou, 2012) and, within bureau-cratic fields such as social work, through minor and stubborn acts of 'deviance' and non-compliance (Carey and Foster, 2011; see also Clarke et al., 2007). People do, in fact, 'find ways of surviving, negotiating, accommodating, refusing and resisting' and do not merely 'act like automatons envisaged in the governmental plans and strategies of the powerful' (Clarke, 2005: 159).

Wacquant in many ways shares Bourdieu's analyses of the social world. However, stretching beyond his late colleague's work, his own, separable, theorisation war-rants isolated attention because his specific conceptualisations on the conjoined evolution of the prison and welfare provide another potentially useful framework enabling a better understanding as to how those he terms neoliberalism's 'castaway categories' are described, dealt with, managed and contained (Wacquant, 2009: 4).

LOÏC WACQUANT: WELFARE WORDS AND NEOLIBERAL PENALITY

> It looks like a prison, it's not the most welcoming of buildings ... The most daunting thing is that when you go in, you don't know where to line up or where you are meant to be going. You walk in a bit doe-eyed, but being there brings you down to reality. You are part of something else now, something you never imagined yourself being a part of. (in Ingle, 2009: 19)

In early 2009, with Ireland deep in an economic crisis, *The Irish Times* produced a feature on the experience on 'life on the dole'. In the final month of the previous year, 23,000 people, many of them never having envisaged they would become familiar with the 'dole office' milieu, had 'signed on' for the first time. Laura Kenneally was a young woman in this position and the remarks above are her initial feelings about the local social welfare office on Cumberland Street in Dublin.

Laura's remarks on the resemblance of the office to a 'prison' relates to what Wacquant terms 'neoliberal penality'[4]. One of Wacquant's chief assertions is that those intent on analysing the evolution of welfare within neoliberalism often fail to take mass incarceration into account (see also Garrett, 2016c). For example, the irruption of the penal state in America has gone 'virtually unnoticed' by those academics focusing on the 'crisis of the welfare state' (Wacquant 2009: xiii). Key definers of neoliberalism on the political left have, therefore, furnished defective analyses because of this lacuna. For example, David Harvey's (2005) respected contributions on the rise of neoliberalism are 'woefully incomplete' because he has 'barely a few passing mentions of the prison' (Wacquant, 2009: 309).

Wacquant's prime, but far from exclusive, focus is the United States which he views as the 'Living Laboratory of the Neoliberal Future' (Wacquant, 2009). In this context, it is vital that we 'construe the prison as a core political institution, instead of a mere technical implement for enforcing the law and handling of criminals' (2009: xviii). Wacquant emphasises the sheer 'grandeur' of the penal state in the US and reveals how the growth in prison numbers is approximately coterminous with the rise of neoliberalism. After 1973, the confined population 'doubled in ten years and quadrupled in twenty' (2009: 114). If it were 'a city, the carceral system of the United States would be the fourth-largest metropolis, behind Chicago' (2009: 114). Wacquant is also particularly attentive to how imprisonment and welfare are racialised (Wacquant, 2009). This is not only of relevance in the United States, given that in 2014 black people comprised 10% of the UK prison population whilst making up only 3.5% of the total population. Indeed, there is an even greater disparity in the UK between the proportion of black people in prison and in the general population than there is in the United States (McVeigh, 2016).

Nowadays, Wacquant (2009: 99) maintains, it should no longer be intellectually tenable to analyse the 'implementation of welfare policy at ground level without taking into account the overlapping operations of the penal institution'. Welfare offices, for instance, are borrowing the 'stock-in-trade techniques of the correctional institutions ... a constant close-up monitoring, strict spatial assignments and time constraints, intensive record-keeping and case management, periodic interrogation and reporting, and a rigid system of graduated sanctions for failing to perform properly' (2009: 101–2). Such practices are undergirded by a 'paternalist conception of the role of the state in respect to the poor, according to which the conduct of disposed and dependent citizens must be closely supervised and, whenever necessary, corrected through rigorous protocols of surveillance, deterrence and sanction, very much like those routinely applied to offenders under criminal justice supervision' (2009: 59–60). In this context, the 'new punitive organization of welfare programs operates in the manner of a labor parole program designed to push its "beneficiaries" into the sub poverty jobs' (2009: 43). Partly evincing the accuracy of Wacquant's perspective, as will be observed in the next chapter, the coercive language of the prison has certainly infiltrated the discourse of welfare dependency with its references to 'repeat offenders' and 'recidivism'.

Within this evolving social order, particular targeted groups, such as 'poor single mothers', are positioned not 'as citizens participating in a community of equals, but as subjects saddled with abridged rights and expanded obligations until such time as they have demonstrated full commitment to the values of work and family by their reformed conduct' (2009: 98). For Wacquant, gender is also significant in that the 'social silhouette' of recipients of Temporary Assistance for Needy Families (TANF), administered and paid under the Personal Responsibility and Work Opportunity Reconciliation Act of 1996 (PRWORA), 'turns out to be a near-exact replica of the profile of jail inmates save for gender inversion' (2009: 98) (see also Chapters 3 and 4). Dorothy E Roberts (2014a: 434) observes how, in the United States, prisons and 'out of home care' for children (involving processes of fostering and adoption) 'function together to discipline and control poor and low-income black women by keeping them under intense state supervision and blaming them for the hardships their families face as a result of societal inequities' (see also Roberts, 2012, 2014b). Furthermore, there may be an implicit eugenicist strand to US incarceration policies and practices in so far as the 'racial bias of the criminal justice system places a disproportionate number of black and Latino men and women in prison at precisely the moment in their life cycles in which nonincarcerated adults typically start building their families' (Smith, 2010: 11).

Wacquant's theorisation has prompted a range of criticisms, with Schram and his colleagues suggesting that the French sociologist could produce a more nuanced reading of developments in the United States. Techniques focused on dealing with welfare and the unemployed encompass various 'incentives' and educative programmes and these are 'no less important than penalties' (Schram et al., 2010: 745). This is not to argue that US welfare is more politically benign, it is merely to recognise that there is a 'wide array of services, classes, incentives, benefits, and sanctions that all aim to turn welfare clients into suitable candidates for low-wage employment' (2010: 745). In short, the modes of governing welfare clients are more varied than Wacquant's analysis appears to maintain. A number of his critics have also argued that he overemphasises the rupture taking place with past practices in terms of how problem populations are currently named, described, confined, managed and regulated. Alert to this criticism, Wacquant argues, however, that the key difference today is the reach and capacity of the State, now 'endowed with budgetary, human and technological resources without equivalent in history' (Wacquant, 2009: 28). At the end of the nineteenth century it 'sufficed for an individual to change his name and move to a different city or region and melt into the surrounding landscape for the authorities to lose track of him' (2009: 28). Today, many States possess the infrastructural and surveillant power enabling them 'to penetrate the population under its aegis and rule over their behaviours' in much more expansive ways (2009: 28).

Since the economic 'crash' some criminologists have detected shifts in how the inflation in actual prison numbers is responded to by neoliberal states. In the United States, on account of concern about the escalating costs of prison during a period of financial cutbacks, various measures have been considered including – outlandishly – using Mexico as a quasi-prison colony. Some Californian counties are also experimenting with various neoliberal ways to reduce costs and increase revenues. Riverside County, for example, decided to charge inmates $140 per night with prisoner debts being recovered from post-prison earnings. In Fremont, inmates are provided with the opportunity to relocate to a safer and quieter area of the prison with such 'upgrades' resulting in a $155 additional charge per night (Aviram, 2016: 270–71; see also Surowiecki, 2016).

AUTONOMIST MARXISM: WELFARE WORDS IN THE SOCIAL FACTORY

Whilst castigating capitalist exploitative practices, Gramsci observed that 'work is the only thing that confers moral impulses' (Gramsci in Bellamy, 1994: 71). Leaving aside the rather tendentious nature of this assertion, it is apparent that a number of the welfare words and phrases to be examined relate explicitly or implicitly to work; for example, welfare dependency frequently connotes notions about the supposedly 'workshy'. Making people work is the 'central goal of schooling, a criterion of successful medical and psychiatric treatment, and an ostensible goal of most welfare policies and unemployment compensation programs' (Glazer in Weeks, 2011: 7). Although insufficiently examined, a saturating 'work ethic' ambience provides part of the moral, political and normative context in which social workers are located (Frayne, 2015). Historically, the enthusiasm (or lack thereof) of a male 'breadwinner' to work provided a key indicator as to whether a family ostensibly in need of assistance, were truly 'deserving' (Woodroofe, 1962; see also Chapters 3 and 4). The degree of respect accorded to a 'client' also tended to be tapered to their preparedness to sell their labour.

In more recent times, practitioners, rooted in a range of multidisciplinary networks, appear intent on promoting the work 'readiness' of 'clients' (McDonald and Chenoweth, 2009; see Chapter 3). This can be seen as a component of the UK 'Looking After Children' (LAC) materials designed, in the 1990s, for social work practice with children and young people in care settings (see also Chapter 8). Specific messages about work and what constitute *appropriate* employee demeanours featured as powerful sub-texts in the vocabularies of these assessment schedules. This was particularly the case in the section of the action and assessment records (AARs) which, directing the attention of the social worker to the 'social presentation' of a young person about to leave public care, was manifestly fixated with grooming compliant workers (Garrett, 2003). The implicit ideological orientation in which the LAC project was marinated was that youthful labour ought to be malleable, flexible and compliant. That is to say, potential labour must be ready and able to exhibit – by way of demeanour and disposition – that it is able to contribute to the processes of capital accumulation and would not attitudinally destabilise or interrupt such processes or the relationships inherent in them.

Given these developments, the theorisation of various writers associated with Autonomist Marxism may also furnish an additional critical lens to look at welfare words. In Italy, Autonomy (*Autonomia*), was an expansive network of extra-parliamentary alliances which united students, the young unemployed and others who were socially and economically disenfranchised (the *emarginati*) (Wright, 2008). Its origins are traceable to the 1960s and the occupations and mass strikes associated with the so-called 'Hot Autumn' of 1969. Such protests were to continue and reach their height in 1977. Antonio Negri (1933–) remains perhaps the most well known Autonomist theorist, but others, such as Kathy Weeks (2011), whose interventions are imbued with a more feminist orientation, have made very significant contributions.

The core feature of this frequently complex body of theorisation maintains that wage labour now *subsumes* all spheres of society. It 'permeates the entire society in a multitude of ways' (Landy, 1994: 221) with 'free time' becoming 'free labour' (Gill and Pratt, 2008: 17; see also Muehlebach, 2012). This analysis highlights 'not the institution of private property, but rather the imposition and organization of work' (Weeks, 2011: 97) In short, capitalism is a 'system built on the subordination of life to work' (Cleaver in Weeks, 2011: 97). Within this theoretical paradigm, work constitutes, therefore, the primary 'basis of capitalist relations, the glue that holds the system together' (Weeks, 2011: 97). From this perspective the problem with work cannot be reduced to the 'extraction of surplus value or the degradation of skill', but extends to the ways that work dominates our entire lives (2011: 13). The fact that one must 'work to "earn a living"' is taken as part of the natural order rather than as a social convention' (2011: 3). Hence, the 'social role of wage work has been so naturalized as to seem necessary and inevitable' (2011: 7). More fundamentally, capital – and the vocabularies, ideologies and disciplines it annexes – continually 'moralizes, normalizes, and mythologizes work' (2011: 92). This results in our tendency to 'focus more on the problems with this or that job, or on their absence, than on work as a requirement, work as a system, work as a way of life' (2011: 3). More fundamentally, because such notions are so embedded, there is a failure to treat and analyse work as a *disciplinary* apparatus. Paradoxically, work locations are more frequently regarded as spheres of 'individual choice rather than a site for the exercise of political power' (2011: 4).

In interpreting work's gradual colonization of the private and domestic sphere, the Autonomists dismiss the notion of a 'work–life balance' given that it is entirely unattainable, for most, within neoliberal capitalism. Countering such conceptualisations, Negri (2005) refers to the 'social factory' or 'the factory without walls', while Lazzarato (1996: 136) prefers the term 'diffuse factory'. Specifically in terms of social work, the 'social factory' concept would certainly seem to relate to the ceaseless spillage of work-related tasks into the private lives of practitioners given employers' promotion of 'flexibility' and the activation of '24/7' responses (Garrett, 2008). Furthermore, the Care Standards Act 2000 resulted in the setting up of the General Social Care Council (GSCC) in England. In 2002 the GSCC published its Codes of Practice which make it apparent that being a social worker is not seen as 'a nine-to-five job, in which there is left a clear separation of work/home/private life' (McLaughlin, 2007: 1274)[5].

Within the 'social factory', labour is squeezed for every scintilla of profit. In the United States this has prompted new efforts to maintain female workers when they are at their most productive and profitable. Hence, new egg-freezing technologies are offered to female employees to try and ensure that they do not become temporarily adrift from the 'work society' (Weeks, 2011) by taking maternity leave. Normally valued at $10,000, this procedure is now provided for free to highly qualified female employees in cutting edge IT corporations, such as Apple and Facebook, keen to encourage staff to defer childbearing. This practice none too subtly conveys the message 'wait and have your kids in your forties, fifties, or even sixties; devote your high-energy, productive years to us' (Fraser, 2016: 115).

Some workers, subject to precarious working conditions characteristic of the lower rungs of the labour market ladder, are often intimidated into working longer shifts, well beyond what is conducive to the health of mind and body (Waters, 2015). Others, however, are induced to work longer hours by more subtle means that lay great emphasis on the 'freedom' and 'liberation' achievable *within* work. Significant also is a 'just be yourself' liberatory managerial discourse that 'asks workers to bring their "authentic" selves from outside work, attempting thereby to incorporate "the whole person into the production matrix"' (Fleming in Weeks, 2011: 107). These approaches seek to 'put some life back into work by appropriating life itself' (Fleming in Weeks, 2011: 231). This aspect is frequently reflected in job advertisements: for example, the supermarket chain Aldi tries to entice graduates by a photograph of a fresh-faced, smart and youthful white woman with the accompanying text having her confide that since becoming an Aldi employee she has become transformed: 'I'm still me, but the most confident, all conquering version of me' (*The Irish Times*, 6 November, 2015).

According to the Autonomists, the period in which we live is one where the 'whole life experience of the worker is harnessed to capital' (Gill and Pratt, 2008: 17). This conceptualization is largely understood in terms of time in that capital is no longer needing to 'buy the entire lifetime of a worker…it is enough to capture isolated fragments of time, moments of attention and operability' (Berardi, 2009: 147). Indeed, this perspective illuminates the situation of those – frequently women – involved in providing care services who are subject to precarious working conditions, uncertain contractual terms and constant and unrelenting surveillance (see also Chapter 8). Their labour is, moreover, 'deterritorialized, dispersed and decentralized' (Gill and Pratt, 2008: 7)

During the 1960s Mario Tronti, amongst other Autonomist writers and activists, called for a 'radical refusal' to participate in capitalist work arrangements. Hence the call for disruptive workplace interventions such as the *autoriduzione* or 'go-slow', absenteeism, the wildcat strike and acts of mass sabotage (Bowring, 2004: 108–9). This refusal does not simply 'pose itself against the present organisation of work; it should also be understood as a creative practice, one that seeks to re-appropriate and reconfigure existing forms of production and reproduction' (Weeks, 2011: 99). Hence, the problem is not simply to liberate production from the control of capital and to restore dignity to labour, it is also vital for 'humanity to liberate itself *from* production by ceasing to treat it as the centre of gravity of all social activities and individual action' (Vincent in Weeks, 2011: 101). In this sense, the word 'refusal' may be somewhat misleading in that it fails to capture the constructive and generative dimension so central in Autonomist Marxist thinking. Virno prefers the term '*engaged* withdrawal' (Virno, 1996: 196, original emphasis). He also relates this to the concept of 'Exodus' (*esodo*) used to 'define mass defection from the State ... The term is not at all conceived as some defensive existential strategy – it is neither exiting on tiptoe through the back door nor a search for sheltering hideaways' (1996: 196). Such a move involves dissidents, within the fabric of capitalism, embarking on generative 'lines of flight' (1996: 203; see also Berardi, 2009). The strategic aim of this project is to create autonomous spaces in which people can arrive at a sense of worth and self-valorization as an alternative to capitalist valorization. One might argue, therefore, that the whole idea of activation relating to workfare, as we shall see in the next chapter, aims to eliminate this form of reasoning and to prevent any opportunity to embark on 'lines of flight' from capitalist domination.

It is not simply that work 'extends across different spaces (the home and, with mobile devices, almost everywhere)', but that the temporality of life is governed by work (Gill and Pratt, 2008: 17). Information and communication technologies play, as many social workers are clearly aware, a significant role given the 'unceasing flow of email, online search, smartphone activities, apps, texts, video meetings, social media interactions, and so forth' (Zuboff, 2015: 76; see also Ryan and Garrett, 2017). As we now become more saturated in a system Zobuff (2015) refers to as 'surveillance capitalism', 'three of the world's seven billion people are now computer-mediated in a wide range of their daily activities far beyond the traditional boundaries of the workplace' (2015: 77). Although not located within the Autonomist Marxist tradition, Melissa Gregg's (2011) examination of 'information, communication and education (ICE) professions' in Australia, also illuminates how the so-called 'flexible workplace' is *remaking* lives around work. On the 'new frontier of mobile and out-of-office work', inhabited also by many social workers, employees 'rarely "count" as work the practices of message monitoring and email checking that are fundamental requirements of professional life' (Gregg, 2011: 167).

Moreover, developments in the future may well include more intensive forms of employee surveillance, including the imposition of sociometric ID badges able to monitor the 'communications behaviour of individuals – tone of voice, posture and body language, as well as who spoke to whom for how long' (Lohr, 2014). Importantly, given the focus in *Welfare Words*, the Autonomists stress that language and communication are, in fact, pivotal in the evolving patterning of work. In the past, factory workers were often perceived by their employers as little more than appendages to the assembly lines; merely 'hands' (Braverman, 1998). In Henry Ford's car assembly factories, for example, workers were deterred from speaking to each other and had to develop a technique they referred to as the 'Fordization of the face' – the ability to speak without moving the lips (Grandin, 2010: 81).

In many respects factory labour was mute because the sheer din within many factories presented an obstacle to verbal communication. In many parts of the world, such forms of production remain broadly similar. However, many of the thinkers associated with Autonomist analyses are attentive to how workers in post-Fordist settings are expected to display skills in loquacity. Employers now 'go out of their way to encourage linguistic cooperation among workers. Previously conceived as a distraction from the production process, horizontal communication – e.g. chatter – has increasingly ... become its very substance' (Fritsch et al., 2016b: 8). Indeed, labour in social work, health, education, the media, and increasingly in other sectors of the economy, is inseparable from the efficacious use of language and good verbal communication skills.

JACQUES RANCIÈRE: WELFARE WORDS, DE-CLASSIFICATION, POLICE AND POLITICS

Franco Basaglia (1924–1980), the founder of 'democratic psychiatry' in Italy, argues that to have a relationship with an individual, it is necessary to establish it independently of the label by which the person has been defined' (in Giordano, 2014: 74). Jacques Rancière's intellectual and political project can be related to this perspective in that he constantly seeks to disrupt accepted ways of categorising and classifying people. His complex philosophical contributions incessantly *dis-order* dominant ways of perceiving and describing the world and the roles that groups and individuals are expected to fulfil. In his own words, he investigates how to 'deconstruct positions, to muck up a certain consensus' (Rancière, 2016: 102).

Such perceptions are, for example, entirely at odds with the notion that workers should fulfil a subservient role within the class system at the core of the politics of the UK Conservative Party. This is not to argue that the Conservative government is anti-working class *per se*. Rather, despite the speech by Theresa May featured at the end of the chapter, its policies seek to ensure that the working class perpetually knows *its place*. In terms of popular television culture, this is also instantiated in historical dramas, such as *Call the Midwife* and *Downton Abbey*, in which 'posh' is rehabilitated and the working class characters evoked are mostly decent, deferential and largely acquiesce with the way things are. In contrast, Rancière encourages us to reflect on how people, especially those perceived by ruling elites as constituting the lower orders, are stationed and stultified. Significantly, for the analysis in *Welfare Words*, this involves their being *fixed* into place through the language used and naming practices deployed. Perhaps implicitly therefore, Rancière encourages us to interrogate the way welfare words function to fasten down particular dominant meanings. His work supports subversive readings and critical engagements aspiring to dis-assemble, de-stabilise and de-classify (see also Garrett, 2015a, 2015b). Within this democratic, even possibly anarchistic, paradigm, the 'democratic voice is the voice of those who reject the prevailing social distribution of roles, who refuse the way a society shares out power and authority' (Hallward, 2005: 34).

Ostensibly a historical study, *Proletarian Nights* (Rancière, 2012) brings the past into conversation with contemporary debates in, and beyond, the French social and political milieu. Drawing from extensive archival work, Rancière highlights how many Parisian artisans do not fit the picture that historians and political thinkers usually present. Focusing on the period 1830–1848, he reveals how many of these workers devoted their night time hours to creative writing, choosing to produce poetry, prose, polemics, letters and diaries. They set out 'to appropriate the language and culture of the other, to act as if intellectual equality were indeed real and effectual' (Rancière, 2003: 219). In Rancière's interpretation, these artisans were committed to conjuring up a form of *active* equality within the confines of the hierarchical world they lived in (see also Rancière, 2016). The 'mere fact of writing', in fact, violated 'class-specific rules of decorum' and can be perceived as 'radically democratizing' (Parker, 2003: xiii, xi).

This fascination with workers wandering beyond the roles allotted to them by the dominant forces in society is a recurring preoccupation in Rancière's philosophical contribution. The shoemaker, whose image is featured on the cover of *The Philosopher and His Poor* (Rancière, 2003) is emblematic. For him, the shoemaker, or cobbler, is the generic name of the person who is not where s/he 'ought to be' (Rancière, 2003: 48). 'Shoemaking remains at the very bottom of the trades', and the shoemaker is the 'least busy with their work, and the least deluded about the glory of the artisan' (Rancière, 2003: 59). In this sense, the figure of the shoemaker is symbolic of a more generalised latent refusal by workers to abide by the rules of the game (see also our discussion on the Autonomist Marxists earlier in the chapter). Thus, the dominant order is 'menaced wherever the shoemaker does something else other than make shoes' (Rancière, 2003: 61). According to Plato, for example, it was important for individuals to maintain their positions within the existing social order and not to 'do anything other than *your own affair* ... if you are a shoemaker, make shoes – and make children who do the same' (Rancière, 1991: 34, original emphasis). This fixation with fixing people is currently present in societies such as India, given the continuing prevalence of a rigidly hierarchical caste system (Shahid and Jha, 2014), but it is, of course, also a preoccupation of societies in the West which, often despite the rhetoric of social mobility, remain rigidly tiered, with people's location being largely determined by class, race and gender.

In contrast, Rancière evokes a world where there is 'recognition of the equal capacity of all for sophisticated complexity of self-understanding and self-performance which exceeds the conservative insistence that the worker must do one thing and one thing only' (Davis, 2010: 22). The 'fundamental idea' he holds onto is that the 'dominated do not need masters or leaders to tell them what they think and what to say. Their plight is not due to false consciousness or ignorance, but to a social organization that systematically makes their voices and their achievements invisible and inaudible' (Deranty, 2010: 6). This perspective, acknowledging the significance of words, is vitally imbued with an awareness of radical possibilities and it can be linked to Rancière's ideas on the 'police' and 'politics': both words which he pulls and stretches beyond the common understanding of what they are ordinarily meant to signify and describe.

'POLICE' AND 'POLITICS'

For Rancière, the 'police' is 'less concerned with repression than with a more basic function: that of constituting what is or is not perceivable, determining what can or cannot be seen, dividing what can be heard from what cannot' (Ross, 2002: 23):

> Policing involves configuring the common world as a stable distribution of places, identities, functions and competencies. The police order defines which places are inside and which are outside, which bodies are in the right place and which in the wrong one, which names fit those places and bodies and which do not. (Rancière, 2007: 561)

It is a sign of 'weakness' and not 'strength' when states inflate police officers [those who he terms merely the 'petty police'] to the 'point of putting it in charge of the whole set of police functions' (Rancière, 1999: 28).

The oppositional counter to 'police' logic is provided by 'politics', an 'extremely determined activity antagonistic to policing' (Rancière, 1999: 29). 'Politics' is the process occurring when the voices of those Rancière (1999: 11) elliptically terms a 'part of those who have no part' suddenly 'grab hold of words' and make themselves heard (Rancière, 2016: 55). This understanding fundamentally departs from the activity ordinarily regarded as politics which, for him, is denuded of any meaningful content and rooted in a form of 'consensus' paradoxically representing the 'disappearance of politics' (Rancière, 1999: 102). For example, in the West, regular elections are held, yet the possibility of genuine change is excluded and the management of affairs is increasingly outsourced to autocratic 'alphabet' bodies such as the WTO, IMF, EU and ECB. Thus, the 'absolute identification of politics with the management of capital is no longer the shameful secret hidden behind the "forms" of democracy; it is the openly declared truth by which our governments acquire legitimacy' (1999: 113).

In contrast, Rancière's own construction of 'politics' entirely 'turns on equality as its principle' and, attentive to the use of words, demonstrates the 'equality of any speaking being with any other speaking being' (1999: ix; 30). Importantly, given this book's focus on words, speech is immensely significant within Rancière's overall philosophy. Significant political transitions involve, as observed earlier, the subversive 'appropriation', by the oppressed, of words that do not ordinarily belong to them (Rancière, 2016: 73). Indeed, many 'revolutionary movements' have started with 'a capacity to turn around' the 'adjectives the people at the top have imposed on the people at the bottom (2016: 71).

Accordingly, political struggle is a struggle to have one's voice 'heard and recognised as the voice of a legitimate partner' (Žižek, 2004: 70). A number of commentators stress this aspect of Rancière's thinking maintaining that 'the political' produces 'a rearrangement of social reality for a refreshed perception, where bodies *and voices* that were neither seen nor heard can be included in a communicative context' (Deranty, 2003: 146, emphasis added). So, for example, the workers in *Proletarian Nights* 'transgressed and subverted the order of things, by claiming the right to be poets, playwrights, philosophers, and so on, that is, the right to have a meaningful voice beyond the constraints of their social destiny' (Deranty, 2003: 152). In this sense, Rancière is attracted to the 'singular voices of isolated individuals who had attempted precisely to throw away the iron cast of class categorization' (Deranty, 2010: 8)

Rancièrean 'politics' stops things 'in their tracks' with the 'presupposition of the equality of anyone and everyone' (Rancière, 1999: 17). 'Politics' may be 'rare, always local and occasional' (1999: 139), but when it occurs the 'whole tissue of congealed expectations and habits that anchor one to one's role or place can evaporate' (Ross, 2002: 105). At these moments the 'dividing up of human beings is called into question' (Rancière, 2016: 162). For example, the eruption of 'politics' can be connected to the 'events' of May 1968 in Paris. As Kristin Ross (2002) reminds us, this was period when students ceased to 'function as students, workers as workers, and farmers as farmers. The movement took the form of political experiments in *de*classification, in disrupting the natural "givenness" of places' (2002: 25). During the weeks of insurrection everydayness seemed to be momentarily transformed. For example, meetings held were 'neither magical nor mythical but simply the experience of incessantly running into people that social, cultural or professional divisions kept one from meeting up with, little events that produced the sense that those mediations or social compartments had simply withered away' (2002: 103).

CONCLUSION

Clearly, not all the theorists mentioned in this chapter are relevant to *all* the welfare words discussed. Gramsci's conceptualisations of hegemony and common sense aid an understanding of the encompassing class and cultural structures in which such words are located. Bourdieu's theorisation, especially his ideas on the role of the State and 'symbolic violence', are useful resources we can deploy in analysing most of the welfare words discussed and particularly those constructing or labelling individuals and groups in a derogatory manner. Wacquant's work, as well as being mindful of the evolution of 'neoliberal penality', suggests that the boundaries between penal/welfare policies and practices are becoming hazy. The Autonomist Marxists helpfully stress the centrality of work within the 'social factory' and indicate how this conceptualisation might illuminate certain welfare words. Rancière's work encourages his readers to have regard to the larger encompassing 'police' structure in which the welfare words are housed.

REFLECTION AND TALK BOX 2

1. During the summer of 2016 when Theresa May became the UK prime minister these remarks were included in her first statement:

   > If you're from an ordinary working class family, life is much harder than many people in Westminster realise. You have a job but you don't always have job security. You have your own home, but you worry about paying a mortgage. You can just about manage but you worry about the cost of living and getting your kids into a good school. If you're one of those families, if you're just managing, I want to address you directly. I know you're working around the clock, I know you're doing your best, and I know that sometimes life can be a struggle. The government I lead will be driven not by the interests of the privileged few, but by yours. We will do everything we can to give you more control over your lives. When we take the big calls, we'll think not of the powerful, but you. When we pass new laws, we'll listen not to the mighty but to you. When it comes to taxes, we'll prioritise not the wealthy, but you. (May, 2016a)

   How can these comments be interpreted in terms of Gramsci's ideas associated with 'hegemony'? Moreover, if you are not located in England, what may be some of the main components constituting hegemony in your own national setting?

2. Earlier in the chapter, reference was made to a letter in James Baldwin's *The Fire Next Time*. How can this passage be related to Bourdieu's 'symbolic violence' concept? Mindful of the current 'Black Lives Matter' campaign, can the same conceptualisation be applied to how the State, in the United States – but also elsewhere – has failed to adequately investigate the deaths of black people at the hands of police officers?

3. The former coalition government in the UK argued that disengaged pupils will benefit from the 'values of a military ethos' and funded projects employing former armed forces personnel to 'improve educational achievement' and teach self-discipline and teamwork (Department for Education, 2012a). How might this relate to some of the ideas on work developed by the Autonomist Marxists?

4. In his analysis of the surveillance which the unemployed are subject to in Australia, Paul Henman (2004: 187) observes: 'The activity of classifying things into groups and the location of where divisions are put are highly political exercises. Such actions have considerable effects and reflect the distribution of power. The way in which categories are defined and who defines them tell a story of power'. Can Rancière's thinking be used to interrogate such stories of power?

FURTHER READING

This chapter has covered, rather quickly, some quite complex theoretical ground. In relation to Gramsci, there is a need to engage with translated extracts from his notebooks and Hoare and Nowell Smith (2005) remains a good starting point. Kate Crehan (2016) has produced a lively articulation of Gramsci's 'common sense' and related themes, applying them to the rise of the Occupy Movement in the United States. Casting her analytical gaze to the political right, Crehan also examines the ascendancy of the Tea Party Movement which was to provide part of the electoral base for Trump's triumph in 2016. Hall and O'Shea (2015) provide a good discussion on neoliberal 'common sense'. The exchanges featured in Bourdieu and Wacquant (2004) furnish an accessible entry into the thought of Bourdieu. Readers might also find my own chapter, in Garrett (2013a: Chapter 7), useful. Wacquant's (2009) focal contribution is *Punishing the Poor*. The work of the Autonomist Marxists influences Kathy Weeks' (2011) lucid feminist engagement with work in contemporary neoliberal societies. I have endeavoured to introduce Jacques Rancière to a social work readership in two articles (Garrett, 2015a, 2015b).

CHAPTER 3

WELFARE DEPENDENCY

Welfare dependency – (usually with negative connotations) dependency on welfare benefits provided by the state, as forming part or all of a person's means of financial support. (*Oxford English Dictionary*)

INTRODUCTION

As observed in Chapter 1, the phrase 'social security', once dominant in the UK in terms of the politics and administration of state benefits, is now rarely used[1]. The prevalent discursive alternative – welfare – is now purposely configured and often experienced by claimants as a heavily surveilled system of social insecurity. In neoliberal parlance, welfare is invariably tainted by the latent risk of dependency. Indeed, the spectre of welfare dependency furnishes the socially corrosive, but still potent, ideological cover for workfare: an 'American invention coined in the 1969 by journalist William Safire on behalf of his patron Richard Nixon' (Barbier, 2014: 74)[2].

A new 'toughness' in relation to welfare has purposely stirred resentment against claimants who are, it is often alleged, undermining the ability of 'hard working families' to claw their way back to prosperity. Those mired in welfare dependency are framed as a burdensome weight serving to impede, with their 'negative' and 'workshy' attitudes and lifestyles, the journey to economic 'recovery'. Activation policies targeted at claimants are also coupled to the 'activation of emotions' against them and their sluggish, inert, and wilfully parasitic lifestyles (Clayton et al., 2015). However, if followed, the dominant discourse suggests the 'pathway' to work will culminate in a bright and 'empowered' sense of 'independence' (see also Connor, 2010).

This inflated, affective dimension to policy discourse was apparent, for example, in the foreword to the UK Coalition government's *Social Justice: Transforming Lives* (HM Government, 2012: 1), where Iain Duncan Smith (Secretary of State for Work and Pensions from May 2010 until March 2016) led his readers on a hellish journey into the house of 'children whose parents are addicted to crack-cocaine'. Here 'Dad has passed out on the mattress in his own vomit, mum is crouched over a table, preparing her fix. What you don't see is the child hidden in the corner crying' (HM Government, 2012: 1). Such interventions are significant in terms of their affective and emotional capacity to potentially solidify hegemonic accounts of welfare dependency (see also Clayton et al., 2015). Here, the focal message conveyed is that people are stuck in the quagmire of dependency simply because of personal deficits and shortcomings. What is more, they can be perceived as guilty, not just of the crime of consuming illegal substances, they are also irresponsible parents for whom we are urged to feel contempt, indignation and an entirely reasonable sense of revulsion. Moreover, the individuals represented remain hazy, falling short of definition as authentic human beings in that their whole lives are defined by the things they lack – agency, aspiration and a capacity to meaningfully care for those around them.

How, then, did the stigmatising of welfare/welfare benefits/welfare dependency constellation come to be so politically and socially charged at this particular conjuncture? The chapter will begin by exploring a cluster of words – welfare, welfare states and social security. Next, largely drawing on the work of Nancy Fraser and Linda Gordon, it will dwell on the evolution of the idea of welfare dependency in the United States (see also Peck and Theodore, 2010a). Although it is vital to recognise that contemporary perceptions of welfare and welfare dependency are not solely derived from the United States, the impact of developments there remains significant because of the discursive and programmatic borrowing from the US by ruling administrations in the UK and elsewhere. The third part of the chapter picks up where the analysis of Fraser and Gordon left off twenty years ago and examines subsequent developments such as the growing focus on conditionality and intensified attempts to adjust the behaviour, attitudes and dispositions of claimants. Following the analysis of Wacquant (see also Chapter 2), it will be argued that the ambience of welfare is beginning, in many international settings, to replicate that of the prison or parole regime. Part four examines the role played by US intellectuals, such as Lawrence Mead, in consistently championing a tougher approach toward the unemployed having recourse to public funds. The fifth component of the chapter focuses on the UK to explore how the discourse of welfare dependency has been assembled and amplified. Next, and relating to Gramsci's ideas on 'common sense' (see also Chapter 2), the impact on public perceptions is explored. Here, the focus will also be on the manifest 'myths' integral to some of the main assumptions on welfare dependency.

WELFARE, WELFARE STATES, SOCIAL SECURITY

Charting the evolution of welfare as a keyword over centuries Williams (1983: 332–3) observes that it was 'commonly used from the 14th century to indicate happiness or prosperity...A subsidiary meaning, usually derogatory in the recorded instances, was of merrymaking...The extended sense of welfare, as an object of organised care or provision, came in the 20th century'. Social historians assume that the British Archbishop, William Temple (1881–1944) 'popularised' the term 'welfare state' (Béland and Petersen, 2014: 2). Wincott (2014) argues that 'the "welfare state" phrase was used in print with reference to the UK as early as the 1920s. Evidence suggests that the phrase was not used between 1945 and 1948 to describe post-war Labour social reforms' (2014: 128). Rather it came into widespread use after social security reform came into operation on 5 July 1948. It is 1949 which 'stands out as the year when the 'phrase "welfare state" broke through into political debate' in the UK (Wincott, 2014: 135). There are, moreover, some indications that the phrase 'welfare state' was used by conservative critics of UK reforms located in the United States.

Historically, in other parts of the Western world, similar keywords capture and express similar political forms. The term *Wohlfahrtsstaat* 'was coined and widely used in Germany before its British equivalent was in general use' (Wincott, 2014: 128). This was employed as early as the 1840s and into the 1870s, but did not form part of the discourse on Bismarck's reforms and was not referred to until the final years of the Weimar Republic in the early 1930s. The word *Sozialstaat* (Béland and Petersen, 2014) is also used. In France, *État-providence* is something of an equivalent (Béland and Petersen, 2014).

Social security is a phrase that first appears to have become significant in the 1930s. In August 1935, as part of the New Deal, President Franklin Delano Roosevelt (1882–1955) signed the Social Security Act 1935. Despite the various groups excluded, it is, it has been argued, the 'most crucial social policy legislation ever enacted' in the United States (Klein et al., 2014: 282). This measure served to popularise the concept of social security and tended to refer not only to all the components of the 1935 Act, but to social programmes in general. In 1942, the International Labour Organisation (ILO) published Oscar Stein's book *Approaches to Social Security* which contributed to the 'diffusion of the concept of "social security" beyond US borders' (Klein et al., 2014: 282). In 1941, Roosevelt and the British prime minister, Winston Churchill (1874–1965) embedded the phrase in point five of the Atlantic Charter, the policy statement defining the Allied goals for the post-war world. *Sécurité Sociale* was also to become an 'enduring "keyword" … in France's social policy language after the 1944 liberation' (Béland, 2014: 143–40).

BORN IN THE USA? *MAKING* WELFARE DEPENDENCY

Article 1 (8) of the US Constitution grants Congress the power to 'lay and collect taxes, duties, imposts, and excises, to pay the debts and provide for the common defence and general welfare of the United States' (Klein et al., 2014: 278–9, emphasis added). Social reformers in the nineteenth century relied on and used this 'general welfare clause' to prompt change. Today, however, welfare is constructed with specific and narrow meanings and is largely associated with public assistance. Moreover, being *on welfare* has become identified with households headed by 'black lone mothers' and in its 'most debased form, this has tended to focus on so-called "welfare queens" in a particularly vitriolic, racialised and gendered politics of poverty' (Clarke in Bennett et al., 2005: 272). The figure of the 'welfare queen' and the wider welfare imaginary furnish condensation symbols, capturing, distilling and politically interpreting a plethora of 'anxieties about morality, politics and the economy' (Gustafson, 2011: 15). Similarly, Scarlett Wilcock (2014: 190) provides an analysis of the 'gendered nature' of the 'welfare cheat' in Australia as depicted in official press releases. She concludes that unlike their 'male counterparts, female "cheats" are additionally subject to high-pitched moral condemnations about their presumed sexual deviance, selfishness or maternal failings. The female "welfare cheat" fuses the neoliberal mantra of "personal responsibility", in which the "cheat" is unambiguously culpable, with gendered assumptions about "bad women"'.

In broad terms, the politics of welfare in the US is prone to circulate around a 'gallery of "self-excluding" groups…dysfunctional families, "persistently delinquent" children, school truants, work avoiders and welfare cheats, bad neighbours, aggressive beggars and so on' (Clarke, 2004: 69). In recent years, for example, the 'Tea Partiers have been obsessed with demonizing the unemployed and the uninsured as undeserving and sucking at the teat of government' (Schram, 2015: 107). Here, a key rhetorical distinction has been made between the productive 'makers' (the employed) and the indolent, freeloading 'takers' (the unemployed having recourse to welfare) (Crehan, 2016). Paul Ryan, the vice-presidential candidate for the Republicans in 2012 and current Speaker of the House of Representatives, has been keen to stress this division (Baumann, 2013). Furthermore, Tom Price, Trump's Secretary of Health and Human Services, holds similar views.

However, welfare has not always framed in so relentlessly negative a manner and neither were claimants presented, so unequivocally, as objects of derision and disgust. In the late 1940s, for example, the *Saturday Evening Post* advised opponents of President Truman's plans to extend the coverage of social security benefits that they needed to tread carefully: 'Who's against welfare: Nobody … Fighting an election by opposing welfare is on a par with taunting an opponent for having been born in a log cabin' (in Asen, 2003: 312). Nevertheless, even during this period there were indications that a more vocal and combative conservatism was emerging which was starkly at odds with the politics of the New Deal and war years (Mirowski and Plehwe, 2009). As a result, post-war attacks on the dangers posed by tax increases and alleged 'statism' became more prominent. Truman, despite the evident complacency of the *Saturday Evening Post*, 'warned his political allies against using the concept "welfare state", as it was becoming a "scare word"' (Klein et al., 2014: 285).

Fraser and Gordon (1997) provide one of the most thorough investigations of the *creation* of welfare dependency in the United States. Echoing Williams, they argue that keywords 'typically carry unspoken assumptions and connotations that can powerfully influence the discourses they permeate – in part by constituting a body of [doxa or], taken-for-granted commonsense belief that escapes critical scrutiny' (Fraser and Gordon, 1997: 122). Excavation of the 'genealogy of dependency' is vital because it carries assumptions about 'human nature, gender roles, the causes of poverty, the nature of citizenship, the sources of entitlement, and what counts as work and as a contribution to society' (Fraser and Gordon, 1997: 122–3). The critical intellectuals' task, therefore, was to dispel the doxa surrounding current US discussions of dependency 'by contrasting present meanings of "dependency" with past meanings ... to defamiliarize taken-for-granted beliefs in order to render them susceptible to critique' (Fraser and Gordon, 1997: 122).

In seeking to comprehend why debates about poverty and inequality are framed in terms of welfare dependency, Fraser and Gordon initially focus on the comments of Daniel Patrick Moynihan, an influential member of the Democratic Party, senator and sociologist. Writing in the 1970s, at the beginning of the neoliberal period, Moynihan maintained unequivocally

> the issue of welfare is the issue of dependency. It is different from poverty. To be poor is an objective condition; to be dependent, a subjective one as well ... Being poor is often associated with considerable personal qualities; being dependent is rarely so. [Dependency] is an incomplete state in life: normal in the child, abnormal in the adult. In a world when *completed men and women* stand on their own feet, persons who are dependent – as the buried imagery of the word denotes – hang. (in Fraser and Gordon, 1997: 121, emphasis added)

Within this framing, therefore, the dependent are deficient, infantile, not fully evolved. This definition is also sub-textually laden with dominant pejorative constructs of the economically dispossessed, women and racialised groups. Furthermore, Moynihan's articulation of dependency remains, allowing for shifts in nuance and differing emphases in different countries, dominant throughout the period of neoliberalism.

Fraser and Gordon also identify how the registers of meaning of the word have been historically fluid and shifting. Beginning with preindustrial English usage, they explain that dependency referred to subordination. However, given the hierarchical composition of feudal societies, 'nearly everyone was subordinate to someone else', and to be dependent did not 'thereby incur individual stigma' (Fraser and Gordon, 1997: 124). During this period, dependency was a 'normal, as opposed to a deviant, condition, a social relation, as opposed to an individual trait ... it did not carry any moral opprobrium' (1997: 125). Detectable attitudinal shifts began to occur from the seventeenth century onwards with the gradual ascendancy of a 'liberal-individualist' politics (1997: 126). With the 'rise of industrial capitalism, the semantic geography of dependency shifted significantly ... What in preindustrial society had been a normal and unstigmatized condition became deviant and stigmatized' (Fraser and Gordon, 1997: 126). Dependency was now more likely to be associated with individual character traits, deficits and shortcomings. In the US, 'racial constructs made some forms of dependency appropriate for the "dark races" but intolerable for "whites"' (1997: 127). In 'the Catholic and early

Protestant traditions, dependence on a master had been modeled on dependence on God' (1997: 127), but this process of transformation was also aided and facilitated by the more individualistic orientation of radical Protestantism (1997: 127). Unsurprisingly, given the rapid embedding of capitalism, wage labour was to become 'increasingly normative – and increasingly definitive of independence' (1997: 127). Consequently, it was those excluded from wage labour and commodification that appeared to 'personify dependency' (1997: 127).

In the 'new industrial semantics, there emerged three principal icons of dependency, all effectively negatives of the dominant image of "the worker", and each embodying a different aspect of nonindependence' (1997: 128). First, the pauper, living on poor relief as opposed to wages, was perceived as 'not simply poor but degraded, their character corrupted and their will sapped through reliance on charity' (1997: 128); second, the colonial native or slave, clearly a part of the evolving global capitalist economy, 'personified political subjection' (1997: 130); third, the housewife. Importantly, what underpinned the envolving semantics was an illusionary and deeply ideological notion that the white workingman constituted the embodiment of independence. Few were able to earn sufficiently to single-handedly support a family and had to rely, given capitalism's exploitative dynamics, on the earnings of wives and children. Although omitted in the analysis of Fraser and Gordon and primarily focusing on England, Marx illuminated how this process worked: the 'capitalist buys children and young persons. Previously the worker sold his own labour-power, which he disposed of as a free agent, formally speaking. Now he sells wife and child. He has become a slave-dealer' (Marx, 1990: 519). Many male workers, in part accepting free market ideology, were, in fact, indignant that factory legislation jeopardised their own exploitation of wives and children (MacGregor, 1996).

Turning to the period 1890–1945, Fraser and Gordon refer to a distinctive form of American welfare dependency which emerged. The United States was, historically and culturally, 'hospitable to elaborating dependency as a defect of individual character' because it 'lacked a strong legacy of feudalism or aristocracy and thus a strong sense of reciprocal obligations between lord and man' which were integral to the older and especially European preindustrial meanings of dependency' (1997: 131). The main definition of economic dependency in this era was simply 'non-wage earning' (1997: 132). By the end of the nineteenth century, this 'definition had divided into two: a "good" household dependency, predicated of children and wives, and an increasingly "bad" (or at least dubious) charity dependency, predicated of recipients of relief' (1997: 132). Reformers toward the end of the century introduced the word 'dependent' into 'relief discourse as a substitute for "pauper" ... in order to destigmatize the recipient of help' (1997: 132). They

> first applied the word to children, the paradigmatic 'innocent' victims of poverty. Then, in the early twentieth century, Progressive-era reformers began to apply the term to adults, again to rid them of stigma. Only after World War Two did 'dependent' become the hegemonic word for the recipient of aid. By then, however, the term's pejorative connotations were fixed. (Fraser and Gordon, 1997: 132)

During the period 1933–1938, the US administration of Roosevelt enacted, as mentioned earlier, a series of New Deal interventionist policies to alleviate the impact of the depression. This development was partly a consequence of, and response to, the emergence of an increasingly militant working class movement. The tangible outcome was a range of programmes to ameliorate the impact of mass unemployment and associated hardships. However, in Fraser and Gordon's reading, the New Deal, and more specifically the consolidation of a two-track welfare system, also served to intensify stigma associated with some forms of assistance. Employment and 'old age' benefits were to be contributory, but Aid to Dependent Children (ADC), to become in 1962 Aid to Families with Dependent Children (AFDC), was to be funded from general tax revenues instead of wage deductions. This created the appearance, for some, that those in receipt of the non-contributory benefits were 'getting something for nothing' (Fraser and Gordon, 1997: 133): despite the fact that ADC and AFDC were only payable subject to 'means testing; moral testing; moral supervision; home visits; extremely low stipends' (1997: 133). Related to this development the 'poor solo mother' was to become 'enshrined' as the quintessential welfare dependant' (1997: 134). President John F. Kennedy, in his 1962 State of the Union address, called for a shift in public welfare 'to emphasise "services instead of support, rehabilitation instead of relief and training for useful work instead of prolonged dependency". The 1962 Social Security Amendments ... put more money behind this agenda with the explicit aim of "ending dependency"' (Klein et al., 2014: 287).

In more recent times, the 'positive countercurrents' associated with earlier semantic constructs of dependency are being diluted and risk being entirely eradicated (Fraser and Gordon, 1997: 134). The idea of a 'family wage' – the notion that a male 'breadwinner' should be able to earn enough for his wife and children – has been eliminated. In what the Autonomist Marxists term the 'social factory' (see also Chapter 1), many families need multiple earners to survive. What is more, family forms have altered and many are, of course, constituted without a male 'breadwinner'. The cumulative impact is that the stigma associated with dependency has increased. With wives' economic dependency 'now contested, there is no longer any self-evidently "good" adult dependency in postindustrial society. Rather all dependency is suspect, and independence is enjoined on everyone' (1997: 135). Independence, however, remains identifiable with wage labour no matter how low-waged or impoverished. This 'norm previously restricted to white workingmen' has been universalised and now applies to everyone (1997: 135).

In one of the most insightful parts of their analysis, Fraser and Gordon (1997: 136) refer to how the 'worsening connotations of "welfare dependency" have been nourished by several streams outside the field of welfare'. Important in this respect is how 'expert' discourses, particularly those rooted in medicine and psychology, associated dependency with pathology. Since the 1980s, for example, experts in these and related fields have begun to write about chemical, alcohol and drug dependency; dependency began to be perceived as a euphemism for addiction. In this context, because 'welfare claimants are often – falsely – assumed to be addicts, the pathological connotations of "drug dependency" tend also to infect "welfare dependency", increasing stigmatization' (1997: 136). Primary definers have also been keen to conflate issues related to drug addiction and welfare dependency. This was, perhaps, best illustrated by Dan Quayle, the US vice-president (1989–1993) who, following the riots in Los Angeles in April–May 1992, referred to the 'narcotic of welfare' (1997: 139; see also Gustavsson, 1991). In the late-1980s there was also a 'spate of books about "co-dependency", a supposedly prototypically female syndrome of supporting or "enabling" the dependency of someone else. In the metaphor that reflects the drug hysteria of the period, dependency here is an addiction' (1997: 137). During the 1980s there was, in fact, something of a 'cultural panic about dependency' with, in 1980, the American Psychiatric Association codifying what was termed 'Dependent Personality Disorder (DPD)'.

More recently, Schram (2015: 113) has highlighted how US welfare 'reform' is now remaking the 'delivery of welfare-to-work services along the lines that parallel addiction recovery programs'. This has entailed welfare agencies putting in place services that are the 'social welfare policy equivalent of a twelve-step program: individuals learn the new "work-first" regime to be "active" participants in the labor force rather than passive recipients of welfare' (2015: 113). Related to the importation of the 'recovery model' into the sphere, welfare-to-work contract agencies now also seem keen to employ 'recovered' and reformed former welfare users. As Schram (2015: 114) notes, this move is entirely consistent with a 'recovery model' philosophy that puts former recipients, deployed as 'success stories', as 'behavioural role models'. Within this paradigm, reliance on welfare becomes constructed less as a social and structural problem and more as a personal mental health issue.

Returning specifically to Fraser and Gordon, arguably the chief drawback with their perspective is that it fails to be sufficiently attentive to resistance and forms of 'counter conduct': 'forms of oppositional conduct geared towards other objectives than those proposed by the apparent and visible official governmentality of society' (Foucault, 2009: 199), for example, movements still attuned to socialist, social democratic and feminist theorisations and rooted in a practical commitment to foster solidarity and/or an ethics of care (McDowell, 2004; see also Chapter 8). Nevertheless, they illuminate how the semantics of welfare have dramatically shifted, especially during the period of neoliberal ascendancy.

WELFARE IN THE SHADOW OF THE PRISON WALLS

The Personal Responsibility and Work Opportunity Reconciliation Act of 1996 (PRWORA), further entrenched the dominant and socially corrosive construction of welfare dependency (Schram, 2015). Introduced in August 1996, when the numbers of those on welfare were actually declining (Seccombe, 2007), this legislation is partly attributable to the project of President Bill Clinton to 'end welfare as we know it' (in Peck and Theodore, 2010b: 205). In his earlier roles as chair of the National Governors' Association (1986–1987) and the Democratic Leadership Council

(1990–1991), Clinton championed welfare 'reform' and endorsed experiments such as 'learnfare', developed in Wisconsin and subsequently emulated elsewhere, which terminated the welfare payments of parents whose children failed to attend school (Abramovitz, 2006).

PRWORA also altered the way in which cash assistance was made available. Although it only cost the nation approximately one percent of GDP from the 1980s into the 1990s (Morgen et al., 2010: 7), AFDC was replaced by Temporary Assistance for Needy Families (TANF) which was introduced as part of the 'reforms' in July 1997. TANF not only made payments conditional on job search efforts, it also established a 'climate of unforgiving behavioral requirements, while decentralizing delivery to states and local administrations' (Peck and Theodore, 2010b: 198). A 60 month time-limit was introduced for TANF assistance, but some states opted to curtail payments after an even shorter period. This legislation also requires states to introduce welfare-to-work programmes and demands that TANF recipients participate in work activities within twenty-four months of receiving their initial assistance (Gustafson, 2011: 45). Unsurprisingly, the myriad of ordeals and inbuilt deterrence mechanisms have led to a significant proportion of those who are income-eligible not receiving any TANF benefits (Morgan et al., 2010: xvi).

Seccombe (2007), deploying a critical and feminist optic, provides a concise overview of national developments following the introduction of PRWORA. Concentrating mostly on Florida and Oregon, she highlights how a number of states introduced policies even more stringent than those imposed by the federal administration. The California Work Opportunity and Responsibility to Kids program (CalWORKs), for example, demands that 'teen parents live with their own parents and attend school to receive cash aid' (Gustafson, 2011: 47). In fifteen states, including California, 'all drug-related charges – from possession of small quantities to major trafficking – will disqualify an individual from welfare receipt for life ... Low-income adults with drug records may receive neither cash aid nor food stamps' (Gustafson, 2011: 55). The State, more generally, is empowered, under PRWORA, to 'intervene in the intimate and sexual dimensions of a poor single mother's life in ways that would be considered legally and ethically unacceptable if these same interventions were aimed at professional women' (Smith, 2010: 4). For those serving in the military and willing to sacrifice their lives, a more robust, less stigmatised, package of welfare is available (Cowen, 2008; MacLeavy and Peoples, 2009).

National TANF caseloads have declined significantly, with a 72% fall in numbers taking place between 1996 and 2008 (Schram, 2015: 112). However, this has not led to an 'escape from poverty' (Morgen et al., 2010: 6). Not untypically, those no longer receiving TANF benefits have gone on to fill poorly-paid and economically insecure jobs (Morgen et al., 2010: 6). Indeed, evidence indicates that the portfolio of 'reforms' introduced under the auspices of PRWORA had an unsurprisingly adverse impact on claimants and their families. This remains the case, despite the increased federal support provided following the 'crash', under the measures introduced by Congress in the spring of 2009. Paxson and Waldfogel (2003) examined the imposition of family caps, lifetime limits, work requirements, sanctions for non-compliance and the restriction of welfare benefits to immigrants. They concluded that these punitive disqualifications increased the number of children in out-of-home care. Furthermore, 'some evidence indicates that strict lifetime welfare limits and tougher sanctions for noncompliance are related to higher levels of substantiated [child] maltreatment' (2003: 85).

Welfare reform and changes to adoption law are very much intermeshed in the United States. Indeed, legislation focusing on the adoption and the wholesale 'reform' of welfare were conjoined in the 'Contract with America' launched by the Republican Party in 1994 (Ortiz and Briggs, 2003). Newt Gingrich, Speaker of the House of Representatives (1995–1999) envisaged more interventionist measures targeted at 'welfare mothers' with orphanages fulfilling a significant role. The Adoption and Safe Families Act 1997 provides that children can be located for no longer than 15 of the prior 22 months in foster or institutional care, before being moved either back to their birth parents or on to adoption. A number of states, going further, 'actually require welfare applicants to endure pro-adoption counselling and educational materials designed to encourage them—solely on the basis of their application for means-tested aid alone, with not even the slightest allegation of child abuse or neglect—to relinquish their custodial rights' (Smith, 2010: 5). This legislation, therefore, heralded a palpably tougher, more punitive approach in relation to mothers, particularly 'welfare-dependent' African-American mothers (Roberts, 2014a, 2014b; Kelly and Blythe, 2000). Bartholet (2007: 194) argues, however, that the legislation ought to 'serve as a model for other countries' domestic laws' on adoption (2007: 194; see also Chapter 9).

Earlier it was noted how discourses of welfare are becoming medicalised. Some theorists, in contrast, stress how the doctrinal ambience of the entire 'reform' endeavour promotes, what Wacquant (2009: 79) refers to as the 'programmatic convergence with penal policy'. At the turn of the decade, Garland (2001: 196) also argued that themes that had come to 'dominate crime policy – rational choice and the structures of control, deterrents, and disincentives ... the responsibilization of individuals, the threatening underclass, the failing, overly lenient system' had begun to 'organize the politics of poverty as well'. More recently, Gustafson (2011: 1) observes that 'while welfare use has always carried the stigma of poverty, it now also bears the stigma of criminality ... Welfare rules assume the criminality of the poor'. Reflecting this drift, biometric imaging is increasingly used within welfare services. In the city of New York, for example, 'applying for welfare mirrors the experience of being booked for a crime; after being interrogated about family and finances, individuals are photographed and fingerprinted' (Gustafson, 2011: 57; see also Seccombe, 2007). Morgen et al. (2010), in their Oregon-located research, report how senior 'welfare-to-work' managers are keen to condemn 'old school social work' and draw on the vocabulary of empowerment, self-sufficiency and personal responsibility to 'reframe' an actual shift in the direction of more punitive approaches.

As Wacquant's (2009: 15) analysis suggests, 'the "clients" of both assistantial and penitential sectors of the state fall under the same principled suspicion: they are considered morally deficient unless they periodically provide visible proof to the contrary'. In the UK this was manifest in the New Labour approach to 'jobseekers' which endeavoured to extend the surveillance of claimants begun during the Conservative administrations of Prime Ministers Thatcher (1979–1990) and Major (1990–1997). More pervasively, the presentation of 'welfare reform' under both New Labour, the coalition (2010–2015) and the present Conservative government (2015–) partly gels with Wacqaunt's perspective. For example, in setting out a vision for 'a radically reformed welfare system', a report published by the UK Department for Work and Pensions casually referred to benefit recipients 'found to be playing the system' as 'repeat *offenders*' (Gregg, 2008: 74: emphasis added). This echoes, from the United States, Anderson and Gryzlak's (2002: 301) and Gurmu and Smith's (2006: 406) passing references to 'recidivism' among welfare recipients. In the southern hemisphere, those refusing to accept the 'coercive authority' of case managers are subject to 'breach' notifications – an Australian framing of non-compliance clearly derived from the criminal justice system and associated with the disciplining, even incarceration, of probation clients (McDonald and Marston, 2005: 388; see also Henman, 2004).

PRWORA is also immensely significant in that it provides something of a tutorial or template for global elites intent on entangling benefit claimants in a web of onerous conditions. Such forms of conditionality operate as behaviour modification programmes aiming to shape conduct and render the impoverished more compliant and ready for commodification within precarious labour market niches. Within this mix of ideas there is also an understanding that the world's poor are rational agents simply requiring some steering – or 'nudging' – to enable them to make 'good' choices which will produce appropriate forms of human capital for themselves and their children (see also the discussion on resilience in Chapter 7).

As part of the post-'89 'new world order', such approaches began to take on a global character. Since the late 1990s Latin America has functioned as the laboratory for what *The Economist* has called 'the world's favourite new anti-poverty device': conditional cash transfer programmes (CCTs). These supply 'monetary benefits as long as recipients can demonstrate that they have met certain conditions' (Lavinas, 2013: 5). Globally, especially since the 'crash' evolving from 2007, the World Bank has operated as the leading advocate of this approach with the acronym CCT becoming 'almost established' as its own 'brand' with 'global conferences and networks of experts designed to spread the concept' internationally (Von Gliszczynski and Leisering, 2016: 335).

In 1997, 'only three Latin American countries had launched such programmes; a decade later, the World Bank reported that "virtually every country" in the region had one, and others outside it were adopting them "at a prodigious rate". By 2008, 30 countries had them, from India, Turkey and Nigeria to Cambodia, the Philippines and Burkina Faso' (Lavinas, 2013: 5). As Lavinas observes, the global spread of

CCTs is part of a wider reshaping of welfare regimes in the developing world and beyond. In many countries social workers are integral to the administration and running of such schemes. In Chile, for example, one of the Latin American countries where conditions are highly intrusive, 'to receive a benefit starting at $24 a month before gradually declining to $11, recipients have to sign a contract committing them to "personalized assistance" with their health, education, employment, family life, housing situation and income, monitored through regular meetings with social workers' (2013: 18).

An important element in the 'new paternalist' approach to welfare lies in the notion that there exists a 'contract' between governments and the governed and it pivots on ideas related to compliance and conduct (Etzioni, 1995: 82–3). In the UK, a 'new politics of conduct' (in Deacon and Mann, 1999: 426) and focus on behaviour is now played out in an array of micro-engagements. Hence, 'conditional' welfare is apparent in numerous welfare domains where behavioural compliance is required before aid or services from the state becomes, or remain, available. Becoming embedded during the period of New Labour, behavioural compliance tests began to be applied to accessing council housing (conditional on behaviour) and even maternity grants (conditional on child health check-ups) (Powell, 2000). These developments and transformations were enmeshed in practices centred in children and families and they often circulated around the 'parenting capacity' of socially and economically marginalised parents, often mothers (Milner, 1993: see also Smart, 1992).

In April 2015, the Australian government announced new measures to compel parents to vaccinate their children. Under a so-called 'no jab, no pay' policy, parents not having children vaccinated were to be denied childcare payments (Collins, 2015: 10). Indeed, it is important to acknowledge that the introduction of CCTs and related practices preoccupied with the conduct of the governed are not solely generated by, or at the behest of, US elites. The United States may be a key location from which neoliberal ideas on welfare and dependency are generated, but the 'neoliberal thought collective' (Mirowski and Plehwe, 2009) is a more complex, geographically and intellectually dispersed body of ideas, networks and relationships. In this context, academic 'expertise' has played a pivotal role in defining and amplifying politically and socially retrogressive ideas that circulate around welfare dependency.

NEOLIBERALISM'S 'ORGANIC INTELLECTUALS' AND WELFARE POLITICS

Although opposed by many more progressive forces in the United States a number of conservative scholars serve as, what Gramsci terms, 'organic intellectuals' of the hegemonic neoliberal project (Hoare and Nowell Smith, 2005; see also Chapter 2). Intent on promoting a new 'common sense', many achieved prominence in the international media. Chapter 4 looks more closely at Charles Murray (1990) and his promulgation of the underclass construct. In what follows the focus is on Lawrence Mead who, although perhaps less well known, provides a good illustration of how US- based primary definers have intervened in welfare politics in the UK and elsewhere in Europe, shaping debates and policy to combat welfare dependency.

Although his main concern is the United States, Mead locates his interventions on dependency and related themes in a more expansive geopolitical framework than a number of other conservative scholar activists. Writing in 1992, he contextualised his perspective on welfare by noting that the 'age of proletarian politics' was passing together with the 'myth of the left, largely derived from Europe, [which] sees working class solidarity leading to democracy and then an ambitious welfare state' (Mead, 1992: 228). Although the neoliberal agenda is discernible before the 1990s in terms of the interventions of conservative public policy figures, it is post-1989 with the geopolitical and ideological vanquishment of the USSR that these interventions become more emboldened and strident. Mead's own views, for example, reflect the triumphalist politics of the 'new world order' spanning the presidential term of George H. W. Bush (1989–1993).

Mead's focal interest is the behaviour and attitudes of the poor and the 'competence' which should be 'expected' of them (Mead, 1992: 211). For him, the poor, 'failing to function in embarrassing ways, force society to assume responsibility for them' (1992: 214). Hence, the key issue for commentators and policy makers is 'how to deal with problems of basic functioning among the seriously poor' (1992: 221). This entails his concentrating on the 'archetypes of dependency ... the jobless youth of the inner city; the homeless man begging in the better parts of town; above all the single mother sitting at home on AFDC' (1992: 212). Here the *sitting* is performing the ideological work and reinforcing the notion that the poor are bereft of ambition and competence because they are invariably 'passive'. The 'poor and dependent' are 'passive' because 'they do little to help themselves' (Mead, 1992: 213). Implicitly aligned with the remarks of Moynihan, mentioned earlier, Mead (1992: 218) maintains that while working 'Americans fear to become like them ... They also envy the poor for their ability to escape responsibility for themselves and transfer it to others. Most people abandon such dependent yearnings in childhood.'

Mead (1992: 213) is keen to point out that by 'passive' he does 'not mean they lack all energy ... but their actions lack purpose and direction'. Given this framing, he hints that a curtailment of citizenship may be necessary because the question has become 'how passive you can be and remain a citizen in full standing' (1992: 213). The people who concern him 'have *personal* problems ... Their struggle is first with themselves, only then with society ... The road toward self-determination does not begin with a civil rights march by people who have their lives together. It begins with Alcoholics Anonymous' (1992: 212). Mead maintains, in fact, that 'typically, social problems do not stem directly from social structure' (1992: 212). In this context, the 'social problem becomes the dysfunction of the poor rather than inequality' (1992: 212). They 'impose the cost on the better-off of paying for government and private agencies to take care of the growing numbers of welfare mothers, drug addicts, and crack babies who cannot fend for themselves. The disadvantaged also undermine American competitiveness, because, lacking skills, they fail to fill the need for competent workers' (Mead, 1992: 218). Mead's 'welfare politics' are also starkly racialised and, in seeking to expand the geographical scope of his analysis, this dimension is replicated: for example, he observes that in 'British cities, a nonwhite underclass is forming with all the features seen in America' (Mead, 1992: 229). What is more, he adds, the Labour Party has 'become the party of racial minorities' (Mead, 1992: 234).

Programmatically, this construction of dependency has a number of consequences. Above all, although Mead does not use the phrase, the main focus lies on children and strategies of 'early intervention' (see also Chapter 6). A 'focus on the young is inevitable. For if the source of degradation is behaviour rather than the scarcity of opportunity, remedies must focus on the stage of life when behaviour is most malleable' (Mead, 1992: 212). In addition, new forms of conditionality are vital since 'today, the key measure is authority: government is advancing if it regulates more of personal conduct' (Mead, 1992: 215). Important here is the tactic of 'help and hassle' (Mead in Peck, 2001: 337): a perception which echoes and amplifies the ideas of behavioural economists, Nichols and Zeckhauser (1982: 372) who argue that cash assistance should only be available to the poor if there are arduous 'restrictions on the choices made by intended beneficiaries'. In the US, and elsewhere, the imposition of such 'excessive and obstructive procedural demands' is also likely to be disproportionately adverse for 'people of color' (Lens and Cary, 2010: 1033).

Many would criticise such indignities and the bureaucracy often associated with claiming welfare benefits but, for Nichols and Zeckhauser, such challenges – or as they preferred 'ordeals' – have to become more integral and woven into the system. The imposition of a regime of 'ordeals' is likely to 'enhance target efficiency' in that the 'demeaning qualification tests and tedious administrative procedures' serve 'a sorting function' (Nichols and Zeckhauser, 1982: 372). According to these influential Harvard-based Reaganite economists, 'ordeals' have to become more integral to welfare benefit systems and not simply function as unfortunate and regrettable side-effects. The fact that many claimants are confused, distressed and humiliated is not an accidental by-product of such assessments or indicative of a fixable malfunction. Rather, the inconveniences caused to claimants furnish proof that the system, purposefully laden with 'ordeals', is actually working.

Clearly, it is possible to detect *endogenous* lineages for 'welfare dependency talk' in the UK and it is not difficult to locate methods that aimed to discipline and punish, to use the more contemporary nomenclature, the *welfare-dependent* (Welshman, 2013; see also Dendy, 1895) [3]. In the late seventeenth century those receiving parish relief were compelled to wear badges, under a statute of 1697, and this can be interpreted as a clear attempt to attach and foster 'feelings of shame' (Higgs, 2010: 61). Over a period stretching from the late-1790s into a new century, Jeremy Bentham (1748–1832) relentlessly campaigned for the setting up of a National Charity Company which would be responsible for coercively 'managing' a million paupers in 'industry-houses' spread throughout 'South Britain' (that is, England and Wales) (Himmelfarb, 1970). The Poor Law 'reforms' of 1834 led to a situation in which most of those successful in obtaining meagre assistance had to endure quasi-incarceration in workhouses. Indeed, these historical practices contribute to the accumulated weight and ideological efficaciousness of terms such as welfare dependency and underclass.

However, underpinning the discussion in this chapter is the understanding that the politics of 'welfare' in the United States, and discourses centring on dependency, have had a major impact in the UK and beyond. Although playing out in complex ways depending on the different political, cultural and social settings, these have affected the tonality of policy-making. Aside from contributing to the formation of what Williams (1977) refers to as 'structures of feeling' on this topic, developments across the Atlantic have influenced the creation of similar, albeit adapted, programmes in the UK. Especially during the period of the New Labour administrations (1997–2010), Tony Blair was a key definer who acted as the transmission belt for ideas, partly originating in US New Right think-tanks and foundations. He appeared, for example, to be particularly intent on discursively re-framing debates on social security as debates pivoting on welfare or, even worse, 'hand-outs' (Hall, 2003). Others in the UK also contributed to the promotion of ideas on welfare dependency and activation (Raffass, 2016).

James Purnell (Secretary of State for Work and Pensions, 2008–2009) played a brief, but not insignificant role, conceding that the policies of New Labour embodied 'an ideological break with the past' (Purnell, 2008). Attentive to the potency of welfare words, he observed that not 'long ago' his 'predecessors were called the Secretary of State for Social Security'. For his government, 'security' was 'something handed down' whereas the 'new title, Secretary of State for Work and Pensions, tells a wholly different story' (Purnell, 2008). Central to this 'different story' was that the welfare state had to be viewed as a 'way out of worklessness and a way up the career ladder, but not a way of life' (Purnell, 2008). This demanded 'tackling inactivity' by introducing 'major reform of inactive benefits' (Purnell, 2008). Hence, there was a need to 'rewrite the terms of the welfare contract' with a re-energised focus on working, seeking work or appropriate training with sanctions to be imposed on the recalcitrant (Purnell, 2008). There would be, glibly avowed Purnell (2008), 'no free riding on the welfare state'. Related to this was the need to have done with the misguided notion that 'welfare recipients ... needed *our* support in perpetuity. That mentality is the enemy of social justice and fair life chances for all'. This intervention was clearly influenced by the tonality which US New Right figures, such as Mead, had vigorously promoted during the previous decade. However, Purnell, along with other New Labour figures, also endeavoured to harness the language of 'social justice' to the project of propelling the workless into a 'dynamic market' economy (Purnell, 2008): the political objective being to encourage 'social justice through independence, not a socially regressive culture of dependency' (Purnell, 2008). Writing before the economic crash, Boltanski and Chiapello (2005) argued that a 'new spirit of capitalism' sought to garner support by rhetorically embracing the themes of social justice and social well-being and Purnell's presentation can, therefore, be interpreted as a good illustration of this tendency. He certainly seemed keen, albeit strategically, to assemble a 'welfare politics' imbued with upbeat themes and motifs whilst seeking to introduce new forms of conditionality and 'Ordeal-ism'. Such tactics were further developed by the hapless Iain Duncan Smith.

Receiving royal assent in March 2012, the Welfare Reform Act (WRA) sought to reduce 'welfare' spending and the budget, introduced the same month, made it clear that the government would aim for cuts of £10 billion by 2016 (Clery, 2012: 3). The main components of the WRA to be introduced over a decade include narrowed eligibility for a range of benefits and a cap on the amount of certain benefits, with Housing Benefit entitlement now being curtailed for social housing tenants whose accommodation is deemed larger than they need. According to Duncan Smith (2014), life under the previous Labour government had been 'blighted' by a 'damaging culture of dependency and worklessness'. It was, for him, a 'sin' that people failed to avail of opportunities to take paid employment (in Wintour, 2010). His government, in contrast, was to benignly propel people on 'a journey, from dependence to independence' and to eradicate 'a damaging culture of dependency'. There was 'a tragic loss of human potential' when 'individuals and families remained trapped in a cruel state of dependency'. Specific policy mechanisms were, therefore, to be introduced or progressed to embed this shift in attitudes and behaviour amongst the unemployed. This included continuing to ensure that those receiving 'Job seekers Allowance' furnished evidence of their obligation to 'seek work, attend interviews, do their best to get the job – and take the job when it is offered'. Those not doing so would face a loss of benefits because the unemployed had to recognise 'you are now in work to find work'. Benefit caps and a panoply of sanctions were also to be deployed to extinguish the 'something for nothing culture' (Duncan Smith, 2014).

More generally and leaving aside the more progressive politics presently adopted by the opposition leader Jeremy Corbyn, the two major UK political parties appeared, for a number of years, to have forged an informal alliance with little disagreement on – what is unproblematically termed – welfare. This was reflected in the temporary Labour leader, Harriet Harman, urging Labour MPs *not* to vote against the government's 'Welfare Reform Bill' in July 2015 (Winter, 2015). According to the then Chancellor George Osborne (2015: 27), this represented an apparent 'settlement' on welfare lying at the 'new centre of British politics'. Given this coalescing of perceptions, and the associated politics it has given rise to, how has the public's view of welfare changed in recent years? In tentatively exploring this question, the British Social Attitudes (BSA) survey, published a few years ago, provides some insights into the evolution of 'common sense' attitudes (Clery, 2012; see also Hills, 2015). Clearly, the impact of anti-welfare rhetoric does not always mechanically produce the outcome that primary definers and articulators require, but there are strong indications that during the period of New Labour such interventions attained the desired effect.

THE POTENCY OF 'COMMON SENSE' NARRATIVES

In 2012, the BSA survey provided data on changing attitudes to welfare (see also Taylor-Gooby, 2013). The research is interesting, but cannot be regarded as an 'objective' and 'scientific' account of the population's seemingly altered perceptions. More emphatically, the document can be read as a *political* intervention implicitly seeking to shape attitudes rather than merely reporting them. This is apparent in two senses. First, as we have seen, a whole series of neoliberal interventions have worked hard to rebrand what was formerly referred to as 'social security' as a more stigmatised and ideologically weighted 'welfare' (Turn2us, 2012; Baumberg, 2016). However, the BSA survey simply frames the relevant chapter featuring the data collected as 'Welfare'. Second, commentary sections ostensibly purport that the approach of the Conservative Party (and before that of the Coalition) and its pursuance of tougher policies and rhetoric relating to claimants were merely mirroring public attitudes revealed in the BSA data. For example, although conceding that a 'shift of opinion was nurtured by a tougher stance towards welfare under the previous Labour government', it is claimed that this shift 'can also be read as evidence that the coalition government's radical Welfare Reform Act is in tune with public opinion, chiming as it does with so many changing attitudes and assumptions' (Clery, 2012: 18). This reading, which clearly gels with that of the current government, is questionable in that it fails to adequately emphasise that politics seek to *form, shape and alter attitudes*. That is to say, public attitudes in the UK may, in large part, be a *consequence* of the mood and 'structure of feeling' which politicians of the right have been striving to create. Indeed, the shifts in public perceptions during the period of New Labour (1997–2010) can be interpreted as reflecting the *success* of neoliberal 'welfare' politics.

In the 2012 report, apparent shifts in attitudes are reflected in the following:

- In 2001 88% agreed that government should be mainly responsible for ensuring unemployed people have enough to live on; 59% think this now.

- In 2001 43% thought that the government should spend more on welfare benefits for the poor, even if it leads to higher taxes, compared to 32% in 2007 and 28% now.

- 62% agree that unemployment benefits are too high and discourage work, more than double the proportion who thought this in 1991 (27%) and a significantly higher proportion than said this was the case in 2007 (54%) (Clery, 2012: 1).

The data suggest that public perceptions on benefits are becoming increasingly bifurcated. The 'relatively high proportions who say government should be mainly responsible for providing welfare when someone is ill or disabled have fluctuated only slightly since the late-1990s' (Clery, 2012: 5) However, agreement 'that the government should be mainly responsible for ensuring unemployed people have enough to live on has fallen…from just over eight in ten in 2003, to less than six in ten now' (2012: 5). In terms of the unemployed 'one in three (33 per cent) think the individual or their family should mainly be responsible, compared with one in ten (10 per cent) who thought this in 1998' (2012: 5). Even in terms of disabled people, there would seem to be a decrease in support for extra spending on benefits (2012: 8).

Public responses to benefit recipients also point to attitudes that seem both 'tougher' *and* ill-informed (see below). Analysing the entirety of the relevant data, the author of the report intimates that it would 'be tempting to conclude … that declining support for the government's role as a main provider of welfare, and for extra spending on benefits, is a direct consequence of the public's view that many social security recipients are undeserving' (Clery, 2012: 11). It

> seems the welfare system is widely viewed as inefficient and poorly targeted – both in terms of who receives support and in terms of its ability to prevent long-term dependency. Since these perceptions are broadly in line with the presumptions underpinning the government's Welfare Reform Act, it seems likely that its implementation will, if attitudes persist, enjoy considerable public support. (2012: 14)

Arguably, this once again represents a somewhat shallow interpretation of the data because it merely situates the 'government' as a passive instrument merely responding to existing public perceptions. As argued earlier, this reading fails to sufficiently acknowledge how the government – a political formation with a distinctive project and series of aims and objectives – seeks to orchestrate public opinion and to maintain a particular 'common sense' on this particular welfare word.

This dimension is illustrated by the fact that the BSA data is longitudinal and is able to track shifts in public perceptions: slightly 'more than half (54 per cent) believe that people would "stand on their own two feet" if benefits were less generous, while only 20 per cent disagree. This is the reverse of the situation in 1993, when only 25 per cent agreed and 52 per cent disagreed with the statement … *We see that most of the increase occurred during Labour's long period in government*' (Clery 2012: 12, emphasis added). It is maintained in the BSA survey that the 'shift of opinion was nurtured by a tougher stance towards welfare under the previous Labour government' (Clery 2012: 18), but this needs, perhaps, to be emphasised to a greater extent. This is not to argue that New Labour interventions were causal in a mechanistic way; the process involving how the public actually responds to politically motivated framing and defining is, of course, complex. Nevertheless, the BSA data certainly suggests that, over a number of years, New Labour provided part of the ideological foundation for later UK governments' amplification of ideas on welfare dependency.

COUNTERING WELFARE DEPENDENCY 'MYTHS'

In his examination of neoliberal welfare politics in the United States, Schram (2015: 84) argues that 'facts rarely have affected the extent to which people allow unexamined stereotypes to influence their attitude toward those "other" people who are allegedly not playing by white, middle-class rules'. Emphasising this point, he asserts that no 'matter how we use statistics to debunk popular myths associated with poverty and welfare, people keep insisting that the welfare poor are those undeserving "other" people who are not playing by the white, middle-class rules of work and family' (2015: 84–85). This, arguably rather pessimistic reading, he attributes to the 'abiding deep semiotic structure of deservedness that undergirds almost all of US political discourse at a most fundamental level' (2015: 107). Facts, so this line of reasoning goes, do not matter: politics simply pivots on which social forces have the best and most compeling 'stories'. This can be connected to the notion, reflected by the arrival of Trump in the Oval Office, that we have entered a 'post-truth' era.

In the case of the UK, it is certainly clear that politically generated and popular perceptions about welfare dependency are rooted in a number of interrelated 'myths'. This was made starkly apparent in an accessible report, issued by a coalition of churches, which was compiled to rebut some of the assertions promoted by the mainstream parties (Baptist Union of Great Britain et al., 2013). Common sense perceptions appeared to crystallise into six myths about the 'poor': that 'they' are:

- lazy and do not want to work

- addicted to drink and drugs

- not really poor, but simply incompetent in managing their money

- on 'the fiddle' and often illegally working or claiming benefits that they are not truly entitled to claim

- enjoying an easy life

- responsible for the 'deficit' prompting the 'austerity' measures impacting on everyone.

As observed earlier, these 'myths', needing to be scrutinised in detail, are reflected in some of the findings of the BSA survey.

First, often occluded in the narrative of welfare dependency is the fact the majority of families living in poverty – deemed 'lazy' or part of an inert and indolent of mass of 'shirkers' – are actually employed. Excluding pensioners, 'there are 6.1 million people in families in work living in poverty compared with 5.1 million people in poverty from workless households' (Baptist Union of Great Britain et al., 2013: 13). However, the 'myth' of 'laziness' is also underscored by the notion that those who are unemployed have been so for many years and are mired in a culture of 'worklessness'. Indeed, 'activation' policies are rhetorically grounded in this misleading notion. However, 'only 0.1% of decade-long benefit claimants are unemployed. The rest are carers (2.2%), lone parents of young children on income support (6.5%) and those on incapacity benefits (90.5%)' (2013: 15). In late-2016, a report from the Joseph Rowntree Trust revealed that there were 7 million people in the UK living in poverty despite their participation in the workforce: 55% of those in poverty were in 'working households' (Walker, 2016). Furthermore, only a 'third of children below the government's absolute poverty line now live in a workless household – two thirds of those classified as poor are poor despite the fact that at least one of their parents is in work' (Institute for Fiscal Studies, 2016).

As the report from the church group maintains, unemployment in the UK is typically short-term, but frequent and is a facet of the 'so-called "low-pay/no-pay cycle", with people moving between insecure low-paid employment and benefits, a trend that increased during the 1990s and 2000s' (Baptist Union of Great Britain et al., 2013: 15). This patterning of precarious working is rooted in, and generated by, structural and economic considerations bound up with the reshaping of capitalist work processes. However, the dominant, deeply ideological, myth-sustaining narrative maintains that people's lack of, or tenuous, attachment to the labour market is a product of family dysfunction producing an inherited culture of worklessness and welfare dependency (Hern, 2013). Jensen and Tyler (2015: 478–9) refer, in this context, to what they term 'benefit broods' defined as a 'cultural figuration of disgust aimed at families that are deemed to have become "excessively" large as a result of over-generous welfare entitlements; "benefit brood" parents are regarded as almost pathologically fertile in their desire to secure greater amounts of welfare payments by having more and more children'. [4]

The figure of the 'troubled family' is now frequently deployed to rhetorically substantiate this idea that idle work units, bedevilled by multiple problems, need 'support' to restructure their dispositions so that they can then slot into the labour force (HM Government, 2012; see also Chapter 4). Underpinning focal representations of such families is the 'myth' that they have been workless for three generations. More pervasively, intergenerational poverty operates as 'a kind of synecdoche, a single part used to represent the whole tangle of problems associated with the poor' (Schram, 2015: 103). Nevertheless, in reality, in 'less than 0.1% of the 20 million working age households there are 2 generations that have never had a permanent job. The numbers of such families, if any exist, are so vanishingly small that no survey has yet been able to detect the much cited three generations of worklessness' (Baptist Union of Great Britain et al., 2013: 16).

Whilst it is frequently implied that the 120,000 so-called 'troubled families' are drug using, there is no evidential basis for this claim (see also Chapter 4). This relates to the second 'myth' which the churches seek to demolish that families who are 'poor' are 'addicted to drink and drugs'. As they maintain, in England, research has revealed that '6.4% of adults demonstrated some form of alcohol dependence with 0.5% showing moderate or severe levels of dependence. National scale research has failed to demonstrate a correlation between alcohol dependence of any degree and income levels' (Baptist Union of Great Britain et al., 2013: 18). Only 4% of those on the 'out-of-work benefits, claim because of alcohol or drug abuse', so to imply that addiction is a 'major cause of welfare bills or poverty' is manifestly incorrect (Baptist Union of Great Britain et al., 2013: 18).

The third 'myth' pivots on the notion that the poverty of the poor is essentially bogus because the substantive issue is that they are merely unable to effectively manage their money. This is, of course, a historically rooted perspective maintaining that those who are 'poor' could, with appropriate tutelage, attain new budget management skills. No evidence exists to empirically support this perspective. However, technology now furnishes new and evolving ways to surveil and further stigmatise claimants. In 2012, for example, a private members' bill was introduced in Parliament by Alec Shelbrooke MP proposing that all benefits to families should be paid using an electronic card which would prevent claimants from spending on items such as 'drugs, cigarettes, alcohol' or 'Sky TV'. Although the bill did not become law, it contributed to the 'tougher' tonality of the welfare politics and policy. Such moves also deliberately function to foster a new 'common sense' on the rightfulness of technological constraints deployed to regulate claimants' consumption. Indeed, Duncan-Smith announced the following year that his government were to test 'prepaid cards' which would only facilitate expenditure on the 'needs of the family' (see also Wood and Salter, 2013).

The fourth 'myth' is that benefit claimants are cheats or at least a 'problem population whose civic probity is by definition suspect' (Wacquant, 2009: 98; see also Chapter 2). This 'myth' is not only integral to welfare dependency discourse in the UK, it is pervasive elsewhere. In the UK, as the BSA survey appeared to reveal, over a third of the public believed that 'most people on the dole are "fiddling"' (Clery, 2012: 11). This perception is amplified and structurally reinforced in how the state concentrates 3,700 DWP staff to investigate welfare fraud, while only 300 specialise in dealing with tax fraud (Garside, 2016: 1). However, benefit fraud actually amounts to a 'relatively small part – 0.9% – of the welfare budget, whereas the government estimates tax fraud to be between 4% and 6% of tax income' (Baptist Union of Great Britain et al., 2013: 21). In 2016 it was reported that benefits fraud costs the government £1.3bn a year, yet the gap between tax owed and tax paid is put at £34bn a year. MPs on the Parliamentary Public Accounts Committee were also of the view that this figure failed to take into account the losses due to aggressive tax avoidance schemes. The Labour Party argues that the tax gap could be as great as £120bn (Garside, 2016).

The fifth 'myth' circulates around the notion that those in receipt of benefits enjoy an easy life and disregards the fact that benefit levels are insufficient to provide for material well-being and abundance. Furthermore, little account is taken of the stringency of qualification clauses and 'caps' impeding access to benefits or radically curtailing amounts payable. As we have seen, partly on account of the influences of the US-based New Right, a series of 'ordeals' now function as obstacles to claiming and maintaining entitlement. Claimants for Universal Credit and Jobseeker's Allowance have to be able to demonstrate they have engaged in work search, be available for work, and undertaken courses and interviews that their JobCentre advisor believes will be beneficial. Over the past few years a so-called Claimant Commitment must be agreed and signed before Universal Credit is paid. If claimants do not comply they face sanctions and the cessation of benefit entitlement.

Throughout Europe, following the near-collapse of finance capitalism, ruling elites deployed slogans and sound bites to justify how the ensuing crisis was – and is – being addressed (Pentaraki, 2013). This relates to the promulgation of the sixth 'myth', contradicted in the report from the churches, that those claiming benefits contributed to the economic crisis. The indolence and dependency of claimants, so goes the argument, led to a bloated welfare state which acted as a brake on prosperity: related patterns of welfare expenditure now add to the 'deficit' and unfairly increase the burden on 'hardworking families'. This factually incorrect and misleading narrative also occludes the entrenched dependency of the rich, whose absence is significant in at least two ways. First, global corporations and holders of wealth *depend* on there being no radical reorganisation of the state resulting in the eradication of gross economic inequalities. Second, on a daily basis, these same dominant interests *depend* on the state to materially serve and act on their behalf. In dramatic and extraordinary terms, this is illustrated by the socialising of privately incurred corporate debts and the 'bailouts' provided when the 'crash' erupted (Callinicos, 2010). Even the Governor of the Bank of England has conceded that many 'supposedly rugged markets were revealed to be cosseted' (Carney, 2014: 3). This twofold structural dependency constitutes, in fact, a shadowy dependency culture at the core of neoliberal state. In the UK, on the day when the former Chancellor George Osborne was to deliver the first Conservative government budget in nineteen years in July 2015, it was revealed that major corporations, such as Amazon, Ford and Nissan, received £93 billion a year in grants, subsidies and tax breaks – £3,500 from each household. A number of major companies were paying little or zero corporation tax (Chakrabortty, 2015; see also Farnsworth, 2006; Farnsworth and Holden, 2006).

CONCLUSION

On account of globalised 'workfare' regimes, social work appears, to varying degrees depending on the jurisdiction, to have become increasingly enmeshed in an 'insidiously manipulative culture' intent on 'easing' the so-called welfare-dependent into low-paid and precarious work (Ehrenreich, 2006: 226; see also Peck, 1998; 2001; Peck and Theodore, 2010a). The 'workfarist turn—towards market-oriented benefit condition-ality, work enforcement, behavioral modification, and individualization—which originated in American cities during the 1960s, has morphed in subsequent decades into something approaching a postwelfare consensus' amongst elites across many parts of the globe (Peck and Theodore, 2010b: 196). Often rhetorically framed by 'activation policies' targeted at the so-called welfare-dependent, such endeavours are better understood, as Offe (1984) argued over thirty years ago, as strategies of 'active proletarianization' aspiring to ensure that the reluctant convert their dormant labour power into wage labour and profit for those owning the means of production and distribution.

Frequently the word 'underclass' is inserted into discourses on welfare depend-ency. Throughout the 1980s and early 1990s, references to poverty often pivoted, in fact, around the so-called underclass. Although this welfare word appeared to have largely evaporated by the beginning of the new century, it now seems to have been reactivated. In 2013, across an international canvas, the Secretary General of Amnesty warned that failure to address conflict situations is effectively 'creating a global underclass' (Amnesty International, 2013). The seemingly uncritical use of this particular welfare word is also detectable in the social work literature; for exam-ple, Houston (2016: 541) refers to a 'growing underclass' and Jönsson (2015: 358) to a 'new underclass'. In our next chapter, therefore, we will turn to examine this, mostly pejorative, welfare word.

REFLECTION AND TALK BOX 3

1. Perhaps an implicit tenet of social work practice is the notion that human beings are social, relational and (inter)dependent entities. For example, while 'condi-tioned in fundamentally significant ways by cultural considerations, dependency for humans is as unavoidable as birth and death are for all living organisms' (Kittay in Lynch, 2007: 553). Kathleen Lynch (2007: 553–4) elaborates

    Even when we are not in a state of strong dependency, we are relational beings ... No human being, no matter how rich or powerful, can survive from birth without care and attention; many would die at different points in their lives, if seriously ill or in an accident, without care. The inevitability of interde-pendency does not just apply in personal relationships, but also in work places, in public organisations, in voluntary groups or other social settings.

    How can this statement be interpreted alongside dominant ideas associated with the phrase welfare dependency?

FURTHER READING

The Lies We Tell Ourselves is a concise dissection of wilfully misleading ideas on welfare benefits (Baptist Union of Great Britain, Methodist Church, Church of Scotland and the United Reformed Church, 2013). One of the main contributions exploring the evolution of workfare is Jamie Peck's (2001) outstanding *Workfare States*. Sanford Schram's (2015) *The Return of Ordinary Capitalism* is also an important critical intervention which includes an examination of ideas circulating around 'dependency' in a 'post-crash' world (see, particularly, Chapters 4 and 5). Many of the welfare words and phrases to be examined in *Welfare Words* are imbued with very specific ideas about gender, 'race' and ethnicity. In terms of the UK, Tracey Jensen and Imogen Tyler (2015) address issue related to gender constructs and 'welfare dependency'. Located in the United States and using a black feminist optic, Dorothy Roberts (2014a, 2014b) looks at the interconnected themes of poverty, child protection and specific surveillance practices directed at African-American families by the neoliberal state. The award-winning film *I, Daniel Blake* (2016), directed by Ken Loach and written by Paul Laverty, provides an alternative to dominant accounts of welfare in the UK. In this way the film can be interpreted, in a Gramscian way, as providing an example of how cultural production can contribute to the assembling of counter hegemonic strategies.

CHAPTER 4

UNDERCLASS

Underclass – a subordinate social class; the lowest social stratum in a country or community, consisting of the poor and the unemployed. (*Oxford English Dictionary*)

INTRODUCTION

At odds with contemporary references to underclass, John Maclean (1879–1923), the Scottish revolutionary socialist, used the word in a very different way in 1918. He spoke of a society moving forward as a 'consequence of an under-class overcoming the resistance of a class on top of them'. Turning to the use of underclass by social scientists, the OED mentions Gunnar Myrdal (1898–1987), the Swedish Nobel laureate economist, sociologist, and politician who, in *Challenge to Affluence* (Myrdal, 1963), stated that technological and structural changes taking place in industrial societies such as the United States had led to the creation of an underclass of the unemployable persons and families at the bottom of a society. Almost half-a-century apart, both these early usages were not pejorative – Maclean, the Marxist, seeking to explain how class societies evolve and Myrdal endeavouring to convey how structural transformations were likely to disadvantageously impact on groups who risked becoming unemployed. Neither was concerned, as later users of the word have tended to be, with the problematic behaviour of an underclass.

Other relatively early uses of the word charted by the OED mostly tend to be associated with the politics of 'race' either in the United States, or, less frequently, in apartheid South Africa. Elsewhere, other writers draw attention to what they perceive as alternative, but still significant, roots and early usage of underclass. Imogen Tyler (2013a: 189) refers to the related word *Untermenschen,* a term popularised by the Nazis but 'first coined' by the American historian, journalist, eugenicist, and political theorist Lothrop Stoddard (1883–1950) in his racist *The Revolt Against Civilization: The Menace of the Under Man* (Stoddard, 1922). According to Stoddard, the term 'Under Man' described civilization's 'inner barbarians, 'degenerate races' and 'defective classes'. Such a perception was reactivated, during the 2016

US presidential election campaign when the National Review castigated those providing, it maintained, the electoral base for Trump.

> [If] you take an honest look at the welfare dependency, the drug and alcohol addiction, the family anarchy…Even the economic changes of the past few decades do very little to explain the dysfunction and negligence — and the incomprehensible malice — of poor white America … The truth about these dysfunctional, downscale communities is that they deserve to die… The white American underclass is in thrall to a vicious, selfish culture whose main products are misery and used heroin needles. Donald Trump's speeches make them feel good. (Williamson in French, 2016)

Mostly focusing on the UK, this chapter begins with a short discussion on how the underclass notion appeared to have been re-ignited around the time of the economic crisis unfolding from 2007/8 (Harkins and Lugo-Ocando, 2016). This, moreover, seemed to coincide with public concerns about child protection services. Next, we will comment on how the word was subsequently deployed to explain the English 'riots' which took place during the late summer days stretching from 6–11 August 2011. In the third part of the chapter, it will be argued that the widespread usage of the underclass term in the United States is of vital significance. The United States has only 4% of the world's population (Christopher et al., 2014) – India and China collectively have 38% – yet the economic, political and cultural weight of the country is entirely disproportionate. In this context, reference will be made to the work of Bourdieu and Wacquant and their assertion that US cultural imperialism, reflected in the exportation of vocabularies and concepts, needs to be taken into account when dwelling on words such as underclass. The fourth section concentrates on Wacquant's insistence that spatiality is crucial in seeking to comprehend labels such as underclass. Finally, turning again to the UK, the chapter dwells on a range of other derogatory conceptualisations used throughout history to describe the supposedly wayward behaviour of the poor. Each of these designations can be perceived as antecedents of the underclass label referring to essentially the same alleged behaviour traits, including fecklessness and lack of foresight.

REDISCOVERING THE UNDERCLASS

In 2008, the underclass construct was frequently used in trying to explain the death of Peter Connelly (Garrett, 2009: Ch. 9; Jones, 2014; Shoesmith, 2016). The 17-month old boy had been subject to a child protection plan put in place by social services in the London Borough of Haringey, following concerns that he had been abused and neglected. In August 2007, the child died from severe injuries inflicted whilst in the care of his mother, her 'boyfriend' and a lodger in the household. Initially, because of restriction placed on court reporting, he was referred to as 'Baby P'. In November 2008 two men were found guilty of causing or allowing the death of a child or vulnerable person. The mother had already pleaded guilty to the same charge. Following the convictions, the death of the child and the, seemingly, inadequate responses of child welfare professionals, dominated political and media accounts.

The Observer, for example, argued that the death of the child 'focused the spotlight once again on child protection services and loopholes in the net designed to protect the most vulnerable children, *as well as broader questions of how to reach an underclass of inadequate parents* raising children in volatile circumstances' ('Put more children at risk into care', *The Observer*, 16 November, 2008: 2, emphasis added). These were, it was asserted, 'families that were straight out of *nightmares* ... an *underclass* ... untouched by the affluence of modern Britain' ('Why children are left to die beyond help's reach', *The Observer*, 16 November, 2008: 18). Similarly, a number of newspaper articles attempted to forge a connection between the cases of Peter Connelly and that of another child, Shannon Matthews, who was alleged to have been kidnapped, but was then discovered to have been hidden by her mother, Karen, and an accomplice, Michael Donovan. Karen Matthews was charged with child neglect and perverting the course of justice. In December 2008, she and Donovan were found guilty on charges of kidnapping, false imprisonment and perverting the course of justice.

In 2017 the BBC was to go on to create a controversial TV drama, *The Moorside*, based on the case. Immediately following the verdict, a senior police officer described the troubled and pathetic Karen as 'pure evil' (*The Observer*, 7 December, 2008: 29–32). According to a leader column in *The Daily Express*, 'the poor' were simply the 'Karen Matthews brigade...able to make welfare dependency a career choice, churning out children they have no intention of supporting' (in Harkins and Lugo-Ocando, 2016: 87). In *The Observer*, Shannon's mother was referred to as a 'representative of a feckless underclass, a broken society, a generation of parents only concerned for their own childish emotions' (*The Observer*, 7 December, 2008: 31).

The newspaper presentation of Matthews, characterised by class spite, was reflected in an article published in *The Independent on Sunday* in November 2008. Here Sophie Heawood (2008: 42) argued: 'It's what seems to be an *underclass*, a level of British society that is not just struggling with poverty – this is way beyond being poor – but often getting by with *subnormal intelligence* levels, living in a world *with no professional aspirations* whatsoever, for generations, where criminality is normality, with people who seem to have not just fallen through the net of literacy or personal improvement, but missed out on education or social development altogether' (emphases added). Her solution to these problems was that her readers should 'join a mentoring scheme to befriend a struggling child ... And how about mentoring adults? Could we create more real-life schemes, and not just TV shows, where people like Karen Matthews can get to know people from less troubled backgrounds? It's the entrenchment of the *underclass* that keeps people there' (Heawood, 2008: 43, emphasis added). Iain Duncan Smith added that there was 'creeping expansion' of a 'more menacing underclass' drawing 'decent' families into the 'code of the street' (Centre for Social Justice, 2008). On occasions, the liberal intelligentsia also mentioned an underclass, with the Scottish novelist and cultural commentator, Andrew O'Hagan (2009) lamenting and bemoaning what he viewed as the contemporary cultural impoverishment of the working class (see also Reflection and Talk Box 4).

'SCUM SEMIOTICS': THE UK 'RIOTS' OF AUGUST 2011

During, and in the aftermath of, the UK 'riots' of 2011, media coverage 'unleashed a torrent of "underclass" appellations' (Tyler, 2013a: 180)[1]. Members of the Coalition government made a series of high-profile speeches in which 'broken society and welfare ghetto narratives ... imbued with class hostility and antagonism' dominated (Hancock and Mooney, 2013: 48). This was exemplified by key speeches by the then Prime Minister David Cameron. In his first statement on the 'riots', Cameron (2011a) argued that 'there are pockets of our society that are not just broken but, frankly, sick'. He continued ... 'when I say parts of Britain are sick, the one word I would use to sum that up is irresponsibility ... a complete lack of responsibility, a lack of proper parenting, a lack of proper upbringing, a lack of proper ethics, a lack of proper morals'. Days later he returned to similar themes, but also incorporated some of the underclass ideas, to be discussed later, associated with the US political scientist Charles Murray:

> I don't doubt that many of the rioters out last week have no father at home. Perhaps they come from one of the neighbourhoods where it's standard for children to have a mum and not a dad ... where it's normal for young men to grow up without a male role model, looking to the streets for their father figures, filled up with rage and anger. (Cameron, 2011b)

Cameron's Conservative colleague Duncan Smith confided:

> For years now, too many people have remained unaware of the true nature of life on some of our estates. This was because we had ghettoised many of these problems, keeping them out of sight of the middle-class majority ... But last month the inner city finally came to call, and the country was shocked by what it saw. (Duncan Smith, 2011)

Former Home Secretary Kenneth Clarke maintained that the disorder was prompted by a 'feral underclass' (Lewis et al., 2011; see also De Benedictus, 2012). Such a perception partly mirrored aspects of a public awareness exercise about the threat of car crime, in the early 1990s, portraying young men as hyenas.

For Mark Easton (2011), the BBC Home Editor, the riots marked the 'return of the underclass'. Similarly, according to Mary Riddell (2011) in the *Daily Telegraph*, the 'riots' were a consequence of what occurs when the 'underclass lashes out'. According to Melanie Phillips (2011), the 'riots' were an 'explosion of elective lone parenthood and dysfunctional behaviour transmitted down through the generations at the bottom of the social heap' (see also Hastings, 2011). Many comments within the mainstream media appeared to frame the 'riots' by sub-textually alluding to zombie films, such as *Return of the Living Dead* and post-apocalyptic horror movies, such as *28 Days Later*. The so-called underclass, thought to have been exterminated since the arrival of New Labour, was arising from the dead to steal fancy trainers from Foot Locker. However, within the sociological and social policy literature, there were a number of contributions that were subtle and critically interrogative (Grover, 2011). In her nuanced examination of the events, Imogen Tyler argues that the 'conceptual and perceptual frame of the underclass was operationalised as a means of explaining and containing the meaning of the August riots as *apolitical*' (Tyler, 2013a: 182–3, emphasis added).

Underclass representations prominent during this period drew on imagery associated with dirt and disease, with Tyler referring to the prevalence of 'scum' and 'scum class' across a number of social media platforms. For her, much of this coverage of the return of the underclass was rooted in 'scum semiotics' (Tyler, 2013b). Moreover, this interpretation can be extended to the more encompassing portrayal of poverty and poor people featured across a range of television programmes, such as *Little Britain*, during the past twenty years (Haylett, 2000; see also 'Judge bans real-life Vicky Pollard from her home', *The Guardian*, 10 May, 2005: 13). Both in terms of fiction programming and 'reality TV', largely spiteful representations purport to reveal what are displayed as the core deficits and shortcomings of poor communities (Raisborough and Adams, 2008).

More measured and sensitive depictions, although far from rhapsodically romanticising working class lives and milieus, have frequently been praised within academic circles, but have found it difficult to counteract more common and socially pernicious mainstream representations (McKenzie, 2015). Tracey Jensen (2013, 2014) dubs recent television representations of the poor as 'poverty porn': a genre of programme, apt to shape unreflective social imaginaries and displaying a 'fetishist fascination' with looking *at* the poor, who are portrayed as deficit, 'ignorant, uneducated and lacking in moral judgement' (McKenzie, 2015: 104–5). Moreover, such programmes have not been confined to the UK; in Australia the documentary *Struggle Street*, for example, was lambasted by many commentators for seeming to mock poor families (Lagan, 2015; see also Archer, 2009). Conversely, some cultural observers have identified a contemporary fascination with 'posh' (Thorpe, 2014). Popular Conservatism has also given rise to the gendered and 'profoundly classed' figure of the 'yummy mummy' (Littler, 2013: 231).

Although not a welfare word evolving within the social science literature, 'chav' has similarly adversely contributed to how those who are poor have been named, depicted and ridiculed (Nayak, 2003; Tyler, 2008; Hollingworth and Williams, 2009; Tyler and Bennett, 2010; Toynbee, 2011; Harris, 2012; Nayak and Kehily, 2014). In terms of its etymology, most 'lexicographers agree that "chav" owes its origins to the Romany dialect word for small child ("chavo" or "chavi")' (Hayward and Yar, 2006: 16). In 2004, the OED referred to 'chav' as the 'buzzword' of the year and the *Independent on Sunday* recorded more than 10,000 references to the word in one week. Indeed, 2004 appeared to be the year in 'which disgust and fascination with chavs peaked in the British press' (Tyler, 2013a: 163). Unsurprisingly, such saturation impacts on the perceptions of the young. For example, research undertaken examining the views of school children, aged 8–13 in unnamed state and private schools, reveals that 'better-off' children viewed their counterparts on 'disadvantaged' housing estates as badly behaved 'chavs', going to 'rough schools' with unemployed parents who do not care for them. These privately educated youngsters perceive the 'chavs' as being located at one end of the social spectrum and the 'rich' at the other, with themselves in the middle (Sutton et al., 2007).

Prior to the 'riots', the omnipresence of 'chav' in popular discourse contributed to the reconstruction or recalibration of the underclass figure. The 'chav' represents

> a popular reconfiguration of the underclass idea...the discourse of the underclass turned crucially upon a (perceived or real) pathology in the working classes' relations to *production* and socially productive labour. Its emergent successor, the concept of the 'chav'...is in contrast orientated to purportedly pathological class dispositions in relation to the sphere of *consumption*...The perceived 'problem' with this 'new underclass' is that they consume in ways which are deemed 'vulgar'... by superordinate classes. (Harward and Yar, 2006: 10; 14, original emphases)

Sociological interpretations of the 'riots' emphasising the relationship of these events to the prevalence of a rampant 'consumer culture' amongst the poor, may also have been – perhaps implicitly – influenced by dominant representations of the 'chav' (Moxon, 2011). Indeed, partial and tendentious readings of these street rebellions, although marinated in voguish social theory, were on occasion prone to lay an undue emphasis on 'politically blind and nihilistic acting out' perceived as central to these multifaceted and disturbing disruptions (Winslow and Hall, 2012).

As we saw in Chapter 2, Rancière stresses the significance of regulating how groups and individuals are situated in a 'police' order. This understanding can also be used to inform our comprehension of how the so-called underclass is expected to remain within their allotted roles, both in terms of physical and symbolic space. This was apparent in terms of some of the media responses in the aftermath of the 2011 'riots'. Not only were the 'rioters' perceived as venturing beyond their confined zones on the 'sink estates', some of them were also transcending their roles within the 'police' order in other ways that were palpably more political. This was evinced in the way in which Carole Duggan, the aunt of Mark Duggan whose 'lawful' killing by the Metropolitan Police prompted the 'riots' in August 2011, was depicted when she questioned how the State was responding to the death of her nephew. Days after the inquest verdict into his death, the journalist Richard Littlejohn (2014), locating his remarks entirely in the context of popular culture and 'poverty porn', reported that the grieving aunt looked like

> Vicky Pollard's granny and spoke in a curious hybrid accent, a cross between Ali G and Liam Gallagher of Oasis … [With] her severe 'council estate face-lift' swept back hairdo, [she] could have wandered off the set of Channel 4's Benefit Street after a session in the boozer with 'White Dee' and 'Black Dee'.

Such comments illuminate the gendered (and frequently misogynistic strand) within underclass discourses. Moreover, they reveal what can occur when individuals, such as Carole Duggan, stray – rather like one of Rancière's wayward shoemakers – beyond their allocated role (see also Chapter 2). Moving out of place, and violating the dominant regime of representation purporting to capture their essence as limited or deficient human subjects, they are scornfully ridiculed.

Particular groups of the population, often constructed as underclass stereotypes, have faced especially coercive policies and practices partitioning them from the more prosperous parts of the population. Perhaps homeless people can be perceived as the paradigmatic group with policies apparently intent on making tough lives even tougher. In his classic *City of Quartz*, Mike Davis (1990) charted how the use of space was increasingly shrinking for homeless people in Los Angeles and other Californian cities. Architecture, and even the design of park benches, were crafted and styled in ways to prevent homeless citizens from resting, sleeping and sheltering. Subsequently, such techniques – along with more punitive attitudes and forms of behaviour management – have become more common in cities elsewhere. Indeed, the phenomenon of 'defensive' or 'disciplinary' architecture can be interpreted as 'a sort of unkindness that is considered, designed, approved, funded and made real with the explicit motive to exclude and harass' (Andreou, 2015).

AN 'ESSENTIALLY AMERICAN INVENTION'?

> Your defendant belongs to a black underclass … which is economically 'redundant'…falling further and further behind the rest of society, locked into a culture of despair and crime – I wouldn't say culture … There is no culture there, it's only a wilderness, and damn monstrous, too. We are talking about a people consigned to destruction, a doomed people… We

do not know how to approach this population. We haven't even conceived that reaching it may be a problem. So there is nothing but death before it. Maybe we've already made our decision. Those that can be advanced into the middle class, let them be advanced. The rest? Well we do our best by them. We don't have to do any more. They kill some of us. Mostly they kill themselves. (Bellow, 2008: 206–7)

These thoughts belong to Albert Corde, the fictional dean of a Chicago college, featuring as the main character in Saul Bellow's *The Dean's December* initially published in 1982 during the period of the first Reagan administration (1980–1984). The former Trotskyist's novel meanders between the United States and Ceaușescu's Romania, but the spectre of the US underclass pervades the plot and floods the narrative. Indeed, ruminations, such as those of Bellow, saturated the politics and culture of the period broadly coinciding with the early evolution of neoliberalism. This identification of an underclass can, in fact, be interpreted as central to the naming practices and vocabulary of neoliberalism in the 1980s and to the interventions of politicians, economists and culture figures associated with this radical project (see also Chapter 2).

Kirk Mann (1994: 81) believes that there is little doubt that the underclass is an 'American invention' and he refers to a speech by Edward Kennedy (1932–2009) in 1978, in which he mentioned this pejorative welfare word. The term was initially promoted by numerous US journalists in the 1980s (Katz, 1993). In this latter context a short series of articles by Ken Auletta, appearing in the *New York Times* in 1981, tends to be viewed as particularly important and influential (Welshman, 2013). Here it was categorically asserted that there was a clear underclass of 9 million Americans who 'do not assimilate' (in Macnicol, 1987: 314). In the *Atlantic Monthly* Nicholas Lemann also wrote on the same theme during the summer of 1986 (Welshman, 2013).

In the 1980s, when the underclass became omnipresent in political and media coverage, it was responded to by a good deal of criticism from many social scientists. This was often because those seeking to define and measure this alleged sub-stratum of society were prone to embedding their scholarship in entirely unexamined normative formulations. Mincy and his colleagues, for example, acknowledge that 'norms are not invariant across cultures or historical periods', but they complacently went on to assert that 'today in the United States it is generally expected that young people will complete their education, at least through high school; that they will delay their childbearing until they are able to support their offspring; that adults who are not old, disabled or supported by a spouse will work; and that everyone will be law-abiding' (Mincy et al., 1990: 248).

In the UK, Dean and Taylor-Gooby neatly summarised that the underclass concept was 'not to define the marginalised, but to marginalise those it defines' (in Welshman, 2013: 11; see also Dean, 1992). Scrutinising the definers, Bagguley and Mann claimed that 'perhaps the real dangerous class is not the underclass but those who have propagated the underclass concept' (in Welshman, 2013: 181). In his classic intervention in these debates, John Macnicol (1987: 314) argued that Auletta's influential journalistic contributions were 'impressionistic, selective and highly misleading. Like previous underclass proponents the US journalist had lumped together an enormous variety of human conditions – "the passive poor" (long-term welfare-dependent), "the hostile street criminals", "the hustlers" and "the traumatic drunks, drifters, released mental patients" etc – into one homogenous group'. Paradoxically, those promoting the underclass concept commonly assumed that there existed a 'relatively fixed and more or less homogenous social grouping' clearly differentiated from the working class (Rodger, 1992: 46).

The criticism directed at the promulgation of the underclass notion failed, however, to dislodge it from its focal location within the politics of welfare in the 1980s and 1990s. This is not to argue that all those using this welfare word were united in their political perceptions as to precisely what had prompted its creation. In general, in the United States, the left and liberals emphasised the 'decline of staple industries, geographical dislocation, political marginalisation, demographic trends, labour market discrimination, and the restraints imposed on inner city inhabitants ... The Right [focused] on the pathology and the culture of the underclass' (Mann, 1994: 82).

Liz Beddoe (2014) draws attention to the racialisation of the underclass in contemporary New Zealand with racialised references to the 'brown underclass' seeping into debates on the situation of impoverished children from Māori and Pacifica families. In the UK, aside from in the early work of Giddens (see below), black minority ethnicities have not tended to be significant in underclass construction. Rather, the term has been apt to conjure images of the white, urban, purportedly feckless poor.

Largely unsuccessful attempts have been made by US conservative intellectuals, such as Mead, to racialise British underclass discourse (see also Chapter 3). Indeed, in the United States, discussion on the underclass has been 'dominated' by the politics of 'race' (Welshman, 2013: 140) and has focused, more precisely, on African-Americans (Reed, 2016). Many authors have used the 'labels "underclass" and "black underclass" almost interchangeably' (Morris, 1989: 126). Moreover, some black writers and academics used the term to try and articulate what they took to be key dynamics within their community. Although perhaps giving more weight to structural than behavioural causes, these interventions accepted the validity of the claim that an underclass was emerging. In this sense, if 'cultural factors were at work, they were evidence of an adaptive response to a wider environment, rather than evidence of a separate subculture' (Welshman, 2013: 150).

William Julius Wilson (1978, 1987) 'attempted to combine structural and cultural interpretations' (Welshman, 2013: 155). He diagnosed that the 'central problem of the underclass was unemployment ... reinforced by an increasing social isolation in impoverished neighbourhoods. What he called "weak labour-force attachment" was caused by two factors: macrostructural changes in the wider society and economy, and the social milieu of individuals' (2013: 154). According to Wilson, if 'underclass minorities have limited aspirations, a hedonistic orientation to time, or lack of plans for the future, such outlooks ultimately are the result of restricted opportunities and feelings of resignation originating from bitter personal experience and a bleak future' (in Welshman, 2013: 154). Thus, while Wilson's understanding might have an affinity with some of the, arguably racist, perceptions of Bellow's Albert Corde, they were, to some extent, intent on illuminating the structural underpinnings of what he viewed as problematic behaviour and attitudes. Many in the black community in the United States, especially those on the left, remained deeply troubled by Wilson's high-profile contributions viewing them as potentially adding to the pathologising of African-Americans. Critics included figures such as Adolph Reed, who lamented the 'poverty of discourse about poverty' (Welshman, 2013: 159; Reed, 2016).

The role of US-based Charles Murray was, for many located in the UK, especially significant given how he functioned as probably the main agent and conduit transporting 'underclass talk' across the Atlantic (Mann and Roseneil, 1994). His *The Emerging British Underclass* (Murray, 1990) was derived from an article appearing in *The Sunday Times* magazine in November of the previous year. Using rather florid prose, Murray explained to readers that he had 'arrived in Britain earlier this year, a visitor from a *plague* area come to see whether the disease is spreading' (1990: 3, emphasis added). The 'question facing Britain is the same haunting question facing the United States: *how contagious is this disease?*' (1990: 23, emphasis added). Having visited Birkenhead on Merseyside and Easterhouse in Glasgow, Murray adumbrated that the appearance of an underclass was related to three main factors or 'symptoms'. First, 'illegitimacy' had to be perceived as the 'the best predicator of an underclass in the making' (1990: 4). This was because 'long-term welfare dependency is a fact, not a myth, among young women who have children without husbands' (1990: 8). One of the main problems was the decline in stigma resulting in too many women giving birth outside of the bounds of a marital relationship. Gelling with the views of many within the contemporary Conservative governments of Margaret Thatcher and John Major, he proposed that a top-to-bottom overhaul of the benefit system was required.

Violent crime and unemployment were two other factors leading to underclass formation, but it often appeared that 'illegitimacy' was at the root of Murray's analysis and public presentation of the issue. He returned to the same thematic preoccupations in the mid-1990s (Murray, 1994). Again having his work published by the right-wing 'think-tank', the Institute of Economic Affairs (IEA), he maintained that the British 'underclass crisis' was beginning to deepen. What is more, he began to refer to this class as heralding the appearance of a mob or 'new rabble' (Murray, 1994a, 1994b, see also Prideaux, 2010).

Despite criticisms directed at underclass discourse in the UK, a number of leading sociologists felt it had some analytical substance. Anthony Giddens (1981: 217) asserted that it was 'hardly possible to resist the conclusion that the existence of a quite highly structurated underclass [was] a fundamentally important phenomenon...conditioning the American experience'. As early as 1973, even before the so-called underclass had begun to become dominant in exchanges relating to poverty, Giddens (1981: 217) argued that the 'underclass was mainly comprised of 'recent migrants to the urban-industrial areas'. However, this was not an occurrence confined to the UK because 'similar developments, less pronounced in nature' could be seen in 'other advanced societies – as a result, for example, of the migration of West Indians and Asians into Britain, and of Algerians into France'. In the Labour Party's centre-left flagship *The New Statesman*, Ralf Dahrendorf referred to the presence of an underclass operating as a 'cancer which eats away at the texture of societies and metastasises in ways which can increasingly be felt in all their parts' (in Welshman, 2013: 167).

Perhaps, the contributions of Frank Field, the former director of the Low Pay Unit and Child Poverty Action Group, were most significant and influential within the British polity. Elected as a Labour MP for the hard-pressed Birkenhead constituency, he wrote a book on what he perceived was an emergent underclass (Field, 1989). Purportedly seeking to 'reclaim the term for the liberal Left' (Welshman, 2013: 171), he argued that important economic and social trends threatened to erode citizenship. For Field, the underclass was comprised of three groups: the long-term unemployed, single-parent families and elderly pensioners. John Welshman (2013: 172) suggests that this intervention reflected Field's endeavour to 'combine behaviour and structural factors' in some ways similar to that of William Julius Wilson. More significantly the Merseyside MP's enthusiasm for the underclass conceptualisation furnished part of the contextual framework for his more encompassing plans for so-called welfare reform in later years. Central here was Field's claim, conducive to the politics of New Labour (1997–2010) and the coalition administration (2010–2015), that there needed to be tougher 'availability-for-work' testing targeting those claiming income support when unemployed. Unsurprising, Field was to serve, albeit briefly, as Minister of Welfare Reform during the Blair's period as prime minister and as 'Poverty Czar' for the Cameron-led Coalition government.

THE 'SYMBOLIC MECCA'

In trying to comprehend the significance of ideas emanating from the United States, the theorisations of Bourdieu and Wacquant are helpful (see also Chapter 2). Writing on the cusp of the new century, they maintained that

> the 'underclass' is but a fictional group, produced on paper by the classifying practices of those scholars, journalists and related experts in the management of the (black urban) poor… Inept and unsuited in the American case, the imported concept adds nothing to the knowledge of European societies. For the agencies and methods for the *government of misery* are vastly discrepant on the two sides of the Atlantic. (Bourdieu and Wacqaunt, 1999: 49, emphasis added)

They dismiss Charles Murray as merely one of countless US scholars whose mission was to 'export intellectual products (often soiled and faded)' (Bourdieu and Wacquant, 1999: 50). Bourdieu and Wacquant acknowledge that the underclass word is likely to have originated in Europe and attribute importance to Myrdal (see above). However, a detour through America transformed the idea 'from a structural concept aiming to question the dominant representation of society' to a 'behavioural category perfectly suited to reinforcing the representation by imputing to the "anti-social" conduct of the most disadvantaged responsibility for their own dispossession' (1999: 49–50).

Bourdieu and Wacquant are especially scathing in their criticism of those acting as transmission belts facilitating the flow of inappropriate vocabularies and their associated concepts into Europe and other parts of the world. Without the role played by such complicit conduits, 'the "globalization" of the themes of American social doxa…would not be possible' (Bourdieu and Wacqaunt, 1999: 46). In comments that have resonance for this book's exploration of welfare words, they also charge that the activities of publishers, those responsible for editing academic journals and philanthropic and research foundations often unthinkingly 'propound and propagate' ideas emerging from the United States or, as they term it, the 'new symbolic Mecca' (1999: 46).

According to Bourdieu and Wacquant (1999: 46), material developments, relating to the internationalisation of academic publishing have been immensely significant and aided the circulation and 'diffusion of "US thought" in the social sciences'. Damagingly, the 'international circulation of ideas … tends, by its very logic, to conceal their original conditions of production and signification' (Bourdieu and Wacquant, 2001: 3). In this context, 'perpetual media repetition' gradually promotes a 'universal common sense' that risks having us forget that certain words, phrases, paradigms and ways of viewing the social world do 'nothing but express, in a truncated and unrecognizable form … the complex and contested realities of a particular historical society … the American society…characterized by the deliberate dismantling of the social state and the correlative hypertrophy of the penal state' (2001: 3).

Partly drawing on Orwell's dystopian *1984*, the two French sociologists returned to address similar themes in another contribution, maintaining that the so-called underclass, along with a cluster of other welfare words, were best interpreted as constituting a 'strange Newspeak' (Bourdieu and Wacquant, 2001: 2). Alternatively, the diffusion of such words might be perceived as helping to constitute a 'new planetary vulgate' obscuring the relevance of a vocabulary and concepts such as 'capitalism' 'class', 'exploitation', 'domination' and 'inequality' (2001: 2)[2]. Hence, prominent and officially sanctioned and propagated welfare words, such as underclass and its associated talk, were functioning, as mentioned in Chapter 1, as a 'screen discourse' blocking engagement with more substantial economic and political questions (2001: 4): such omissions were generated by the 'imperialism' of 'neoliberal reason' (2001: 5). By 'imposing on the rest of the world categories of perception' corresponding to its social structures, the United States was 'refashioning the entire world in its image' (2001: 4).

These, palpably polemical, interventions by Bourdieu and Wacqaunt are intentionally provocative and potentially contribute a good deal to our understanding of transmission and amplification of welfare words originating from, or having their meaning decisively deflected in, the United States (see also Hall et al., 1978). Their analysis emphasises how words, such as underclass, need to be interpreted within the context of neoliberalism (see also Chapter 1). Nonetheless, it might also be contended that the pair's reasoning is overly strident and insufficiently attentive to critiques articulated *within* the US on the globalisation of culturally specific ways of perceiving and policy-making. Perhaps Bourdieu and Wacquant also fail to capture the significance of historically embedded *national* forms of 'common sense' located beyond the United States (see also Chapter 2). This is reflected, as we will see, in terms of how current underclass stereotypes can be related to previous British formulations dating back centuries.

In her examination of the construction of the 'dole bludger' in 1970s Australia, Verity Archer (2009) provides a fascinating illustration of how US and 'home' factors became dialectically intertwined. In this instance, New Right advocates in Australia, located in 'think-tanks' such as the Institute for Public Affairs (IPA) and the Centre for Independent Studies (CIS), acted as conduits for the ideas of US-based neoliberal ideologues. In this way, such organisations provided the infrastructure for the organic intellectuals of Australian neoliberalism to act, with great energy and purpose, in destabilising a fragile Keynesian consensus. In the UK also, even before Murray's interventions, there were indigenous and embedded discourses historically naming, labelling and pathologising the poor. Before turning to briefly explore this dimension, however, the solo work of Wacquant, first discussed in Chapter 2, warrants renewed consideration because it usefully highlights the importance of spatiality and place within dominant and dominating underclass constructs.

PLACING THE UNDERCLASS: 'BAD' NEIGHBOURHOODS AND SOCIAL DETRITUS

In the UK, the images and vocabulary attached to underclass stereotypes have been heavily influenced by the iconography of the so-called 'sink estate' (Hanley, 2007; see also Hanley, 2016). Another US importation, this phrase focuses on particular places which, in the 1990s, were variously described as part of 'No Go Britain' and 'estates from hell' (Victor et al., 1994). Into the twenty-first century, council estates have been positioned in elite depictions as 'holding pens for the undeserving poor' (McKenzie, 2012: 129). For even vaguely leftist commentators, such as Will Hutton (2007), the council house 'ghetto' was a 'living tomb' with dominant discourses dwelling on the idea that public housing tenants constitute 'a socially excluded, economically inactive and politically apathetic "underclass"' (Watt, 2008: 347). TV programmes frequently help to solidify such stereotypes; a notable example of this being the 2012 BBC *Panorama* documentary 'Trouble on the

Estate', featuring the Shadsworth estate on the outskirts of Blackburn, Lancashire, which prompted several complaints[3].

For New Labour, and subsequent governments, the council estate appeared to be the theatre in which the performance and regulation of 'anti-social behaviour' was enacted (see Garrett, 2007a, 2007b). In this context, Wacquant encourages us to think about processes of 'advanced marginality' and the connected production of 'territorial stigmatization' (see, for example, Wacquant 2007, 2008, Ch. 8; 2009). 'Advanced marginality' refers, in broad terms, to an emerging 'yet distinctive regime of urban poverty' associated with 'new forms of exclusionary closure translating into the expulsion to the margins and crevices of social and physical space' (2008: 232). A core element of this process is the 'symbolic splintering' of the working class (2008: Ch. 8). This is connected to the fragmentation and denunciation of particular fractions of the class which are constructed as a form of social detritus or waste.

Linking this to the evolution of the underclass label, Wacquant relates how this development is frequently associated with the identification of particular locations in official and popular exchanges and, as discussed in Chapter 2, what Gramsci terms 'common sense' perceptions. Rather 'than being disseminated throughout working-class areas, advanced marginality tends to concentrate in isolated and bounded territories increasingly perceived by both outsiders and insiders as social purgatories, leprous badlands at the heart of the postindustrial metropolis where only the refuse of society would accept to dwell' (Wacquant, 2008: 24). Discourses of 'vilification proliferate and agglomerate' about such territories and are generated 'from below', in the 'ordinary interactions of daily life', as well as 'from above', by journalistic, political and bureaucratic fields (Wacquant, 2007: 67).

In the US literature on the underclass, such areas are categorically and unambiguously defined as 'bad neighbourhoods' (Mincy et al., 1990: 451). These are characterised as places where the 'incidence of nonconformity to existing norms is high', with Mincy et al. (1990: 451) confidently 'measuring' 'non-conformity' across four indicators: adolescents dropping out of high school, single parenthood, welfare dependency and male joblessness. More critically, Adolph Reed (2016: 273), concentrating on how images of a black underclass dominated responses to urban reconstruction following hurricane Katrina, maintains that housing projects in which poor people are clustered are presented as 'alien, dangerous hearts of darkness' and that such 'underclass ideology is also directly implicated in the proliferation of approaches to policing that routinely flout civil rights and liberties and approximate the terroristic style of an occupying army'.

In the UK, in recent years, particular territories – the 'neighbourhoods' and 'estates' which are 'ghettoised' – are depicted as zones inhabited by a feral underclass beyond the norms of civility shared by the rest of the community. Such constructions also 'chime with the new conditionality regimes and reductions in benefits for tenants' (Hancock and Mooney, 2013: 55; see also Chapter 3). The intervention, therefore, of primary definers such as Cameron and Duncan Smith, along with a host of likeminded commentators and media pundits, perform potent ideological work in that the 'construction of place through territorial stigmatization obfuscates fundamental structural and functional differences underlying the uneven spatial distribution of poverty and disadvantage, and displaces questions of culpability away from the state and private sectors' (Hancock and Mooney, 2013: 53). Moreover, changes to benefit entitlement, especially the introduction of the so-called housing 'benefit cap', is resulting in substantial reductions in rental support for many families and this will socially engineer a higher degree of social class and income segregation between wealthy and poorer localities (Hammett, 2010).

Wacquant's 'advanced marginality' and 'territorial stigmatisation' concepts are useful in aiding the assembling of a sociological interpretation of why some particular localities – subjected to what Bourdieu refers to as 'symbolic violence' – are belittled, cheapened and degraded in hegemonic underclass discourses. His theorisation helps to explain why it is that certain geographical spaces are constructed as 'symbolic locations' and are deployed as signifiers for crime and an assortment of threats and troubles (Campbell, 1993). In terms of cities, in England particularly during the period of the Thatcher administrations in the 1980s, Liverpool often fulfilled this role (Lane, 1987). Across the Irish Sea, Limerick (and parts of Dublin) have served a similar function (Hourigan, 2011).[4] Within each of these urban locations, specific, impoverished neighbourhoods are then identified as pariah micro-zones within the wider city: for example, Toxteth in Liverpool and the localities of Moyross and Southill in Limerick (McMorrow, 2006).

Importantly, areas subjected to 'territorial stigmatisation' are localities where practitioners, such as social workers, go about their work on a daily basis and some of the research literature highlights the role of such 'external actors' in producing and amplifying stigma. Hastings (2004: 240), for example, refers to how 'the policies and practices of local authority workers such as housing officers and social workers, as well as the police force, can perpetuate myths about particular places as well as contribute to their material deprivation by failing to see them as deserving of their share of public resource'. Given such findings, there needs, perhaps, to be greater recognition of communal tenacity within stigmatised localities and an acknowledgement of the collective unwillingness of residents to bend in the face of economic adversity (McKenzie, 2015).

LOOKING BACKWARDS: LOCATING THE UNDERCLASS IN HISTORY

In her study of St Ann's, in Nottingham, Lisa McKenzie (2015: 9) observes that 'symbolic violence' has been 'visited on the poor for many generations in the UK, often through the language of the "underclass" and the negative connotations attributed to those it describes'. Indeed, various versions of the underclass concept have featured prominently in social and political debates in the past. Some writers locate similar concerns as long ago as the seventeenth century Poor Law, given the preoccupation with vagrancy and an aspiration to neatly separate 'deserving' and 'undeserving' claimants (Welshman, 2013; see also Chapter 3).

Marx's comments on the lumpenproletariat, from the nineteenth century, have been referred to by those seeking a more leftist lineage for underclass theorisation. His perception was rooted in his encompassing model of capitalism's evolution and, in this context, a surplus population of workers becomes

> the lever of capitalist accumulation, indeed it becomes a condition of the existence of the capitalist mode of production. It forms a disposable industrial reserve army [and] creates a mass of human material always ready for exploitation. (Marx, 1990: 784; see also Braverman, 1998; Smith, 2011)

The lumpenproletariat is, therefore, a part of the 'lowest sediment of the relative surplus population' which always 'dwells in the sphere of pauperism' (Marx, 1990: 784). More specifically, it is comprised of 'vagabonds, criminals, prostitutes' and three additional groups rendered surplus to production: first, those 'suffering the impact of a crisis of trade'; second, 'orphans and pauper children'; third, a collection of individuals including the 'demoralized, the ragged' and those 'unable to work' because their skills are no longer fitted to the current mode of production, the aged, the victims of industrial accidents and widows (Marx, 1990: 794).

Taken from the first volume of *Capital* published in 1867, these comments are situated within Marx's wider structural analysis of how the system operates and he is not interested in moralising about the behaviour of the social strata identified. Somewhat earlier, however, in his commentary on the rise of Bonaparte, his perceptions of this 'lumpen' class were more critical given his stress on how it provided a base from which the forces of reaction could recruit individuals to assist in the liquidation of the workers' uprising in France (Marx, 2000; see also Tyler, 2013b).

In terms of other prominent 'classical' Marxists, Nikolai Bukharin (1888–1938) maintained that in the lumpenproletariat we find 'shiftlessness, lack of discipline, hatred of the old, but impotence to construct or organize anything new, an individualistic declassed "personality" whose actions are only based on foolish caprices' (in Matza, 1967: 291). Gramsci, in his prison notebooks, analyses the role played by the lumpenproletariat in Italian society. Referred to in Italy by 'the picturesque name of *morti di fame*' (down-and-out, literally, 'dying of hunger'), he outlined this group's composition and reactionary political role (Gramsci in Hoare and Nowell-Smith, 2005: 203, 272–273).

However, the underclass notion has tended to be mostly 'propagated by those of a conservative outlook' (Macnicol, 1987: 299). Some of their historical definitions, enunciated by various 'experts' heavy with 'symbolic capital' (Bourdieu, 1991), include: the 'social residuum' of the 1880s, the 'social problem group' of the 1930s, the 'problem family' in the 1950s (and 1990s) and the so-called 'troubled family' of today (Tepe-Belfrage and Montgomerie, 2016; see also Chapter 3).

INDUSTRIAL RESIDUUM

Toward the end of the nineteenth century, it was the 'industrial residuum' which was positioned as the underclass of the period. The 'industrial residuum' – for some writers, merely the 'residuum' – featured as a focal concern from approximately the early 1880s until the commencement of the First World War in 1914. The residuum label appears to have been first used by John Bright MP for Birmingham in a debate on the Second Reform Bill in 1867 (Welshman, 2013). According to Bright, those constituting the residuum were all in a 'condition of dependence' and prey to being taken advantage of and exploited by unscrupulous members of society. Their identification also coincided with the 'age of classic social investigation' during which Charles Booth (1840–1916) became 'arguably the most influential writer' on the residuum (Welshman, 2013: 16; see also Brown, 1968). Others, such as Samuel A. Barnett (1844–1913), exhibited an interest in the theme advocating the inception of labour colonies for recalcitrant workers. Barnett was associated with the establishment of the first university settlement Toynbee Hall in east London in 1884. The forerunners of modern-day social work, the Charity Organisation Society (COS) were also prominent promoters of the residuum conceptualisation (Bosanquet, 1895a, 1895b). Here, the interventions of Helen Dendy (later Bosanquet) (1860-1925) are illustrative and exerted an important influence on social policy. She contributed, for example, to the Majority Poor Law report published in 1909 (see also Dendy, 1895). Somewhat unconvincingly, Welshman (2013: 33) argues that Dendy can be viewed as providing 'perceptive and sympathetic descriptions of working class life' and in this sense her perspective can be regarded more favourably than that of her contemporary, and oftentimes opponent in relation to 'reform' strategies, Beatrice Webb (1858–1943) (see also Webb and Webb, 1968 [1932]).

Those discursively situated within the residuum were perceived as an economically unproductive layer of social outcasts and they featured prominently in social science and popular literature. Pearson (1975: Ch. 6) highlights that 'sewage' and a cluster of related metaphors were prevalent in the descriptions of this group and its alleged characteristics and proclivities. Indeed, sewage and 'drains were the guiding metaphors for those who were depicted as the deviants of the time' (1975: 161). Central within this perspective was the prominence of 'cloacal imagery' (1975: 162): the residuum referring both 'to the offal, excrement and waste which constituted the sanitary problem, and ... to the lowest strata of society that constituted the social and political problem'. Contagion and contamination were other recursive themes within underclass narratives and it was echoed, as discussed earlier, in Murray's interventions a century later.

SOCIAL PROBLEM GROUP

During the inter-war years in the UK, the underclass was re-conceptualised as the 'social problem group' which differed from the preceding industrial residuum on account of its 'more precise hereditarian causation' (Macnicol, 1987: 297). Interventionist remedies envisaged as dealing with this group included targeted sterilisation (Macnicol, 1987: 300). A significant role was played by the Eugenics Education Society (often referred as a simply the 'Eugenics Society') founded in 1907. In 1923, it established a committee to consider research projects scrutinising Poor Law applicants. With a view to ascertaining if pauperism was inter-generational, family lineages of social problem groups were to be traced and applicants were to be compared and measured against a random sample of purportedly 'normal' citizens (Macnicol, 1987: 305). Despite the enthusiasms and aspirations of those involved, even the 'most enthusiastic eugenic ideologue found it impossible to collect family pedigrees of a quality sufficient to prove the case' (Macnicol, 1987: 302). E. J. Lidbetter (1877–1962), a Poor Law official in the East End of London produced *Heredity and the Social Problem Gro*up. Yet, even after many years of research, the findings were generally vague and inclusive serving to damage the cause of the eugenicists (Macnicol, 1987). Investigative work was also carried out by David Caradog Jones (1883-1975) who was to become a lecturer in sociology at the University of Liverpool. In his tripartite categorisation of the 'abnormal', he included those with some form of disability; others with moral failings and a third group defined through its dependence on welfare (Welshman, 2013: 73; see also Perkins, 2016 for a contemporary spin on this concept).

A Mental Deficiency Committee (or 'Wood Committee'), appointed in 1924, reported in 1929 that the 'social problem group' was comprised of 'approximately the lowest 10% in the social scale of most communities' (in Macnicol, 1987: 302). Given the sheer scale of the perceived problem

> [Sterilisation] offered an appeal on several levels. It was seen by eugenicists as a crucial measure, the successful implementation of which would lead to the spread of 'eugenic consciousness' throughout society. It would cost little to implement (by contrast, institutional segregation was prohibitively expensive) and thus appealed to the fiscal retrenchment mentality of the professional middle classes to which eugenists tended to belong. (Macnicol, 1987: 303)

Debates about consent taking place at this time prompted suggestions that sterilisation could become compulsory for those individuals perceived by scientific expertise to be 'unfit' (Macnicol, 1987: 303). A Committee for Legalising Eugenic Sterilisation was organised by Carlos Blacker (1909–1975) of the Eugenics Society and an unsuccessful Private Member's Bill was introduced by a Labour MP, Major Archibald Church (1886–1954). Remarkably, a 1932 report drawing on the 10% notion, counted the potential targets of the eugenicists to be up to '4 million persons in England and Wales, who are the great purveyors of social inefficiency, prostitution, feeblemindedness and petty crime, the chief architects of slumdom, the most fertile in the community' (in Macnicol, 1987: 304).

In 1934 the Brock Committee recommended voluntary sterilisation should be legalised, but medical opinion was not unified and opposition was encountered from the Roman Catholic Church and many in the Labour Movement. Arguably, a form of 'left-over eugenics' was, however, detectable in the introduction of the 11+ examination. Mapped out in the Norwood Report in 1943, this test aspired to gauge the 'intelligence' of school children so as to allocate them a place within a new tripartite system of secondary education.

This fixation with eugenics stretched to many parts of the globe (see, for example, Broberg and Roll-Hansen, 1996). In 2007, Indiana passed the first US sterilisation law 'in light of concerns about miscegenation and racial degeneracy' (Meloni, 2016: 71). In 1927, Buck v Bell upheld state law allowing the superintendents of insane asylums to order the sterilization of an inmate with an inherited condition of insanity or mental disability whenever they deemed that such an operation would advance the interests of the inmate and society as a whole. In Californian alone, over the period 1909–1929, some 6,255 people were sterilised with 1,488 of these subjected to the rather elastic diagnosis of 'feeble-minded' (in Stehlik, 2001: 376). A contemporary report summarising the Californian programme, titled 'Sterilisation for human betterment', rhapsodised that such interventions were undertaken in a spirit of 'constructive charity' (in Stehlik, 2001: 376).

The Nazis enacted the Law for the Prevention of Hereditarily Diseased Offspring in July 1933, legalising compulsory sterilisation of those judged to be suffering from hereditary disorders, including feeblemindedness. In this context, a number of social historians have examined responses to 'asocial families' and other 'social outcasts' (see, for example, Pine, 1995; 1997; Gellately and Stoltzfus, 2001; Kunstreich, 2003). In some countries, practices of sterilisation carried on, and even increased, after the Second World War (Hietala, 1996; Mottier and Gerodetti, 2007; Swansen, 2007). Indeed, 'eugenic thinking never really went away' (Burdett, 2007: 8; see also Hauss and Ziegler, 2008). In 2010, a senior academic in the UK proposed the sterilisation of parents abusing their children (Pemberton, 2010). More recently, it has also been confidently detected that the 'number of children born to welfare claimants tracks the generosity of benefits with increases in the generosity of benefits being followed by deliberate increases in their rate of reproduction via altered contraception usage' (Perkins, 2016: 4). Similarly, within the political sphere, a Conservative Party member of the House of Lords has expressed his concerns about excessive 'breeding' amongst the poor ('Pressure to sack peer who thinks cuts will encourage the poor to "breed"', *The Guardian*, 26 November, 2010: 1–2). The Conservative government's plans to limit child tax credits to two children can also be interpreted as 'reminiscent' of 'eugenics policy' (Wintour, 2015). In the United States, Anna Marie Smith (2010: 11) maintains that much of 'contemporary social policy is an expression of neo-eugenics' and it is possible to observe the 'training of a myriad of forces upon the poor that effectively discourage them from forming kinship groups and bearing and rearing children on their own terms'. Amrita Pande (2016) has written on how neo-eugenics impacts on and informs practices of commercial surrogacy in India (see also Chapter 9).

PROBLEM FAMILIES

In the UK, by 1947, the Eugenics Society had formed a Problem Families Committee and, according to the minutes of one of its meetings, such families were thought to exhibit four distinguishing characteristics: intractable in-educability; instability or infirmity of character; multiple social problems; and a squalid home (in Welshman, 2013: 83). The problem family conceptualisation lacked, however, the core eugenicist element vital to the social problem group discourse. It primarily arose from concerns about the medical condition and 'anti-social behaviour of some of the inner city school children evacuated to rural reception areas during the Second World War' (Macnicol, 1987: 297). In *Our Towns*, the influential Women's Group on Public Welfare (1943) adumbrated that a 'submerged tenth' 'still exists in our towns like a hidden sore, poor, dirty and crude in its habits, an intolerable and degrading burden to decent people forced by poverty to neighbour with it'. Within this group were 'problem families' always on 'the edge of pauperism and crime, riddled with mental and physical defects'.

In terms of the primary definers of the problem family, aside from the Eugenics Society and its associates, three other groups appear to have been significant: the Family Service Units (FSU) evolving out of the voluntary activities of pacifists during the Second World War; medical experts including doctors concerned with public health; a wide coalition of academics and practitioners in the social work profession (Welshman, 2013: 81). Macnicol (1987) perceives the problem family in rather less pessimistic terms compared to its 'social problem group' predecessor. Perhaps, mirroring the social-democratic reformist zeal associated with the 1945 Labour government, individuals in such families were not perceived as the passive victims of poor genetic endowment and considered potential targets for sterilisation and/or segregation. Rather, they tended to be viewed as amenable to character reform through the personalised intervention of social workers intent on fostering therapeutic relationships (Philp and Timms, 1957; Hall, 1960). Thus, to better coordinate interventions, local authorities were encouraged to assemble comprehensive lists of these families, as they would later be exhorted to do with the so-called troubled families (Welshman 2013; see also Blacker, 1952).

In the early 1950s, Spinley (1953) provided an account of 'one of the worst slums in London' describing a district that was 'notorious ... for vice and delinquency... a major prostitution area' and the 'blackest spot in the city for juvenile delinquency'. The author sought to provide her readers with a picture of a typical house in the locality:

> The most noticeable characteristic of the house is the smell, indeed on a
> first visit the middle-class stomach may find it impossible to stay longer

than five minutes. These strong odours are partly due to the fact windows are not opened and so no current of air can carry away the smells of cooking, lavatory bucket, mattress wet in the night, and the baby's vomit hurriedly wiped up. (Spinley, 1953: 40)

The focus of comment and intervention was 'highly gendered', targeting the 'domestically incompetent mother' (Macnicol, 2015: 4), often described as wayward, slovenly and 'feckless' (Starkey, 2000).

In the late-1950s, social workers and academics connected to the profession became increasingly lukewarm about the term, but the problem family remained attractive to other medical specialisms, such as psychiatry, into the 1970s (Wooton, 1959; Welshman, 1999). Furthermore, into the period of New Labour in the 1990s, Tony Blair was eager to excavate the phrase and put it into circulation once again (see *The Guardian*, 26 July 1993). For example, the problem family was a key component of New Labour's discursive framing of 'antisocial behaviour', with the White Paper, *Respect and Responsibility – Taking a Stand Against Anti-Social Behaviour*, drawing laudatory attention to the 'Problem Family Manual' produced by Kent Police (Home Office, 2003: 55). During the same period, this ideological category began to be uncritically deployed once again in professional discourse of social work (Cleaver and Freeman, 1995: 51–53). More recently, a lecturer at the prestigious King's College, Cambridge, has confidently asserted that adults in 'problem families, on average, display personality profiles that are significantly less conscientious and agreeable than those of adults of … comparison families' (Perkins, 2016: 19).

In broader historical terms, however, the problem family can be interpreted as something of a 'conceptual stepping stone between the social problem group ideas of the 1930s, and the cycle of deprivation notion of the 1970s' (Welshman, 2013: 81). This latter conceptualisation will be explored in Chapter 5.

TROUBLED FAMILIES

In his discussion of the 'category' of the family, Bourdieu (1996: 25) argues that the State 'performs countless constituting acts which constitute family identity as one of the most powerful principles of perception of the social world and one of the most real social units'. In our current period, the Conservatives can be viewed as fulfilling a vital role in 'constituting' and reifying the troubled family, a particularly problematic and seemingly dysfunctional aberration from the ideal (see also Atkinson, 2014).

The phrase – troubled family – has quickly become prominent, even if on occasions used sceptically, within the social work and social policy literature (see, for example, Hayden and Jenkins, 2014; 2015; Morris, 2013; Bond-Taylor, 2015; Davies, 2015). The OED states that 'troubled' can be defined as 'disturbed; disquieted; disordered; agitated; afflicted'. The term, 'troubled family', was used in the title of a book by Carolyn Webster-Stratton and Martin Herbert (1994) based at the Parenting Clinic at the University of Washington in Seattle. As observed, Tony Blair was especially prone to refer to the problem family. However, during the period of the Gordon Brown administration (2007–2010), problem families gave way to the troubled families which would become the symbolic targets for the Coalition (2010–2015) and two subsequent Conservative administrations (2015–).

While Blair and Brown were prime ministers, a whole range of interventions were triggered, focusing on impoverished families. This included the introduction of controversial 'intensive family support projects' (later referred to as 'family intervention projects' or simply FIPs) with the residential elements of such projects being dubbed 'sinbins' in parts of the media (Garrett, 2007a). A renewed interest in early intervention, informed by evolving approaches in neuroscience, was apparent and this also contributed to the tonality of policy-making in this era (see also Chapter 6). Subsequently, Cameron praised the work of the FIPs and appointed the garrulous Louise Casey as Head of the Troubled Families Unit in the Department for Communities and Local Government (see also Casey, 2012). One of her key roles was to lead the 'nationwide task of getting to grips with the number of troubled families – and working out where they are' (Cameron, 2011c). Picking up one of Blair's pet themes, Cameron charged that his government's initiative had to be viewed as integral to a wider agenda, that of 'fixing the responsibility deficit'. To perform the arduous task of 'turning around the lives' of the 120,000 troubled families, 152 English local authorities were to receive approximately £450 million before the end of the government's term in 2015. In 2013, it was announced that the Troubled Families Programme (TFP) would be 'rolled out' to a further 400,000 families.

The initial figure of 120,000 was reported to have been loosely derived from a Family and Children Survey (FACS), conducted in the middle of the previous decade, which identified 2% of families being 'severely multiply disadvantaged' (Levitas, 2012: 4). These families were found to have at least five of the following seven criteria:

- No parent in the family is in work

- Family lives in overcrowded housing

- No parent has any qualifications

- Mother has mental health problems

- At least one parent has a long-standing limiting illness, disability or infirmity

- Family has low income (below 60% of median income)

- Family cannot afford a number of food and clothing items (in Levitas, 2012: 5).

As is clear from Cameron's speech, however, the focus shifted to the problematic behaviour of these families.

> Whatever you call them, we've known for years that a relatively small number of families are the source of a large proportion of the problems in society. Drug addiction. Alcohol abuse. Crime. A culture of disruption and irresponsibility that cascades through generations. (Cameron, 2011c)

Indeed, 'crime and anti-social behaviour', one of the key criteria for inclusion in the TFP was not included in the FACS survey (Hayden and Jenkins, 2014). In this sense, so-called troubled families are, in effect, tainted with criminal and anti-social behaviour, despite the foundational research not having identified this as an issue. Subsequently, additional claims were made, on the basis of interviews with just 'sixteen families', that troubled families were characterised by a history of sexual abuse (Casey, 2012); a theme emphasised in some of the media coverage (Shipman, 2012).

In June 2015, Cameron stated that the TFP was a 'total success' and had, in fact, 'turned around' the lives of 99% of families involved (Levitas, 2014; Bawden, 2015). However, a number of academics and other commentators have expressed concern that such claims of unbridled success are deeply misleading (Levitas, 2014; Butler, 2014; Crossley, 2016). Such scepticism was substantiated in an analysis by the National Institute of Economic and Social Research (2016) which was 'unable to find consistent evidence that the programme had any significant or systematic impact'.

CONCLUSION

Thirty years after its formulation it, Macnicol's (1987: 315–16) critique of the underclass appellation remains apt. He asserted that this welfare word lacks weight as a meaningful and convincing social science concept because it is 'essentially an artificial administrative definition relating to contacts with particular institutions of the state (e.g. social workers, welfare agencies, the police etc.). As such it is a statistical artefact in that the size of the underclass will be affected by a great variety of factors – criteria of eligibility, efficient registration, take-up of benefits – including, crucially, external factors that dictate the level of unemployment. Nevertheless, as a concept, the underclass is usually supported by those wishing to 'constrain the redistributive potential of state welfare' and it thus tends to reoccur, in various guises, as part of a broader conservative 'aetiology of social problems'. In this sense, following Gramsci, we can also say that the underclass designation and its promulgation are components of a wider hegemonic class project (see also Chapter 2). Moreover, when the substantial impact of US discourses becomes dialectically enmeshed with genealogies of the term underclass in the UK, they produce a socially corrosive cocktail.

In the next chapter the focus will be on the seemingly more benign phrase 'social exclusion'.

REFLECTION AND TALK BOX 4

1. In his lucid dissection of the underclass, John Macnicol (1987: 296) argues

    The concept of an intergenerational underclass displaying a high concentra-
    tion of social problems – remaining outside the boundaries of citizenship,
    alienated from cultural norms and stubbornly impervious to the normal
    incentives of the market, social work intervention or state intervention –
    has been reconstructed periodically [and] while there are important shifts
    of emphasis between each of these reconstructions, there have also been
    striking continuities. Underclass stereotypes have always been part of the
    discourse on poverty in advanced industrial societies.

    Do you agree with this statement? Do you feel that social work practice is
    influenced by underclass or similar derogatory stereotypes? Can your percep-
    tions apply to a particular area of social work activity, such as child protection?

2. What is your view of Andrew O'Hagan's statement, featured in the UK *Guardian*
    newspaper, shortly after the economic 'crash'?

    By the late 1990s, the working class were no longer a working class – their
    traditions, habits, jobs, even in some places their speech, were given over
    to new forms of transcendence offered by celebrity culture and credit
    cards and the bogus life of the fantasy rich…It gives no one joy to observe
    that the English underclass…is now the most conservative force in Britain,
    in some quarters fascistic, hopped up on vengeance, tabloids, alcopops and
    sentiment…Disenchantment is the happy code that informs every byway
    of the underclass: service jobs, celebrity dreams, Lotto wins, leisured pov-
    erty on pre-credit crunch credit cards. (O'Hagan, 2009: 3)

FURTHER READING

Perhaps a good place to begin to understand the contemporary and invariably pernicious, deployment of underclass is the work of Charles Murray (1989). John Macnicol's
(1987) historical 'pursuit' of the underclass and its precursors provides invaluable
insights. John Welshman's *Underclass* (2013) also usefully charts the evolution of this
and similar welfare words aimed at the poor and socially marginalised. Pat Starkey
(2000) provides an informative discussion on how the role of the 'mother' is frequently
the focal concern of professionals. Her analysis relates to the problem family, but it
contains components that inform our understanding of how the role of women is

articulated in relation to other similar constructs such as the Troubled Family. My own, and for some controversial, analysis of some of the research on 'intensive family support projects' – the so-called 'sinbins' – may also be an additional and helpful resource for readers (Garrett, 2007a). Hayward and Yar (2006) explore the 'chav' phenomenon. The newspaper article by Gallagher (2012) is important in that, for me, it provides an illustration of 'hate speech' directed at the impoverished, as well as showing how this type of speech often fuses together different welfare words: in this instance underclass and adoption (see also Chapter 9). Wacquant's (2007) conceptualisation of 'territorial stigmatization' and related ideas can be found in a short article in *Thesis Eleven*.

CHAPTER 5

SOCIAL EXCLUSION

Social exclusion – Exclusion from human society (or from a specific milieu); exclusion or isolation from the prevalent social system and its rights and privileges, esp. as a result of poverty or membership of a particular social group. (*Oxford English Dictionary*)

INTRODUCTION

In May 2014 a high profile conference, organised by the Inclusive Capitalism Initiative, took place in London. Speakers included key figures, such as Mark Carney (2014), the Governor of the Bank of England, and Christine Lagarde, the Managing Director of the IMF. The event was co-hosted by Lady Lynn Forester de Rothschild, a member of the famous Rothschild banking dynasty and one of the world's wealthiest families. In attendance were luminaries such Prince Charles and former US president Bill Clinton, the latter responsible for the repeal of the Glass–Steagall Act – which de-regulated Wall Street – and US welfare 'reform' (see also Chapters 3 and 4). A neoconservative pressure group, the Henry Jackson Society (HJS), was the initiator of the event and it stated that the 'urgency of the London riots and the on-going effects of the financial crisis, austerity cuts and the Occupy Wall Street movement' had first prompted it to promulgate the notion of 'inclusive capitalism' (Brading, 2012).

In seeking to articulate a new narrative on 'inclusive capitalism' and criticising the concentration of wealth in the hands of a few, Lagarde (2014) referred to the 'need to ingrain a greater social consciousness' which would 'seep into the financial world and forever change the way it does business'. Carney's contribution was the most extensive mapping of the construct. Setting his ideas against those of 'market fundamentalism', he asserted that only by 'returning to true markets ... can we make capitalism more inclusive' (Carney, 2014: 3–4). However, within this new, somewhat folksy paradigm, 'business ultimately needs to be seen as a vocation, an activity with high ethical standards, which in turn conveys certain responsibilities' (2014: 8). If such moves were made, it would lead to the return of a 'more trustworthy, inclusive capitalism … in which individual virtue and collective prosperity can flourish' (2014: 10).

This chapter examines in greater detail the whole idea of inclusivity and, more specifically, social exclusion. Writing in the *European Journal of Social Work*, toward the end of the twentieth century, Washington and Paylor (1998: 335) argued that 'the developing usage of the concept of social exclusion offers social work an opportunity to establish a professional focus which can be used in practice throughout the member states of the European Union'. By the 'turn of the century, social exclusion had become a Third Way buzzword in the UK' (Silver, 2010: 189; see also Giddens, 1998, 2001; McLennan, 2004). However, there were indications that social work practitioners and some academics were a little more sceptical (Ward, 2009). New Labour's Social Exclusion Unit (SEU) was perceived by some as a 'middle class institution, run by middle class people to impose middle class solutions on people who do not want them' (Chadda, 1999). Despite such scepticism, as illustrated by the contributions of Carney and his colleagues, there may be a resurgence in inclusion talk. Indeed, more recently, addressing the 'problems of social exclusion' was a rhetorical pivot for Dame Louise Casey's heavily criticized and racialized review of 'opportunity and integration' in the UK (Casey, 2016: 7, 1).

Hardly featuring in the discourse of social work and social policy in North America (Chaskin, 2013), social inclusion has, however, had a detectable impact in Australia. Bearing the 'imprint' of the New Labour approach to social exclusion in the UK, the South Australia Social Inclusion Initiative, begun in 2002, was to become nationally influential (Silver, 2010; see also Hunter and Jordan, 2010). At the inaugural Social Inclusion Conference in January 2010, the then Minister for Social Inclusion, Julia Gillard, launched the government's national statement on social inclusion, *A Stronger, Fairer Australia* (Silver, 2010). Furthermore, social exclusion – and its rhetoric antithesis, social inclusion – continues to feature prominently in policy documents associated with the European Union with the Europe 2020 Strategy giving 'new impetus to efforts to address poverty and social exclusion across the EU' (European Commission, 2013: 3). Central to this agenda would be the policy aim of preventing 'the transmission of disadvantage across generations' (European Commission, 2013: 2).

The chapter is divided into four parts. Initially, it concentrates on the history of social ex/inclusion – as an idea – and here the particular focus will be on France. The second part of the chapter examines New Labour and how it was apt to use these terms in the UK. The third part of the chapter explores if these welfare words can be perceived as helping to pragmatically provide traction for more progressive policies relating to social work and social policy. Here, the focus is on *In from the Margins: Roma in Ireland* produced by the Irish Immigrant Support Centre (NASC, 2013). Finally, the discussion hones in on some of the difficulties with the notion of social exclusion, concentrating on Marxist critiques and those rooted in the work of Foucault.

FRANCE: *L'EXCLUSION SOCIALE* AND THREATS TO THE 'SOCIAL FABRIC'

Whilst remaining alert to differing models, nuances and political paradigms, Hilary Silver (1994: 536–7) summarises that exclusion is 'a "keyword", in Raymond Williams' sense, in French Republican discourse' (see also Chapter 1). It not 'only originated in France, but is deeply anchored in a particular interpretation of French revolutionary history and Republican thought' (1994: 537). David Byrne (1999: 8) claims that social exclusion reflects 'the somewhat surprising synthesis of social Catholicism and republicanism'. From this perspective, '"exclusion" is conceived not simply as an economic or political phenomenon, but as a deficiency of "solidarity"' (Silver, 1994: 537; Dobbernack, 2014). Such thinking can be connected to the work of Émile Durkheim (1858–1917), in which 'exclusion threatens society as a whole with the loss of collective values and the destruction of the social fabric' (Silver, 1994: 534).

Exclusion, and its linked conceptualisations, appealed to the secular Republic tradition in France because poverty was associated with the *ancien régime* and notions of Christian charity. Alternatively, it was subsumed with the more encompassing category of 'inequality' and perceived as part of the labour question. In contrast, ideas around inclusion cohered with 'the distinctively "social" idea of "solidarity"' originally legitimised during the years of the Third Republic spanning from 1870 to 1940 (Silver, 1994: 537). Perhaps exclusion also achieved prominence because it was 'evocative, ambiguous, multidimensional and elastic' enabling it to be defined in many different ways (1994: 536).

The social commentator Jules Klanfer was one of the first to use the term *L'exclusion sociale*, which was also the title of his 1965 book. Here, social exclusion is said to concern 'people who are unable to enjoy the rewards of economic prosperity due to irresponsible behaviour' (Béland, 2014: 150). However, the coining of the term is usually attributed to René Lenoir, whose book *Les Exclus: Un Français sur dix* was published in 1974, when he was the Secretary for Social Action in the Gaullist government of Jacques Chirac (1974–1976). For Lenoir the 'excluded' were those adrift from mainstream society due to, for example, disability, mental illness, and poverty. Even if the 'meaning of "exclusion" has changed since the mid-1970s, Lenoir's book is considered the founding document of the modern social exclusion discourse in France' (Béland, 2014: 150). In this context, the 'inverse of exclusion is thus "integration" and the process of attaining it, "insertion"' (Silver, 1994: 542).

During the 1980s, as a number of social and political crises occurred, 'exclusion came to be applied to more and more types of social disadvantage' (Silver, 1994: 532). However, 'insertion' focused mainly on young people leaving school and not entering employment. Introduced in 1988, the *Revenu minimum d'insertion* (RMI) [minimum income to enable social integration] drew on the Republican 'rhetoric of "solidarity", "cohesion", "social bonds"' (1994: 534). The RMI was made available for those, of working age, who were unable to claim contributions-based unemployment benefits. However, it was also related to more sustained attempts to activate and insert people into work (see also Chapters 2 and 3). In 2009 the RMI was replaced by the *Revenu de solidarité active* (RSA).

As deployed within French political discourse, social exclusion stretches beyond the economic domain, hinting at a wider and more ambiguous social and cultural malaise. In the late 1980s and towards the end of the twentieth century, whilst relating to unemployment, the term referenced other forms of societal instability and uncertainties: 'family instability, single-member households, social isolation, and the decline of class solidarity based on unions, the labour market, and the working class neighbourhood and social networks. There were not only material but also spiritual and symbolic aspects to this phenomenon' (Silver, 1994: 533). In the 1990s, exclusion talk in France was also connected to official concerns about the situation of residents living in the deprived suburbs – the *Banlieues* (Béland, 2014; see also Falconer, 2006; Balibar, 2007). In more recent times, the dangers of exclusion have been fused to fears about the threat of Islamic youths becoming 'radicalised'.

Importantly, social ex/inclusion also became 'diffused through international policy networks' particularly within Europe and, more specifically, the European Union (Béland, 2014: 143). This process probably commenced in the 1980s when Jacques Delors served as European Commission President (1985–1995). A Roman Catholic, economist and member of the French Socialist Party, he was President Mitterrand's Minister of Finance in the early 1980s. Delors emphasised the need for a strong social dimension to the European project and following this 'logic, the fight against social exclusion became a European issue' (Béland, 2014: 151). Supporters of this perspective argued that the pleas to combat social exclusion operated as a shield to protect the most vulnerable against the worst excesses of rampant neoliberalism. However, critics countered that the phrase was used merely as a rhetorical device tactically deployed to try and win the support of organised labour and social movements for the project to enlarge and expand the EU. A more fundamental and emphatic criticism is that the politics of social ex/inclusion were not a politics intent on rebutting neoliberalism, rather they actually helped to constitute and further embed neoliberalism (Bourdieu and Wacquant, 2001).

UK: RECYCLING OF THE 'CYCLE OF DEPRIVATION' AND HYPER-VALORISING PAID WORK

Even when imported from elsewhere, welfare words and concepts relating to poverty are fluid and alter their meaning to gel with hegemonic national paradigms (see also Chapter 2). To better understand New Labour's amplification of social ex/inclusion talk in the UK, it is important, therefore, to have regard to the cycle of deprivation theory which, emerging in the 1970s, placed the emphasis on the cultural disposition of the poor themselves.

Keith Joseph (1918–1994), the Secretary of State for Social Services in the Conservative government of Edward Heath, referred to a 'cycle of deprivation', in a speech given to a Pre-School Playgroups Association in late-June 1972. An important ideologue, influential in shaping what was to become 'Thatcherism', he maintained that the process he was referring to was one in which multiple deprivations and social disadvantage was transmitted inter-generationally. For Joseph, this could be connected to an excess of births, and unregulated fecundity, occurring in mothers from the lower social classes. A large-scale Department of Health and Social Security (DHSS)/Social Science Research Council (SSRC) research programme followed directly from his speech (Welshman, 2013: 119).

In a later intervention, in October 1974, Joseph avowed, that 'a high and rising proportion of children are being born to mothers least fitted to bring children into the world' (Welshman, 2013: 122). Moreover, many of these mothers in social classes IV and V were often unmarried, deserted, or divorced as well as being of low intelligence and low educational attainment. Such women were 'producing problem children, the future unmarried mothers, delinquents, denizens of our borstals, subnormal educational establishments, prisons, hostels for drifters' (Joseph in Macnicol, 1987: 294). The solutions Joseph proffered were far from clear, but he indicated that there was a need for more family planning and enhanced 'preparation for parenthood' (1987: 294). Certainly, the shadow of the Eugenics Movement appeared to fall across these speeches by a senior politician nicknamed the 'Mad Monk' by his critics inside and beyond the Conservative Party (Denham and Garnett, 2001; see also Chapter 4).

Macnicol argues that Joseph's views were reflective, not only of historical perceptions of the poor, but were also illustrative of a new interest in poverty during this period. The 'rediscovery' of poverty was apparent, in England, with the publication of Coates and Silburn's (1970) *Poverty: The Forgotten Englishman*. However, developments in the United States, including the 'war on poverty', were also influential. Michael Harrington's (1928–1989) *The Other America* had a significant impact in policy circles, particularly within the Democratic Party (Harrington, 1962). These writers emphasised how the poor were radically different and culturally separated from what was constructed as the societal mainstream. Harrington expressed this succinctly with his assertion that there was 'a language of the poor, a psychology of the poor, a world view of the poor. To be impoverished is to be an internal alien, to grow up in a culture that is radically different from one that dominates society' (Harrington in Macnicol, 1987: 298).

Oscar Lewis (1914–1970), a professor of anthropology at the University of Illinois, based his theorisation on empirical work undertaken in Mexico in the 1950s and in Puerto Rico during the following decade. By the 1960s, his 'culture of poverty' thesis began to be widely known. Although not situated within right-wing or what was to evolve into a distinctly neoliberal politics, Lewis' ideas appeared to gel with those crafting a more retrogressive perspective on welfare. This was because of the anthropologist's focus on how behaviours and beliefs learned and instilled in childhood could produce multigenerational poverty. His understanding of a culture of poverty implied, in his evocative phrase, a 'design for living' passed down from generation to generation (Lewis in Ortiz and Briggs, 2003: 42). Perhaps this partly sympathetic perspective has some similarities with facets of Bourdieu's 'habitus' conceptualisation (see also Chapter 2). However, in the United States it was the neoconservatives who latched onto Lewis' ideas.

Coates and Silburn felt that Lewis' theory had 'parallels with what they observed in the course of their research in Nottingham' (Welshman, 2013: 115). Various UK initiatives can also be interpreted as reflecting a similar 'preoccupation with culture deprivation, and environment' (2013: 112). For example, the introduction of Educational Priority Areas (EPAs), although not associated with any direct reference to the culture of poverty, 'seemed inspired by American initiatives' (2013: 112). Similarly, Community Development Projects (CDPs), announced by Harold Wilson's Labour government in 1969 as part of a larger Urban Programme, were 'a direct copy of the Community Action Areas that had been created during the "War on Poverty" in America' (2013: 113).

New Labour initiatives, such as the Sure Start programme for under-fives introduced in 1998, excavated and used the phrase 'cycle of deprivation' (Welshman, 2013: 119); at the same time, the naming of Sure Start drew on and semantically alluded to the US Head Start begun in the mid-1960s as part of President Johnson's Great Society initiative. At the launch of the Social Exclusion Unit (SEU), Prime Minister Blair asserted: 'Social exclusion is about income, but it is about more. It is about prospects, networks and life chances. *It is a modern problem likely to be passed down from generation to generation*' (in Alcock, 1998: 20, emphasis added). Alistair Darling, then Social Security Secretary, echoed such sentiments, claiming: 'Many of these people live on the worst estates. They will die younger, *statistically there is a good chance their exclusion will pass on to their children*' (Darling, 1999, emphasis added).

Unlike previous Conservative administrations, New Labour was prepared to refer to poverty. As Walker (1999: 139) argues, before 1 May 1997 [the date of New Labour's election victory], poverty had been 'a proscribed word in official circles for a political generation'. Furthermore, there was a stated commitment to eradicate child poverty within twenty years (Lister, 2001; Piachaud and Sutherland, 2001). Nonetheless, New Labour governments never endeavoured to build a consensus in favour of redistribution. Rather, their preferred orientation was to shift the focus of debate to social exclusion.

Even by the mid-1990s, and still in opposition, social ex/inclusion had become central to New Labour's social justice discourse (Commission on Social Justice, 1994). By the following decade the term began to dominate the Blair government's conceptualisation of, and response to, poverty. Described by the press as 'ghetto busters to tackle poverty' (Wintour, 1997), New Labour's SEU was launched, following a speech by Blair at Stockwell Park School in Lambeth, in December 1997. Initially, priority tasks for the SEU centred on truancy and school exclusion, so-called 'rough sleepers' and rundown estates. Subsequently, it turned its attention to 'teenage pregnancies' (Department of Health, 2000). Indeed, given its frequent focus on the intergenerational *reproduction* of social exclusion it is unsurprising that New Labour dwelt on motherhood (see also Chapter 6). In this context, pregnant teenagers were significant on account of their proclivity to transmit their 'misconceived negativity about education, training and employment' (Colley and Hodkinson, 2001: 341). Rooted in what was aptly dubbed 'Anglicised communitarianism', at the heart of such endeavours were plans to create a network of supervisory and tutorial relationships that would re-invigorate and re-moralise (Deacon, 2000: 11; see also Etzioni, 1995).

Conceptual criticisms of social ex/inclusion talk can be applied beyond the UK and this wider dimension will be returned to later in the chapter. Here, however, a little more attention will be given to the critique of Ruth Levitas, whose focus is mainly on the particular variants of the discourse which emerged in the UK. She maintained that social exclusion

> represents the primary significant division in society as one between an included majority and an excluded minority. This has implications for how both included and excluded groups are understood, and for the implicit model of society itself. Attention is drawn away from the inequalities and differences among the included. Notably, the very rich are discursively absorbed into the included majority, their power and privileges slipping out of focus if not wholly out of sight. At the same time, the poverty and disadvantage of the so-called excluded are discursively placed outside society. (Levitas, 1998: 7)

What resulted from this flawed and misleading analysis was 'an overly homogeneous and consensual image of society – a rosy view possible because the implicit model is one in which inequality and poverty are pathological and residual rather than endemic' (Levitas, 1998: 7).

In the UK, according to Levitas, the practice of social exclusion was embedded in three different discourses or ideal types. First, a redistributionist discourse (RED) evolving within social policy during the long period of Conservative rule (1979–1997). Influenced by Peter Townsend's (1979) *Poverty in the United Kingdom*, this discourse was not apt to use the phrase social exclusion but, in seeking to redefine poverty as a condition of relative deprivation, it fitted with the notion of social exclusion. Important here was the argument that many people lacked the financial means to participate in society's ordinary living patterns, customs and activities. Amartya Sen (2000: 4) relates such approaches to social exclusion to Aristotelian accounts viewing an 'impoverished life as one without the freedom to undertake important activities that a person has reason to choose ... Thus, the view of poverty as capability deprivation (that is, poverty seen

as the lack of the capability to live a minimally decent life) has a far-reaching analytical history.' In a UK context, he also maintains that the focus of Adam Smith
(1723–1790) on the 'deprivation involved in not "being able to appear in public
without shame" is a good example of a capability deprivation that takes the form
of social exclusion' (Sen, 2000: 4; see also Brown, 2015, Ch. 1).

Second, Levitas referred to a moral underclass discourse (MUD), amplified by the
interventions of figures such as Charles Murray, and circulating around underclass
stereotypes (see also Chapter 4). This can also be regarded as a gendered discourse
whose 'demons are criminally inclined, unemployable young men and sexually irresponsible single mothers, for whom paid work is a means of social discipline' (Levitas,
1998: 7–8). What MUD implies is that the structure of the society is basically sound
and it is the behaviour, attitudes and dispositions of these particular inhabitants which
is the core problem. These individuals, mired in welfare dependency and 'hand-outs',
needed to have their easy access to benefits terminated. This was, in fact, a social
exclusion discourse, on occasions, promulgated by Blair (2006a) who lambasted those
with an 'inability to live a life free from the charity of others'. For these people, poverty
was not 'just about poverty of income, but poverty of aspiration, of opportunity, of
prospects of advancement' (Blair, 2006a).

The third discourse, identified by Levitas as a social integrationist discourse
(SID), can be perceived as that characterising the approach to social ex/inclusion in
the EU and New Labour. Undermining the legitimacy of those deciding not to participate in wage labour, this approach views paid work as the sole and vital
mechanism ensuring the elimination of social exclusion and the fostering of social
cohesion (Gough and Olofsson, 1999; see also the discussion on the Autonomist
Marxists in Chapter 2). A problem here is that this perspective masks, or obscures,
the inequalities *between* workers. Since women are paid significantly less than men
and are far more likely to be in low-paid jobs, it also functions to obscure gender
inequalities in the labour market. Relatedly, it is unable to address issues connected
to work which goes unpaid. Because it ignores unpaid work and its gendered distribution, this particular paradigm also implies an increase in women's total
workload. Equally important, this discourse erases from vision the inequality
between those owning the bulk of wealth and the rest of the working population.

Since the demise of the New Labour administration in 2010, the social ex/inclu-
sion theme has waned and is less frequently mentioned within UK discourses on
social work and social policy. Nevertheless, the idea that social exclusion – along
with its socially disruptive potential – was likely to pass down through the generations was reactivated following the 'riots' of 2011 (see also Chapter 4). For Melanie
Phillips (2011), the disturbances were an 'explosion of elective lone parenthood and
dysfunctional behaviour *transmitted down through the generations* at the bottom of
the social heap' (emphasis added).

During the initial period of Cameron's prime ministership, it was maintained that
the aspiration should be to dismantle 'the old-fashioned state... the heavy-handed
state' and to construct a 'Big Society' (Cameron, 2010: 10). Perhaps something of a

rhetorical substitute for social inclusion, this notion was 'about a real cultural shift – we know that the era of big government... didn't work. We want to build a Big Society where local people feel empowered' (Cabinet Office, 2010: 1). As a narrative or binding ideology, the 'Big Society' may have 'flopped', but the current UK Conservative-led government is still 'retreating from the sphere of social reproduction, placing the associated costs onto the unpaid realms of the home and the community' (Dowling and Harvey, 2014: 870; see also Chapter 8). Despite the occasionally more inclusive language, Theresa May's government remains intent on ushering in a 'permanently shrunken state' (Toynbee, 2010: 27).

However, some continuity with New Labour is apparent in approaches to children and families. For example, 'parenting support' has been 'expanded and developed under the umbrella concept of "early intervention" – a policy rationale which argues that intervening pre-emptively in social problems conceptualised as emanating from "dysfunctional" individuals, families or communities, reduces the later social and economic costs of such problems' (Macvarish et al., 2015: 249–50; see also Chapter 6). Alongside this 'narrowed focus' on 'parenting', there has also been a political 'closing down of structural explanations for poverty, inequality and arrested social mobility' (Macvarish et al., 2015: 249; see also Lee et al., 2014).

IRELAND: SOCIAL EXCLUSION AND THE ROMA COMMUNITY

As we will see, powerful arguments exist, contesting the notion that social in/exclusion is a useful concept or organising motif which might aid in the creation of a more benign, even progressive, social policy.[1] Whilst remaining somewhat sceptical of this discourse, some writers still perceive its potential utility. Ruth Levitas (1998), as observed, was one of the main social policy critics of New Labour's preoccupation with this theme, yet she remains of the opinion that it 'may lead beyond itself, into the very critique of capitalism' (1998: 6). Can, therefore, the rhetoric of social ex/inclusion be utilised to further progressive social gains in the area of social work and social policy? To explore this question in a little more detail, the focus will shift to Ireland and the situation of the Roma community. This minority ethnic population can, perhaps, be perceived – if the phrase is used warily – as a paradigmatic socially excluded community. It has been estimated that there are '10 to 12 million Roma in Europe, and approximately 6 million in the EU, making them the largest minority group in Europe ... Although historically nomadic, 80% of Roma in Europe are now settled' (NASC, 2013: 9). In April 2011, with the adoption of the EU Framework Strategy on Roma Integration, the European Commission highlighted the fact that 'many of the estimated 10–12 million Roma in Europe face prejudice, intolerance, discrimination and social exclusion in their daily lives' (NASC, 2013: 4).

Excluding indigenous Irish Travellers, members of the Roma community in Ireland are largely of 'Romanian, Hungarian, Polish and Czech origin. As such, they are citizens of the European Union and under EU law have the same rights as any other EU citizen resident in Ireland' (NASC, 2013: 9). Today there are estimated to be '5,000 Roma in Ireland but there is very little accurate data available as Roma ethnicity is not collected in immigration, employment, or other Government statistics' (NASC, 2013: 10). The Roma population appears relatively small compared to other western European countries such as Bulgaria, Slovakia, Hungary, Spain and France.

Approximately half a million Roma, nearly a quarter of the European Roma population, were murdered during the Holocaust (NASC, 2013: 16). Furthermore, as the 'quintessential migrant group' (NASC, 2013: 15), the Roma community has frequently been the target of neo-fascist groups. Perhaps more troubling, the political mainstream has resorted to the targeting of Roma communities (McGarry, 2017): for example, the series of high-profile French expulsions of Roma migrants by the government of Sarkozy in 2010 (Badiou, 2008; see also Bowers, 2013). In Ireland, Roma have mostly escaped this form of state intervention, but evidence exists that they are still apt to be perceived as social pariahs who can be *legitimately* subjected to processes of exclusion and expulsion.

In 2012 a Eurobarometer Report on discrimination in Europe, published by the European Commission, revealed that in 'Ireland 38% "totally disagree" that society could benefit from better integration of the Roma community and 37% "totally agree" ... By contrast, in Sweden 87% agree that society could benefit from better integration of the Roma and there is also broad support for the integration of Roma in Finland (78%), Lithuania (74%) and Hungary (72%)' (in NASC, 2013: 19). Respondents were also invited to indicate on a scale from 1 to 10 how comfortable they might feel if their children had Roma schoolmates: overall, 34% of 'Irish respondents indicated that citizens in their country would feel uncomfortable if their children had Roma schoolmates (28% answered fairly comfortable and 25% responded comfortable) (2013: 20). As NASC concludes, such findings serve to 'highlight the unease that exists in Irish society with regard to the Roma community' (2013: 19).

The Roma community are an at-risk group in terms of their health status with a 'higher infant mortality rate, lower life expectancy and a higher rate of diseases' (NASC, 2013: 58). A United Nations Development Programme report on five countries noted that 'Roma child mortality rates are 2 to 6 times higher than for those of the general population ... Roma women are a particularly at risk group in terms of health' (2013: 58). In short, the lives of many Roma are precarious and characterised by persistent poverty and hardship.

Ireland's National Traveller/Roma Integration Strategy (Department of Justice, 2011) has been criticised for simply restating and summarising what was 'already in place' as opposed to identifying a more meaningful strategic direction (NASC, 2013: 41). Whilst acknowledging the potentially socially progressive legislative framework seeking to promote equality, critics point to the various exemption clauses and delays in seeking redress are acting as obstacles to combating structural discrimination (NASC, 2013). Referring to the

Macpherson Inquiry into the death of Stephen Lawrence, NASC (2013: 34) assert that the inquiry's definition of 'institutional racism' has analytical usefulness in trying to grasp how the Irish state and its agents interact in negative ways with the Roma community[2].

In October 2013, the accuracy of the NASC assessment was starkly affirmed and received international media attention when children from two Roma families were removed by police officers. These police interventions occurred days after the removal of a child, called Maria, from a Roma family in Larissa in Greece (Commissioner for Human Rights, 2013). In Ireland, a seven year-old girl was taken from her home in west Dublin and placed in the protective care of the Health Service Executive (HSE). Another child, a two-year-old boy living in Athlone in the Irish midlands, was also removed from his family. On both occasions, official concerns were prompted because the children did not resemble the appearance of their Roma parents: eventually both children were reunited with their families.

The actions of the police and social workers, along with the initial media reporting, were underpinned by stereotypical and racialised perceptions of Roma (Pavee Point Traveller and Roma Centre, 2013; Logan, 2014). They were certainly linked to historical myth that Roma are 'child stealers'. Primarily what triggered the hasty and ill-judged removals and enforced detentions was a rather crude form of racial profiling. The two children were subjected to aggressive intervention and excessive public exposure by the police and child protection services because they did not look like Roma were *expected* to look.

In responding to the removal of the Roma children from their families, Pavee Point Traveller and Roma Centre (2013) argued that 'serious child protection concerns' did, in fact, jeopardise the welfare of Roma children, but such concerns were manifestly connected to structural considerations: for example, to lack of 'access to doctors, medical care and participation in education'. Concerns were 'further exacerbated in the context of recent budget cuts to education supports'. Unfortunately, there was now a 'real danger that precipitative action, undertaken on the basis of appearance [and racial profiling]' would 'create the conditions for an increase in racism and discrimination against the Roma community living [in Ireland]' (Pavee Point Traveller and Roma Centre, 2013). A subsequent inquiry, undertaken by the Children's Ombudsman, stated that 'ethnic profiling' had, in fact, played a role in the removal and temporary confinement of the children in foster care placements (Logan, 2014; see also European Union Agency for Fundamental Rights, 2010).

Perhaps, if it is momentarily accepted the social ex/inclusion binary might prise open a space for a more progressive social policy relating to the Roma community, facets of Nancy Fraser's contribution relating to the politics of recognition can also be introduced; more specifically, her discussions on what she terms the 'principle of parity of participation' and the promotion of embedded social arrangements that permit all (adult) members of society to interact with others as peers (Fraser, 2003: 36).

Here, the aim is to preclude 'institutional norms that systematically depreciate some categories of people and the qualities associated with them' (2003: 36) (3). Although Fraser's theorisation can be criticised for failing to properly articulate the role of the neoliberal state (Garrett, 2013a: Ch. 9), it might still conceivably form part of a pragmatic approach to help tilt the balance in favour of the Roma community. In this sense, using social ex/inclusion talk might be viewed as aiding in the construction of a strategy of 'radical incrementalism' (Schram, 2105). This is defined by Schram (2105: 184) as a process in which there is a 'push for change' but also a recognition that that it will not necessarily be as great as desired. At the same time any change prompted would do more than merely 'fine tune the existing system'. Applied to the Roma Community in Ireland, this might include a whole series of steps seeking their 'parity of participation' in civil society. Such a programme might aim to advance seven interrelated demands:

- Access to employment with the trade union 'rate for the job'

- Access to decent housing

- Access to all state welfare benefits

- Access to health care

- The cessation of harassment and targeting, particularly of Roma women, by the police

- Within schools, more sustained initiatives to combat the marginalisation of the Roma community

- An end to racist stereotyping in the media.

Prompted by the demands of the Roma community and organising around this strategy could conceivably bring about incremental social gains. However, it is important to examine some of the conceptual criticisms countering claims that the social ex/inclusion talk can furnish a useful vocabulary for progressive politics.

WHAT'S WRONG WITH SOCIAL INCLUSION TALK?

Goodin (1996: 351) charges that 'inclusion talk' is apt to 'subsume a wide range of other concrete issues ... In its imperialist mode, inclusion talk threatens to submerge and subvert other equally genuine concerns – concerns which are logically better expressed, and politically better pressed', in terms of more familiar words and phrases. This might include, therefore, reference to poverty, capitalism, exploitation, domination, racism and so on. Mindful of this suggestion, particular attention will now be accorded to Marxist informed critiques and those associated with Foucault and governmentality theory.

ILLUSTRATING THAT CAPITALISM IS FUNCTIONING?

Marie Moran has criticised the importation of social ex/inclusion talk into Ireland. For her, 'progressive aspects of the discourse of inclusion are conflated at a rhetorical level with more regressive or conservative meanings, while at the level of policy implementation, the radical aspects are easily and typically sub-sumed to their less progressive counterparts' (Moran, 2006: 182). Social ex/inclusion, perceived in this way, provides only the narrowest space, barely discernible, in which to construct a politics oppositional to neoliberalism. In this sense, having recourse to social ex/inclusion talk, when seeking to address the lot of the Roma community or any other group, may risk tumbling into a conceptual and political trap. This is especially the case in Ireland, given that initiatives rhetorically rooted in bland, mantra-like aspirations to combat social exclusion are ubiquitous, omnipresent and 'generally heavily endorsed or even celebrated within public discourse' (2006: 182–3).

More universally, the voluntary and willed exclusion of the comfortably wealthy tends to be rendered absent in social ex/inclusion talk. Parents able, for example, to pay to educate their children in private schools are not ordinarily viewed as indulging in a form of willed social exclusion. Similarly, Atkinson and Flint (2004) explore 'gated communities' and the desire, on the part of the rich in the UK, to withdraw from the wider citizenry. In Silicon Valley, 'a digital overclass' discuss 'secession' from the wider United States (Giridharadas, 2013). Such sustained segregationist endeavours, driven by an impulse of the rich to set themselves apart from 'what are deemed to be surplus populations', are rarely framed in terms of social exclusion (Frase, 2016: 130). On a wider and more global scale, as revealed in 2016 in the leaked papers relating to off-shore Panama accounts, the financial scheming of the super-rich does not tend to be perceived in terms of their opting to exclude themselves from democratically constituted nationally determined taxation regimes. Rather, as discussed earlier, social exclusion is generally posited as a problem associated with the 'poor' or – more commonly within the discourse – the 'disadvantaged'. What gets obscured within this framing is the social justice dimension and associated understandings that socially progressive policy should not simply seek to ameliorate the lot of the 'disadvantaged'. Rather, the focus should be on elites with measures taken to redistribute their wealth and social advantages in order to try to create and nurture a more equitable social and economic order.

As mentioned, New Labour, in the UK, was frequently criticised for using the term social exclusion to mask poverty and the related questions of income and wealth distribution. More fundamentally, social exclusion should not be perceived as an aberration, but as a constitutional ingredient of the capitalist system. As Byrne (1999: 130) lucidly concludes, 'if social exclusion is inherent in a market-oriented flexible post-industrial capitalism, then it is impossible to eliminate it by any set of social policies directed at the excluded alone'. Unemployment and the resultant social and economic exclusion is 'a function of the internal dynamics of capitalism, which, by necessity, maintains a reserve army of labour in order to undermine the security and bargaining position of the mainstream employed' (Moran, 2006: 186). The unemployed are not outside or excluded from the system and so perceiving them as such simply 'masks the manner in which the routine undulations of capitalism ensure the existence of a working class that shifts from employment to unemployment in line with the inevitable peaks and troughs of capitalism' (2006: 186).

Similarly, Ruth Levitas (1996: 5) criticises the 'hegemonic' discourse of social ex/inclusion because 'social divisions which are endemic to capitalism' are presented as 'resulting from an abnormal breakdown in social cohesion'. The concept also erases issues connected to low pay in that work is usually perceived as *the* mechanism of social inclusion: to consider 'integration as solely effected by paid work is to ignore the fact that society is – and certainly should be – more than a market' (1996: 18). Implicitly, such criticisms may also be connected, of course, to the theorisation of the Autonomist Marxists explored in Chapter 2.

Simon Winslow and Steve Hall (2013), although perhaps not entirely happy to be referred to as Marxists, still display an affinity with Marxist-informed critiques when they hone in on the main assumptions which often lie at the foundations of social ex/inclusion talk. Expanding the criticisms of Levitas, Moran, Byrne and others, they suggest that the plight of so-called 'excluded populations' should not be considered 'external to or separate from the organising logic of global neoliberalism' (Winslow and Hall, 2013: 2). That is to say, the capitalist system generates, sustains and materially benefits from their exclusion. Such arguments are also aligned with Marxist theorisation concerning the creation of a 'relative surplus population' within capitalist labour markets, referred to in Chapter 3.

In their account of contemporary 'marginalised subjectivities', Winslow and Hall (2013: 7) are especially scathing in their criticisms of academic colleagues who, perhaps aware of the intellectual shallowness of much thinking around social ex/inclusion, still opportunistically use these welfare words to secure research funding for politically tame projects. More funtamentally, most social democratic thinking about social exclusion, in seeking to reintroduce the 'excluded' into the civic mainstream, merely aims to reinsert resource-poor workers into the very system of relentless socio-symbolic competition that expelled them in the first place (Winslow and Hall, 2013: 6). Moreover, adrift in the 'stultifying world of policy production' (Winslow and Hall, 2013: 11), some academics, complicit in moves to further exploit the already impoverished, are not performing any beneficial or socially progressive role. Winslow and Hall caustically conclude that rather than 'figuratively patching up the poor with neatly organised CVs, new qualifications and a taste for entrepreneurial accomplishment, then sending them out once again to do battle in the unforgiving and precarious advanced capitalist labour market, it might be more productive to address the source of social conflict and competition' (Winslow and Hall, 2013: 6–7; see also Bailey, 2016).

ILLUSTRATING GOVERNMENTALITY?

Turning again to France, where the chapter commenced, the ascendancy of the social ex/inclusion theme and its acceptance across the mainstream left/right continuum might be interpreted as the product of the defeat of the revolutionary left in May 1968. During the weeks of insurrection all social and economic relations seemed likely to be transformed (Ross, 2002). In contrast, social ex/inclusion tends to 'promote a functionalist understanding of the social in which the objective is cohesion rather than justice' (Clarke, 2013: 17). In this sense – and very much still influenced by the events of '68 – Rancière can be perceived as a critic of social ex/inclusion (Rancière, 1999; see also Chapter 2). Relatedly, Foucault (2008: 202), in his lectures at the Collège de France in the late-1970s, maintained that within social ex/inclusion discourse the *social* operates as a stable given with political actors seeking merely to safeguard 'players from being excluded from the game'. There 'must now be a rule of non-exclusion' and the function of the 'social rule, of social regulation, or of social security in the broadest sense of the term, is purely and simply to ensure non-exclusion with regard to an economic game' (Foucault, 2008: 202). Those influenced by Foucault, particularly governmentality theorists, remain therefore coolly sceptical about political commitments to counter social exclusion and, in this context, Nikolas Rose's analysis of the inclusion/exclusion binary is reflective of their critical orientation.

The foundation for Rose's perspective is the identification of, what he terms, 'ethnopolitics'. This is a form of politics aiming to 'regenerate and reactivate' ethical values, regulate individual conduct and bolster the maintenance of civil order. 'Ethnopolitics' aspires to bind 'individuals into shared moral norms and values: governing through the self steering forces of honour and shame, of propriety, obligation, trust, fidelity, and commitments to others' (Rose, 2000: 324). Rose argues that contemporary 'control strategies' associated with 'ethnopolitics' can be separated into 'two families': those aiming to regulate conduct by 'enmeshing individuals within circuits of inclusion and those that seek to act upon pathologies through managing a different set of circuits, circuits of exclusion' (2000: 324).

As for the circuits of inclusion, people are no longer solely integrated into disciplinary institutions, such as schools, factories and barracks, in the way they were in the past. Rather, argues Rose, a myriad of other means now exist which enmesh and retain us. Within contemporary 'control' societies this process of forced inclusion is much more insidious, much more pervasive than before (Deleuze, 1995). Thus, one is always in 'continuous training, life-long learning, perpetual assessment' and so on (Rose, 2000: 325). Furthermore, control techniques are no longer top-down and centralised, but are more dispersed and flooded with enhanced and omnipresent surveillance capacity (Lyon, 2006).

Unlike writers associated with Marxist-informed critiques of social ex/inclusion talk, governmentality theorists are not primarily interested in the economic domain and Rose's work is illustrative of this major deficit and conceptual failing. However, he does recognise how the 'continual incitement to buy, to improve oneself' helps to sustain capitalist patterns of consumption (2000: 325). In theoretical terms, Rose's perceptions also partly articulate processes taking place in fields such as social work with its new modes of professional registration, regulation and the focus on mandatory and continuing professional development (Cole, 2006).

Tougher stances on 'law-and-order', the increase in prison population, and 'strategies for the preventive detention of incorrigible individuals, such as paedophiles', illuminate the tonality and trajectory of policy and practice (Rose, 2000: 330). Vital here is the 'administration of the marginalia' delineating which individuals warrant moving into the circuits of exclusion (2000: 333). In this context, the assessments conducted by a plethora of different, but interlinked, professionals fulfil a significant role in sifting the population. In terms of the actual day-to-day activity of the 'control workers', the 'focus of the risk gaze' is 'organized and packaged by structured risk assessments, risk schedules, forms and proformas, database fields' (Rose, 2000: 333). Despite such endeavours, the 'technological imperative to tame uncertainty and master hazard' will remain fragmentary and incomplete (2000: 333).

The task of 'control workers' – the police, social workers, doctors, psychiatrists, mental health professionals – is to ensure that the community is adequately protected from 'risky' individuals (2000: 333). These will tend to be the 'usual suspects' – the 'poor, the welfare recipients, the petty criminals, discharged psychiatric patients, street people' (2000: 333). They are encouraged to be self-reliant and to restructure their conduct with a whole range of techniques and programmes being made available to enable and facilitate their efforts (see also Chapter 3). Entirely in tune with ideas pivoting on self-realisation and empowerment, these subjects 'are to do the work themselves, not in the name of conformity', but to make themselves 'free' (2000: 334). Indeed, the 'beauty of empowerment is that it appears to reject the logics of patronizing dependency that infused earlier modes of expertise' (2000: 334).

However, many of those excluded are not, as was often the case in the past, the targets of reform and rehabilitation. They are simply identified as needing to be safely contained. Hence, the evolution of a 'new archipelago of confinement is taking place' (2000: 335). Rose (2000: 334) also maintains that a 'whole variety of paralegal forms of confinement are being devised, including pre-emptive or preventive detention prior to a crime being committed'.

Although his contribution was written before heightened official concerns about migration, this part of Rose's analysis certainly would seem to have new global resonance today (Tazzioli, 2015). More specifically, perhaps his perspective can be conjoined, or brought into conversation with, the emerging academic field of 'detention studies' (Mountz et al., 2013; see also Furman et al., 2016). This area of analysis encompasses the 'use of incarceration by states to contain people who are not necessarily charged with crimes. These groups include a wide variety of individuals: migrants, asylum seekers, refugees, terrorism suspects, political dissidents, and "enemy combatants"' (Martin and Mitchelson, 2009: 465). Indeed, in many jurisdictions, 'imprisonment practices are now aimed at *non-criminals*, namely, administrative detainees and persons suspected of associating with terrorist networks' (2009: 465, original emphasis). Furthermore, despite the millions of migrants being 'displaced from NATO's arc of war and fleeing, among other things, French and British bombs' (Watkins, 2016: 27), EU debates on their plight are apt to circulate around how best to manage and engineer territorial *exclusion* (Hall, 2010; Neocleous and Kastrinou, 2016).

CONCLUSION

Critics of Rose and other governmentality theorists argue that they 'direct our attention to the governance of subjectivity and of the micro-social', but 'resemble foreign correspondents … unwilling to intervene in those events' (Fitzpatrick, 2002: 14). More fundamentally, governmentality theory often seems to rule out the possibility of human agency failing to appreciate, as does Gramsci, the significance of resistance and potentially transformative oppositional practices (see, particularly, Dean 1999: see also Chapter 2). Nevertheless, Rose still furnishes a useful optic through which we might critically consider social ex/inclusion. What is more, his perspective indicates that social workers, along with a plethora of 'control workers', could begin to unpack these welfare words rather than merely amplifying exhortations, from within and beyond the social work profession, to combat social exclusion. Unsentimentally, the theorisation of Rose suggests that sifting and assessing those who might be excluded is, in many instances, one of social work's prime functions. Identifying those who can be legitimately excluded, from a particular place or type of relationship, is an important activity and should not, in and of itself, be decried. Despite, for some, the seductive allure of postmodern relativism, it seems entirely fitting to exclude ideological neo-fascists from, say, becoming school teachers. Problems, of course, occur when decisions pertainingto exclusion are governed, structured and ordered – as they frequently are – by an insular, self-serving neoliberal rationality.

More generally, this chapter has viewed social ex/inclusion rather warily. They are welfare words filling a vacuum once 'the horizon of political hope has been delimited to a single political-economic system', the project of neoliberal modernisation (Davies, 2016: 127). Rhetorically, the only-game-in town simply becomes one of seeking out a measure of 'fairness' within an economic and social order in which the structural maintenance of gross inequality is actually a vital, integral ingredient (Byrne, 2017).

Tony Blair viewed 'early intervention', in the lives of children and families, as a vital element of New Labour's 'poetic vision' of ending social exclusion (Blair, 2006a). The next chapter will, therefore, explore this seemingly 'common sense' approach to working with children and families.

REFLECTION AND TALK BOX 5

I.   Refer again to the ideas of Ruth Levitas on RED, MUD and SID. Are these convincing conceptualisations of social ex/inclusion talk? Do any of them apply to such talk in your national setting/workplace? Is there another conceptualisation which better articulates the processes occurring?

2.   Perhaps recalling his own experiences, Goodin (1996: 344) speculates that references to exclusion are able to summon and evoke 'deep rooted intuitions traceable all the way back to the schoolyard. We all keenly recall, from whatever temporal distance, the pain that can come from being cold-shouldered and maliciously cut out of the games of our schoolmates'. Hence, because social exclusion is able to avail of these sub-textual – even sub-conscious – components, its opponents can encounter obstacles in articulating the case *against* it. Do you agree with the contention that this dimension is significant in relation to these welfare words?

FURTHER READING

Ruth Levitas' (1996) critique of social in/exclusion was written shortly before the arrival of the first Blair administration in the UK. Over twenty years old, it remains an important intervention and a useful entry-point into some of the debates circulating around this particular phrase. Beverly Silver (1994), also from the 1990s, presents an accessible account of the evolution of the term. Drawing on Foucault's theorisation, Nikolas Rose (2000), provides an interesting perspective on social in/exclusion. Nikki Ward's (2009) article also merits attention, particularly for a social work readership. The present Governor of the Bank of England articulates his ideas on 'inclusive capitalism' in Carney (2014). Readers keen to know more about the situation of the Roma community, Irish Travellers and asylum seekers might view my own piece in the journal *Patterns of Prejudice* (Garrett, 2015c).

CHAPTER 6

EARLY INTERVENTION

Early – Absolutely or relatively near to the beginning of a period of time: opposed to late. (*Oxford English Dictionary*)

Intervention – The action of intervening, 'stepping in', or interfering in any affair, so as to affect its course or issue. (*Oxford English Dictionary*)

INTRODUCTION

The year prior to being succeeded as prime minister by Gordon Brown, Tony Blair explained to a BBC interviewer that more consideration had to be given to intervening in particular families, before a child was born, 'pre-birth' (Blair, 2006b). Expanding and frequently focusing on the figure of the 'teenage mum', he asserted that there were approximately '2.5 per cent of every generation ... stuck in a lifetime of disadvantage and amongst them are the excluded of the excluded, the deeply excluded' (Blair, 2006a). Given the number of 'severely dysfunctional' families with 'multiple problems', it was wrong to continue 'pussy-footing around the issue' (Blair, 2006b). Being 'hard-headed' meant recognising that from a very early age there was scope for a 'system of intervention' where families were offered support, but also that there would be 'some sense of responsibility and discipline injected into the situation' (Blair, 2006b). The then prime minister also drew on the literature relating to human capital arguing that the 'Nobel economist James Heckman famously showed that the return on human capital was very high in the early years of life and diminished rapidly thereafter' (Blair, 2006a; see also the discussion on human capital and resilience in Chapter 7).

Whilst arguing that more 'than anything else, early intervention' was the crucial means to ensure social inclusion, Blair remained rather hazy about what this might look like in policy terms. Aside from his support for the Family Intervention Projects – which would provide the groundwork for subsequent UK governments' Troubled Families Programme – there was little that was new or specific (see also Chapter 4 and Garrett, 2007a). However, there was a revitalised focus on parenting and, in November 2006,

it was announced that a new network of parenting experts was to be established cover-
ing over seventy areas. Midwives and health visitors were also exhorted to become
more attentive to screening families regarded to be 'at risk'. The following year, a
National Academy of Parenting Practitioners was established and a scheme, devised by
David Olds, developmental psychologist at the University of Colorado, called Family
Nurse Partnerships was introduced (Dodds, 2009; see also Lee et al., 2014).

Even during the New Labour period, marginal, but lucid, criticisms emerged
from within the social work literature criticising the over-emphatic and populist
emphasis on early intervention in the lives of children and families (Gray, 2014). In
a searing contribution focusing on these welfare words, Andrew Pithouse (2008:
1537) points out that the 'assumption that early intervention "will work" in tackling the multiple overlapping needs of children seems taken for granted by
government in their policy aspirations'. The whole idea that if 'we tackle problems
early, then there is more chance of success' is typically cast as a fine example, of
'therapeutic good practice and common sense' (2008: 1537; see also the discussion
on Gramsci in Chapter 2). Nonetheless, the available literature is simply unable to
answer 'deceptively simple questions such as the optimal disposal of resource to
deliver the desired impact, how to identify and prioritize sizeable numbers of users
who will respond well to treatment, and whether interventions will achieve inter-
mediate and long-term benefits' (2008: 1538). Relating his remarks to New
Labour's flagship Sure Start programme, Pithouse argued that 'extensive national
evaluation after three years implementation showed very few significant differences
compared to Sure Start-to-be areas' and there was even 'some indication of adverse
effects in the most disadvantaged families' (2008: 1538).

One of Pithouse's main criticisms dwelt on the fact that those pressing for more
robust and widespread forms of early intervention rarely examined, or indicated any
intellectual curiosity in, the normative underpinnings of such thinking. In this context, strategies of early intervention should not be crudely and misleadingly
perceived as a neutral "plug-in" entity that can simply "work" unproblematically
wherever it is introduced (2008: 1539). Indeed, some of the

> knowledge base about 'what works' in early intervention stems from
> schemes deemed successful by the use of measures and cultural assump-
> tions which no longer map across to today's problems and forms of
> practice and evaluation. What once evidently succeeded in an earlier time
> and another place (say, in some long-vanished homogeneous US indus-
> trial small town) may not transplant, say, to a contemporary large UK
> metropolitan local authority that features highly differentiated ethnic
> sub-cultures, fragile or transient family structures, marginal economic
> opportunities, over-stretched public services. (Pithouse, 2008: 1542)

Furthermore, early intervention may not be welcomed by some intended recipients and could lead to labelling and stigmatization. Turning to practical issues

associated with the actual provision of services, Pithouse speculated that early intervention, in the form of targeted and specialised forms of practice, could undermine and dilute the resources available for more universal services. Hence, unproven early intervention schemes could siphon off resources and scarce skills for 'no good purpose' (Pithouse, 2008: 1544). Subsequently, Mike Stein (2011) echoed this criticism of 'irrational, morally flawed and naïve' early intervention schemes for failing to 'give equal recognition to the needs of vulnerable teenagers as to those aged three and under'.

Despite such pointed criticisms, with the subsequent UK Coalition and Conservative governing administrations, advocacy of early intervention would seem to have been bolstered by the purported and, seemingly, unequivocal scientific authority of neuroscience. Indeed, this dimension has given rise to developments replicating, in part, the 'explicit linking of brain science claims and early years policy and practice' which had become more pronounced in the late-1990s in the United States (Edwards et al., 2015: 168). More generally, this 'turn towards brain science' can be perceived as international in scope (Edwards et al., 2015: 171; see also De Vos and Pluth, 2016; Rose and Rose, 2016).

This chapter, therefore, explores the revitalised discourse of early intervention. It begins by referring to the evolution, since the 1960s, of what Joelle Abi-Rached and Nikolas Rose (2010) term the 'neuromolecular gaze'. Next, the chapter highlights the apparent significance of the visual and new imaging technologies in promoting neuroscience. The third part focuses on how, in the UK, neuroscience is being emphatically deployed across the mainstream political spectrum to amplify the argument for early intervention into the lives of children and families. The chapter concludes by examining two central elements: the questionable 'brain science' laying too great an emphasis on infant years; and how this, apparently, more 'objective' and scientifically grounded approach shares affinities with older embedded ideas associated with attachment theory.

THE EVOLUTION OF THE 'NEUROMOLECULAR GAZE'

Neuroscience seems to provide a potentially alluring and 'attractive grammar for living' perhaps because it combines both 'therapeutic and objective, scientific meanings, operating across moral, ethical, and scientific registers' (Thornton, 2011: 408). Nevertheless, this is a relatively new field of scientific investigation with the term 'neuroscience' only having been coined in 1962 (Abi-Rached and Rose, 2010). Allan Hobson, one of the key US figures associated with the rapid evolution of neuroscience, suggests that the development of the 'new molecular style of thought' was partly attributable to discontent with the dominance of psychoanalytical approaches and what was viewed as a lack of scientific rigour (Hobson in Abi-Rached and Rose, 2010: 27).

In the United States in the 1960s there was enhanced interest and funding in the brain sciences by governmental agencies, philanthropic organisations and, significantly, the burgeoning corporate pharmaceutical industry (Abi-Rached and Rose, 2010). However, before the 1970s, despite the current prominence of neuroscience within discourses focused on children and families, the term 'neuroscientist' hardly 'existed' (2010: 28). It was only in 1973 that neuroscience developed as 'a discipline in its own right, when Amherst College became the first institution to offer an undergraduate degree in neuroscience' (2010: 28). Fifteen years later, the first UK undergraduate course was introduced at Cambridge (Abi-Rached and Rose, 2010). In 1990, President George H.W. Bush, responsible for fathering one of the less cerebral occupiers of the White House, designated the 1990s as the 'Decade of the Brain' and this unsurprisingly prompted additional expenditure and research (Bush, 1990).

As observed, Abi-Rached and Rose refer to a 'neuromolecular gaze' to summarise a 'hybrid style of thought, approach, language and perception that reduces understanding of complex phenomena to a molecular understanding gathered around the brain, and which means that intervention in the brain can shape behaviour' (in Edwards et al., 2015: 172). This 'gaze' is increasingly omnipresent with, often crudely formulated, 'biologised accounts of the formative impact of early experiences on brain development' beginning to 'shape politics, key social policy legislation and early intervention initiatives, as well as … everyday practices among health care providers and early years educators' (Edwards et al., 2015: 168). Nonetheless, a good deal of what is derived or 'is "known" from neuroscience is speculative' (Walsh, 2011: 22; see also Pickersgill, 2011).

The 'medical model' – in the shape of neuroscience and as it relates to discourses of early intervention – should not be pre-emptively and foolishly rejected out of hand. Indeed, it is essential of course, to have regard to the materiality of the body (see also the discussion on bodywork in Chapter 8). We are 'biological organisms … and our activities and thoughts can be understood only by situating us properly with a brain in a body in an eventful world abounding with objects and people' (Dawson and Fischer in Yaqub, 2002: 1082). As Majia Holmer Nadesan (2002: 426) remarks, when considering the 'discursive aspects of scientific knowledge' we need to recall that we are 'embodied, corporeal beings' having 'bio-material conditions of possibility for our senses, mobility and sociality'. Hence, neuroscience may have much to offer and could beneficially contribute to, for example, less harsh responses in the area of youth justice (Walsh, 2011). A US neuro-psychologist, Gary Marcus, argues

> Our early-twenty-first century world truly is filled with brain porn, with sloppy reductionist thinking and an unseemly lust for neuroscientific explanations. But the right solution is not to abandon neuroscience altogether, it's to better understand what neuroscience can and cannot tell us, and why. (in Edwards, et al., 2015: 174)

EVERY PICTURE TELLS A STORY

As a number of commentators have suggested, neuroscience has been harnessed to support particular solution-focused social policies not necessarily on account of 'its actual explanatory capacity, but for its persuasive value' (Edwards et al., 2015: 175). Perhaps especially during periods of welfare retrenchment and neoliberal cutbacks, this 'persuasive' aspect gives this range of ideas a certain appeal. In this context, despite the focus of *Welfare Words* being on *words*, it is vital to emphasise the immense importance of the visual (Rose, 2016).

Technological advances, particularly the introduction of functioning magnetic resonance imaging (fMRI), enable pictures of the brain to accompany early intervention's new vocabulary impacting on social work and social policy relating to children and families. Often lacking, and uninterested in encouraging deeper, analytical engagement, brain images 'shout science' (Poerksen in Wastell and White, 2012). Indeed, Tallis charges that such images are 'a fast acting solvent of critical faculties' (in Wastell and White, 2012: 280). Many neuroscientists, in fact, are alert to the limitations of brain imaging techniques and the related risks of data misinterpretation, given that what appears to be compelling visual evidence actually fails to address important dimensions or lines of inquiry (Ramani, 2009): for instance, that 'blood flows in one part of a brain are shown as "lit up" on an fMRI scan does not mean that the rest of it is inactive' (Edwards et al., 2015: 174). In short, the images are far from the straightforward and unambiguous representation of the actual totality of brain activity.

Moreover, brain science 'findings' may be occasionally inaccurate, misleading, inconclusive and mostly shaped by implicit normative understandings, yet such flaws risk becoming mere superfluous distractions when viewers are presented with brightly coloured, simplistic and, apparently, objective neuro-images. In this sense, pictures risk being deployed as substitutes for meaningful interrogation of the messy social world with its array of ethical and political dilemmas. Davi Johnson Thornton (2011: 402), for example, is troubled by the 'supreme status' which the brain imaging, associated with neuroscience, has quickly achieved. Furthermore, this development is providing a basis for the evolution of early childhood development policy and practice in social work and related fields. Who can, it is implied, doubt the 'biological truths' which are pictorially displayed for all to see (Thornton, 2011: 402)?

Stamm's (2007) *Bright from the Start*, along with a range of other books intended as popular and accessible guides on how to mould, wire and optimise the potential of children, rely on brain images to convey, especially to mothers, how their 'every mood and affection has an immediate, physiological impact that can be constantly visualized and measured' (Thornton, 2011: 402). Diffusing neuroscience expertise and vocabularies, the aspirant mother is able to 'look inside [a baby's] brain' to incessantly monitor and recalibrate how nurturing interventions can be maximised (Stamm in Thornton, 2011: 410). As discussed later, mothers on the lower rungs of the class ladder may face more emphatically severe interventions if they fail to learn from and act on this emerging knowledge. In the UK, Martin Narey, for example, advocates more strident policies of adoption and he uses neuroscience to support his assertions (see also Chapter 9).

More generally, Donato Ramani (2009) usefully delineates three dimensions amplifying neuroscience in different, but interrelated, ways. First, he refers to 'neurorealism', which is a perspective in which the evidence emanating from neuroimaging is perceived as real and objective: a sort of 'visual proof ... despite the enormous complexity of data acquisition and image processing'. In this instance, viewers are presented with, it would seem, final and compelling 'proof' of what people have always felt to be 'real' and 'true' but, until now, nobody had been able to visualise 'pain, feelings, fear, pleasure, even faith': in other words, fMRI could function as 'validation' of what has previously been considered 'evanescent and impalpable' (Ramani, 2009: 2).

Second, Ramani detects 'neuro-essentialism' in perspectives maintaining that, looking at the brain, we 'should be able to catch the true essence of personality (i.e. "brain cannot lie"), the origin of individual differences (differences between man and woman, homosexuality, vices etc.) and so on' (Ramani, 2009: 2). Third, 'neuropolicy' refers to the 'political use of neuroimaging findings to promote specific issues' or policy solutions with the neuroimaging or 'visual proof' having a powerful influence (2009: 2).

Each of these overlapping dimensions impacts on how strategies of early intervention are unfolding in the UK. Furthermore, within the international social work literature, this new interest in brain science is, on occasions, producing outlandishly incomplete and reductive accounts of the choices people make in the circumstances in which they find themselves. One contribution from Australia, for example, refers to the excess cortisol a baby received in her mother's womb 'causing her to develop an anxious temperament' which 'may lead her, as an adult, to move to a high security environment, such as a gated community' (Cameron and McDermott, 2007: 37). Of more serious concern, Karen Healy (2016) communicates how the suicide of a fifteen-year-old Aboriginal boy was interpreted by the Western Australian coroner as largely attributable to neurological changes prompted by childhood neglect. Failing to use a more encompassing critical optic, there was little recognition of how the continuing 'effects of European colonisation, institutionalised racism, violence and economic exclusion' are also immensely significant factors contributing to high suicide rates among Aboriginal teenage males (Healy, 2016: 1453). Unsurprisingly, given the narrowness of the focus, the coroner merely concluded her report by calling for child protection practitioners to better integrate recent 'advances' in neuroscience in their work with children viewed as vulnerable (2016: 1453). In this way, neuroscience can also be perceived as a 'screen discourse' partly functioning to hide an interrogation of structural questions circulating around power, domination and racialised subjugation (Bourdieu and Wacquant, 2001: 4).

NEUROSCIENCE AND THE EVOLVING VOCABULARY OF EARLY INTERVENTION

Perhaps influenced by the thoughts and assertions of Blair, mentioned at the outset of the chapter, the Iain Duncan Smith-associated Centre for Social Justice drew attention to brain science in *Breakthrough Britain: The Next Generation* published in 2008. Being reared in the context of a stressful or impoverished relationship, involving continuous criticism and verbal abuse, can, it is argued, damage brain tissue, due to the 'toxic levels of stress hormones "cascading" over the brain' (Centre for Social Justice and the John Smith Institute, 2008: 43). As is recognised in the field of epigenetics in physiology, in such instances the dynamic 'interplay' between genes and the environment is vital:

> In essence, some of our genes will be expressed in a particular way, depending on the environment in which we find ourselves. So for example, some of the genes which code for chemical activations that restore well-being after a stress reaction may be 'tuned down' by adverse parenting experiences in childhood. Similarly, genes which can place us at risk of later problems may only be 'turned on' by adverse parenting. (Centre for Social Justice and the John Smith Institute, 2008: 44)

According to the report, a 'neuron footprint' serves to reveal how this 'interplay' has unfolded for particular individuals. In the context of 'everyday medical practice', in fact, the 'earliest years of infancy and childhood are not lost but, like a child's footprints in wet cement, are often life-long' (Centre for Social Justice and the John Smith Institute, 2008: 149). An emphasis on the very early years of a child's life, should not, moreover, be 'confined to those children who are at most risk of social exclusion' (2008: 133; see also Chapter 6). This scientific revelation has, it is avowed, profound implications for evolving social policy.

The Family Nurse Partnership programme, mentioned earlier, now requires that practitioners raise the subject of brain development during the initial visit to a pregnant mother as a way of underlining the 'crucial significance of participation in the programme and the associated imparted advice' (Edwards et al., 2015: 179). Mothers are also given a sheet titled 'How to build your baby's brain' which includes a list of activities which, it is claimed, will 'enrich neural connectivity' (Edwards et al., 2015: 179). Programmes such as this establish a new 'common sense' around how – and why – the state intervenes in the domestic sphere (see also Chapter 2). In this process its agents, such as social workers, doctors and health visitors, have the purpose and scale of their interventions and incursions into families recalibrated. Parents – more often mothers – are referred to in 'flattering terms as "sculptors" and "architects" of the physical infant brain' and are enjoined to become responsible for optimizing the potential of their offsprings (Macvarish et al., 2015: 258).

Perhaps unsurprisingly, as soon as early years intervention advocates in the United States began to promote the first three years of life as critical for brain development, middle class parents, intent on maximising their household's store of human capital, became 'consumers of brain-based products and activities that would help their children to achieve educationally (which then left them even more anxious)' (Edwards et al., 2015: 182).

The fixation with neuroscience was prominent in *Early Intervention: Good Parents, Great Kids* (Allen and Duncan Smith, 2008). Moreover, in 2010, following the assembling of the Coalition government, a policy focus informed by brain science continued to resonate, with Allen producing two more reports published by the Cabinet Office (Allen, 2011a, 2011b; see also Wintour, 2008; Stein, 2011). Each reiterated the point that the early years of a child's life were crucial in that they furnished a narrow – *now or never* – period in which to get things right. Derived from an image used by the neuroscientist Bruce Perry in an article six years earlier, the report's cover showed the difference in size between the brain of a 'normal' three-year-old and that of a three-year-old victim of 'extreme neglect' (Allen, 2011a). Alongside the former, one single gold ingot is used to signify the government's investment in 'early intervention', the latter is flanked by two stacks of ingots, representing the excessive public cost of not intervening early: 'Low Attainment', 'Benefits', 'Failed Relationships', 'Poor Parenting', 'Drug Abuse', 'Teen Pregnancy', 'Violent Crime', 'Shorter Life', 'Poor Mental Health' (Allen, 2011b).

Those who are 'neglectful or depressed parents (or suffering from mental disorders) or who are drunk, drugged or violent, will have impaired capacity' to provide the necessary 'social and emotional stability' (Allen, 2011a: 15). This perspective was also lodged within historically rooted ideas, especially relating to attachment theory (see below). Thus, 'research' revealed that 'insecure attachment is linked to a higher risk for a number of health conditions, including strokes, heart attacks and high blood pressure, and suffering pain ... from headaches and arthritis' (Allen, 2011a). In contrast, 'people with secure attachment show more healthy behaviours such as taking exercise, not smoking, not using substances and alcohol, and [even, somewhat oddly] driving at ordinary speed' (2011a: 15). Illuminating the accuracy of some of the Marxist Autonomist insights (see also Chapter 2), Allen also appeared, on occasions, to conflate 'life' and 'work'. The Labour MP stated, for example, that suitably tapered forms of early intervention could aid in the production of 'life ready' subjects possessing the 'social and emotional capability to enter the labour market'. Such individuals would also grasp and understand the 'importance and the social, health and emotional benefits of entering work' (2011a: 9).

International advocacy of neuroscience-based intervention has been dubbed the 'First three years movement' (Thornton, 2011). Comprised of an alliance of 'child welfare advocates and politicians', it claims that 'social problems such as inequality, poverty, violence, lack of educational achievement, mental and physical ill-health, can be ameliorated or prevented if policy can secure functional infant brain development' (Macvarish et al., 2015: 253). In the lead up to the 2015 UK General Election, such thinking produced the Cross-Party Manifesto (2014) publication *The 1001 Critical Days: The Importance of the Conception to Age Two Period*. Receiving support across the mainstream political spectrum, and even signed by John McDonnell who went on to become the Labour Shadow Chancellor, it highlights how this movement, as proposed by Blair, is 'increasingly extended back before year zero, into gestation' (Macvarish et al., 2015: 257). A development hinting that expectant mothers, particularly those viewed as potentially 'risky', may become subject to more 'support' and enhanced surveillance.

The prime instigator of the Manifesto was the former investment fund manager and unsuccessful candidate for the leadership of the Conservative Party, Andrea Leadsom. She advised *The Guardian* that there was a need for 'stiletto-sharp interventions' which are 'brief, sharp, very focused' and which aim to 'get mum, dad or carer to the point where they are good-enough parents' (in Rustin, 2012).

> The worst thing ... is the parent who is inconsistent – you know: sometimes when I cry *my mum* hugs me and other times *she* hits me. That is where the baby develops an antisocial tendency. Kids who go and stab their best mate, or men who go out with a woman and rape and strangle her – these are the kinds of people who would have had very distorted early experiences. (in Rustin, 2012, emphases added)

Reductively simplistic in terms of how the psychology of rapists and murders is constituted, such comments – together with the wider cultural and political paradigm in which they are discursively situated – unsurprisingly generate a range of interrelated criticisms. However, such perceptions remain influential and are, perhaps, impacting more on decision-making in instances where 'parenting capacity' is subject to scrutiny. For example, in a Department for Education and Family Justice Council commissioned report, Brown and Ward (2012) identify how neuroscience-based developmental time frames should guide court decision-making in care proceedings. Should this occur on a widescale basis, it could result in the more rapid removal of a child from their family of origin (see also Broadhurst, et al., 2015).

DECIPHERING EARLY INTERVENTION

In some quarters within social work there may be a tendency to frown upon, even to reject, what is loosely referred to as the 'medical model' in which neuroscience is located. Such a stance may be related to something of an inferiority complex within the 'field', grounded in the understanding that social work is unfairly bereft of the 'symbolic capital' associated with the medical professions (see also the discussion on Bourdieu in Chapter 2). Alternatively, this perspective can be understood as driven by a more potentially liberatory project aiming to free the profession, and the users of services, from the narrowness and insularity of medical and positivistic approaches. 'Science with a capital "S" can sometimes be accredited with an explanatory power that it does not possess' (Walsh, 2011: 35). Such a view is likely to be informed by recognition of just how damaging the dominance of the 'medical model' has been in the past, particularly for those using health and social services regarded as 'deviant' or 'abnormal'. It would, however, be problematic to frame this issue within a crude binary logic – 'social' versus 'medical' model – because in most areas of their day-to-day work practitioners will take a more hybrid approach. Moreover, neither the 'social' nor the 'medical' can be rendered as entirely fixed and static constructs.

In what follows, the aim will be to articulate two core facets of early intervention discourse. First, the focus is on the questionable science often deployed to rhetorically inflate the significance of early intervention, particularly, the marked infant determinism and the stress usually placed on 'early plasticity and later rigidity' (Nadesan, 2002: 405). Second, it will be suggested that neuroscience perception of the vital significance of the early years is, perhaps, especially seductive for fields such as social work, because it coheres with the valorisation of more embedded, and traditional, ideas associated with attachment theory.

'BRAIN SCIENCE'

The 'most repeated claim about the infant brain is that it is distinguished from the adult brain by its capacity for extremely rapid "growth" (Macvarish et al., 2015: 257). As observed, the notion that the early years are the narrow 'window' available in which adult carers can fruitfully and productively intervene in the life of an infant is central to neuroscience and its amplification in media discourses. However, the main criticism of this form of reasoning is that it places far too great an emphasis on early interactions and lends insufficient attention to a child's – and subsequently adult's – constantly evolving 'habitus' and fuller sense of their place in the world (see also Chapter 2). Moreover, as well as boosting the strategies of corporations to market developmental children's toys at middle class consumers (Nadesan, 2002), this increasingly dominating discourse can be interpreted as kindling new anxiety and guilt in *all* parents, but particularly those impoverished parents already subjected to the disproportionate surveillance of the state (Wastell and White, 2012).

Here, one of the main criticisms is that the brain does *not* cease to exhibit plasticity after the first few years. Whilst accepting that brain development during this period is tremendously significant, it is important to recognise that the patterning of brain development is 'nonlinear, a complex web of recursive loops' (Walsh, 2011: 35; see also Malabou, 2008). A young child's brain is *not* irrevocably 'wired' after the age of 3 with the very early experiences producing and determining the life course of an individual. Located across a range of disciplines including neuroscience, many researchers, in fact, question the validity of such brain-based claims-making and express concerns about the direction of policies.

One of the chief critics is Bruer, who maintains that the focus on early years and brain development is, in part, a public relations ploy to garner additional funding for research (in Edwards et al., 2015: 175). He also cautions that many of the findings are extrapolated from animal-based research and that there are clearly manifest 'neurological differences between humans and the animal subjects that problematise the external validity of these studies' (Nadesan, 2002: 406). While critical of those relying uncritically on animal studies, Bruer still points out that some animal-based studies indicate that adults *can* and *do* continue to learn throughout their lives and that there is no compelling evidence revealing that 'children do, in fact, learn more quickly or more deeply' than adults (Nadesan, 2002: 406). Skills not untypically increase over time.

Bruer marshals a range of inter-related criticisms and he is sceptical about the normative assumptions embedded into research and policy in this area suggesting that there are too many generalisations made by 'academics who have very little experience of what it's like to be from a working class home or an impoverished background, and they are attempting to impose these middle-class views on everybody' (Bruer in Smith, 2014: 36). For example, the 'rich, complex environments' that parents and carers are exhorted to provide for children in their early years, appear to share many of the 'features of upper-middle class, urban, and suburban life' (Bruer, 1997: 10). Related to the criticism, and focusing on the frequent class-based nature of the discourse associated with brain science, Bruer chides that it is misleading to privilege certain environments as more beneficial than others for neural development of sensory-motor and visual skills. Such stimuli tend to be 'ubiquitous' and

> available to any organism that inhabits any reasonably normal environment ... available in any child's environment, unless that child is abused to the point of being raised in a sensory-deprivation chamber ... In short, experience-expectant brain plasticity does not depend on specific experiences in specific environments ... Cultural variations in child reading suggest that there are many equally successful ways to provide the normal environment needed for brain development. (Bruer, 1997: 8)

In discussing the cultural preoccupation with neuroscience discourses and how these have impacted on early intervention, it also important to recognise how more rooted professional thinking remains influential.

TOO ATTACHED TO ATTACHMENT THEORY?

As suggested earlier, evolving technologies and brain imaging techniques are central to the neuroscience discourse aiding the promotion of strategies of early intervention. However, when stripped down, neuroscience-driven strategies of early intervention can be read as a mere 'reformulation of old and contentious tenets of mother–child attachment theory' (Edwards et al., 2015: 176). What is more, despite such strategies

and approaches often being couched in gender-neutral language with copious references to 'parenting', it still can appear that it is mothers – and more so if they are poor
– who will be the targets of intervention given they are seen as the 'core mediators of
their children's development' (Edwards et al., 2015: 176).

In the reports of Graham Allen, discussed earlier, prevalent gender-neutral
terminology is apt to give way to female pronouns and ample references to the
role of mothers. In his first report, for example, he refers to the 'emotions in the
exchanges between mother and baby' (Allen, 2011a: 13) and 'the mother's mental state' features as a sub-heading for one section of his discussion (Allen,
2011a: 15). Elsewhere, he focuses on research which, readers are informed, has
analysed and found a manifest 'link' between 'low maternal responsiveness' and
problems with the behaviour of infants and young children. More specifically,
this research has

> found a link between low maternal responsiveness at 10–12 months to
> aggression, non-compliance and temper tantrums at 18 months; lower
> compliance, attention-getting and hitting at 2 years of age; problems with
> other children at 3; coercive behaviour at 4; and fighting and stealing
> when the child is 6. (Allen, 2011a: 16)

Pivoting on the mother–infant dyad, attachment theory and its lexicon has become
'one of the most enduring discourses aimed at explaining and defining normal (and
hence normative) maternal and child roles in the last century' (Thornton, 2011:
407). Historically significant here are figures such as the British developmental
psychologist John Bowlby (1907–1990) (see also Clarke and Clarke, 1976). His
understanding was that the first three years of a child's life are the most important
for the 'bonding of an infant to their mother' (Allen, 2011a: 73): these thirty-six
months establish the essential foundation for *all* subsequent adult growth and psychological development (see, for example, Bowlby, 1990). The insights of Bowlby
need, however, to be understood in the context of the hegemonic economic and
gendered order of the Cold War. His theorisation, and much of that derived from
it, has been subject to sustained and convincing critiques from feminist scholars
(Birns, 1999; McNay, 2008). Nonetheless, Bowlby's views remain at the core of
present-day education and practice as it relates to child and family social work.
Bowlby also continues to inform contemporary social theory, especially some of the
strands associated with the politics of recognition (Honneth, 1995; see also Garrett,
2013a: Ch. 9).

In the context of the focal concerns of this chapter, attachment theory is now
operating as an implicit resource for neuroscience-informed frameworks for intervention. This is not to argue that this body of theory merely replicates that of the
1950s and 1960s. In the past, the mother–infant bonding process was perceived as
mostly biologically determined and a *natural* outcome of interactions between the
normal mother and her child (Thornton, 2011). According to some writers in the

field of cultural studies, influenced by governmentality theory, contemporary attachment theorisation lays greater emphasis on the mother needing to constantly work on 'the self', primarily through 'actions directed inward; toward feelings, attitudes, and desires' intent on achieving 'personal freedom' and 'self-realization' (Thornton, 2011: 409). Hence, there is a detectable tendency, perhaps especially in US parenting advice books aimed at a financially comfortable segment of the female population, to 'frame instruction as a progressive advancement over the more archaic (defined as repressive, intrusive, even patriarchal or sexist) instruction of the past' (Thornton, 2011: 410). Although these more contemporary renderings of attachment theory remain moralistic and sexist, the 'good mother' is not a 'socially or biologically imposed norm to which women must conform; rather, mothering is a limitless pursuit of the self and its values of enjoyment, happiness, and fulfilment' (Thornton, 2011: 413).

CONCLUSION

Notwithstanding the discursive hype, early intervention talk in the UK does not always appear to be matched by investments in practice. For example, it has been reported that cuts are adversely impacting on local councils' ability to provide such services. Action for Children, National Children's Bureau and The Children's Society (2016: 2) reveal that, 'between 2010–11 and 2015–16, spending by local authorities on early intervention services for children, young people and families fell by 31 per cent in real terms'. Nevertheless, it is still important to dwell on this 'current vogue for tracing the origins of social failure to early-life factors' (Macnicol, 2015: 5).

Across an array of childcare arenas, concerns about the capacity of parents – usually mothers – to nurture their children are historically rooted, and clearly pre-date the emergence of neuroscience-based claims. Consequently, in trying to arrive at a rounded assessment of such claims, they need to be situated alongside earlier patterns of class-based and gendered modes of understanding and reasoning. As suggested in Chapter 2, Gramsci's comments on how residues from the past impact on and shape contemporary concerns remain instructive. Certainly, neuroscience 'has latched very easily' on to classed and gendered psychological ideas about childrearing which have been hegemonic for decades (Edwards et al., 2015: 173).

Given cuts to services, early intervention, it is maintained, is a manifestly 'smart' and common sense approach. Moreover, the science at the core of its explanatory logic appears to suggest that it is *beyond* politics. How could any reasonable person conceivably dispute the solid 'truth' of science? Despite the manifest affinities with neoliberal forms of rationality, brain science tends to be presented as the antidote to 'outmoded ideas about social class as shaping life chances' (Edwards et al., 2015: 181). Within the evolving dominant paradigm, the relationship between the parent as child is, in the words of Jan Macvarish and her colleagues, constructed and calibrated as 'both naturally foundational to society but also too risky and important to be left to the unseen vagaries of the private realm' (Macvarish et al., 2015: 252). This furnishes part of the context for the centrality of early intervention, where 'expert-led, neuro-scientifically-informed parenting support' is seen to be 'necessary to train the parent in the correct way to nurture the child' (Macvarish et al., 2015: 257). Moreover, underpinning early years' intervention is a 'cultural deficit model' that tends to guarantee that it is the impoverished that are perceived in terms of 'risk, with little consideration given to wider structural and economic factors' (Edwards et al., 2015: 180).

Early intervention talk fuses, therefore, a back-to-basics attachment theory-driven approach to children and their mothers with a more 'evidenced-based', visualised and futuristic perspective. Added ideological ingredients suggest that the assortment of ideas associated with early intervention promise not only to save the hard-pressed taxpayer money, they point the way for the aspirational parent to know how *she* can maximise their child's potential to become a socially well-adjusted individual psychologically primed and nurtured to succeed in a hyper-competitive market economy. In this sense, it has strong affinities with resilience, the next welfare word to be explored.

REFLECTION AND TALK BOX 6

1.   Writing in *Newsweek* approximately mid-way into George H W Bush's 'Decade of the Brain', Sharon Begley (1996) argued

> It is the experiences of childhood, determining which neurons are used, that wire the circuits of the brain as surely as a programmer at a keyboard reconfigures the circuits in a computer. Which keys are typed – which experiences a child has – determines whether the child grows up to be intelligent or dull, fearful or self-assured, articulate or tongue-tied … Yet, once wired, there are limits to the brain's ability to create itself. Time limits. Called 'critical periods', they are windows of opportunity that nature flings open, starting before birth, and then slams shut, one by one, with every additional candle on the child's birthday cake. (Begley, 1996)

2.   Relate these remarks to the activity of child protection social workers.

3.   Look at the images of the brain featured on the front cover of Allen's (2011b) *Early Intervention: Smart Investment, Massive Savings*
     https://www.gov.uk/government/uploads/system/uploads/attachment_data/
     file/61012/earlyintervention-smartinvestment.pdf

How can these ubiquitous pictorial displays be connected to some of the themes explored in the chapters on welfare dependency (Chapter 3) and underclass (Chapter 4)?

4.   The UK's *The Daily Telegraph* newspaper maintains that:

> the improvements in parental care required are not huge: simply ensuring that *mothers* play with their children in the first three years of their lives, empathise with them and make them feel safe, makes a very significant difference to the physical architecture of the developing brain, which in turn can make the difference between whether a child develops into a normal, fully socialised teenager or an out-of-control hoodlum (Palmer, 2010, emphasis added)

What is being conveyed about the role of mothers?

FURTHER READING

Andrew Pithouse's (2008) article in the *British Journal of Social Work* is a succinct critique of some of the core assumptions underpinning early intervention. Insight into the increasing centrality of neuroscience to early intervention is provided by the two reports produced by the UK Labour MP Graham Allen (2011a, 2011b). Similarly, the Cross-Party Manifesto (2014) on the significance of the 1001 'critical days' for children is a significant and accessible document. More sceptical accounts, both in the same issue of *Critical Social Policy*, are those of Ros Edwards et al. (2015) and Jan Macvarish et al. (2015). Charlotte Walsh (2011), looking at neuroscience from a somewhat different angle, cogently argues that it may contribute to potentially more lenient judicial decision-making in the area of youth justice. Jan De Vos and Ed Pluth's (2016) *Neuroscience and Critique* is a lively and informative book. The US cultural theorist Davi Johnson Thornton (2011) suggests that early intervention and omnipresent ideas associated with entrepreneurship can by analysed in tandem. On Twitter, Neurobollocks is also worth dipping into: https://twitter.com/neurobollocks?lang=en

CHAPTER 7

RESILIENCE

Resilience – The action or an act of rebounding or springing back; rebound, recoil. (*Oxford English Dictionary*)

INTRODUCTION

Resilience is a prominent welfare word within the 'self-help', 'life skills' and 'coaching' book market[1]. Here bestselling titles, many of them originating in the United States, include *The Seven Habits of Highly Effective People* (Covey, 1989), *The Resilience Factor: 7 Keys to Finding Your Inner Strength and Overcoming Life's Hurdles* (Reivich and Shatte, 2002), *The Resiliency Advantage: Master Change, Thrive Under Pressure and Bounce Back from Setbacks* (Siebert, 2005), *The Power of Resilience: Achieving Balance, Confidence, and Personal Strength in Your Life* (Brooks and Goldstein, 2006). Each title echoes core concerns of 'positive' psychology and conveys the 'can-do' vibe of the genre. Seen from this perspective, resilience can – as suggested at the end of the previous chapter – be a vital attribute to add to the kitbag of hardened individual subjects intent on training to achieve psychological fitness for the rigours of neoliberalism's relentless and unending competition.

Resilience is also omnipresent within the academic literature of social work. The *British Journal of Social Work* has published a plethora of articles with resilience or resilient in their titles since Trotter's (2000) contribution: three were electronically published in the space of just over a week in October 2012 (Adamson et al., 2012; Ungar et al., 2012; Wu et al., 2012). Reflecting the international scope of the journal, papers have originated from authors based in Canada (Gilgun, 2005; Ungar, 2008; Ungar et al., 2012), China (Hong Kong) (Fu Keung Wong, 2008; Wu et al., 2012), England (Schofield and Beek, 2005; Murray, 2010; Kinman and Grant, 2011; Rajan-Rankin, 2014), New Zealand (Adamson et al., 2012) and the United States (Bailey et al., 2013). The thematic focus has varied with resilience being associated with a shifting constellation of other words and phrases including: assessments, cross-cultural practice, educational outcomes, gun violence, long-term foster care, mental health, migrant children, offending, sexualities, well-being, work-related stress, youth. Significantly, resilience research occasionally has the sheen of 'radicalism' by virtue of it being associated, particularly in the US literature, with individuals and groups possessing 'negative symbolic capital' (Bourdieu in Bourdieu et al., 2002: 185; see also Chapter 2): for example, socially and economically groups who are frequently poor and subject to racism and racialisation (see, for example, Jenson et al., 2013: 106–7).

The World Bank (Lundberg and Wuermli, 2012a) and the International Monetary Fund (IMF) locates the restoration of resilience as one of the prime aims in its 'global policy agenda' during a period of faltering economic recovery (IMF, 2013). Furthermore, the theme of the 2013 World Economic Forum, held in Davos-Klosters, was 'resilient dynamism' (Tapscott, 2013; see also Adams, 2015). More expansively, perhaps, resilience can be interpreted as not only a welfare word, but as evolving into one of the key cultural and political categories of our time (Chandler and Reid, 2016). Invariably, it is also viewed as an asset. In contrast, this chapter aims to produce a critical overview of resilience and to *stretch* the relevant literature so as to create the space for a pluralistic and questioning discussion of this particular welfare word. Underpinning the exploration is the recognition – present throughout this book – that words and concepts, such as resilience, need to be interrogated and situated within encompassing economic, social and political contexts. This is because narratives and 'metaphors play an important role in the shaping of policy: policy makers need to tell "stories" and these often support and reinforce prevailing relations of power' (Harrison, 2013: 99).

Central to the discussion in this chapter is the proposition that the promiscuous and mobile discourse pivoting on resilience has largely escaped critical scrutiny within social work and social policy and has far too swiftly become part of its 'common sense' (see also Chapter 2). Hence, it can appear self-evident, established and settled once and for all that resilience furnishes a convincing conceptual framework for thinking about, for example, social work interventions with a range of client groups. Relatedly, most studies looking through a resilience optic fail to look more closely at a range of other welfare words and phrases present in the same discursive orbit. Gilligan (1999: 187), for example, refers to how social work interventions, informed by the research on resilience, might assist young people 'such as those in care, to "join or re-join the mainstream"' (see also Chapter 8). Yet, this 'mainstream', its margins and exclusionary modalities and practices, is left unexplored: similarly, phrases, such as 'pro-social behaviour' and 'world of work', despite being politically charged, are not interrogated (Gilligan, 1999: 187, 192).

Starting with an overview of the origins and definitions of resilience, the chapter focuses on some of the main characteristics of resilience-driven research approaches and forms of intervention. This will be followed by a summary of some of the main criticisms levelled at resilience. The lines of criticism will then be extended by concentrating on how resilience is incorporated and amplified in both military and mainstream neoliberal discourses. It will then be suggested that there is a need to theoretically conjoin notions of resilience with ideas relating to human capital. The chapter concludes with a brief exploration of attempts to tilt resilience talk in slightly different, more socially and politically progressive, directions.

ORIGINS AND DEFINITIONS

Resilio originates from Latin and means 'to jump back' (Mohaupt, 2009: 63). How resilience is defined, in a contemporary sense, relates to the disciplinary context in which it is being promulgated, but most definitions lay emphasis on the dynamic ability to adapt, cope and transcend disruption or longer-term adversity. Despite much debate 'amongst researchers concerning its conceptualization, resilience is generally defined as positive adaptation despite adversity' (Bottrell, 2009: 323). Thus, one who is resilient may be 'considered irrepressible; buoyant; enduring; flexible: the person who bounces back – unchanged – from exposure to trauma' (Vickers and Kouzmin, 2001: 96). Harrison (2013: 98) reiterates that resilience basically entails the 'capability to "bounce back" from adversity. Such adversity includes economic recession, natural disasters, climate change, and the psychological effects of stress and family breakdown.' The term conveys 'the idea of positive responses from individuals in the face of adversity' and 'implies the ability to withstand setbacks or even the capacity for individuals to use their problems as an impetus for positive change' (Harrison, 2013: 98).

Across the resilience literature, there is little agreement on which discipline initially began to use the term (see also Table 1 in MacKinnon and Derickson, 2012). Some argue that its origins are in physics and engineering where resilience captures the ability of 'materials to "bounce back" after shocks and resume their original condition' (Mohaupt, 2009: 64). Others have suggested that medicine provided a significant impetus for the promulgation of ideas pivoting on resilience. Within the medical/health promotion field, Aaron Antonovsky's focus on factors that support health and well-being, rather than on those that cause disease, has been viewed as significant. Hence, his concept of 'salutogenesis' has been 'implicit' in the more popular idea of resilience (Canvin et al., 2009: 239). Examining genealogies of resilience as they relate to neoliberal and security discourses, Walker and Cooper (2011) highlight the work of Crawford S. Hollings (1973) within ecosystems science in the 1970s (see also Adger, 2000). However, in her concise survey, Mohaupt (2009: 64) concludes that 'most of the literature cites social psychology as the place of origin for the concept where it dates back to the 1940s'.

Although the origins of resilience remain contested, its social psychology foundations appear to have had the most impact on social work. It was in the 1980s that 'a real paradigm change from risk research to resilience research' occurred (Mohaupt, 2009: 64). During that decade, some of most influential published empirical studies include that by Garmezy and Rutter (1983), who undertook a long-term survey of 200 children in the United States, and Werner and Smith (1988), who tracked over 600 people in Hawaii over a thirty-year period. Here, the core research focus was on the factors and processes which led to 'successes' despite adverse circumstances. Furthermore, a concentration on children, particularly in the psychology literature, remains apparent today as 'childhood resilience is one of the most extensively researched areas in the field' (Mohaupt, 2009: 64). What is more, some commentators have detected in the 'resilience of children' a reason for all of us to be more existentially 'hopeful about the future' (Sharry, 2011).

RESEARCH APPROACHES, PROGRAMMES, FORMS OF INTERVENTION

Resilience research – or as some prefer 'resilience science' (Masten, 2014: 7) – is a diverse field, whose advocates tend to lay different emphases on particular issues and themes. However, in simple and broad terms, there are a number of key conceptual underpinnings which highlight a loose unity in the research strategies adopted. First, acting as something of a counterweight to the 'deficit' models perceived to be formally characterising practitioner interventions, there is an emphasis on 'strengths' or 'assets' and on the ability of individuals to cope with fraught situations. Hence, particular attention is paid to 'internal' and 'external' 'protective factors': in children, internal 'attributes … range from problem-solving skills, aspirations, social competences, intellectual/cognitive skills, self-regard and self-esteem' (Mohaupt, 2009: 65). External factors, frequently narrowly conceived, relate to 'family characteristics' and key 'institutions such as the school or community' (2009: 65–6). Second, there is an awareness of the dual significance of 'inputs' (the exposure to risks and adverse circumstances) and 'outcomes'. The latter dimension, as Mohaupt (2009: 65) explains, involves 'studying whether coping mechanisms lead to outcomes within or above the expected range. This should be assessed by comparing the outcome to a context specific reference group (e.g. same age group, social and cultural context, etc.)'. Third, resilience should be understood as a dynamic unfolding rather than as a static occurrence. Hence, it is vital for researchers to track the same individuals over a lengthy period of time (e.g. Garmezy and Rutter, 1983; Werner and Smith, 1988).

Fourth, forms of intervention seeking to embed a resilience orientation have tended to initially take hold in particular institutional settings (such as schools, and the military), and have subsequently been applied to the domestic sphere.

Consequently, the institutional 'target' populations (school pupils, soldiers) might be perceived as providing a template for interventions aiming to shape how families conduct themselves and to nurture what are perceived as the necessary resilient characteristics. Later in the chapter, the focus will be on the US Army, but it is apparent that the school is increasingly furnishing a domain of experimentation for resilience-driven approaches. In the UK, the Promoting Alternative Thinking Strategies programme (PAThS) teaches resilience as a component of pupils' social and emotional education. Rooted in 'a "whole school approach", the programme involves all staff including playground supervisors and canteen assistants whilst also encouraging parents and carers to help children practise skills at home, thereby promoting their transfer and reinforcement' (Ecclestone and Lewis, 2014: 200). Influenced strongly by positive psychology and cognitive behavioural therapy (CBT), resilience is one of 'several, interrelated constructs that comprise "emotional well-being", including optimism, emotional literacy (especially self-awareness, empathy and emotional regulation), altruism, self-esteem and stoicism' (Ecclestone and Lewis, 2014: 196). This assortment implicitly identifies, therefore, the core characteristics and attributes deemed necessary to manage and regulate oneself to attain the behavioural competencies to live appropriately in the world. In February 2013, the All-Party Parliamentary Group on Social Mobility (2014) held a 'summit' to launch a *Character and Resilience Manifesto*. Here, it was spelt out that the aspiration was to 'encourage a refocusing of schools' policy to ensure that the development of Character and Resilience and associated skills move from the periphery to become ... the "core business" for all schools' (All-Party Parliamentary Group on Social Mobility, 2014: 34). As with the armed forces, one of the key messages within the sphere of the school is that resilience is an *attitude* that can be learned, nurtured and cultivated. In this sense, resilience training can be perceived as an expansive, colonising system of tutelage and social control. Moreover, it can be interpreted as a technique of 'massification' (McNay, 2009: 57).

Fifth, many of the resilience-based approaches are directly influenced by developments in the United States and this is apparent in terms of initiatives taking place in UK schools. Reflecting some of the theorisation of Bourdieu and Wacquant, mentioned in Chapter 4, US 'education policy and practice over the past 20 years has been a powerful influence' on high-profile initiatives (Ecclestone and Lewis, 2014: 198). This is signalled not only by the introduction of PAThS, but by the appearance of other programmes imbued with a positive psychology orientation such as the Social and Emotional Aspects of Learning Strategy for Schools (SEAL) initiative and the Penn Resilience Programme (Ecclestone and Lewis, 2014).

In what follows, and before examining the military fascination with the same theme, some of the criticisms directed at resilience-focused research will be briefly outlined.

QUESTIONING TALES OF 'ORDINARY MAGIC'

First, in terms of the operational changes resilience researchers seek to trigger, the proposed shift from a 'deficit model' to an 'asset model' could lead to an 'over-reliance on prevention programmes' (Mohaupt, 2009: 66; see also Gray, 2014). Prevention operates at the 'deep level of cultural order or common sense' (Freeman, 1999: 233). Moreover, this fascination with prevention illuminates the positivist and empiricist roots of social science. Specifically in terms of the dominant tendencies within resilience research, this is rooted in the 'paradigm of developmental disorder and positivist (observable, measurable) conceptions of social transactions, which may be targeted for intervention' (Bottrell, 2009: 325). As well as potentially diverting resources from other worthwhile areas of provision, resilience programmes risk being perceived, particularly during a period of ongoing budget cuts, as 'a panacea for managing social problems' (Hine, 2005: 128). What is more, an array of 'theoretical and moral questions' underpin the delivery of preventive interventions to children and families (2005: 128).

A second, and substantial, criticism directed at the resilience literature relates to value judgements and normative reasoning. The criteria for 'assessment of positive or mal-adaptation is embedded in socio-cultural assumptions and historically specific societal expectations' (Bottrell, 2009: 324). More recently, such criticism has prompted greater attentiveness to sociocultural factors (Masten, 2014), but resilience theory still tends to disconnect 'from analyses of social inequalities and questions about the status of young people in society' (Bottrell, 2009: 322). How, for example, is the notion of 'positive outcomes' and ideas pivoting on 'success' or 'coping' arrived at? Such questions highlight the tendency in the mainstream literature towards value-laden attributions. In global terms, definitions created by, for example 'white, middle-class, male academics in the Western World, have their limits in their applicability to other countries – especially developing countries' (Mohaupt, 2009: 66; see also Christopher et al., 2014). Alert to the charge that resilience research is 'anchored in a Eurocentric epistemology', Michael Ungar's constructivist approach to global resilience research studies is much more context-sensitive (Ungar, 2008: 222). Along with colleagues in Canada, he furnishes accounts of how more participatory and culturally nuanced defining practices involving the 'target groups' themselves can try to arrive at more negotiated and pluralistic accounts of 'success' and 'positive' outcomes (Ungar, 2008; Ungar et al., 2012).

However, a damaging conceptual binary at the core of such approaches is illuminated by the suggestion that concerns about 'community and cultural factors' are only viewed as relevant in terms of the engagement of 'Western' researchers with target populations situated in 'non-Western' cultures (Ungar, 2008: 221). Such an analysis risks implying that those situated in the 'Western' world form an undifferentiated whole, not divided by class and other intersecting processes of separation, demarcation and exploitation. This dimension is recognised in the fascinating work of Dorothy

Bottrell (2009) focusing on young females' narratives in an inner-city suburb of Sydney, Australia. She suggests that to meaningfully comprehend their adaptive behaviours 'requires understanding the social processes of differentiation that underpin the girls' accounts' (Bottrell, 2009: 331): an approach running wholly counter to normative models of resilience which are likely to 'preclude non-conformist forms and to categorise them in psychopathological terms' (2009: 329).

In contrast, a number of US research studies appear to deploy notions of 'culture' to erase the significance of the economic oppression and racialization prompting the 2013 formation, by Alicia Garza, Patrisse Cullors and Opal Tometi of the Black Lives Matter campaign (see also McVeigh, 2016). Jenson et al. (2013: 160) merely prefer to blur such issues by referring, for example, to variations in 'academic achievement between youth of color from low income families and [those rather anachronistically termed] Caucasian youth'. Moreover, the same researchers seek to entirely expunge class whilst encouraging resilience programme evaluators to be 'sensitive' to racial, ethnic gender and sexual orientation differences (Jenson et al., 2013: 106–7).

Some US-based authors are beginning to concede that there are 'gaps' existing in resilience theorisation especially in relation to structurally embedded poverty:

> We must be cautious that the concept of resilience is not used in public policy to withhold social supports or maintain inequities, based on the rationale that success or failure is determined by strengths or deficits within individuals and their families. It is not enough to bolster the resilience of at-risk children and families so that they can 'beat the odds'; we must also strive to *change the odds* against them. (Walsh in Seccombe, 2002: 287–8, emphasis added)

Inescapably, seeking to 'change the odds' means, as some of the supporters of Bernie Sanders' failed bid for the Democratic candidacy in the 2016 presidential election recognised, combating mass poverty and dismantling the exploitative neoliberal economy that produces and sustains it. Figures released by the US government on children (from birth to seventeen years) reveal that, in 2013, 20% (14.7 million) lived in poverty and 21% (15.8 million) lived in households classified as 'food insecure' (Federal Interagency Forum on Child and Family Statistics, 2015: vii). According to a report by the National Center on Family Homelessness (2014), nearly 2.5 million children experienced homelessness in the United States in 2013, an 8% rise nationally from the previous year. The National Low Income Housing Coalition reports that there is no longer a 'single state or county anywhere in the country where a full-time minimum wage worker can afford even the average one bedroom apartment' (Oxfam America, 2016: 4). However, during the Obama administrations the situation of the impoverished was often worsened by specific political decisions. In 2014, for example, the US Congress cut

one of its premier safety net programs, the Supplemental Nutrition
Assistance Program (SNAP) – better known as food stamps – by
$8.7 billion, causing 850,000 households to lose an average of
$90 per month. In fact, since 2010, federal policymakers have cut 85%
of US federal programs supporting low income families. (Oxfam
America, 2016: 4; see also Chapter 3)

A third related criticism concentrates on the way in which the wider societal and
political context is minimised in so far as dominant theories of resilience usually
focus on the individual. Although some attempts have been made to craft the idea
of 'social resilience' (Cacioppo et al., 2011; Hall and Lamont, 2013), ordinarily
there is a wholly 'inordinate focus first on the individual as the unit of observation
and second on intra-psychic functioning and individual behaviour as the object of
analysis' (Boyden and Cooper, 2007: 5). Resilience research is, therefore, vulnerable to accusations of being far too 'actor centred, ignoring any structural forces'
(Mohaupt, 2009: 67). For example, the structurally generated scale of poverty in
the United States, mentioned earlier, and the enormous disparities in wealth is not
the focus of research interest. Instead, and despite 'growing recognition of the
importance of analysing contexts, "resilience" research remains principally preoccupied with the individual and assumes the individualised nature of adaptation'
(Bottrell, 2009: 336). Such criticism can be related to the charge that resilience,
functioning as a distraction, 'can de-politicise efforts such as poverty reduction
and emphasise self-help in line with a neo-conservative agenda instead of stimulat-
ing state responsibility' (Mohaupt, 2009: 67). Attention is, therefore, 'diverted
away from the state and other actors with the power and moral responsibility to
intervene and bring about change, with populations living in poverty being
charged with using their own resources to support themselves through crisis'
(Boyden and Cooper, 2007: 5).

In the area of organization studies, Margaret Vickers and her colleagues criticise
the valorisation of the trait of individual resilience within agencies subject to neoliberal restructuring processes; oftentimes this results in 'an inaccurate and
inappropriate reification of such traits in organizational actors' (Vickers and
Kouzmin, 2001: 96). As a consequence there is a willed failure to acknowledge that
workers 'may be permanently damaged, traumatised and alienated as a result of
their experiences with New Public Management' (2001: 111). Approaching this
phenomenon from a more psychodynamic viewpoint, the authors suggest that managers, 'assuming an ongoing resilience of colleagues may be employing Freudian
defence mechanisms such as denial or repression to cope with the situation' (Vickers
and Kouzmin, 2001: 101).

Next, extending the critique of this particular welfare word, the focus will be
on how resilience discourses can be better understood by having regard to their
military usage. Despite this dimension being neglected in discussion of resilience
in, for example, social work, exploration of this facet of resilience is vital because

it highlights the tangled roots of this theorisation. Moreover, there is a need to examine the military sphere because there are signals that the programmatic experimentations taking place within the army – perhaps particularly the US Army – are being assembled as preliminary measures which are also applicable to the civilian domain in the United States and beyond.

RESILIENCE AND MILITARY LOGIC IN AN ERA OF 'ENDLESS WAR'

As commented on in Chapter 4, a good deal of mainstream political and media attention focused on the role of the so-called underclass in the English riots of 2011. Following these events, a Riots Communities and Victims Panel (2012: 7) established by the Coalition government stressed the importance of 'personal resilience' in enabling young people to 'recover' from 'setbacks'. Significantly, *After the Riots* maintained that the military furnished an example as to how this attribute might be 'built in adolescence and through adulthood' (Riots Communities and Victims Panel, 2012: 51):

> An example of this comes from the US Army which has developed the Master Resilience Trainer, which forms part of the Comprehensive Soldier Fitness Programme. It teaches officers how to build emotional fitness in their soldiers through training, placing as much emphasis on character as physical fitness. (Riots Communities and Victims Panel, 2012: 51)

Today, in much Western military thinking, resilience is viewed as 'an indispensable resource and necessary characteristic of modern warriors, and human beings more generally' (Howell, 2015: 15–16). Over the past decade, resilience programmes have been introduced into the armies of Australia, Canada, the Netherlands, and the United States (Howell, 2015). A number other countries are also involved in resilience activities coordinated through NATO's Mental Health Training task group (Howell, 2015). This aspect has gained attention within the area of 'security' studies, particularly in the work of Howell (2015: 16), who convincingly argues that the US military is also being used as a 'site of experimentation in the production of an austere science of psychological resilience that is overtly pitched as a tool for civilian settings' (2015: 16).

Throughout history, war has often provided the impetus for new social policy thematic preoccupations and programmes in the field of welfare (Dwork, 1987; Cowen, 2008). In a contemporary sense, resilience can be viewed as providing a case example of this dimension of welfare's evolution. In the UK, as part of a more encompassing initiative seeking to imbue schools with a 'military ethos', a 'growing number of former soldiers' are being 'employed to boost resilience' in children (Weale, 2015; see also ForcesWatch, 2015). However, it is in the US, partly because of the sheer numbers of its armed forces personnel, that this military component to the evolution of policy and practices is most pronounced (Howell, 2015). This is driven by two key factors. First, given there is a perception that this is an epoch of endless and changing types of war, it is argued that the soldiery needs to be more psychologically attuned and better able to endure and emerge victorious: hence, the US military has identified resilience as a core component in the training of combat troops (Cacioppo et al., 2011). Second, resilience thinking needs to be connected to the drive to reduce the cost of health spending on the military. Both these dimensions will be briefly examined.

RESILIENCE AND THE CRAFTING OF AN 'INDOMITABLE' SOLDIERY

In the United States, the Comprehensive Soldier Fitness (CSF) programme was conceived in 2008 and launched the following year. Significantly, so as to emphasise the role of spouses, intimate partners and the nexus of the family, it was rebranded the Comprehensive Soldier and *Family* Fitness (CSF2) programme in 2012. Nowadays it is officially perceived as a vital form of intervention given the 'need for a resilient Army capable of meeting the persistent warfare of the foreseeable future' (Seligman and Fowler, 2011: 82; see also Matthews, 2014). Perhaps especially, it seeks to produce and nurture the 'manpower for a kind of warfare that goes among the people ... fostering this expansion of warfare by creating the human resources necessary to carry out this kind of extensive and persistent form of war' (Howell, 2015: 23).

CSF2 is, according to the estimations of its promoters and advocates, the 'largest deliberate psychological intervention in history' (Lester et al. in Howell, 2015: 16). This may initially appear self-serving and hyperbolic, but Howell counsels that the claim has elements of truth. With over a million test subjects (US Army soldiers and civilians) required to participate, and military spouses encouraged to take part also, CSF2 can certainly be regarded as the 'largest psychological *experiment* in human history' (Howell, 2015: 16, original emphasis). In this context, a Global Assessment Tool (GAT 2.0) is a significant instrument. Given one million soldiers will be using this online self-reporting questionnaire, it constitutes an 'unprecedented database for the prospective longitudinal study of the effects of psychological variables on physical health, mental health, and performance' (Seligman and Fowler, 2011: 84–5).

CSF2 perceives fitness as an encompassing totality integrating dimensions beyond the physical fighting body of the soldier. According to Howell, four domains are identified: *Emotional* fitness (having the ability to be positive, optimistic, able to exert self-control and possess the requisite stamina); *Social* fitness (having the capacity to make and retain friends, evolving good communication skills, being implicitly able to deal with racial and gender-based diversity); *Spiritual* fitness (holding onto a body of beliefs, principles, or values which can sustain); *Family* fitness (being nestled within familial relationships which can function as unpaid resources of support)[2].

Perhaps every welfare word, in order to become embedded in 'common sense', requires a champion: an intellectual 'personality' possessing scientific knowledge and often, but not always, garlanded with praise and recognition within his (and it is usually *his*) own field of scholarly endeavour and beyond. Whilst he may not have coined the word or elaborated his associated conceptualisations, he possesses the right mix of 'symbolic capital', and often media acumen, to *push* it out into the world (see also Chapter 2 on Bourdieu). Such primary definers have the attention of senior figures within the political 'field' and they may also reap lucrative financial rewards. As discussed earlier, with the underclass notion, Charles Murray fulfilled such a role (see also Chapter 4). The former American Psychological Association (APA) president Martin E.P. Seligman, generally regarded as a 'main architect' of CSF2, is a similar figure in relation to resilience (Howell, 2015: 19; see also Benjamin, 2010). His aspiration is to install resilience training as 'common sense' as part of a project to build an 'indomitable' US army (Burling, 2010). The author of *Authentic Happiness: Using the New Positive Psychology to Realize Your Potential for Deep Fulfilment* (Seligman, 2015), he is also Director of the Positive Psychology Center, University of Pennsylvania.

RESILIENCE, THE MILITARY AND NEOLIBERAL AUSTERITY

The rise of resilience within the US Army is also partly attributable to a drive to reduce the cost of health spending in the military and within the Department of Veterans Affairs (VA) (Howell, 2015). These costs are significant because of the scale of US involvement in wars and because of the increased price of corporate pharmaceutical products. Moreover, according to the dominant reasoning, if resilience training is an effective preventative measure in terms of reducing mental health care expenditure on soldiers and their families, it may serve as a model for the wider civilian population as neoliberal states look to cut the costs of welfare. What is more, there is clearly a cross-fertilisation and dialectical enmeshment facilitating the evolution and spreading of the 'science' and practice of resilience across both the military and civilian spheres.

The aspiration to have military resilience permeate the civilian field is a recursive preoccupation. According to Peterson et al. (2011: 16) maintaining that resilience assessment and training techniques developed and deployed within the military are similarly applicable in other spheres such as 'schools, businesses, police and fire departments, hospitals, community mental health centers, and the like – any and all settings where doing well is recognised, celebrated and encouraged'. The academic promoters of military resilience, such as Seligman, are explicit and their comments merit quoting at length:

The use of resilience training and positive psychology in the Army is consciously intended as a model for civilian use. The bulk of health care costs in civilian medicine go not to building health but rather to treating illness. The Army's emphasis on building psychological fitness preventively is intended to be a model for the future of medicine generally. Imagine that building emotional, social, family, and spiritual fitness among young soldiers noticeably reduces morbidity, mortality, and mental illness, offers a better prognosis when illness strikes, and cuts down on treatment costs ... The implications for public education and for the corporation may be just as sweeping ... If it turns out that soldiers given this training perform better in their jobs, are more engaged, have more meaning in their lives, enjoy better relationships, and have more fruitful employment when they return to civilian society, this will ground a new model for our public schools. (Seligman and Fowler, 2011: 85)

Indeed, as observed earlier, resilience training, heavily influenced by the work of Seligman and kindred academic figures, is now being embedded into UK schools (All-Party Parliamentary Group on Social Mobility, 2014: 43–4).

RESILIENCE AND NEOLIBERAL REASONING

More generally, resilience 'science' might be interpreted as a more potentially pervasive form of neoliberal governance percolating into an array of institutions. Following the 2008 'crash', the APA issued the following statement emphasising the importance of 'staying resilient' – and remaining politically inert – during 'tough economic times':

The current economic situation is a major stressor for eight out of ten Americans, according to a 2008 survey by the APA. With constant reminders from newspapers, television and the internet, it's hard to avoid the doom and gloom narrative about the economy... However, you can handle stress in positive ways and implement tactics to help you better manage and develop your resilience .... Maintain a hopeful outlook – *No one can reverse what has happened*. But by being resilient, you can change how you interpret and respond to events. (APA, 2009, emphasis added)

Thus, resilience is deployed to explain how families and individuals should respond to the collective instabilities and uncertainties engendered by neoliberal economics which are taken for 'granted as an immutable external force akin to the forces of nature' (MacKinnon and Driscoll Derickson, 2012: 261). In this sense, the dominant discourse on resilience demands, as Neocleous (2013: 7) asserts, 'acquiescence, not resistance'. Similar criticisms have been made by Harrison (2013: 99) who detects an 'overemphasis on the ability of those at the sharp end of economic downturns to "bounce back"': resilience is an 'ordinary magic' which people can, it is implied, conjure up when the welfare state is dismantled (Masten, 2001). Within this paradigm the role of professionals becomes merely one of exhorting and 'empowering' people to manage their own risks (O'Malley, 2010). This is conveyed, as mentioned, in a welter of popular self-help books advising people not only how to achieve their dreams, but also stressing that it is they who are entirely responsible for their present situation. As one of these books claims:

> You must recognize that *you alone* are the source of all the conditions and situations in your life. You must recognize that whatever your world looks like right now, *you alone* have caused it to look that way. The state of your health, your personal relationships, your professional life – all of it is *your* doing, yours and no one else. (Hernacki in Ehrenreich, 2006: 81–82, original emphases)

This leading narrative depoliticises and diverts responsibility away from those in power and from more structural considerations. Related to this dimension, there is a detectable gendered subtext to resilience talk since the 'cost' of resilience within families is often carried by women (Hozić and True, 2016). A report by the Liverpool Mental Health Consortium (2014: 27), on the impact of austerity, has its women respondents referring to 'sleeplessness, stress, anxiety, worry, depression, and feeling overwhelmed, isolated and suicidal'. Relatedly, what has been dubbed the 'new thrift' sub-textually appeals to the 'virtuous resilience of pre-feminist times' (Forkert, 2014: 42).

Whilst noting the different tendencies within the literature, resilience can still be interpreted as, at root, part of neoliberalism's hegemonic lexicon and socially corrosive rationality (see also the discussion on Gramsci in Chapter 2): integral to the mind-sets and practices that Keil (2009) identifies with 'roll-with-it' neoliberalisation. Indeed, writers aiming to situate resilience at the core of approaches to a range of social problems frequently make ideological assumptions about the role, and the purported incapacity, of the 'reformed' welfare state to intervene. The front cover of *Resilient Nation* (Edwards, 2009) baldly asserts: 'Next generation resilience relies on citizens and communities, not the institutions of state'. The trope of resilience can, of course, also be interpreted as a discursive element integral to the plans to 'reform' welfare (Harrison, 2013; see also Chapter 3). More recently, ideas associated with 'creativity' – often combined with 'thrift – have also been harnessed to this project. However, as Kirsten Forkert (2016: 11) observes, within the context of austerity 'creativity' is 'stripped of any oppositional or transgressive aspects' and is frequently used discursively to refer to the resilience and 'ingenuity of citizens to adapt and "problem-solve" in the face of cuts to the welfare state'.

Resilience research is mostly focused on trying to identify the core ingredients which, despite the erosion of the welfare state 'safety net', might enable individuals and families to adapt and cope inside of capital's turbulent circuits of economic and social reproduction. Here the ovreriding question is: how can human capital be safeguarded irrespective of the hardship and related forms of stress and pressure generated by regulated capital? (See, for example, Lundberg and Wuermli, 2012a; Wuermli et al., 2012). A European research consortium, exploring patterns of resilience during socioeconomic crises among households in Europe, illustrates the fixation with this question. Assuring readers that what are ambiguously termed 'European social ethics' will ensure that 'resilience is not an alternative, but a complement to the welfare state', the researchers suggest that 'what is intriguing is that ... some vulnerable households can be observed to be developing resilience by performing social, economic and cultural practices and habits that effectively protect them from greater suffering and provide sustainable patterns of coping and adaption, with less than expected or completely without welfare state interventions' (Institute for Employment Research and the Research Institute for Federal Employment Agency, 2014: 8; 7). The authors then go on to confide:

> Governments and welfare-state institutions are not the only mechanisms to provide safety nets against the impact of the socioeconomic crisis. Citizens, their families and households should not be treated as passive social agents who are exposed to unemployment and poverty ... At least some of them have access to materially useful assets and resources that have been developed over time, such as knowledge, social networks, strategies, habits and practices that save them from deprivation or reduce their exposure to socioeconomic hardship. Resilience of families and households depends on these accumulated resources. (Institute for Employment Research and the Research Institute for Federal Employment Agency, 2014: 7)

Indeed, within dominant theories of resilience it is possible to detect a 'valorisation of individuals as managers of their own risks' (O'Malley, 2010: 499). Within this paradigm, it is only those lacking the correct behavioural attitudes and competencies to maintain sufficient and robust stocks of appropriate human capital that will be targeted for intervention by a residual welfare state.

Within this framing, 'social security in the broadest sense of the term, is purely and simply to ensure non-exclusion with regard to an economic game' (Foucault, 2008: 202; see also Chapter 5). This relates to what Foucault (2008: 144) identifies as the 'individualization of social policy and individualization through social policy'. In the post-Second World War period, such a radical approach could not become wholly operative, because of political opposition associated with the strength of the labour movement and the post-war social democratic consensus, yet by the late 1970s, social policy increasingly tended to 'follow this programme, at least in those countries increasingly aligned with neoliberalism' (Foucault, 2008: 144). Developments in this area reflect, moreover, the short, prescient remarks which Foucault (2008) made on human capital – weeks before Thatcher came to power in the UK – in his spring lectures at the Collège de France in 1979. In what follows, therefore, the aim is to briefly explore this body of theory as it relates to contemporary ideas circulating around resilience.

RESILIENCE AND HUMAN CAPITAL

According to the early German proponents of neoliberalism, known as ordoliberals, a key function of social policy was actually to let inequality flourish. Articulating their perspective over the period from the 1930s into the 1950s, they argued that governments 'must not form a counterpoint or a screen … between society and economic processes' (Foucault, 2008: 145). Neither must governments 'correct the destructive effects of the market on society' (Foucault, 2008: 145). US supporters of neoliberalism shared this perception, but their thematic preoccupations were somewhat different. Importantly, one of their main interests was the theory of human capital which envisioned extending economic analysis and reasoning into domains ordinarily perceived to be non-economic (Foucault, 2008: 219; see also Adamson, 2009). This amounted, in fact, to the 'generalization of the market form throughout society'(McNay, 2009: 59).

In this context, Foucault stresses the significance of the US-based Theodore Schultz (1902–1998) and Gary Becker (1930–2014): both highly influential articulators of the idea that inequality and relentless competition characterises social life. Another key figure is James Heckman (1944–) whose ideas, as mentioned in the previous chapter on early intervention, so captivated Blair. According to their paradigm, explains Foucault (2008: 227), human capital is comprised of both 'innate' or 'hereditary' components and 'acquired' ones, with the latter relating more closely to our discussion on resilience.

'Acquired' capacities can be assembled during the period of a lifetime with individuals being perceived as 'abilities-machines' (Foucault, 2008: 229). Educational 'investments' are of the utmost significance. For example, the 'time parents devote to their children outside of simple educational activities' (2008: 229). More 'educated parents will form a higher human capital than parents with less education – in short, the set of cultural stimuli received by the child will all contribute to the formation of those elements which make up a human capital' (2008: 229). In terms of the formation of a child's human capital, what some refer to as 'proximal processes' occurring within the family are crucial (see for example, Wuermli et al., 2012: 48). In this context, Foucault also paid attention to the evolution of attachment relationships (see also the discussion on this theme in Chapter 6). According to his theorisation, US neoliberals were increasingly fascinated by

> how the mother–child relationship, concretely characterized by the time spent by the mother with the child, the quality of care she gives, the affection she shows, the vigilance with which she follows its development... all constitute...an investment which can be measured in time. (Foucault, 2008: 244)

Consequently, 'everything comprising ... the formative or educational relationship, in the widest sense of the term, between mother and child, can be analysed in terms of investment, capital costs, and profit – both economic and psychological profit – on the capital invested' (Foucault, 2008: 244). Those promoting this form of analysis were, he argues, interested in a 'whole environmental analysis' of a child's life which might enable them to 'calculate, and to a certain extent to quantify, or at any rate measure...the possibilities of investment in human capital' (2008: 230).

As Wendy Brown (2015: 38) asserts, a direct consequence of applying such assumptions is that the social world becomes saturated in an ethos of radical inequality:

> When figured as human capital in all that we do and in every venue, equality ceases to be presumed natural in relation to one another...In legislation, jurisprudence, and the popular imaginary, inequality becomes normal, even normative. A democracy composed of human capital features winners and losers, not equal treatment or equal protection.

Foucault's own genealogy of neoliberalism is ambiguous and lacks political clarity, but it is important to spend a little while summarising his remarks because the focal questions he identifies these neoliberals as posing are ones also posed by those supporting the idea that resilience-based thinking has to be central to social and public policy. For example, what in the 'child's family life will produce human capital? What type of stimuli, form of life, and relationship with parents, adults and others can be crystallised into human capital?' (Foucault, 2008: 230). These questions are also, of course, implicit in the discourse on early intervention examined in Chapter 6. Clearly, when Foucault delivered his Paris lectures he was unable to predict the rise and subsequent dominance of neoliberalism. Neither was he able to foresee the subsequent scale of the assaults on the welfare state associated with the neoliberal project. However, his comments on human capital certainly take on a resonant aptness in the first quarter of the twenty-first century.

A few years after the unfolding of the financial 'crash' commencing in 2007, the World Bank published an edited collection titled *Child and Youth in Crisis: Protecting and Promoting Human Development in Times of Economic Shocks*. The chief concern of the contributors was 'how best to protect the most vulnerable from lasting harm and the degradation of human capital' (Lundberg and Wuermli, 2012b: 4).

What can families do to withstand 'shocks' to 'human capital development'? (Lundberg and Wuermli, 2012b: 4). Potentially, readers are advised, the answer can be found in creating a 'comprehensive framework for analyzing the impact of aggregate economic shocks on human development during the critical formative years of a young person's life, between conception and about 25 years' (Wuermli et al., 2012: 29). Moreover, a 'crisis can cause families and societies to underinvest in human capital, leading to lower growth' (Wuermli et al., 2012: 41).

This 'comprehensive framework' pivots on the importance of individual and family resilience and strains to fuse the perspective of Becker, Schultz and other rational choice theorists with that of Urie Bronfenbrenner (1917–2005) and his ecological systems theory or bioecological model of child development (Wuermli et al., 2012: 48). Both areas of theorisation, maintains this World Bank publication, have gaps which the other can fill in order to arrive at a more rounded comprehension as to how to deal with economic 'shocks'. Capitalism is presented as a 'given' and there is a tendency to refer to generic titles – 'economists', 'policy makers', the 'global development community' – implying a unity of approaches, interests and politics within such diverse fields. However, the volume clearly merits exploration because it furnishes a good contemporary illustration of the relevance of Foucault's understanding of how human capital theorisation gels with, and helps to constitute, neoliberal rationality.

It is, for example, asserted that a family will ordinarily seek to 'enhance the human capital of its members' and can be regarded as the prime 'investor' in relation to their child or children (Wuermli et al., 2012: 38). The decision 'on how much to invest is based on their expectations of the net returns to the investments' (2012: 38). Such 'investments' include 'education (whether from formal schooling, training, work experience, or on-the-job learning), physical and mental health, personality, and psychological states, and social relations' (2012: 39).

Conceding that the literature derived from economics reductively focuses mainly on formal education and training, the contributors claim that the research associated with ecological systems theory is more attentive to spheres beyond the school. It is also recognised that the rational choice economic model is insufficient because it fails to incorporate and emphasise the importance of interactions at multiple levels (micro, meso, macro and chrono) stressed in the bioecological model. Consequently, the aim should be to integrate this within a more context-sensitive framework acknowledging the importance of, for example, 'proximal processes' (Wuermli et al., 2012: 48). Considered one of the 'driving forces of development', such processes include regular face-to-face interactions over extended periods of time with people, objects, or symbols, which promote the realization of the genetic potential for effective biological, psychological, and social development' (2012: 48). Although often 'neglected' by 'economists', child and youth development is a process bound up with 'an intricate mesh of interacting systems, actors, and processes, embedded in contexts' (Lundberg and Wuermli, 2012b: 9). Again echoing some of Foucault's comments in his Collège de France lectures, emphasis is also given to the 'effects of attachment-related issues' pertaining to 'early infancy' (Lundberg and Wuermli, 2012b: 8; see also Harms, 2015, Ch. 5). Relatedly, the World Bank publication is attuned to the significance of the 'life-course' perspective which the authors connect to Bronfenbrenner's theorisation of the chronosystem.

Similar to the European research consortium report discussed earlier, this approach does not seek to eliminate the role of the state. Indeed, the state is often the engine orchestrating the introduction of resilience into the 'social body or social fabric' (Foucault, 2008: 241). As mentioned, this is occurring in terms of the plethora of programmes being introduced into miltary and school institutions. Significantly, however, the welfare role of the state begins to alter in terms of *how* it intervenes in the lives of families. As the World Bank collection makes clear, the focus is on 'targeting' and 'monitoring' particular segments or slices of the population, with particular reference to selective 'preventative targeting' focused on indicators such as 'high-risk' neighbourhoods or 'high-risk single mothers' (Wuermli et al., 2012: 83–4). Ideally, within the neoliberal rubric, even these interventions will be undertaken by private, often for-profit organisations, which are merely subject to quality control by the slimmed down welfare state.

REMAKING RESILIENCE?

> I get knocked down
> But I get up again
> You're never gonna keep me down
> I get knocked down
> But I get up again
> You're never gonna keep me down
>
>   (Tubthumping by Chumbawamba, 1997)

The dominant and evolving resilience paradigm is a complex amalgam fusing parts of human capital theory, ecological systems theory, positive psychology and an expansionist military logic: each of which are marinated in neoliberal rationality. Yet, one may ask, can this capacity to 'get up again' be imbued with some of the anarcho-punk spirit of Chumbawamba's lyrics above? More theoretically, is it possible to shape a counter-hegemonic form of resilience potentially capable of destabilising and displacing dominant neoliberal accounts and narratives? While there may seem to be little scope for reworking the concept, on account of its prime focus on individual agency within 'given' social and political structures, some maintain that resilience can, in fact, be cast in more progressive terms and re-routed in the direction of a more critical theory and practice (see also Chapter 10).

The social geographers Danny MacKinnon and Kate Driscoll Derickson (2012: 254) note that the resilience concept could potentially be employed to 'frame particular forms of activism, some of which are anti-capitalist in nature'. However, in tune with the discussion in this chapter, they are unconvinced such a framing is beneficial because of the clearly 'normative political yearnings' underpinning resilience talk (2012: 255). The whole idea of resilience 'derived from ecology and systems theory, is conservative when applied to the social sphere' in that it 'privileges established social structures' largely shaped by unequal power relations and injustice. It 'also closes off wider questions of progressive social change which require interference with, and transformation of, established "systems"' (2012: 254). Mostly 'externally defined by state agencies and expert knowledge', resilience discourse is more likely to 'reproduce the wider social and spatial relations that generate turbulence and inequality' (2012: 254). Not entirely convincingly, they suggest that 'resourcefulness' is an alternative framing perhaps better able to 'animate politics and activism that seek to transform social relations in more progressive, anti-capitalist and socially just ways' (2012: 255). According to this perspective, resourcefulness couples attributes of tenacious durability with inadequate resourcing and is situated within an ethic more alert to structural, political economic considerations. Unlike resilience, resourcefulness aspires, they maintain, to deal directly with inequality and failures to ensure that groups and communities have 'parity of participation' in decisions impacting on them (Fraser, 2000; see also Chapter 5). In this way, resourcefulness stresses forms of learning and mobilisations based, not on 'expert' accounts, but on 'local priorities and needs as identified and developed by community activists' themselves (2012: 263).

Approaching resilience from a different direction, some of the literature exclusively focused on Israel/Palestine is suggestive of approaches more likely to destabilise extant power relations. In this context, a number of researchers focus on the Palestinian notion of *Sumūd* conceived as a practice of everyday, non-violent resistance to Israeli occupation and aggression (see, for example, Richter-Devroe, 2011; Johansson and Vinthagen, 2015). *Sumūd*, 'literally persistence or steadfastness, is a term often used to describe a type of inner strength or hardiness of Palestinians to confront and live through the extreme conditions' (Johansson and Vinthagen, 2015: 110). The word, and the practice, emerged within the Palestinian community in the 1970s and 1980s and it politically emphasises the importance of maintaining a presence on the land and seeking to retain distinctive cultural tradition, despite Israeli policies of ethnic cleansing (Morris, 2004).

CONCLUSION

In contrast to these more critically nuanced inflections of resilience, this chapter has mainly dwelt on the dominant, doxic paradigm which seems to leave little leeway to enable such a re-crafting. Indeed, resilience appears to be an 'inducement to putting up with precarity and inequality and accepting the deferral of demands for change'. Hence, resilience talk can be interpreted as rooted in a more pervasive, omnipresent and evolving programme of neoliberal economic and cultural transformation (Diprose, 2014–15: 45).

Perhaps also, at the core of the resilience talk lies a palpable tension – an oscillation between the optimistic and pessimistic: individuals and families, armed with an appropriate supply of human capital, have the means to become 'better' neoliberal subjects, but the wider context may become, as in the post-apocalyptic film *The Road* (2009), more cataclysmically blighted, irredeemably and irrevocably worse. In short, perhaps a latent catastrophism shadows the more 'positive' aspects of resilience (see also Reid, 2016).

Within the framework, as observed, the notion of human capital features prominently. The next chapter will move, however, from capital to care. Less of a buzzword than resilience, care is also a welfare word subject to an array of different interpretations within the economic and cultural fabric of neoliberalism.

REFLECTION AND TALK BOX 7

1. There is, suggest Kathryn Ecclestone and Lydia Lewis (2014: 196), acceptance that the state should 'sponsor initiatives to develop individuals' and communities' resilience' given that that the theme now 'permeates the policy arenas of compulsory schooling, adult community education, child and family welfare, physical and mental health'. Do you detect this permeation? If you are a practitioner, does the notion of resilience impact on and change your day-to-day work?

2. What do you see as the main threads linking early intervention (Chapter 6) and resilience?

3. In the World Bank report discussed earlier, Lundberg and Wuermli (2012b: 3) argue that:

    > Human capital accumulation at all stages—from the antenatal environment through early childhood and adolescence—helps facilitate the transition to a healthy and productive adulthood and break the intergenerational transmission of poverty. Shortfalls or setbacks at any stage of the life course may have severe consequences for individual development as well as for the growth and development of successful communities.

    Why is human capital – its acquiring, safeguarding and multiplying – so centrally located within resilience talk?

FURTHER READING

Sarah Mohaupt (2009) provides a concise overview of the resilience literature and some of the key ideas associated with the concept. The article by Mark Neocleous (2013) in *Radical Philosophy* is a pithy and robust critique. Given its multidisciplinary orientation, the Taylor and Francis published journal *Resilience*, introduced in 2103, may also be a useful resource. Resilience is a focal word across a number of theoretical and practice spheres and Kathryn Ecclestone and Lydia Lewis (2014) have furnished a good exploration of what is occuring within educational settings in the UK. Alison Howell (2015) contributes a fascinating account of resilience in the context of the US military. As noted elsewhere, many of the welfare words examined in this book are founded on dominant gender constructs and Elizabeth Harrison (2013) and Dorothy Bottrell (2009) explore this dimension in their empirical work on resilience, respectively in England and Australia.

CHAPTER 8

CARE

Caring – Compassionate, concerned; *spec.* with reference to professional social work, care of the sick or elderly, etc. (*Oxford English Dictionary*)

INTRODUCTION

The journalist, Madeleine Bunting (2016: 23) avows that care, the verb from which the adjective caring is derived, is

> a small word, so pervasive and overloaded with meanings that its significance has often been easy to overlook. It's the care given by parents that nurtures us into adulthood, and it's the care given by others that supports us in old age and as we die; and in-between, care is the oft overlooked scaffolding of our lives, on which wellbeing and daily life depend.

Although in recent years there may have been more attempts to lay down what exactly constitutes good care, care remains 'notoriously hard to define, measure and secure' (Lewis and West, 2014: 2). Stretching this reasoning a little further, it it is impossible to confine measures pertaining to the quality of care to the 'efficient and able performance of tasks' because the 'rationality of care is other orientated, defying bureaucratic rationality' (2014: 3). It is, for example, very difficult to comprehensively codify when it is appropriate for a social worker to touch a client (Lynch and Garrett, 2010). Nevertheless, in the early 1990s, and specifically in relation to social work with children and families, the influential and deeply ideological 'looking after children' (LAC) materials officially endeavoured to create an expansive scheme to identify precisely how the care of children should be constituted (Parker et al., 1991; Ward, 1995; Garrett, 2003; see also Chapter 3)[1]. Similar moves have been made across other sectors to try to formulate what constitutes good care practices. Bad care, harmful care, hurtful care is much more palpable especially when it teeters into its antonym – abuse. However, even here, there are ambiguities and child care case law, for example, reflects the scope of deliberations on this issue.

Care is central within a range of discourses impinging on social work and social policy in connection, for example, to the evolution of community care, the long-term care of the increasing proportions of older people, the treatment of children and young people in the public care system and debates about the recognition of unpaid carers. Furthermore, 'self-care', a notion so prominent within social work and simi-lar 'caring' professions, is often mobilised to help deepen 'neoliberal objectives to dismantle public welfare resources and shift responsibility for care onto individual citizens' (L. Ward, 2015: 45; see also Farris, 2012; Muehlebach, 2012). All these issues and themes focus, to differing degrees, 'on what care means, its uses and abuses, what it costs, how it is supported, how it is delivered, and by whom' (Williams, 2005: 471). Underpinning a range of these issues are complex factors, and more abstract considerations related to the use of time and who is empowered to organise its distribution across a multiplicity of, what I will term, 'carescapes'.

As will be discussed later, contemporary theoretical engagements recognize that care requirements stretch across a person's lifecourse and caring arrangements are fluid and complex: a 'carer one day may be a care recipient the next. Care may also be reciprocal and interdependent rather than one way' (Phillips, 2007: see also Barnes, 2015). This alertness to the shifting nature of caring relationships is resistant to rigid classifications of carer/cared for and might also be more theoretically inter-preted as gelling with a Rancièrean aspiration to subvert the stultifying and static categorisations, and *fixing* practices, frequently integral to 'police' orders (see also Chapter 2).

Care, not unlike other welfare words, shifts in meaning across time:

> Whereas care in the late twentieth century was associated with the 'welfare' or 'support' of a person, or a 'liking of' or a 'responsibility to' a person, in the past it had more negative associations. In Anglo-Saxon the meaning of the word was sorrow, anxiety, burden or concern. (Phillips, 2007: 14)

As John Harris (2002: 267) pointed out during the period of New Labour, any analysis of care policy and care practices has to be attentive to how these are politically and economically articulated within particular 'welfare regimes'. The post-war social democratic state, despite its flaws and normative gendered fram-ing, was rooted in notions of 'community and collectivism' (2002: 270; see also Chapter 1). In contrast, during the years of Conservative rule in the 1980s and 1990s, a neoliberal emphasis was placed on 'self-responsibility and self-reliance', virtues implying that only 'people who could take care of themselves could be proud of themselves' (2002: 271). The evolution of policy meshed with an array of 'reforms' introducing quasi markets into the health sector, social work and social care services. Subsequent UK governments have not attempted to reverse these trends. Discursive shifts have become embedded with home care, rather like pizzas, now invariably 'delivered' in 'packages'.

During the 1990s, carers became more central within care policy in the UK with the Carers (Recognition and Services) Act 1995 (implemented in July 1996) enabling them, under section 1 of the legislation, to request that local authorities make a separate assessment of their 'ability to provide and continue to provide care' (in Harris, 2002: 274). This development has been interpreted as reflecting the growing strength of the carers' lobby and, in part, a policy development to be welcomed. The 2001 Census revealed, in fact, that there were 5.2 million people providing informal care in England and Wales (in Lloyd, 2006). However, some commentators note how the evolving policy visibility of carers fits with the aspiration to 'roll-back' or reconfigure state services. The 'often-quoted slogan of carers' organizations that carers save the economy £57 billion a year highlights the importance of carers to the national economy and asserts a moral case for greater attention' (Lloyd, 2006: 952). More recent figures indicate that there are now over 6 million carers (mainly women), in the UK providing unpaid labour with a contribution producing exchequer savings of £119 billion per year (in Skeggs, 2014: 11). Without this 'gift of free caring labour' by the millions of unpaid carers, 'capital would have significant problems and costs reproducing, servicing and sustaining the future, present and ex-workforce' (Skeggs, 2014: 12).

Our personal understanding, feelings and expectations about care will also be deeply rooted in our biographical experience, upbringing and what Bourdieu terms 'habitus' (see also Chapter 2). Crucial here, of course, is the issue of gender and, tellingly, most of the references in this chapter will be to the work of female scholars. The Dutch feminist Selma Sevenhuijsen observed, in the late-1990s, that policy developments in her homeland draw upon a 'silent logic of the "natural" provision of care within family and kinship networks, where it is self-evident that it will be women, rather than men, who, whenever the need arises, care spontaneously for others' (in Hughes et al., 2005: 265). Such assumptions 'remain remarkably robust across a variety of cultures' (in Hughes et al., 2005: 265). What is more, the gendered dimension central to processes of neoliberalism have, if not always explicitly but surreptitiously, further embedded the gendered relations of care and carework. That is to say, it is women who

> disproportionately remain the invisible infrastructure for all developing, mature, and worn-out human capital – children, adults, disabled and elderly. Generally uncoerced, yet essential, this provision and responsibility get theoretically and ideologically tucked into what are assumed as preferences issuing naturally from sexual difference, especially from women's distinctive contribution to biological reproduction. It is formulated, in short, as an effect of nature, not of power. (Brown, 2015: 105)

It might be countered that this set of circumstances predates the evolution of neoliberal rationality and was woven into the fabric of social democracy and welfare capitalism. However, neoliberalism serves to intensify these manifestly gendered arrangements because of the 'shrinking, privatization, and/or dismantling of public infrastructure supporting families, children and retirees' (2015: 105).

This chapter is a little different to earlier chapters in that the main focus is on definitions and debates around this welfare word which have not always been instigated and generated in a top-down way by primary definers. Instead, we will dwell more on those who have contested dominant understandings and hegemonic meanings to try to arrive at new paradigms. The first section of the chapter will concentrate on feminist ethics of care. Since the 1980s, in fact, there has evolved a vast feminist literature on care and the present survey does not purport to be either comprehensive or exhaustive since it can, of course, only signal some of the main issues and debates. Some of this theorisation found its way into the academic literature of social work with writers attempting to apply some of the core conceptualisations in relation to practice in general (Clifford, 2002), and more specifically to working with older people (Ash, 2010), those with learning difficulties (N. Ward, 2015) or, less frequently, with children and families (Cockburn, 2005; Holland, 2010).

The second section refers to the fact that the feminist ethic of care sits uneasily with aspects of the theorisation of the disability movement (Hughes et al., 2005). This will be followed by a short section on care as 'bodywork', with Tangenberg and Kemp (2002: 9) suggesting, for example, that in its 'theoretical and practice framework social work pays little attention to the body'. Similarly, it has been argued that the corporal is insufficiently encompassed in most of the literature associated with feminist care ethics given that this tends to dwell more on the affective aspects of the care relationships than the material ones (see also Wolkowitz, 2002; Cohen, 2011).

The fourth part of the chapter focuses on a somewhat different approach to this welfare word and situates what is occurring to care practices within a framework emphasising political economy. Hence, the prime focus is on how neoliberal managerialism is adversely impacting on the jobs of those employed as care workers. Here, one of the chief concerns is to illuminate that the labour process, associated with a multiplicity of care roles and tasks, is becoming more fragmented, more surveilled and riper for even greater exploitation. Despite its potentially beneficial impact, technology is apt to render the work arid, when its deployment is driven by the imperative to extract more surplus value from the hard-pressed caring workforce (Taylor, 2014). Using a broadly Marxist optic, the contributions of Canadian academic, Donna Baines, are significant in this regard highlighting the 'prevailing social order's systematic tendency to create unsatisfying work' (Bellamy Foster, 1998: ix). This perspective is at odds with the implicitly reformist logic of the feminist ethic of care which implies that a change in values might bring about transformative impact *within* the social and economic fabric of capitalism.

Angie Ash (2010: 206) ponders why it is that some people living in – what are paradoxically referred to as – care homes are 'destined to die in a place' where staff swear in front of them. More generally, a litany of reports and inquiries published across decades expose a 'shameful absence of care' (Lewis and West, 2014: 2). Indeed, it can often seem that this particular welfare word is strategically deployed to mask or shield what are, for residents, or patients, abusive realities (McCann, 2014). With 35,810 allegations of abuse investigated by English councils in 2013–14, almost 100 every day (Brindle, 2014), it is unsurprising that the prospect of moving to a care home frightens 'two-thirds of Britons' (ICM poll cited in Carvel, 2007).

The final section of the chapter, drawing on Wardhaugh and Wilding's (1993) classic discussion, refers therefore to the 'corruption of care' within institutional settings. Published a quarter-of-a-century ago, their article still contains significant messages helping to illuminate why care practices may become degraded and abusive.

FEMINIST CARE ETHICS

In the 1970s, research often perceived 'informal care' as a form of oppressed labour with female carers accorded little recognition or financial support from the patriarchal state (Williams, 2005; see also Finch and Groves, 1983). During the following decade shifts occurred within the feminist literature with Williams identifying a move against the idea that women were simply 'victims' having the burden of care foisted on them. Instead, women's commitment to caring should be celebrated and interpreted as evidence of the essence of a 'woman-centred culture' (Williams, 2005: 475). Within this paradigm, caring was not to be misinterpreted as unwanted labour reluctant women were compelled to undertake, it was a distinctive facet and attribute of women's lives.

Influential here was the work of the US feminist and psychologist Carol Gilligan and, particularly, her *In a Different Voice,* published at the beginning of the 1980s. Gilligan asserts that women and men think and act differently with the norms of the latter more likely to circulate around an ethic of justice. In contrast, sensitivity to the 'needs of others and the assumption of responsibility for taking care lead women to attend to voices other than their own and to include in their judgment other points of view' (Gilligan, 1982: 16). An 'overriding concern with relationships and responsibilities' is 'inseparable from women's moral strength' (1982: 16–17). Associated with this analysis is the assertion that men take for granted the caring roles women undertake. Alternatively, they are keen to marginalise and misrecognise what is occurring.

Gilligan's contribution remains significant and can be related to the work of those, such as Kathleen Lynch (2010), who have analysed the 'carelessness' characterising neoliberal and gendered institutions such as Irish universities. Unsurprisingly, however, given facets of her theorisation, Gilligan has also been vulnerable to accusations of essentialism since her perspective is 'almost entirely gender-focused' and 'with some exceptions, towards an undifferentiated category of womanhood' (Williams, 2005: 476). Similar criticisms were directed at the work of Nel Noddings (1984) whose *Caring: A Feminine Approach to Ethics and Moral Education* was published in the mid-1980s. According to the US ethicist the mother–child relationship is the central and paradigmatic care relationship. Many feminist critics were alert to how this understanding seems to construct care as merely residing in a 'private relationship between two individuals, one of whom occupies a powerful position vis-à-vis the other', was overly narrow and delimiting (Barnes, 2015: 32; see also Beasley and Bacchi, 2007). What is more, not every carer or potential carer is a mother and so not everyone is able to develop the capacity to 'care through the practice of caring for a vulnerable infant' within the affective perimeters of a mother–child relationship (Barnes, 2015: 32). Relatedly, it is important to understand that care takes place 'beyond dyadic relationships within which relationships between those identified as care givers and care receivers are embedded' (2015: 35). In this sense, networks – perhaps wider families or organisations – are significant. More fundamentally, the early care ethics contributions of writers such as Noddings failed to embrace a more political and structural account of the contexts in which caring evolves.

Still within the parameters of feminism, a 'second-generation' of care ethicists (Beasley and Bacchi, 2007) emerged in the 1990s, paying renewed attention to the complexities of caring as a social practice. Research began, for example, to better acknowledge and recognise the role of disabled people as active carers and children as carers. Analyses took note of the different sites of care lying outside the conventional nuclear family (Williams, 2005). Moreover, questions pertaining to 'race' and caring began to feature in the literature (Forbat, 2004). As will be discussed later, there was also an acknowledgement of how various forms of caring stretched across and *beyond* the container of the nation-state. More broadly, these developments in feminist ethics were rooted in a belief that greater sensitivity in the area of care practices might 'impact on the way we think about politics and the way political decisions are reached' (Barnes et al., 2015: 5). For example, Selma Sevenhuijsen (1998), and others, emphasised how an ethics of care is a vital element of citizenship.

Relevant here is the work of the US political scientist Joan Tronto (1993) and what has been described as her 'ground-breaking' *Moral Boundaries: A Political Argument for an Ethic of Care* published in the early 1990s (Barnes et al., 2015: 3). Tronto (2010: 159) charges that 'while we can turn to family life to intuit some key elements of good care, to provide good care in an institutional context requires that we make explicit certain elements of care that go unspoken and that we take for granted in the family setting'. She is also keen to identify that 'family care rests upon clearly understood lines of *power* and obligation' (2010: 161, original emphasis). Hence, there should be wariness about becoming 'too nostalgic' for the arrangements of the past given this could result in the construction of an ethical framework founded upon misleading and 'sentimental views of the family' (2010: 61–62).

According to Tronto, providing care is not simply a concern of women or an activity undertaken, on a paid basis, by those often subject to exploitative forms of labour. For her, receiving care is a marker of our existential vulnerability and is defined as an:

> activity that includes everything that we do to maintain, continue, and repair our 'world' so that we can live in it as well as possible. That world includes our bodies, our selves, and our environment, all of which we seek to interweave in a complex, life-sustaining web. (Fisher and Tronto in Tronto, 2010: 160)

Caring is delineated as being comprised of four elements or qualities: *attentiveness* to the needs of others; a sense of *responsibility* beyond proscribed rules and duties; *competence* in the provision of care; *responsiveness* to the vulnerability of care receivers. Tronto also differentiates between four phases of activity in which these qualities come into play: caring about, taking care of, care giving and care receiving. What is more, 'conflict, power relations, inconsistencies, and competing purposes and divergent ideas about good care could affect care processes' (Tronto, 2010: 160). For example, the care 'deficit' present in the wealthy countries of the global north is simply being passed 'down the line and into other states' (Tronto, 2015: 21).

Etched into the theorisation of revolutionary Marxists such as Rosa Luxemburg (1871–1919) was a belief that capitalism is only able to reproduce itself because of its 'capacity to globalize exploitation' (Federici, 2004: 17). Indeed, since the turn of the new century, perhaps one of the main departures in terms of feminist care ethics has been a recognition of the global patterning of care practices (Robinson, 2006; Barnes et al., 2015) and the need to 'transcend' national frameworks (Tronto, 2015: 21). As well as

> diminishing public provision and recruiting women into waged work, financialized capitalism has reduced real wages, thus raising the number of hours of paid work per household needed to support a family and prompting a desperate scramble to transfer carework to others. To fill the 'care gap', the regime imports migrant workers from poorer to richer countries ... This scenario fits the gendered strategies of cash-strapped, indebted postcolonial states subjected to IMF structural adjustment programmes. Desperate for hard currency, some of them have actively promoted women's emigration to perform paid carework abroad for the sake of remittances. (Fraser, 2016: 114)

Migrant workers, primarily female but also male, increasingly help wealthier nations address what is frequently termed the 'crisis in care' (Muehlebach, 2012: Ch. 7;

see also Robinson, 1999; Bunting, 2005). These workers, frequently vilified in anti-immigration discourses, primarily emanate from those parts of the 'world where there is a need for cash to those parts of the world where there is a demand for caregivers and a willingness to pay for their services' (Kittay, 2014: 62). In the UK, this dimension has come to the fore following the Brexit vote on 23 June 2016:

> Potential changes to immigration policy post-Brexit could have serious consequences for the social care workforce unless the necessary work is done now to mitigate any risks. Around 1 in 20 (6%) of England's growing social care workforce are European Economic Area (EEA) migrants, equating to around 84,000 people. (*Independent Age*, 2016: 2)

Some authors lay emphasis on the complicated sense of agency exercised by migrant workers and are reluctant to perceive them as merely the victims of global processes of dispossession and dislocation (Christensen and Guldvik, 2014). Those looking favourably on the workings of the market also perceive neoliberal globalism as making available new and potentially beneficial choices. Such a perception is often wedded to the notion that the remittances that migrants send home aid the economies and wellbeing of the families left behind: for example, remittances to the West African country of Liberia amount to a staggering 18.5% of its GDP (Legrain, 2016: 7). Others are, however, less sanguine, with Barnes et al. (2015: 6) referring to the 'care deficits' left behind when migrants leave their homelands.

Related to the recognition of how the dynamics of care provision is now more likely to traverse the boundaries of particular states is an acknowledgement that a carer does not necessarily have to be 'physically present for the care receiver' (Barnes, 2015: 34). For example, Italy and Spain are two European countries with a high proportion of elderly carework being undertaken by immigrant women (Muehlebach, 2012: Ch. 7). Whilst such women will clearly be providing proximate services to these older people, it does not mean their caring for their own children and for other family members, perhaps remaining in their countries of origin, has been extinguished. Despite a lack of bodily tending and touching, other forms of care for those remaining at 'home' are still likely to be provided. Although such care may be provided at a distance and not 'hands-on' it can still, to some extent, be undertaken using modern communication technologies.

RE-ARTICULATING 'CARE' AS 'ASSISTANCE', 'HELP' AND 'SUPPORT'

Marked differences exist in how 'feminist scholars' and 'disability activists' regard care and caring (Hughes et al., 2005: 260). Clearly there is a need to be sensitive to the fact that these categories are not tidy and separable groups and that, for example, a 'feminist scholar' might also be a 'disability activist'. Nevertheless, the tensions and conflicts that Bill Hughes and his colleagues identify do prompt further deliberation on fundamental issues circulating around care and highlight the fact that this welfare word is subject to conflicting perceptions and interpretations (see also Lloyd, 2001).

The main contention is that with 'feminist scholars' the emphasis is laid on 'the giver of care (usually female)', whilst for 'disabled activists' and others located within the field of 'disability studies', it is the 'recipient of care (male or female)' who is the chief concern (Hughes et al., 2005: 260). Hughes et al. (2005: 260) summarise the differing positions by arguing there is a:

> tendency in feminist thought to valorize the caring relationship for its potential to symbolize and be the very embodiment of genuine intimacy and reciprocity that cannot find expression in a society dominated by the male imaginary. For the Disabled People's Movement (DPM), care is often demonized and its organization is regularly represented as a significant barrier to the emancipation and independence of disabled people.

Hence, the DPM in the UK has 'dropped the discourse of care' preferring terms such as 'personal assistance, help or support'. It also 'dislodges gender critique' in that where feminists see 'care in terms of its role in the making of men and women, disability activists see it primarily in terms of the infantalization and disempowerment of disabled people' (Hughes et al., 2005: 261).

Although care 'as a concept is waterlogged with benign and pastoral connotations', the DPM 'drawing on the practical experience of disabled people...has seen into its darker heart' (Hughes et al., 2005: 262; see also Shakespeare, 1997; 2000). Hence, care and caring is perceived, often through a Foucauldian lens, as complicit in modalities of domination and discipline with micro-technologies of power and persuasion, operating through powerful social work and associated discourses, constituting 'the disabled body as dependent, burdensome, incapable, tragic and repulsive and the carer as charitable, altruistic, stalwart, saintly and dependable' (Hughes et al., 2005: 268).

However, the DPM is criticised for its 'pragmatic and materialist interpretation of care that is commensurate with its masculinist ethic and idealises masculinist notions of autonomy' (Hughes et al., 2005: 263). Hence, there is an emphasis on disabled people being better able to use direct payments to restore agency to purchase the services of Personal Assistants (PAs). This mechanism, according to this reasoning, enables the disabled person to exercise agency and creates more choice. Consequently, 'as "master" of "his" own destiny, and with PA at "his" command, the disabled person is able to acquire control over many of the mundane but vitally important aspects of everyday existence which, hitherto, were delivered, if at all, to a timetable that suited the "carer"' (Hughes et al., 2005: 263). Within this paradigm, therefore, the terminology of 'carer' and 'cared for' is eliminated in so far as the latter becomes the 'employer' and the 'carer' the employee.

As a model of care valorising formal contractual relationships, the DPM's approach is starkly at odds with the ethics of care articulated by feminists since the 1980s. Arguably and perhaps unwittingly, it appears, instead, to chime with central tenets of the neoliberal agenda. Hughes and his colleagues are scathing in their critique, maintaining that the DPM and the 'male protagonists', constituting its leaders, are 'trying to put some hair back on the chests of the poor unfortunates who have been confined in feminized spaces' (Hughes et al., 2005: 268). The DPM strategy is also considered to be 'wrong-headed' because transforming 'care into Personal Assistance means buying into the logocentric and patriarchal heritage of the enlightenment' (Hughes et al., 2005: 268). What is needed, they assert, is a willingness to make common cause with carers and this is inseparable from recognising that the 'cared for' and 'carer' relationship is assembled, constituted and maintained in more complex ways than the DPM allows for.

Whilst some of the criticisms levelled at the 'transformation of care into cold contract' by 'malestream disability studies' are certainly persuasive (Hughes et al., 2005: 269; 270), Hughes et al. arguably fail to adequately incorporate a rounded understanding as to how neoliberal economics function to structure policy, practice and relationships. This dimension is turned to, toward the end of the chapter, by looking at contributions informed by labour process theory focusing on the erosion of care. First, however, the significance of the body and bodywork will be briefly discussed. This crucial material aspect of care is, it has been contended, frequently neglected by the literature which tends to concentrate more on the 'social, emotional and interpersonal' facets of caring (Twigg, 2000: 394).

CAREWORK AS BODYWORK

The carework central in areas such as community care has been conceptualised and analysed in ways that simply 'neglect its nature as "bodywork"' (Twigg, 2000: 389). Evoking images of sculpted gym-goers glistening with sweat, 'bodywork' has tended to be equated with work undertaken on one's own body to maintain or enhance personal attractiveness, health and wellbeing. Twigg (2000: 389), however, suggests that 'carework' can also be conceived and interpreted as a form of 'bodywork'. This argument is echoed by Rachel Lara Cohen (2011: 189) in her observation that 'since health and social care services require workers to work on, with and sometimes inside the bodies of others, bodies are both the object of labour and the material of production'.

In the final decades of the twentieth century, a new sociology of the body began to evolve and this was reflected in the founding of a journal entirely devoted to the theme, *Body & Society*, in 1995. Nevertheless, the focus of scholarly interest in this new sub-discipline was predominantly on the body as a 'site of consumption and pleasure' with sociologists' gaze drifting towards young, sexy bodies (Twigg, 2000: 393). Twigg, however, suggests that this orientation fails to adequately analyse the body integral to carework – the body which is frequently impaired, decaying, subject to pain and requiring aid and assistance. Writing in 2000, and seeking to explain why the body is occluded in discourses on care, she contends that a range of factors operate as obstacles. Turning to the health sector, she persuasively suggested that the dominant discipline within the field – medicine – deals with the body in a 'particular and circumscribed way, constructing it in terms of the object body of science, distant and depersonalised' (2000: 389–90). Medical practice actually limits involvement with the body with 'professional status' being 'marked out in terms of distance from the bodily' (2000: 390).

Nursing is organised hierarchically and as 'staff progress, they move away from the basic bodywork of bedpans and sponge baths towards high-tech, skilled interventions; progressing from dirty work on bodies to clean work on machines' (2000: 390). A new emphasis on the 'psychological dimensions of the patient' and an emerging tendency to 'academicise nursing' might also indicate a 'further flight from the bodily in pursuit of higher status forms of knowledge and practice' (2000: 390). Specifically within the field of social gerontology, there is a 'desire to combat an excessive focus on the body and its decline' (2000: 392). This has, perhaps, become more embedded given the frequent contemporary focus on 'active aging' (Muehlebach, 2012).

However, the failure of the academic and policy literature to evoke the 'front-line realities' in areas such as community care could also be connected to the ascendancy of neoliberal managerialism. Twigg (2000: 392) charges that

> Managerialist discourse is itself notably disembodied, drawing on traditions like economics, accountancy, organisation and methods that prize abstraction and emotional distance. The body has little place in these analyses; indeed it represents just those qualities of embedded, messy, concreteness that such forms of analysis aim to transcend.

NEOLIBERAL LABOUR CARE PROCESSES

Earlier in the chapter, reference was made to the work of Joan Tronto who maintains that one of the chief characteristics of good care is attentiveness and that a skilful carer will always be alert to the particular and changing needs of the cared for. Whilst not seeking to deny the importance of attentiveness, writers utilising a labour process theory perspective maintain that attentiveness needs to be situated within a more encompassing analytical framework incorporating the wider political economy. Irrespective of their ethical commitments and aspirations to provide a good service, many paid care workers have their ability to be attentive diluted due to the intensified pace of work, forcing them 'to rush and quietly neglect service users' (Baines and Van Den Broek, 2016: 13).

Neoliberal policy and practice in this area relentlessly aspires to re-order the temporal world of care workers and to forcefully instil quicker performance rhythms leading to enhanced productivity. Indeed, this, in turn, is likely to impact on the private or familial lives of workers, especially those subject to 'zero hours' contracts, both in terms of their ability to care for those around them at home and in terms of the stresses of work beginning to flood into private and intimate relationships beyond the workplace. According to the UK Office for National Statistics (ONS), the proportion of workers on such contracts has increased from one in ten of the sector's workforce to one in seven in 2016. Data from the ONS reveals that 'between April and June ... about 113,000 of the 769,000 workers who provided at-home care for vulnerable people or were employed in care homes were on contracts with no guaranteed hours. At approximately one in seven, that total represents a substantial and rapid increase on 2015, when one in 10 care workers were on zero-hours' (Osborne, 2016: 8).

Instead of being able to realise and exemplify professional ethics in relation to care practice, 'workers frequently find themselves enacting a cutbacks policy agenda [and in] so doing, social workers and other care workers become, in effect, part of the austerity agenda, injecting neoliberalism into the lives of service users and communities' (Baines and Van Den Broek, 2016: 2; see also Muehlebach, 2012). In homecare visiting services this may result in workers being compelled to visit more clients in a shorter period. Where workers are 'constantly, systemically (not arbitrarily) rushed and compelled to provide thin, technical, tightly controlled allotments of care to those in need. Workers can do little to change this system-wide neglect and are expected to operate as if the care they are providing is acceptable while knowing that it is not' (Baines and Van Den Broek, 2016: 7). Relatedly, an ability to be truly attentive to needs may be fragmented because of cuts in homecare services or because vacancies have been left unfilled. Some homecare recipients may be left bereft of *any* attention, because they cannot afford to pay for services previously not subject to charging policies.

Similar points can, of course, be made in relation to the service provided to children and young people in public care. This line of analysis makes the connection, therefore, between poor quality jobs *and* the poor quality of care provision. These are 'often treated as separate issues despite being intertwined' (Lewis and West, 2014: 11). For example, in Ireland it became apparent in 2010 that no reliable data existed on the deaths of children in contact with social workers. As a result an Independent Child Death Review Group (ICDRG) was established to tabulate the fatalities (Shannon and Gibbons, 2012). However, the task of the ICDRG was complicated because of the disarray of care files relating to the children whom they investigated. Oftentimes these files were 'poorly kept' and many 'records were handwritten and barely legible, files themselves were often incomplete, and important notes were scribbled on pieces of paper and data such as birth dates were entered differently on different forms' (Shannon and Gibbons, 2012: ii).

However, it is not unlikely that such shoddy work practices, and lack of appropriate attentiveness and care within the *care* system, was attributable to unfilled vacancies and a consequential speed-up of work across the social work sector. Indeed, a number of child death inquiries mention – usually in passing and without further investigation – that poor social work care practices had occurred in the context of shortfalls in staffing numbers and, more generally, inadequate resourcing (Garrett, 2014b). More recent evidence continues to point to deficiencies in the Irish system: more than 130 children went missing from state care facilities in 2015 with one region not even maintaining information on the numbers of those missing (McMahon, 2016). Furthermore, almost 1,000 high-priority cases involving potentially at-risk children had still to be assigned a social worker by the end of 2015 (D'Arcy, 2016: 2). Clearly, instances such as these prompt a series of questions: what is structurally generating organisational carelessness and inattentiveness across carescapes? Why is it that the care ethics, articulated by feminist scholars, is frequently denuded of real meaning in terms of many people's actual experience of paid carework?

It might be argued that caring is offered as a gift, and as such, it offers a counter-hegemonic glimpse of a 'different way of being in the world' (Skeggs, 2014: 13). Nevertheless, within paid care work, it is increasingly difficult to transcend the logic of capital and researchers across different continents have illuminated the deleterious consequences of the New Public Management (NPM) in embedding neoliberal rationality within care practices. This can also be viewed alongside what I have termed elsewhere social work's 'electronic turn' enabling employers to better dictate, monitor and incessantly surveil the patterning of work and individual productivity (Garrett, 2005). In countless countries, companies – new and old – are actively developing software and miscellaneous apps, using GPS technology, to monitor dispersed and harried workers providing services to service users in their homes. In Ireland, for example, the Finnish-developed and deceptively cheerfully named, 'NurseBuddy', is just one of these surveillance apps used to track and monitor social care staff (http://nursebuddy.co/).

Despite the appearance of robotic carers, and the corporate hype frequently associated with their deployment, the social reproduction and maintenance of human beings cannot be entirely reducible to mechanization (see also Dyer-Witheford, 2015; Leiber, 2016). As Silvia Federici comments, carework is associated with the 'satisfaction of complex needs, in which physical and affective elements are inextricably combined, requiring a high degree of human interaction' (in Farris, 2012: 190–1). Unlike the production of commodities, such as cars or fridges, carework is still very much reliant on 'living labor' (Farris, 2012: 191). More generally, Moser and Thygesan (2015: 113) take an optimistic position in relation to the beneficial possibilities technology provides within the field of care services and especially in terms of how it may aid the shaping of 'care at a distance'. It has also been maintained that the 'interneting of things' and the 'wiring' of the homes of the elderly and infirm might 'ease the load' of 'adult children too tied up in their own lives to visit' (Hinsliff, 2016: 29).

Grounded in her work in Canada and Australia, Baines' contention is that, despite social service provision being rhetorically motivated by notions of social justice, the NPM 'systematically strips out the work of caring content' (Baines, 2004: 268; see also Baines, 2013). Within Canadian social service organisations, there has been an expansion in the reliance on the 'altruism' of workers on account of the explicit expectation that they 'perform unpaid, volunteer work within their own organization to fill the "caring gap"' created by cutbacks and the creation of 'lean' work organisations (Baines, 2004: 268). This can involve extending the work hours, staff needing to take work home, their working through lunch and breaks, and so forth. One of the 'strongest findings', in her empirical studies of mostly female care staff, is the 'prevalent sense of regret, or even mourning, over the loss of caring relationships with clients' (2004: 278).

The NPM, and similar managerial approaches, frown on subjects lacking the will to be manageable and methodically strategise to reduce the scope for professional discretion in how work tasks are ordered, transacted and completed. This is not to argue that it is possible to entirely extinguish this space for individual decision-making and judgement, given that social work and related services 'cannot actually function *without* discretion' (Scourfield, 2013: 917, original emphasis). Paradoxically, as Bourdieu argues, the 'rigidity of bureaucratic institutions is such, that ... they can only function, with more or less difficulty, thanks to the initiative, the inventiveness, if not the charisma of those functionaries who are the least imprisoned in their function. If bureaucracy were left to its own logic ... then bureaucracy would paralyse itself' (Bourdieu in Bourdieu et al., 2002: 191). However, the neoliberal playbook still hinges on curtailing the sphere of discretion and on ensuring that management retain the uncontested right to manage. In this sense, the NPM can be viewed as the antithesis of the social-democratic debates taking place in the 1970s, when Williams' *Keywords* was first published, promoting 'workers control' (Coates and Topham, 1972). NPM, and similar techniques of management, ultimately aim to entirely eradicate even the memory of these counter positions envisioning more democracy within workplaces.

A report produced by Social Care Ireland, found that 90% of social care workers across a variety of social care settings had 'experienced workplace violence' (Keogh and Byrne, 2016: 3). Some locations were found to have a significantly higher prevalence of violence, with 'all social care workers in Children's Residential Services and 92% of those working in Disability Services having experienced workplace violence' (2016: 3). Indeed, more pervasively, one further consequence of the deterioration in the working environment across various carescapes, is that staff appear to be increasingly subject to violence from those in receipt of a service. This issue has been far from prominent, yet it is beginning to emerge within the academic literature on carework.

Baines and Van Den Broek (2016: 9) maintain that the use of coercion in care settings is attributable not only to the abuse which workers encounter in interactions with managers, it is also apparent in 'sudden and unexpected client violence'. Both verbal and physical, such occurrences are reported by careworker respondents in Canada and Australia with outbursts connected to 'under-served, angry and desperate' clients often feeling 'pushed to the edges of their endurance' (2016: 10, 9). The aetiology of this violence may be specific forms of illness (such as dementia or psychosis), yet attacks on workers can also be interpreted as 'exacerbated and sometimes set in motion by the complex overlay of inadequate government funding levels, and the insistence on the use of competitive performance management models that decrease front line autonomy through the enforcement of tightly scripted, standardised portions of barely adequate, technical care' (2016: 9). This data also reveals that patient violence against nursing staff, for example, is more prevalent in workplaces where staffing numbers are 'thinned' and the performance of tasks, for the remaining workers, is consequently speeded up. What is more, 'reforms' often inject social toxicity into the working environment in the form of 'horizontal violence': a form of 'meanness and bullying among co-workers caused by inadequate resources and a lack of autonomy and employee power' (2016: 10).

COMMODIFICATION AND CORRUPTION

Clearly a range of the themes identified in the research of Baines and Van Den Broek illuminates the deterioration taking place within care services. Almost on a daily basis, the media reports one or more 'scandals'. Although the complexity of abuse cannot be imputed to a single cause, one contributory factor generating abusive practices is likely to be the incessant penetration of commodified and marketised carework. Beverley Skeggs (2014: 11) observes that essential to

> the maintenance and future of capital, capitalists have long tried to give responsibility for the reproduction of the workforce to either the family and/or the State. The shift in the re-organization of reproductive labour has been driven by capital. As wages decrease the male breadwinner 'family wage' is not enough and more women are drawn into the workforce, creating a crisis in care provision.

However, this 'crisis' contributes to care becoming an opportunistic site for greater and more extensive capital accumulation (see also Gallagher, 2014). Given this development, it is vital to recognise that, for the private sector, the determining motivation is to drive down labour costs and increase profitability (Boffey, 2014). This factor has become increasingly important with regard to the 'delivery' of care for older people in the UK since the introduction of the

NHS and Community Care Act 1990 relating to the adult and learning disability sectors where large corporate providers now prominently nestle (Harris, 2003; Humber, 2016). Residential care is, therefore, perceived as 'a commodity ... to be traded and exploited for its surplus value like any other commodity' and as a consequence 'the quest for profitability means that business values, reductions in costs and income generation have been prioritised above the quality of care' (Scourfield, 2007: 162; 170).

The structural *carelessness* integral to the evolution of neoliberal social policy was highlighted, in 2011, by the abuses committed against residents at Winterbourne View hospital in Bristol owned by the Irish investors Castlebeck (O'Toole, 2012). A Serious Case Review, undertaken for the South Gloucestershire Safeguarding Adults Board, was scathing in its assessment that whilst the 24-bed hospital charged the NHS on average £3,500-a-week to treat each patient, this was 'no guarantee of patient safety or service quality' for 'uniquely disadvantaged' individuals (Flynn, 2012: 145). Castlebeck cynically, but entirely attuned to neoliberal rationality, prioritised 'decisions about profitability, including shareholder returns, over and above decisions about the effective and humane delivery of assessment, treatment and rehabilitation' (Flynn, 2012: 144). Similarly, the financial collapse of the care home chain Southern Cross furnishes evidence of the sheer recklessness of privatisation (Coward, 2011; Scourfield, 2012). Nevertheless, privatization continues with, for example, 43 social workers being transferred to Virgin Care in Bath and North East Somerset in April 2017 (Turner, 2017).

Milton Friedman asserted, in the early 1960s, that the 'only social responsibility of business' is to maximise enhance profits and stockholder value (in Eagleton-Pierce, 2016: 170). Imposed regulatory mechanisms ensure that there are limitations as to the sovereignty of private companies in the area of care provision (Brindle, 2014), yet the extraction of profits remains the paramount consideration despite the promotional vocabulary and imagery usually deployed to deny this fact. In capitalist societies, it could not really be otherwise. In Ireland, one of the largest private providers of nursing homes, Mowlam Healthcare, provides 1,400 beds across 25 elderly care facilities. It does not, however, publish accounts and its shares are held by another financial entity with an address in the British Virgin Islands (Keena, 2015). With the number of people aged over 65 due to increase by 38% in the period to 2021, and the number aged over 85 years of age to grow by 46% over the same period, the sector is poised to expand. However, there are criticisms from nationally located private operators that Irish banks are reluctant to lend. This is viewed as particularly irksome given the lurking 'foreign venture capitalists and vulture funds' viewing the care sector as 'sexy' and ripe for takeovers (Keena, 2015: 5). In terms of children's services, care costs are three times more when private companies are used, yet nine companies continue to exploit, and profit from the gaps in public provision (Gartland, 2016).

The embattled public care sector is unable, of course, to exist entirely beyond neoliberal rationality given the dominance of NPM and cuts to services. In 2013, for example, the UK Francis Inquiry investigating the 'conditions of appalling care that were able to flourish' in the Staffordshire hospital observed that the management's 'thinking during the period under review was dominated by financial pressures...to the detriment of quality of care' (Francis, 2013: 7, 13). At the time of writing, criminal investigations are taking place in the west of Ireland relating to the abuse of residents at the Áras Attracta care home, housing 100 people with intellectual disabilities (Áras Attracta Swinford Review Group, 2016). These abuses were secretly filmed by the national TV broadcaster RTE and screened in December 2014. The *Irish Times* health correspondent reported some of the 'shocking scenes' as follows:

> In the single most shocking incident Mary Maloney (75) who cannot speak and has a severe intellectual disability, is force-fed in a chair by a care assistant. The staff member pulls her back in the chair by her hood and pins Ms Maloney's arm down using her knee while shoving a beaker into her mouth. When Ms Maloney tries to remove the beaker, the care assistant pins her arm behind the chair ... The footage also shows Ivy McGinty (53), who is also unable to speak and has severe autism, being pinched, prodded, poked and kicked by staff, seemingly for no reason. She is frequently ordered to sit in a chair, face the wall and keep her head down. Keys are rattled in her face because it is known she does not like this and on one occasion a staff member comes in and sits on her as a joke, though this too causes her distress ... During many of these incidents other staff members attend to mobile phones or do paperwork without intervening. (Cullen, 2014a: 1)

Whilst noting the concern of whistleblowers over a number of years, the same correspondent later observed that perhaps the 'most chilling aspect' of the TV programme was the 'casual and routine nature of the abuse meted out to vulnerable residents. The kicking, hitting, pinching, prodding and dragging was performed by staff without any sign of anger or any other strong emotion' (Cullen, 2014b: 3). Being aware of economic processes and associated deleterious cuts to services is likely to contribute to an understanding of abuse and wider shifts taking place within carescapes, but it is still important not to be analytically reductive. Most instances of abuse cannot, of course, be *entirely* explained by economic determinants. In this context, Wardhaugh and Wilding's exploration of what they refer to as the 'corruption of care' remains an important contribution to the literature. After over a decade of unbroken Conservative rule in the UK, it was hardly surprising that the neoliberalisation of care services would have a damaging impact. However, in the wake of reports examining instances of institutional abuse, Wardhaugh and Wilding (1993) endeavoured to unpack what was occurring to contaminate and corrupt care practices. The core question, for them, was how do institutions, organisations, and staff supposedly committed to the ethic of care and respect for others, become corrupted and abuse their power and their clients? Their investigation is significant because of its aspiration to identify particular contributory factors which, especially when occurring simultaneously as a toxic constellation, were likely to generate abusive practices.

After their scrutiny of reports on abuse in care settings they refer to eight key propositions, or circumstantial factors, we might think of as 'warning lights' or 'signals' that care practices are becoming corrupted in institutional settings with residents left increasingly vulnerable[2]. According to Wardhaugh and Wilding (1993) these factors can be connected to:

- The neutralisation of normal moral concerns

- The balance of power and powerlessness in organisations

- Particular pressures and particular kinds of work

- Management failure

- Enclosed, inward-looking organisations

- The absence of clear lines and mechanisms of accountability

- Particular models of work and organisation (such as 'batch living' entailing the segregation of particular and vulnerable 'client' groups)

- Certain 'client groups' being viewed as 'less than fully sentient beings' because of, for example, age and/or disability.

Underpinning the sociological perspective of Wardhaugh and Wilding is their dismissal of the notion that abuse in institutional care settings is solely attributable to the actions of 'bad apples' or, more extremely, 'evil' individuals. In terms of the factors listed above, some require additional elaboration. For example, the assertion that the corruption of care depends on the neutralisation of normal moral concerns is important in both historical and contemporary contexts. Thus, for people to be abused in institutional settings, they have to be perceived and regarded as 'beyond the bounds of moral behaviour which [normally] governs relations' between people (Wardhaugh and Wilding, 1993: 6). The abused individual or group come to be seen as 'less than fully human' (1993: 6). Victims are perceived as not 'like us', worthless, ambiguously problematic: freighted in fact, with Bourdieu's 'negative symbolic capital' (in Bourdieu et al., 2002: 185; see also Chapter 2). Turning to Ireland, this might contribute to a better understanding of the treatment, in the past, of children in industrial schools and those within homes for 'unmarried mothers' (Garrett, 2013b; 2016a; 2017). Important here were the ritualised admission procedures serving to denude residents of a sense of individuality and personhood (see also Foucault, 1991 [1977]). As a result, moral issues became matters of organisation or technique with people becoming merely 'specimens of a category' (Bauman in Wardhaugh and Wilding, 1993: 7).

Wardhaugh and Wilding are partly influenced by the sociological exploration of the late Zygmunt Bauman (1925–2017). More specifically, his theorisation of the Holocaust and the treatment accorded to Jews and other pariah populations (Bauman, 1989). Bauman argues that these groups, who the Nazis were intent on eliminating, had to be excluded from normal social life, depersonalised and dehumanised before deportation and extermination (Garrett, 2012b). Wardhaugh and Wilding are not arguing, of course, that the corruption of care practice crudely replicates the horrors of the Holocaust. However, their reading is reflexively and humanly sensitised to detecting elements linking genocide and, for example, the types of institutional abuse of children in care taking place when they were writing in the early 1990s (Staffordshire County Council, 1991).

It is also possible to see how Wardhaugh and Wilding's contribution relates to the empirical work of Baines and Van Den Broek mentioned earlier. In their article, the British scholars referred to pressurised work in care settings serving, over time, to contaminate or corrupt care. This might involve scarce resources and an emphasis on merely 'getting by' resulting in a pernicious organisational preoccupation with control and order. Not dissimilarly, Baines and Van Den Broek (2016: 10) maintain that 'workers absorb and buffer' this type of pressure, but most of the care workers they interviewed indicated nevertheless that 'to keep up with their workloads, they have few options other than to increase their control of service users'.

CONCLUSION

Care is a welfare word which has a 'warm and loving quality to it, and it is difficult to wholly detach it from this halo effect. Simply to describe work as carework takes it into a special realm of value' (Twigg, 2000: 393). Looking at a number of approaches to care, this chapter began with feminist care ethics. Next, it referred to the perspective of the DPM and then briefly explored the perspective of those seeking to locate 'bodywork' at the centre of debates on care.

Perhaps a central strand, or tension, running through the chapter relates to how feminist care ethics and approaches rooted in a labour process theory, attempt to challenge, explain and respond to neoliberalism. The former advocate care practice as a virtue and as a way to meaningfully oppose a 'perceived contemporary crisis around the maintenance of social connectedness' (Beasley and Bacchi, 2007: 280). However, writers such as Tronto, a prominent definer and amplifier of feminist care ethics, arguably lack a sufficiently robust analysis of capitalism. This shortcoming is evinced and magnified in a tendency to use vague phrases, such as the unspecified 'changes in the nature of modern life' accounting for changes in care practices (see, for example, Tronto, 2010: 161). Elsewhere she refers to the 'present moment, when the costliness of labor-intensive care is foremost in the minds of citizens' (Tronto, 2010: 163). More emphatically, one of the criticisms of the approach of Tronto and others using a similar optic is that they can only provide a series of 'meliorist reforms that tinker at the edges of inequality' (Beasley and Bacchi, 2007: 280). In short, they only furnish a 'restricted challenge' (Beasley and Bacchi, 2007: 285). This, however, is not to totally disparage the idea that a more intense 'focus on the need to develop humane, tolerant human relations' is required if neoliberal hegemony is to be challenged within, and beyond, carescapes. The 'vocabulary' of those promoting a feminist ethics of care is also 'somewhat levelling' in that it recognised that 'all of us do undertake and need care' (Beasley and Bacchi, 2007: 285).

Those more alert to the political economy and labour processes might be criticised for implicitly suggesting that a 'golden age' of care and caring existed prior to the neoliberal offensive. However, their central contention that carework, like many other forms of work in neoliberal societies, is increasingly degraded by the driving imperative of incessant and unremitting capital accumulation appears to be entirely warranted.

Child adoption is, of course, a very specific form of care: legally mandated and enforced permanent, substitute, non-biological parental care for children. The next chapter, therefore, will explore aspects of this particular welfare word.

REFLECTION AND TALK BOX 8

1. In the early 1980s, Carol Gilligan (1982: 17) maintained that women's place 'in man's cycle has been that of nurturer, caretaker, and helpmate, the weaver of those networks of relationships on which she in turn relies. But while women have thus taken care of men, men have, in their theories of psychological development, as in their economic arrangements, tended to assume or devalue that care'. What is your view of her perspective?

2. Rachel Lara Cohen (2011: 190) argues:

   Notwithstanding professional or compassionate commitment to patients, work and employment in health and social care settings is played out on the same territory as other work in capitalism. This territory is marked by persistent, albeit not always predictable, conflict and constraint... When organisations are in the public sector this imperative is somewhat altered, but increasingly the public sector is also subject to pseudo-market mechanisms, incorporating targets, audits and rewards for cost-cutting.

   If you are a social worker practitioner, or located in similar area of work, how do you relate this comment to your experience?

FURTHER READING

Nancy Fraser (2016) provides an excellent short exposition on how the 'crisis' in care can only be properly understood if we locate it within capitalism's contemporary evolution. Marian Barnes and her colleagues (Barnes et al., 2015) introduce their readers to some of the main issues presently related to feminist care ethics. As mentioned earlier, Bill Hughes and his colleagues illuminate some of the tensions and oppositions relating to feminist perspectives and the Disabled People's Movement on care. Neoliberal care processes are examined by Donna Baines and Diane Van Den Broek (2016). My own article on the use of e-working in social work and related areas may also be of interest to readers (Garrett, 2005). Similarly, my chapter on those historically excluded from care in Ireland may be worth reading (Garrett, 2013a). The classic reading on the 'corruption of care' is that provided by Wardhaugh and Wilding (1993) in *Critical Social Policy*.

CHAPTER 9

ADOPTION

Adoption – The action or practice of legally or informally taking a person into any relationship; esp. the taking of a minor who is not one's offspring into the legal relationship of child. (*Oxford English Dictionary*)

INTRODUCTION

In spring 2012, an article in the UK's *Daily Mail* newspaper focused on a problem which was, readers were advised, acting as an obstacle preventing children being adopted (Gallagher, 2102)[1]. Children were denied a '*loving* home and the prospect of a good start in life' and left to '*languish* in the care system' because of the names they have been given by their families (Gallagher, 2012, emphases added). The author, a member of an adoption board charged with approving adoptive parents, explained:

> For some reason there is currently a fashion, among those whose children are forcibly removed, for calling little girls after drinks — hence two recent babies called Chardonnay and Champagne. There is also a tendency to name girls after jewels, though often misspelt: Rubie, Emmarald, Jayde, Chrystal. So we on the adoption board who are trying to place these children in loving homes are confronted with Gemma-Mai, Courtney-Mai, Alexia-Mai, Lily-Mai, Shania-Rae and so on, names which will mark them out for their whole lives as members of a peculiarly British underclass. Simply put, the children's names do not fit with the social demographic of the people coming forward to give them homes. (Gallagher, 2012)

This writer feels so 'sorry for potential adopters, those hard-working and educated people, with their good intentions and bright smiles'. Lacking the 'cultural capital' (Bourdieu, 2002) to appropriately name their children, the families of origin are causing a blockage in what is now often referred to as the adoption 'pipeline'

(Bartholet, 2007: 166). The names of the children make 'their less-than-middle-class backgrounds all too obvious. And most prospective parents don't want to adopt children who are named after someone's favourite celebrity or tipple... Naturally you want a new child to blend in with your existing family — but will Chardonnay ever fit in with Henry, James and William? No' (Gallagher, 2012). Referring back to Rancière, the names chosen by their biological parents brand their children as irredeemably inferior within a 'police' order governed by class-based imperatives and associated cultural assumptions (see also Chapter 2).

Gallagher maintains that the 'problem' with the names is illustrative of a more significant flaw associated with adoption policy and practice: that an adopted child needs to keep in contact with or have some sense of their 'roots' and familial heritage. This often leads to the retention of first names and also produces considerable disadvantages for adopters keen to provide 'loving' homes.

> Adoptive parents often think they will get a few pages about the child they are being offered, covering basic information. Instead they get a file the size of the Yellow Pages, full of details that would make your hair stand on end. For some reason known only to social workers, the reports disclose often unsavoury and unnecessary information that is off-putting to those new to the system and from immaculate homes. A typical example might read: 'Chrystal-Mai suffered from nits for 18 months and was excluded from nursery. She misses her daddy who is in jail serving 15 years for distributing paedophile images.

It might be contended that this newspaper article, so suffused with class loathing and contempt, merits little consideration and, unsurprisingly, it is entirely aligned with the world view and 'common sense' attitudes of *The Daily Mail*. Indeed, of all the British tabloid newspapers analysed during the period August 2007 – August 2012, it was *The Daily Mail* and *The Mail on Sunday* which were most likely to use the underclass word and feature underclass related articles (Harkins and Lugo-Ocando, 2016). This, in itself, does not render this particular piece any less spitefully toxic, but there is a need to dwell on it at such length because it illuminates how many of the welfare words and associated concepts, explored in this book, are so intermeshed. Here, of course, the blending of underclass and adoption is most apparent (see also Chapter 4).

Furthermore, Gallagher's article provides a good route into a number of themes examined in this chapter. Even if the tonality is somewhat different, her views reflect, in some respects, something of the drift of more mainstream opinion and policy on child adoption practices in recent years (Neale and Lopez, 2017). These too appear to hanker for a return to a type of adoption which evolved, in the UK, between the late-1920s and the 1950s–60s, when there was greater availability of babies and adoption was conceived as a neat and tidy 'secret' event resulting in the definitive rupturing of the adopted child's relationship with her/his birth mother and family of origin. Within this former approach to adoption, birth mothers were rendered entirely superfluous after the transference of parental responsibility had taken place (see also Broadhurst et al., 2015).

Into the new century, governments in the UK and the United States have had an itching preoccupation with child adoption. Blair, sensing his party was inexplicably becoming 'somehow out of touch with gut British instincts' observed that the 'adoption issue worked well' and that it might be politically expedient to trigger a series of other 'eye catching initiatives ... entirely conventional in terms of their attitude to the family' (see 'What the memo tells us about Tony Blair's style of leadership', *The Guardian*, 18 July 2000). Astutely media-conscious, this sophisticated political operator clearly felt that promoting a populist child adoption agenda was electorally to his advantage.

More broadly, the adoption of children will always command a measure of political and public attention because it touches on a host of substantial and emotive issues centred on, for example: constructions of 'childhood' and of children's rights at particular junctures in history; the rights of parents versus the rights of the state; how notions such as 'good enough parenting' are assembled and amplified (Adcock and White, 1985); how societies are economically structured to enable some parents, but not others, to adequately care for their children and to enable them to flourish; the commodification of children and the new markets in child welfare services; neo-colonial practices and how affluent citizens in the West relate to the 'developing' world and to those areas formerly residing behind the so-called 'iron curtain' (Bartholet, 2007: 160). Moreover, the discourse on this welfare word is, as will be discussed later, laden with questions pertaining to 'race'.

The chapter begins with a necessarily truncated history of how the practices connected to this welfare word have changed in recent times. Moving on, the focal interest will be on England and Wales and on how policy has been shaped during the period of the Coalition and Conservative governments from 2010. The next section of the chapter tries to analyse and interpret the contemporary politics of domestic adoption. By way of a coda, the 'globalisation' of adoption and inter-country adoption will be examined and here the focus will be on the stances taken particularly by US-based participants in debates on inter-country adoption (ICA). Media interest in this dimension of adoption was amplified following a spate of inter-country adoptions by US celebrities. Indeed, the Irish bookmaker Paddy Power was criticised for offering odds on the next celebrity couple to adopt an African orphan. Under the title 'Out of Africa – Celebrity Baby Craze', the press release stated: 'Angelina Jolie did it and so too has Madonna, and we are not talking about bedding some of the hottest men in Hollywood' (Cullen, 2006). Having controversially adopted a child from Malawi, Madonna told Oprah Winfrey in 2006, 'if everybody went there [Africa], they'd want to bring one of those children home with them and give them a better life' (Dubinsky, 2008: 339). Following her own advice, Madonna subsequently adopted three more Malawian children.

CHANGING ADOPTION PRACTICES

The US state of Massachusetts initiated the first modern adoption law in 1851. The legal adoption of children was introduced, in England and Wales, in 1926. Northern Ireland followed in 1929 and Scotland in 1930 (Teague, 1989). Adoption in the Republic of Ireland was only introduced in 1952. Over the past four decades significant changes have taken place in relation to the dynamics of the adoption process. First, on account of the contraceptive pill, social liberalisation and the waning in stigma associated with unmarried births, the numbers of children adopted in England and Wales radically diminished during the final thirty years of the twentieth century from approximately 20,000 each year in 1970 to 4,100 in 1999 (Performance and Innovation Unit, 2000: 10). The most drastic decline related to the numbers of babies adopted. In 2012, Michael Gove, then Secretary of State for Education in the UK Coalition government, reported that only '60 babies' were adopted that year (Gove, 2012a: 3). Adoption is now more likely to involve children in public care – or 'looked after' under the Children Act 1989 – who are older, have been at the centre of child protection concerns, or who have disabilities or other special or complex needs. Many of these children will have been removed, on a compulsory basis, from their parent(s). Within Europe, Spain has the highest adoption rate, the 'second in the world, behind the United States' (Marre, 2012: 89).

Second, there is now greater openness in the adoption process (Department of Health, 1999: Ch. 5). Over the past twenty-five years adoption has 'moved progressively from the "clean break" philosophy and its lifelong impact' has tended to be recognised (Kirton, 2013: 102). A more 'open' approach results, in some instances, in 'contact arrangements' between the child and their family of origin after adoption has taken place (Dutt and Sanyal, 1991; McRoy, 1991). Birth mothers have pressed for greater openness in adoption (Howe et al., 1992). Such changes were also prompted by the gradual acknowledgement, on the part of mainstream professional opinion, that some form of contact or at least awareness of one's origins is important in relation to the 'identity needs of adoptees' (Kirton, 2000: 108). Opposition to this trend is still evident, as reflected in Gallagher's comments and, indeed, in the drift of more recent policy-making.

However, the retreat from the secrecy surrounding adoption was also partly driven by the demands of adoptees themselves who wanted to discover more about their birth families (Feast and Howe, 1997). In the early 1970s, Triseliotis (1973: 1), examining the experiences of adoptees who searched for biological parents, observed that Scotland and Finland were at this time 'the only countries in the Western world where an adopted person can obtain from official records information that could lead to the tracing of the original parents'. In Scotland, this right to information had been provided under the Scottish Adoption Act 1930. In England and Wales, the Adoption Act 1976, as amended by the Children Act 1989, required the Registrar General to set up an Adoption Contact Register to enable adopted people to contact their birth parents and other relatives. Related to these developments is an awareness of the significance (and inadequacy) of post-adoption services (Expert Working Group on Adoption, 2012).

Third, there is more willingness to recognise the abuse associated with adoption practices in the past. This is not universally accepted, however, and in the late-1990s it was charged that 'tormented birth mothers describing their regrets' had become, 'along with sexual and reproductive peculiarities', the 'stock-in-trade of television talk shows' (Morgan, 1998: 7). The Natural Parents Support Group has lobbied the UK parliament for a public inquiry to examine the injustices occurring during the years of mass adoption in the 1950s and 1960s. The Movement for an Adoption Apology (2011) has called for an official political statement expressing regret for policies and practices coercing women, often in fraught situations, to relinquish children. In November 2016, Cardinal Vincent Nichols, head of the Catholic Church in England and Wales, apologised for its part in the 'hurt' caused to young unmarried women pressured into 'handing over their babies for adoption in the 1950s, 60s and 70s' (Sherwood, 2016: 3). Beyond the UK, the Australian prime minister issued a state apology in Parliament House in Canberra on 22 March 2013 (Gillard, 2013). In terms of research agendas, in the 1990s, some attention also began to be paid to the marginalisation of birth fathers within adoption processes (Clapton, 1997).

Fourth, sexual orientation forms a part of recent debates on child adoption. Controversy resulted following a late amendment to New Labour's Adoption and Children 2002 Act, permitting adoption by unmarried (including same sex) couples. Nevertheless, in 2009/10, 91% of those adopting children from the care system were couples, of which only 2% were unmarried same sex couples. Nine per cent were single people and these tended to be mostly female (93%) (Department for Education in Ali, 2014b: 78). Gay, bisexual and transgender people are invited to 'step forward' to adopt and the adverts targeted at potential adopters are now pictorially reflecting this invitation (Williams, 2015). Many Roman Catholic charities in the United States chose to close their adoption services following the introduction of state laws compelling agencies to consider same sex couples as potential adoptive parents if they were to continue to receive state funding. For example, the large social services provider Catholic Charities, based in Illinois, opted to shut down its adoption services rather than comply with non-discrimination laws enacted in November 2010 (Goodstein, 2011).

ENDING THE 'CRUEL RATIONING OF HUMAN LOVE': THE UK COALITION AND CONSERVATIVE GOVERNMENTS

Under both the Coalition and Conservative governments, the tonality of adoption policy-making altered and this was apparent in, for example, a detectable scepticism toward notions of 'openness'. Although 'much more familiar with the prison service than social services' (Butler, 2014: 491), Martin Narey was appointed the Coalition government's 'adoption tsar'. Earlier, his views had been prominently aired in the media which reported him calling for less effort directed at 'fixing families that can't be fixed' with more 'children being taken away as babies' and adopted (in McVeigh, 2009). Narey's *Our Blueprint for Lost Children*, although somewhat hastily assembled and anecdotal, furnished part of the foundation for significant policy departures. Narey chose to ignore or criticise open adoption and enquired why can't 'adopters cannot be regarded as the "real and only" parents' (in Kirton, 2013: 99). Such views, mirroring those featured in the *Daily Mail* piece referred to at the chapter's outset, degrades and disregards families of origin. Moreover, such perceptions would seem to be 'very much at odds with those of adopted children themselves' whose families of origin remain, in varying ways, of real and continuing significance (Kirton, 2013: 99).

Gove (2012a), who was himself adopted as baby, aspired to raise the profile of child adoption. Seeking to garner the support of child welfare professionals, Gove's ministerial foreword to *An Action Plan for Adoption: Tackling Delay* he indicated his awareness of how adoption had changed and was less 'straightforward' then when he was a child in the late-1960s and early 1970s (Department for Education, 2012b). Babies, for example, were only 'rarely relinquished' by their birth mothers and adoption was now more likely to follow a period of 'neglect or abuse and time in care' (Gove, 2012a: 3). However, Gove's main intention was to ensure that the present adoption system promoted 'successful and early adoptions and does not thwart them' (Gove, 2012a: 3). Apt to idealise adoption, he still acknowledged that adoption was 'not suitable' for all children removed from their birth parents. With many of the 65,000 children in care, though, the adoption option needed to be explored and, if appropriate, progressed with revitalised energy by all involved. His government 'strongly' believed that adoption was the 'best permanent option for more children' than were currently benefiting from it (Department for Education, 2012b: 6). Particular attention needed to be given to 15,680 children, under the age of five, presently in care (Department for Education, 2012b: 6).

Despite the 'major overhaul' of legislation and practice, triggered by Blair, adoption and its associated practices had, claimed Gove, 'slipped back down the agenda' (Department for Education, 2012b: 11):

> there are many more than just the three thousand or so adopted last year, who need, and deserve, all that being adopted by a loving and caring family means. That adoptions are at their lowest point for a decade means *a cruel rationing of human love for those most in need*. (Gove, 2012a: 3, emphasis added)

Within the official and published discourse, un-named adopters proclaimed that the adoption system empowered them to make 'confident little people' (Department for Education, 2012b: 13). However, even those 'fortunate children' who were eventually adopted waited 'too long' given that the 'average wait between their coming into care and being united with their adoptive parents was twenty one months

(Gove, 2012a: 3). Dangers inherent in delay were potentially disastrously deleterious for children: attachment problems resulted and evolving discoveries in neuroscience emphasised the risks associated with delay (Department for Education, 2012b: 14; see also the exploration of this theme in Chapter 6). As will be discussed later, it was also argued that delay was interconnected with the issue of 'race' and placements (Department for Education, 2012b: 21–3).

More generally, it was claimed it was 'too simplistic' to assume that '*speedier adoption*' would prompt more adoption breakdowns (Department for Education, 2012b: 17, emphasis added). The Gove 'plan' hinged on commitments to:

- legislate to 'reduce the number of adoptions delayed in order to achieve a perfect or near ethnic match between adoptive parents and the adoptive child' (Gove, 2012a: 3);

- require *swifter* use of the national Adoption Register to find the right adopters for a child wherever they might live;

- encourage all local authorities to seek to place children with their potential adopters in anticipation of the court's placement order;

- radically *speed up* the adopter assessment process;

- introduce a '*fast track*' process for those who have adopted before or who are foster carers wanting to adopt a child in their care (Gove, 2012a: 4, emphasis added);

- develop a 'national Gateway to adoption' as a consistent source of advice and information for those thinking about adoption (Gove, 2012a: 4, emphasis added);

- introduce, as 'part of a new tougher approach to addressing underperformance in the adoption system', a 'new performance scorecard' (Department for Education, 2012b: 41; see also Department for Education, 2014).

The following year, the Coalition government returned to dwell on the same pre-occupations in *Further Action on Adoption: Finding More Loving Homes* (Department for Education, 2013). The 2013 report stressed that the evolving 'vision' was one of a regional 'system with fewer adoption agencies operating at larger scale with clear incentives to respond to the needs of all children waiting for adoption' (Timpson, 2013: 3; see also Timpson, 2015). The government was also to take powers enabling it to 'require some or all local authorities to outsource adopter recruitment and assessment' (Department for Education, 2013: 21). A national 'Gateway' to adoption was reported to be up-and-running with a full online service to be available by 2014. A consortium, First4Adoption, was to provide the service which would serve as an information portal or hub for potential adopters (Department for Education, 2013: 9).

Despite the numbers of children being approved for adoption by the courts (from just over 3,000 in 2009-10 to 4,200 in 2011–12), the numbers of children moving in with adoptive families was rising at a much slower pace (from 3,100 to 3,500) (Department for Education, 2013: 10). As a consequence there were 'over 4,600 children with a placement order waiting to be able to move in with a new family' (Department for Education, 2013: 10). In short, there was something of a blockage in the adoption 'pipeline' (Bartholet, 2007: 166). This was connected to the fact that a core asset – the numbers of potential adopters – was not keeping up with the numbers of children requiring adoptive placements. Hence, there was a need for 'more than 600 additional adopters each year to keep up with the grow-ing number of children waiting to be adopted' supplemented by '2,000–3,000 on top of that to reduce the backlog' (Department for Education, 2014: 10). According to the government, the focal obstacle was that the system did 'not treat and value adopters as it should' (Department for Education, 2013: 13). One new innovation, therefore, would be to symbolically allocate to every adopter an 'adop-tion passport' providing speedier access to a range of universal and specialist post-adoption support services (Department for Education, 2013: 36; see also Expert Working Group on Adoption, 2012).

The Children and Families Act 2014 made the adoption process easier and swifter. Importantly also, under the terms of the Adoption Reform Grant, annual funding in excess of £100 million was made available to local authorities. Alongside monies associated with the Troubled Families Programme (TFP), this also enables the government to exercise more financial and policy leverage given local authorities are 'still having to manage significant reductions in their overall budgets' (Butler, 2014: 421; see also Chapter 4 featuring a discussion on the so-called Troubled Family).

Over 5,300 children were adopted in 2015 – 72% more than in 2011 (Department for Education, 2016a). The following year, with an aspiration to 'revolutionise sup-port for the most vulnerable children' and to free the process of adoption from the 'shackles of council red tape', a 'brand-new' four-year adoption strategy was 'unveiled' by the Education Secretary Nicky Morgan (Department for Education, 2016a). Also described as a 'watershed moment – a new line in the sand', the strategy would, for example, provide every child adopted from care with a designated teacher and 'virtual school head'. In addition, 'therapeutic services' would be made available for all adopted children and the 'selfless' families caring for them (Department for Education, 2016b).

INTERPRETING CONTEMPORARY DOMESTIC ADOPTION POLITICS

The evolving position of both the Coalition and the Conservative government should be situated alongside a range of contextual issues and themes. These include the continuing ramifications of the death of Peter Connelly in 2007 ('Baby P'), which appeared to reveal, certainly according to potent media forces, that social workers were tardy in removing children from damaging and potentially lethal familial circumstances. Alternatively, having been removed, children were later carelessly restored to dangerous familial environments. The political and media preoccupation with underclass families and the developing focus on the so-called troubled families is also significant (see also Chapter 4). In the 1970s, a not 'dissimilar interest in "problem families" went hand-in-hand with a rapid rise in the number of children in public care in the context of an ideological preference for "rescue" rather than rehabilitation' (Butler, 2014: 420). Perhaps also, for some primary definers and commentators, developments in neuroscience and brain imaging technology reinforce the vital importance of a child's early years and this is viewed as providing an important impetus for swiftly removing children from damaging families (see also Chapter 6).

Certainly, the numbers of children in local authority care are, at the time of writing, drastically escalating in England and Wales (see also Bywaters et al., 2015; Bywaters et al., 2016a, 2016b). Ian Butler (2014: 420), for example, refers to an 'unprecedented rise in the absolute and relative numbers of children and young people coming into public care in the UK'. In January 2016, it was reported that there were '1,092 care applications in December, a 17% increase on the same period last year, and the highest ever demand for that month'. It was the 'fifth time in 2015–16 that care applications have gone over 1,000 in a month, and the third month in a row that this has happened. Before the current financial year, care applications had only surpassed 1,000 in a month three times' (Stevenson, 2016; see also Broadhurst et al., 2015). In this context, assertive adoption policies and practices are increasingly perceived as a solution to an array of problems which these children, and the society they live in, face.

It is apparent that evolving Conservative policy is nestled within the hegemonic framing Blair and New Labour put in place (Kirton, 2013). At this particular historical juncture there are, however, at least five distinctive strands helping to constitute Conservative politics on adoption. First, there is an antipathy toward the welfare state and a rooted scepticism that public sector professions are sufficiently committed to the type of marketised 'transformation' perceived as vital. In recent years there has been a strategic and politically instrumental willingness to recognise and praise social workers. Cameron did so at his party's conference in 2013 and Gove (2013) replicated this with the recognition of 'just how difficult – how challenging – how important and how inspiring – the role of social workers is'. Nevertheless, those undertaking such roles are mostly perceived as an obstacle to embedding a more proactive policy of child adoption and, more generally, they are viewed as lacking the appropriate ideological disposition to assist in the attainment of more encompassing social and welfare 'reform'. Hence, the establishment of 'Frontline' as a 'fast-track' route into social work for a potential 'officer class' more likely to be attuned to the Conservative world view (Murphy, 2016; see also MacAlister, 2012; Narey, 2014). However, specifically in relation to adoption and despite government criticisms, there is no tangible evidence that social workers are guilty of inefficiency and 'widespread poor practice' (Kirton, 2013: 100).

Second, both implicitly and explicitly, neoliberal discourses on consumption are increasingly mimicked and risk becoming embedded. As early as the 1920s, in the United States 'adoption culture' exhibited a proclivity to 'treat children as consumer goods and to view the choice of child as a deserved consolation for families unable to produce children biologically' (Cartwright, 2003: 86). This facet to contemporary adoption practices is magnified given the evolving visual culture of adoption. Moreover, the 'self-presentation' of most US adoption agencies, with names such as *Heart to Heart Adoption* or *Children's Hope*, trade on the 'vulnerability and cuteness of waiting children, always pictured as isolated, alone, devoid of parents, communities, nations, waiting for rescue. "I found my son in Guatemala", proclaims a popular t-shirt (or mouse pad, or coffee cup) available from a US adoption agency website' (Dubinsky, 2008: 339). With web technologies, potential adopters are merely one click away from viewing the image of an adoptable child; a digital practice too uncomfortably similar to browsing on Amazon for an item of jewellery or a power-tool. US-based sites such as Precious.org (https://www.precious.org/) and Children Awaiting Parents (www.childrenawaitingparents.org/), for example, contain pictures and search and sorting facilities rendering them uncomfortably similar to other sites displaying consumer goods and services. In the US, the moment of acquisition, the day a child is chosen to be adopted, is frequently celebrated as 'Gotcha Day' (Dubinsky, 2008).

Clearly, domestic adopters in the UK do not literally purchase children as market commodities, but the pervasive incursion of elements of market discourse perhaps reflects Wendy Brown's (2015:10) understanding, referred to in Chapter 1, that that neoliberal rationality 'transmogrifies every human domain and endeavour, along with humans themselves according to a specific image of the economic'. In this sense, discourses of consumption, reflective of this hegemonic neoliberal rationality, are seeping into UK child adoption policy language and practice especially as these relate to the figure of the potential adopter. Even *'where money is not at issue'*, these individuals are being configured as 'market actors' (Brown, 2015: 31, emphasis added). What is more, because of their economic and cultural milieu potential adopters may be responsive to an evolving paradigm in which they are unambiguously assembled as the 'customer' (Expert Working Group on Adoption, 2012). In this context, emphasis is placed on the need for radical 'approaches to improve customer service' (Expert Working Group on Adoption, 2012). Similarly, the Department for Education (2016b: 30) is keen to utilise the skills of 'marketing and customer insight experts' in luring, winning over and retaining potential adopters (Department for Education, 2013: 30).

Market logic is also apparent in a heightened attentiveness to the speed of response to these adoption 'customers'. Historically, temporal questions often focused on children 'drifting' or 'waiting' too long in care on account of inadequate care planning. Alertness to such dangers helps, in fact, to constitute part of the doxic knowledge of the bureaucratic field of child and family social work. However, the issue of time is now as likely to focus on the velocity of agency responses to potential adopters. The entire thrust of Gove's plan hinged, as observed earlier, on creating 'swifter' adoption processes and 'fast tracks'. Likewise, 'scorecards' incorporate metrics relating to speed of response to enquiries (Department for Education, 2012b: 17). Such a valorisation of speed of response chimes, of course, with corporate customer service approaches, with the underlying assumption being that technology can 'accelerate the delivery of products' and 'welfare solutions' in the 'here and now' (Pithouse, 2008: 1545). As one of Suki Ali's (2014b: 77) respondents told her, one of the 'problems with the government is that they talk about having a John Lewis customer service meaning, you know, the customer being the adopters'. There are also some indications that a muddled understanding of local authorities' target-driven culture is adversely impacting on the perceptions of parents who have children embroiled in care proceedings (Broadhurst et al., 2015: 91).

A quicker speed of response may not, of course, always be in the best interest of the children concerned and this has been a criticism levelled at attempts to transform policy from Blair onwards (Hilpern, 2008). This is because assessment processes are *necessarily* complex and time-consuming. Indeed, the emphasis on swiftness, removal and adoption application was criticised by Judge Sir James Munby, president of the High Court family division, who in the case of *Re B-S*, complained about the 'recurrent inadequacy of the analysis and reasoning put forward in support of the case for adoption (in Tickle, 2014). There will also be instances where it is better for children to remain in foster care for a lengthy period, than to be on a 'fast track' to permanent adoption (Hill, 2012). Noting the increase in the number of adoptions, the vice-chair of the British Association of Social Workers (BASW) maintains that the 'policy imperative' to introduce quicker forced adoptions could mean 'we may well look back on this period in horror as we do now to the forcible removal of thousands of children to Australia in the 1930s, 40s and 50s without their parents' knowledge or consent' (in Tickle, 2015: 36).

Attention should also accorded to the ways in which children – as the 'products' – are discursively and materially situated within the evolving politics of adoption. Arguably, the current political lukewarmness toward 'openness' can be connected to a desire to replicate the fixity of contracted ownership for purchased items. Legal adoption wholly and unequivocally transfers parental responsibility to the adoptive parents, so practices of 'openness' can be interpreted as rendering fuzzy or ambiguous 'ownership' of the child. Furthermore, the government's partiality to return to a closed system of child adoption – often referred to as 'plenary adoption and associated with a definitive break with the family of origin – is 'highly unusual in global terms', with England and the United States making vastly more domestic use of it than other Western countries (Kirton, 2013: 104). In the latter, many regard this model as 'unacceptable and express puzzlement about the need for such a "possessive" approach to children" (2013: 104). Perhaps strategies aiming to legally fix and stabilise a child's status, by extinguishing 'openness', also provide an illustration of Rancière's theorisation as to how individuals are situated at specific places inside of 'police' orders (see also Chapter 2). Hence, the preoccupation with categorically defining which family a child is a member of eliminates, in some senses, any ambiguity attached to their role and place within a specific grid of relationships and associated cultural expectations.

Following the same line of analysis, the enthusiasm for 'adoption parties' may also be significant. Such arrangements, popular in US states such as Massachusetts, prompt the potential adopters to partake of a 'much greater role in initiating matches' with children (Department for Education, 2013: 34). On occasions also called 'placement activity days', these are events designed to provide an opportunity for potential adopters to briefly engage with a number of children prior to making a decision about whether or not they wish to adopt a particular child (Department for Education, 2012b). In this way, the 'customer' is afforded the opportunity to shop around, to peruse and select from an array of 'goods'. Referred to as 'cattle markets for kids', 'fashion parties' or 'speed dating for toddlers' (in Moorhead, 2014: 1), the 'adoption party' innovation has not sat comfortably with many child welfare professionals. Before closing in 2015, partly due to funding difficulties, the British Association for Adoption and Fostering (BAAF) was involved in such events. A director of child placement at the Association conceded, however, that the 'parties' illustrate how 'we are moving up the tariff of risk in the ways we are being forced to seek out families for these children' (in Hill, 2009: 6). Similarly, Action for Children refers to the 'high risk' for the children involved since they will be 'aware that they are being picked or not picked at the parties, no matter how sensitive the pre-party preparation has been' (in Hill, 2009: 6).

Third, within the Conservative politics of adoption, a new emphasis is being placed on the authenticity and lived experience of those primary definers mapping out more assertive approaches. Expressed a little more theoretically, particular actors are bringing very specific types of 'symbolic capital' into the policy arena and using it as a political resource in forging a new 'common sense' around this particular welfare word (see also Chapter 2). Like Michael Gove, Edward Timpson, the Parliamentary Under-Secretary of State for Children and Families (2012–2015), had direct experience of the issue in that he has two adopted brothers. Born into a family that also fostered eighty-seven children, he witnessed, he claimed, 'babies addicted to heroin go into spasms' (Timpson, 2015: 3). He was also someone recognising the 'enormous benefits that adoption can bring' (Timpson, 2013: 3). A similar rhetorical strategy was apparent in a letter mailed to a national newspaper in January 2011, where the correspondent corroborated Martin Narey's rather simplistic plans to increase the number of adoptions, castigating the 'misplaced emphasis' on 'political correctness' in social work. In this instance, not only was the writer able to refer to his 'Professorship and Directorship of a Centre of Social Work and Social Policy' he was keen to confide to readers of *The Guardian* that he was, in fact, an 'adoptive person' himself. In each of these instances, the devisers, enunciators and supporters of adoption 'reform' deploy autobiographical data to try to disarm criticisms. Each of them, unlike, it is implied, most of their critics, have 'been there', having personally experienced adoption.

Here, 'primary experience, unmediated by theory, reflection, speculation, argument' is used like a trump card in a game (Hall et al., 1978: 152). Putting it into play in this way is meant to signal that experience is more meaningful and far 'superior to other kinds of argumentation because it is rooted in reality' (Hall et al., 1978: 152; see also Kaul, 2016).

Fourth, as was the case during the Blair period, the impact of US policy and practice remains influential even though it tends not to be perceived as such. For example, as suggested in Chapter 3, the US Adoption and Safe Families Act (ASFA) 1997 flagged a more directive, assertive and combative engagement with birth parents. Placing a 'strong emphasis on shortened timeframes for terminating parental rights and on adoption promotion', the ASFA undercuts the 'potential for strengthening family preservation services' (Kelly and Blythe, 2000: 36). Furthermore, US champions of this legislation, essentially of a form of top-down, class-driven social engineering, view it as a global template for more proactive and assertive policies: the 'spirit' of this legislation can also 'help animate efforts to free increased numbers of children for adoption, and ease the barriers to international adoption' (Bartholet, 2007: 170). Albeit with significant differences, the recent policy on adoption in England can be situated on the same ideological terrain. It is also apparent that policies to 'speed up' adoption processes partly replicate discursive tropes found in the US discourse (Roberts, 2012, 2014a, 2014b). The following section of the chapter will focus on a fifth dimension related to child adoption – that of 'race' – and here once again what has occurred in the United States is likely to have been influential (see also Chapter 4).

'WE DON'T NEED WHITE COUPLES': 'RACE' AND ADOPTION

In 2016 it was estimated that the cost of raising a child to the age of 21 is £230,000, more than the 'price of a semi-detached house in Britain' (Collinson, 2016). Unsurprisingly, therefore, it is largely financially comfortable, white, middle class couples who are able to afford such costs and they constitute the 'majority of adopters both domestically and transnationally' (Ali, 2014a: 93). Yet it is this group, often belligerently aggrieved, which has frequently featured within adoption 'stories' and related feature articles. Oftentimes, but not always, the grievances aired are of prospective adopters seeking to gain approval and complaining about how what might be termed the 'weight of whiteness' affects child adoption assessment (see also Lawrence and Stocks, 2011; Doughty, 2012; Harley, 2015). Such is the burden of people who perceive – often because of alleged institutionalised 'political correctness' – that their whiteness is hampering their opportunities to access, extract and legally relocate the biological children of others within their own family units. They are affronted because, despite their cultural capital, they are unreasonably unable to 'make the grade' to secure children to adopt (Woods, 2011; see also the discussion on Bourdieu in Chapter 2).

'We don't need white couples', an article in the *Daily Telegraph,* provides an example of this perspective (Woods, 2011). It is prefaced with a sub-editor's explanation that the author's 'dream of adopting a child came to an end' because of the 'prejudiced' attitude of local authorities and now she was simply left with the 'trauma' of failing to adopt. The author herself then begins by implying that the presence of books around the house was bound to act as an obstacle in that the cultural capital symbolised by her and her partner's bookishness and middle class sensibility had no currency within the field of adoption assessment. While in the circles in which the family ordinarily move, books represent a laudable mark of distinction, in the outlandish world of adoption assessment, they are likely to function as a form of 'negative symbolic capital' due to the hegemonic 'political correctness' pervasive amongst local authority social workers (Bourdieu in Bourdieu et al., 2002: 185):

> There we were, two middle class professionals, with a happy, healthy five-year-old daughter, living in a nice house with a garden being vetted about our suitability to adopt a child in care, desperately in need of a family where he or she wouldn't be sexually abused or emotionally starved or physically mistreated. (Woods, 2011)

For the author, 'race' proves to be a particular stumbling block in that she has been advised, via an Adoption Team helpline, that 'white adoptive parents' are not needed. This was the reason, she avows, why many white couples chose to adopt on an inter-country basis where less of an emphasis is placed on the 'race' and ethnicity of adopters. Domestically, however, 'safeguarding a child's cultural heritage' appears to take 'precedence over their day-to-day wellbeing and life prospects' (Woods, 2011). Palpable, therefore, is a racialised and class-based sense of affront and hurt attributable to the attitudes of 'mean-spirited' local authority adoption services.

Suki Ali (2014b: 68) maintains that 'race' became 'a feature of adoption debates in the 1950s'. Probably because of new patterns of immigration and shifts in the racial composition of the population, it gradually evolved into a more central issue. During this period, and into the 1960s, there was also growing awareness of the disproportionate number of minority ethic children in the care system (Ali, 2014b). In 1965, attempts began to be made in the UK to recruit parents for black and ethnic minority children. The British Adoption Project (BAP) had the specific remit to locate substitute parents for – in the language of the day – 'coloured children' (Ali, 2014b: 68). Such initiatives targeted 'white middle class parents' and, in 1970, a Home Office Advisory Council 'endorsed transracial placements' (Ali, 2014b: 68). Research projects on the transracial adoption of children, situated with the BAP, appeared to indicate that such placements were 'broadly successful' (Ali, 2014b: 68). However, these studies were later criticised with 'negative accounts' beginning to be produced by those who had themselves been transracially adopted (Ali, 2014b: 68). In this context, it is also important to note that invariably discourses circulating around transracial adoption are not referring to adoption taking place across the boundaries of 'race', they are tending to exclusively refer to the placement of black children with white substitute parents (Flynn, 2000). Moreover, in more recent years, this discourse has frequently highlighted 'a continuing belief in "white" British superiority, masquerading as post-race pragmatism' (Ali, 2014b: 81).

In the early 1980s, the Association of Black Social Workers and Allied Professionals (ABSWAP) challenged the hegemony of child placement policies founded on a liberal and assimilationist perspective. Here, the critique focused on the damaging consequences for black children placed with white adoptive and foster carers, but, more broadly, it drew attention to the impact of racism in British society (Small, 1982; Small with Prevatt Goldstein, 2000). Such criticisms were informed by a new self-confidence on the part of black professionals within local authority social services departments. As 'Black workers groups' were being formed in cities such as Liverpool, the influential New Black Families scheme was launched in 1980, in the London Borough of Lambeth, setting out to recruit substitute black families for black children in care. This new attentiveness to issues of 'race' and identity was gradually incorporated into practice guidelines for children in contact with social services. Importantly, these developments reflected the contemporary ethos of 'state multiculturalism', which stressed the 'complementarity of different cultures' whilst aspiring to 'manage diversity and produce integrated British citizens' (Ali, 2014b: 69).

A shift began to occur in the late 1990s, with Paul Boateng, a junior minister in the first New Labour government, engaging in what often seemed to be a personal crusade to promote transracial adoption. He and his ministerial colleagues may also have been influenced by the US Multi-ethnic Placement Act (MEPA) 1994 and the provisions on Removal of Barriers to Interethnic Adoption in 1996 (Brooks et al., 1999); particularly given the cross-fertilisation of projects and strategies linking Blair's New Labour and Clinton's Democrat administration. The circular *Adoption – Achieving the Right Balance* issued in August 1998, hinted at such convergences and asserted it was 'unacceptable for a child to be denied loving adoptive parents solely on the grounds that the child and adopters do not share the same racial or cultural background' (Department of Health, 1998: para 14). Significantly, however, *Adoption Now: Messages from Research* (Department of Health, 1999), an overview of adoption research published in October 1999, concluded that placement with a 'family of a different ethnic and cultural background should be unusual and should be based on specific reasons for individual cases' (Department of Health, 1999: 159).

Following the publication of the inquiry into the death of Stephen Lawrence and the fresh alertness to 'institutional racism', this was clearly a more restrained intervention on the question of 'race' and child placement than was apparent in some of the contributions of Boateng (MacPherson, 1999). More measured and informed by research evidence about what was actually taking place in practice, *Adoption Now* cautioned against any radical departure from the principles of the Children Act 1989 and the dominant approach which had evolved and been implemented in the 1980s and 1990s. Subsequent Department of Health reports reinforced the importance of 'race' and ethnicity for children and their families (O'Neale, 2000; see also Sissay, 2012). Blair's prime ministerial review of adoption had little to add on 'race' and the placement of children (Performance and Innovation Unit, 2000).

However, more recently, a pervasive emphasis on the 'failures or excesses of multiculturalism' appears to signal a return to the assimilationist policy of previous decades (Ali, 2014b: 69). A recalibration of policy and rhetoric was illustrated by the speech of Coalition prime minister David Cameron (2011d), to an international security conference in Munich in February 2011, in which he castigated the 'doctrine of state multiculturalism' for encouraging 'different cultures to live separate lives, apart from each other and apart from the mainstream ...We've even tolerated these segregated communities behaving in ways that run completely counter to *our* values (Cameron, 2011d, emphasis added). What was required, Cameron asserted, was a 'much more active, muscular liberalism'.

Importantly, this 'common sense', which the Conservatives, and others, continue to promote around issues of 'race' and culture, now informs debates on adoption (Loughton, 2010). The 'concept of delay itself has been deeply racialized [and it is] almost invariably the notion of proposing a 'ban' on transracial adoption that 'dominates debate, policy documents and ministerial pronouncements' (Kirton, 2013: 101). This can be interpreted as an 'attempted "final push" to remove barriers to transracial adoption, long a cause célèbre for both the media and the politicians' (2013: 101). Speaking at an event at the Coram Foundling Museum in London, Michael Gove, asserted:

> Thousands of children are currently in the care system waiting to be adopted. Every day they wait is a day they're denied the loving home all children deserve. But politically correct attitudes and ridiculous bureaucracy keep many of those children waiting far too long. Edicts which say children have to be adopted by families with the same ethnic background and which prevent other families adopting because they don't fit left-wing prescriptions are denying children the love they need. (in Department for Education, 2011: 2)

Two factors are often disregarded when this matter is placed in the wider public domain by primary definers such as Gove. First, the reasons *why* a disproportionate number of black and minority ethnic children are in care (Ali, 2014b). This omission replicates a similar lack of curiosity in the United States (Roberts, 2012, 2014a, 2014b). On account of this, issues related to questions of 'race', class and power are eased from the analytical frame. Second, the dominant tendency of 'invoking a singular category of "race" cannot provide a full picture' (Ali, 2014b: 71). Drawing on a welter of research literature, Ali (2014b: 71) usefully articulates some of the complexities which come to light if the category 'black and minority' is unpacked given the somewhat different care dynamics relating to Black African and Black Caribbean, Pakistani, Bangladeshi and Indian children.

However, the Department for Education's (2012b: 21) *An Action Plan for Adoption: Tackling Delay* starkly asserts that the 'delay faced by black children … needs particular attention', challenging the belief 'in some parts of the system … that ensuring a perfect or near perfect match based on the child's ethnicity … automatically outweighs other considerations' (Department for Education, 2012b: 21).

In 2013, the Coalition government finally announced it would amend the law to address what it perceived as an 'imbalance' (Department for Education, 2013: 34). In England – but not in Wales – the Children and Families Act 2014 marks a 'crucial symbolic landmark' in repealing the 'ethnicity clause' featured in the New Labour-prompted Adoption and Children Act 2002 (Kirton, 2016: 2). The intention, therefore, is clearly to promote the transracial adoption of black and minority ethnic children. More fundamentally, the current Conservative government is ideologically committed to minimising the relevance of 'race' and ethnicity and of grossly over-simplifying both the 'processes and experiences of adoption' (Ali, 2014b: 68).

INTER-COUNTRY ADOPTION (ICA) IN THE 'NEW WORLD ORDER'

Having been rebuffed in their attempts to adopt domestically, many wealthy and middle class couples turn to inter-country adoption (ICA). Four such couples recounted their experiences of dissatisfaction with adoption processes in the *Daily Mail* (Lawrence and Stocks, 2011). Each of them had their applications rejected for the 'most spurious reasons', but was able to 'fulfil their dreams' elsewhere. One couple informed readers:

> One social worker admitted there would be three things that would make it difficult for us to adopt in the UK: we were white, middle class and heterosexual. It just felt like political correctness gone mad. Like other couples in our situation, we were finally forced to look overseas, and we adopted our son three years ago from Guatemala, when he was 11 months old.

Clearly, being assessed as 'good enough' to adopt a child from abroad, but not domestically, might prompt concerns about the laxity of assessments relating to those seeking to extract children from other jurisdictions.

In global terms, ICA is largely a phenomenon stretching from the Second World War with the 1990s and early years of the next century being the peak period (Bartholet, 2007). For example, the numbers of adopted children from other countries arriving in the United States ballooned from 8,333 in 1994 to 22,884 in 2004 (Bartholet, 2007, Appendix A). The United States was – and remains – the world's leading 'receiving' country with some 'two-thirds of all internationally adopted children' being taken there (Bartholet, 2007: 166)[2]. However, figures published by the US State Department (2015) reveal that the number plummeted to 6,441 in 2014.

The mid-twentieth century Korean War (1950–1953) led to South Korea's 'opening up' for potential US adopters. As a result of the war, many children were orphaned or abandoned and some faced discrimination having been fathered by US servicemen. Adoptions continued from Korea, in considerable numbers, until the issue became politically ignited during the Seoul Olympics in 1988 when 'political forces launched a campaign castigating the government for "selling" the nation's children to affluent foreigners' (Bartholet, 2007: 160). On account of these protests and the availability of new and alternative supply chains, the number of Korean children being adopted into the United States drastically declined from 2,620 in 1990 to 370 in 2014 (Bartholet, 2007; US State Department, 2015).

Children move from 'south to north, east to west, poor to rich, brown to white. Over 50 per cent of them end up in one country alone: the United States' (Dubinsky, 2008: 340). Even the most prominent and vocal of supporters of ICA concede that it is not simply attributable to the 'objective needs of children for homes or the desire of prospective parents for children' because fluctuations in the flow of children are inseparable from 'political attitudes within both sending and receiving countries, and the international community' (Bartholet, 2007: 159). ICA is, in fact, invariably connected, even if only implicitly, to inequalities pertaining to states, classes, ethnicities and genders. Events in the former USSR provide a good illustration as to how ICA has to be situated within the broad context of global politics and economics.

As neoliberalism began to take hold in the former Eastern Bloc, whole swathes of life, formerly beyond the market-based modes of calculation and appreciation, were rapidly commodified. Indeed, this rationality began to saturate ICA practices in many countries. In 2001 Romania headed the list of countries having children adopted by US parents (2,594) (Bartholet, 2007: Appendix B). Moreover, researchers reporting on the country observed that every discussion on ICA circulated around commercial terms, such as 'auction', 'market' and 'price' (Corbett, 2002).

Across many parts of Eastern Europe, intensive assaults on public health provision resulted in death and hardship on a mass scale (Klein, 2007). For example, beginning in the early 1990s in the Russian Federation, there was a 'marked increase in male mortality over and above the historical trend' and the number of additional deaths during 1992–2001 is estimated at an astonishing 2.5–3 million. As a UN report remarked, in the 'absence of war, famine, or health epidemics there is no historical precedent for the scale of loss' (United Nations Development Programme, 2005: 23). Mass impoverishment and commodification, along with Westerners having greater access, formed potent contextual factors leading to inflated numbers of children being extracted and taken by adoptive parents to the United States, and a number of other countries, in the 1990s and into the new century (Bartholet, 2007: Appendix, B).

The growth in the number of children enmeshed in ICA processes was, therefore, analytically inseparable from the evolution of the 'New World Order', and the period in the 1990s which witnessed the belle époque of US 'global hegemony' (Davies, 2016: 127). Relatedly, economic 'shocks' – alongside war and natural disasters – have tended to furnish the terrain on which the global politics of ICA is mapped, with children moving and being relocated to adoptive families in the 'more privileged countries of the world' (Bartholet, 2007: 193). Historically, 'word of fast, easy placements of infants and toddlers spreads' and particular, usually impoverished, countries 'become "hot spots"… Typically, the children offered for placement will have characteristics valued by American adoptive parents' (Oreskovic and Maskew, 2008: 107). As the 'popularity of the country increases, competition for available infants becomes more intense' (2008: 109).

Since 1 May 1995, the Hague Convention on the Protection of Children and Co-operation in Respect of Intercountry Adoption (Hague Convention, 1993) has functioned as a form of global governance regulating ICA practices. As they have become gradually embedded, the provisions of the Convention have prevented some of the abuses so manifestly present during the ICA 'boom' years. In order to map some of the diverse responses to the Convention, the focus will initially be on the perceptions of Elizabeth Bartholet, an esteemed professor at the Harvard Law School. She maintains that adopters are too fettered by legal and other restrictions and so children are left to suffer. More broadly, Bartholet can be perceived as one of the chief promoters of ICA who advocates for policies that might better facilitate potential US adopters accessing and extracting children from their families, and countries of origin. Next, attention will turn to the critique directed at her perspective from Johanna Oreskovic and Trish Maskew (2008). All three authors are situated in the United States and, despite ICA processes being dissimilar in many respects in different countries their exchanges provide insights that have universal resonance.

COMBATING 'ANTI-ADOPTION FORCES': MAKING THE CASE OF ICA

According to its supporters, ICA is of considerable significance beyond the child/parent(s)/adoptive parent(s) triad because of its potent political symbolism: given the 'realities of today's world … it also pushes us forward on a path to creating a more just world' (Bartholet, 2007: 158). Adoptive parents, acquiring children through ICA, 'demonstrate the human capacity for love across lines of difference, as a positive force for good in a world torn apart by hatred based on racial, ethnic, and national differences' (Bartholet, 2007: 182). Thus, the extraction of children from the country of origin can be perceived as a form of benign, humanitarian interventionism chiming with the rhetoric of US and NATO foreign policy imperatives.

In advocating their position, figures such as Bartholet imply that they are giving voice to an embattled, minority position which is confronted by a plethora of international forces. Powerful supra-national bodies, such as the United Nations Children's Fund (UNICEF) and the UN Committee on the Rights of the Child, are accused of negative bias against ICA (Bartholet, 2007: 152). Similarly, the European Parliament is criticised for being 'dominated by forces' that consider

ICA to be 'inherently a violation of children's human rights' (Bartholet, 2007: 157). Paradigmatic of the EU's position, for example, were the pressures placed on Romania in 2004, to prevent ICA, except in circumstances where the adopters are the child's grandparents. Whilst Bartholet recognised that efforts to enforce rules against the sale of children were 'appropriate', 'so-called reform moves' resulted, for her, in thousands of children 'abandoned in institutions' being denied the chance of adoption (Bartholet, 2007: 162).

The Hague Convention is deemed to be flawed because international 'human rights organizations' allegedly blunted its original goals, by excluding a provision requiring signatory nations to proactively *facilitate* ICA. With its emphasis on preventing adoption abuses, the Convention appears, in Bartholet's views, to 'effectively close, not open, opportunities for adoption' (2007: 154), creating countless 'additional barriers' and 'new bureaucratic hurdles' (2007: 175). Such measures are prompted by 'anti-adoption forces' seeking to use the implementation of the Convention as another 'opportunity to mount a battle to limit or close down international adoption, as has happened in Guatemala' (2007: 175). On account of their interventions, additional administration is also likely to unfairly 'increase the expense' of ICA for prospective parents in the US and elsewhere (2007: 175).

One 'unduly restrictive' article in the Convention, of particular concern to Bartholet (2007: 176), is the stipulation that each sending and receiving country must have a 'Central Authority' with overall responsibility for the oversight and the regulation of ICA. However, the state having a 'monopoly' constitutes a problem because of the 'risk' that adoptions would be 'unduly limited or effectively closed down, given government proclivity to regulate in a negative way' (2007: 176). Entirely attuned to pervasive neoliberal perceptions, Bartholet's (2007: 176) preference is that the state should retreat so as to preserve the role of private adoptions, with non-governmental agencies and 'intermediaries' continuing to play a pivotal role (2007: 176).

Bartholet (2007: 179) maintains that the 'social science and child development expertise' reveals just how harmful it is to children to 'grow up on the streets or in institutions'. In contrast, overemphasising children needing to remain in their countries of origin, opponents of ICA are seen as deluded by 'extreme romanticism, without any grounding in the available evidence and without support in common sense' (Bartholet, 2007: 180). The choice, for many children, is stark: between 'life – and often death – in orphanages or on the streets in their home country and, for a lucky few, life in an adoptive home abroad' (2007: 181). Moreover, the numbers of children requiring ICA is potentially enormous given there are

> said to be some *100 million children with no available caregivers* – 65 million in Asia, 34 million in Africa, and 8 million in Latin America and the Caribbean. UNICEF estimates that at least 2.6 million children worldwide live in institutional care, noting that this is a significant underestimate. (Bartholet, 2007: 182–3, original emphasis)

According to this perspective, ICA is not a crudely selfish endeavour pursued by relatively wealthy citizens from the US and elsewhere in the West. It can also be perceived as politically progressive in that, aligned with aspects of feminist thinking, it rejects genetic essentialism and the associated fetishism of familial blood ties. ICA also has potent and beneficial outcomes for the sending countries placing 'helpful pressure' on officials in these countries and on people in 'richer countries of the world to improve conditions for children in orphanages and on the streets' (Bartholet, 2007: 184). Indeed, ICA helps to bring much needed new funding to poor orphanages in sending countries (2007: 184).

Perhaps one of the major challenges that Bartholet encounters is the well-documented abuses associated with ICA, particularly in the 1990s and early 2000s when the practice was most rife and unregulated. However, for her, critical reports on ICA are simply reflective of the manipulative agenda-setting capacity of the 'anti-adoption forces' preoccupying her. Opponents make some 'arguments that are simply absurd, but are nonetheless seriously problematic ... because they are sometimes believed and thus give adoption an unjustified bad name' (Bartholet, 2007: 186). In 2007 she argued that Guatemala, from where she herself adopted a child, was the place where the main 'battle' was being fought (2007: 190). By 2014, the number of children adopted from Guatemala was a mere 29 (US State Department, 2015: Table 1). However, in 2006, around the time she was writing, despite its relatively small size, more children were adopted into the United States from Guatemala (4,135), than from any other country apart from China (no. 6,493) (Bartholet, 2007: Appendix B). Many suggested that the sheer numbers of children taken from Guatemala at least hinted at major problems. This was clearly not the perception of Bartholet (2007: 190–1), who accused those calling for reform, of doing 'devastating harm to thousands of Guatemalan children every year, condemning them to spend unnecessary months and years in damaging institutions, denying them any opportunity for a normal family life'.

'DISTURBING AND PROBLEMATIC' QUESTIONS: CONCERNS ABOUT ICA

Unsurprisingly, Bartholet's perspective on ICA has prompted detailed criticisms. Oreskovic and Maskew (2008: 76), who like her have acquired children via ICA, argue that her position occludes a range of 'disturbing and problematic' questions including 'child-buying, coercion of vulnerable birth parents, weak regulatory structures, and profiteering'. Underpinning the critique is the assertion that Bartholet tactically inflates the number of children actually available for ICA. Empirically, they maintain, her assertion that there is a global pool of millions of potentially adoptable children lacks credibility. They also counter Bartholet's tactic of equating placement in an orphanage with the desire of parents to permanently relinquish their children. This notion requires a more 'searching investigation' because of the complexities associated with recourse to orphanages in many parts of the world (Oreskovic and Maskew, 2008: 76). Many parents, they argue, may use orphanages in a temporary and expedient way, but this does not mean that they or the wider family have permanently relinquished children. Moreover, the population of children located in orphanages is not that targeted by US adopters. UNICEF estimate that 88% of the world's orphans are *over* the age of five. In contrast, children adopted by US citizens tend to be *under* the age of five years (in Oreskovic and Maskew, 2008: 80). Children are not, as Bartholet would have her readers believe, remaining in orphanages simply on account of the allegedly restrictive policies being championed by 'anti-adoption forces'. It is more likely to be because they do not meet the 'well-documented preference of adoptive parents for infant and toddler girls' (Gravois, 2004; Oreskovic and Maskew, 2008: 81).

Oreskovic and Maskew (2008: 122) also question Bartholet's apparent failure to adequately address the 'growing body of work' produced by many adoptees chronicling 'alienation both from birth and adoptive cultures, significant identity and role confusion, and profound degrees of depression and anger over the loss of identity, family and heritage'. Article 8 of the UN Convention on the Rights of the Child, the right to identity, notably includes 'nationality, name and family relations as recognised by law'. For children adopted beyond their countries of birth, the notion of 'open adoption' – discussed earlier – has no real impact. Evidence gathered in Ireland, for example, indicates most adopted children do not remain in contact with anyone in their country of birth (Green et al., 2007: 13). The same research study also states that adoptive parents can appear 'disinclined to accept the extent to which their children might be struggling with issues of difference, for example, making comments about how they did not notice their child's skin colour any more or that they forget that they were adopted. This contrasted with an acute awareness of difference on the part of many of the children' (2007: 14).

Consistent with her aspiration to keep the state at a distance, Bartholet's preference for a private agency system as opposed to a 'Central Authority' regulation of ICA mandated by the Hague Convention also merits further scrutiny. The US has ratified the Convention, but the overwhelming majority of international adoptions are arranged privately. Oreskovic and Maskew identify a range of concerns with such reliance on private agencies. For example, many of the agencies enter into contracts with parents which contain stringent terms excluding them from liability should any medical issues subsequently arise with the children adopted. Such contracts can also contain 'gagging clauses' preventing adoptive parents from speaking publicly about aspects of ICA practices (Oreskovic and Maskew, 2008). US Adoption agencies have not tended to feel even legally bound to ensure that the post-placement reports required by many sending countries are completed. Such omissions were connected, for example, to the plight of a five-year old Russian girl, Masha Allen, allowed to be adopted by a single male, who sexually abused her for over six years (Oreskovic and Maskew, 2008: 85). Private agencies also depend too much on 'in-country intermediaries, many of whom are unlicensed and whose activities are not closely monitored' (Oreskovic and Maskew, 2008: 86). Controlled government systems – such as those established in China – having offices tasked with facilitating and controlling ICA, 'do a better job of preventing child buying activities' (Oreskovic and Maskew, 2008: 89). In contrast, countries such as Guatemala, Cambodia and Vietnam – without robust central state systems – have been embroiled in scandals related to child buying, bribery and miscellaneous related scandals.

Perhaps the main charge levelled at Bartholet is that she downplays the sheer scale of adoption abuses associated with ICA. Payments provided to birth mothers are rationalised by her suggesting that a distinction must be made between those made to 'induce relinquishment and humanitarian assistance provided *after* relinquishment'. However, such a distinction may not be so clear-cut since 'the *known* possibility of assistance, whether pre or post relinquishment, has the same effect: It creates an *incentive* to relinquish, particularly when the birth family is destitute or in crisis' (Oreskovic and Maskew, 2008: 105, original emphases). Hence, by 'minimizing the ethical significance of payment in connection with relinquishment Bartholet can then cast the human rights community's legitimate concern with the integrity of process as mere anti-adoption sentiment' (Oreskovic and Maskew, 2008: 105). On the whole, human rights objections have focused on only a handful of places: Romania in the early 1990s, Cambodia in 2000–2001, Vietnam and Guatemala later the same decade. Unsurprisingly, these are countries afflicted by extreme poverty, war or other forms of unrest and, with the exception of Romania, these are also countries that have been subject to various forms of military interventions by the United States. As a result of this constellation of adverse circumstances, they lack adequate child welfare and social work infrastructures and this negatively impacts particularly on women.

In the late-1990s and into the new century, Cambodia furnished insights into the 'shadowy world of illicit child procurement networks that can operate in a laxly-regulated system particularly vulnerable to abuse' (Oreskovic and Maskew, 2008: 111). This is not to suggest this situation was attributable to something inherently abusive about the people of Cambodia. Rather, the problems associated with its child adoption practices have to be situated within a wider framework alert to Cambodia's history as a Western colony. In the late-1990s, the country was also war ravaged and locked into a subjugated role within the global political economy. Specifically, relating to the births of children, records were normally maintained at 'village level if at all' and actual certificates of birth were not ordinarily produced unless a child was to be adopted (Oreskovic and Maskew, 2008: 111). Initially, potentially adoptable boys outnumbered girls, so what occurred was what 'you would expect to happen in an under-policed free market: Market pressure built up, until certain enterprising Cambodian adoption suppliers, or "facilitators" stepped in and found a way to meet demand' (Gravois, 2004). Involved in at least one 'celebrity' adoption, an American adoption facilitator, Lauryn Galindo, was subsequently imprisoned by a US court for her illegal practices.

In 2001, the American Ambassador to Cambodia referred to how the growing interest in adoption had prompted the building of new orphanages to be erected 'expressly to keep the parade of Americans happy and that, more worryingly, these orphanages are filled with children who seem custom-ordered to suit American tastes' (Corbett, 2002). As one aid worker confided it was the 'cute and cuddlies' who were most prized, meaning children who were healthy, young and preferably female.

Significant here was the role played by various 'facilitators' in ensuring the flow of children to the United States was maintained (Oreskovic and Maskew, 2008: 115).

As mentioned above, Guatemala was championed by adoptive parents fleeing 'political correctness gone mad' at home and for a number of years the country was converted into a 'virtual baby farm' supplying 'infants as if they were a commodity' (Nicolson, 2004; Lacey, 2006). The US was the chief destination and between 1995 and 2005, US families adopted '18,298 Guatemalan babies, with the figure rising nearly every year' (Nicolson, 2004). The paperwork deemed necessary could be dealt with in just one visit. At the beginning of the 1990s, just 257 children were taken to the United States by adoptive parents; in 2000 1,518 were taken from the country by US adopters. However, in 2006 the number of Guatemalan children adopted into the United States reached 4,135 (in Bartholet, 2007: Appendix B).

Contextually, Guatemala's recent history includes a US-engineered coup (1954), a civil war (1954–1996), human rights abuses, desperate poverty and a prolonged health emergency (Dubinsky, 2008). In tandem with these inflicted forms of social suffering and distress, the country of 12 million people emerged as a 'hot spot' for foreigners intent on finding and extracting a child for adoption. Children adopted from Guatemala, during the peak period of transfers to the United States, also tended to come primarily from an unregulated 'private system developed by Guatemalan attorneys and foreign agencies' (Oreskovic and Maskew, 2008: 117). Significant here was the role of *jaladores* who tracked down pregnant women or women with small or very young children to convince them to relinquish their children for a fee. They, in turn, were paid a finder's fee for locating such women (Oreskovic and Maskew, 2008). Such pivotal figures tended to be doctors, social workers, nurses, teachers or other community figures perceived as possessing sufficient 'symbolic capital' to undertake the role (see also Chapter 2).

More generally, by 2010, the global number of children being adopted via ICA fell to the lowest level since 1997, yet this figure was still estimated to be 50% higher than in 1987 (Selman, 2012: 393). In terms of the United States, in 2014, China was the country most children were adopted from (2,040). Within Europe, Ukraine, experiencing turmoil and civil unrest, was slowly beginning to emerge as a new 'hot spot' for US adopters (521). Relatedly, there are indications that Ukraine is an increasingly favoured location for Westerners seeking to have children via surrogacy, given the relatively inexpensive transactional costs and the fact that legislation there is 'protective of the intended parents' (Wayman, 2016: 9; see also Pande, 2016). Beyond Europe, Ethiopia (716) and Haiti (464) now also feature prominently in the ICA statistics published by the US State Department (2015).

CONCLUSION

Returning to the current presentation of adoption and its prominence in political and popular discourses in the UK, there are risks that many parents – perhaps anxious that their children might be adopted – may be alienated and deterred from approaching local social services for family support. The political centrality of adoption word might also lead to a further diminution in such services. More generally, it is apparent that both domestic and inter-country adoption has to be situated in the context of neoliberal economic and cultural practices. Furthermore, adoption continues to lie at the intersection of a range of converging issues rooted in social divisions and cleavages associated with social class, 'race' and ethnicity, sexual orientation, gender roles, age, (dis)ability and, in the case of ICA, neo-colonialism.

REFLECTION AND TALK BOX 9

1. How can some of the issues raised in relation to child adoption be connected to the discussion on the underclass featured in Chapter 4?

2. In May 2016, the British Association of Social Workers (BASW) instigated an enquiry focused on child adoption. It stated:

    > There has been a relative absence of discussion within the profession of the issues of rights and ethics, in what is an increasingly contested and complex area of work ... In most cases today, adoption is non-consensual and involves removing the rights and responsibilities of birth parents, and severing the relationship of a child with his or her birth parents and families, most of whom are among the most disadvantaged people in society. (BASW, 2016)

    Is BASW right to be concerned about recent developments?

FURTHER READING

In terms of the trajectory of policies in England and Wales, a number of recent articles examine the politics of 'race'. In this context, the work of Suki Ali (2014a, 2014b) is excellent. Derek Kirton (2016) has also explored this aspect. Ian Butler (2014) charts how more coercive approaches toward certain families are becoming more embedded. The Movement for an Adoption Apology (2011) illustrates how mass adoption, in the past, resulted in oppressive practices. In Australia, the national apology given by Prime Minister Julia Gillard (2013) highlights how abuses took place, of course, also beyond the UK. Turning to inter-country adoption, the exchange involving Elizabeth Bartholet, Johanna Oreskovic and Trish Maskew provides a good example of the opposing positions taken in debates circulating around the theme.

CHAPTER 10

CONCLUSION

INTRODUCTION

Only occasionally catching a blurred glimpse of the location names on the platform signs, the express train driver speeds, station to station, without stopping. The approach taken in this book has been more akin to a train moving at a slower pace and pausing at a number of stations. Passengers – rejecting the term 'customers' – could amble around for a while and explore a few places that people talk about a lot, but rarely visit and really get to know. The seven stations punctuating the journey were the book's 'welfare words': 'welfare dependency', 'underclass', 'social exclusion', 'early intervention', 'resilience', 'care' and 'adoption'.

Writing at the beginning of the 1960s, the Swedish sociologist Gunnar Myrdal (1960: 122) claimed:

> We have come a very long way from the old quasi-liberal state as it existed half a century ago. The Welfare State is now developing further almost automatically. The social and economic reforms accrue merely as by-products of economic progress, which itself is spurred by the reforms in a cumulative fashion. No hard fights are now necessary. The reformers become largely dispensable.

Looking backwards, it is striking how sanguine and complacent the supporters of the social democratic pact, giving rise to the welfare state, actually were. In the UK, perhaps stretching from the end of the Second World War until the period of Thatcherism, a broad swathe of 'left and right political opinion supported this social democratic consensus on the welfare state, allowing it to be represented as apolitical and value-free' (Harris, 2002: 268).

In his popular *The Ministry of Nostalgia*, Owen Hatherley (2016) remarks that:

> The attacks on social democracy by the 1960s generation that benefitted from it most – as statist, or even 'totalitarian' – now seem hysterical, devoid of any real sense of historical perspective. For them the 'welfare

state' was normal, familiar, and rather boring, a perspective it is hard not
to find outright offensive today. Their politics were based on the assumption that affluence, social peace and equality were permanent rather than
the brief historical aberration that they were.

It is, of course, possible to question the notion that the welfare state was benignly
altruistic and inclusive. As observed in the introductory chapter, when thinking
about the welfare state, there is a need to avoid retrospectively misreading and
valorising, seemingly, progressive and benign post-war 'Fordist' welfare arrangements and structures. Historically, welfare states always had 'something to do
with the management or regulation of "problem" populations' (Clarke, 2004: 1;
Fletcher, 2015). Tracy Jensen and Imogen Tyler (2015: 471) argue that what
remains of the post-war welfare state today was 'indelibly shaped by struggles
against disciplinary welfare regimes and against the forms of patriarchy and
state-racism it reproduced'.

More generally, welfare states, such as that assembled following the introduction
of the UK Beveridge reforms, were a complex 'interaction of three main factors':
the struggle of the working class against their exploitation; the requirements of
industrial capitalism for a more efficient environment in which to operate and, in
particular, its need for a highly productive labour force; recognition by property
owners of the price that had to be paid for political security (Saville, 1957: 2). The
creation of state-managed Fordist welfare regimes was, in this sense, 'saving the
capitalist system from its own self-destabilizing propensities—as well as from
the spectre of revolution in an era of mass mobilization. Productivity and profitability required the "biopolitical" cultivation of a healthy, educated workforce with
a stake in the system' (Fraser, 2016: 109).

Foucault (2009: 216) argues that the Beveridge Plan and 'all the projects of economic and social interventionism' developed during the Second World War were the
outcome of a 'series of pacts' which were to characterise the period of 'embedded
liberalism' (Harvey, 2005). Such 'pacts', occasionally implicit, promised 'to those
who were asked to go to war and get themselves killed – a certain type of economic
and social organization which assured security (of employment, with regard to illness
and other kinds of risk, and the level of retirement)' (Foucault, 2009: 216). However,
the German ordoliberals defined their politics in opposition to Beveridge and a
more interventionist state and were to act as a geographically dispersed 'thought
collective' for a range of neoliberal blueprints (Mirowski and Plehwe, 2009).

Neoliberals have been the curators of neo-welfare: fostering and promoting a new
state of welfare aspiring to replace welfare states. Within the EU, in recent years, it has
been Greece which has had to face the most 'radical' experimentation in this regard.
The Greek working class has been the target of a 'gigantic disciplining operation –
a huge experiment in violent downward social mobility and neoliberal adjustment and
restructuring' (Stavrakakis, 2013: 315). Emblematic in this respect, is the acronym
'PIIGs' (Portugal, Italy, Ireland, Greece and Spain), deployed, on one level, merely as a

shorthand for the EU's most indebted national economies toward the end of the 2000s, on the other, as an insidiously dehumanising metaphor, justifying the use of large number of disenfranchized citizens, as 'guinea pigs' in the EU neoliberal lab (2013: 315).

Some of the main, and emerging, characteristics of neo-welfare, in locations such as the UK, include:

- A commitment to ensuring that welfare provision is sufficient to maintain the required levels of social reproduction and social stability to offset the risk of mass resistance and widespread public disturbances

- Privatisation of many areas of public welfare provision

- Precarious working conditions

- Increased 'third sector' provision and promotion of a 'new philanthropy'

- More indebtedness given it is 'increasingly through debt ... that capital now cannibalizes labour, disciplines states, transfers wealth from periphery to core, and sucks value from households, families, communities and nature' (Fraser, 2016: 113)

- Enhanced conditionality and surveillance: in the future, this may entail a greater use of algorithmic monitoring devices producing metrics indicating an individual's degree of willingness to appropriately care for their own welfare and that of their family

- Increased (dis)entitlement relating to 'othered' populations such as asylum seekers

- Inflated rhetoric circulating around innovation, entrepreneurship, empowerment, participation.

Many of these dimensions can be detected, and have shaped contemporary under-standings of some of the welfare words explored in the earlier chapters.

'CHANGE HAS GOT TO COME': RHETORICALLY RECALIBRATED NEOLIBERALISM?

> It's been a long, a long time coming
> But I know a change gon' come, oh yes it will
>
> (Sam Cooke, 1964)

> It feels like your dreams have been sacrificed in the service of others. So change has got to come (Theresa May, 2016b)

At this current conjuncture, it appears that neoliberalism is being rhetorically recalibrated. In the UK, it has been maintained that the Brexit vote and the associated 'ructions of 2016 may signal a pivot from punitive to compensatory neoliberalism, as spending cuts and monetary policy reach their political and economic limits' (Watkins, 2016: 27). However, as Nancy Fraser (2016: 103) maintains crashing through such 'limits' is, in fact, inherent to capitalism. Furthermore,

> when capital's drive to expanded accumulation becomes unmoored from its social bases and turns against them ... the logic of economic production overrides that of social reproduction, destabilizing the very processes on which capital depends—compromising the social capacities, both domestic and public, that are needed to sustain accumulation over the long term. Destroying its own conditions of possibility, capital's accumulation dynamic effectively eats its own tail.

However, at the time of writing, shifts may be detectable in the tonality of policy as this relates to questions pertaining to welfare provision and, more broadly, the role of government. Seemingly, a longing for earlier forms of *nationally* 'embedded liberalism' (Harvey, 2005), discussed in our opening chapter, has started to seep into the rhetoric deployed by primary definers, such as UK Prime Minister Theresa May. Enunciating the 'new centre ground' of British politics at the Conservative Party conference in October 2016, May (2016b) contended that this was the time for

> a new approach that says while government does not have all the answers, government can and should be a force for good; that the state exists to provide what individual people, communities and markets cannot; and that we should employ the power of government for the good of the people.

If this politics were to be pursued it would serve to maintain and nurture a 'country of decency, fairness and quiet resolve ... a Great Meritocracy' (May, 2016b). This rhetorical positioning is partly a reaction to challenges from the nationalist right, within her own party, UKIP and the insurgent left within the Labour Party. Following the Conservative Party debacle in the 'surprise' General Election in 2017, the 'threat' posed by a revitalised democratic–socialist project has been magnified. However, in some respects, May's rhetoric was foreshadowed by the narratives circulating around 'inclusive capitalism' referred to in Chapter 5 (see also Carney, 2014). Such moves can be interpreted as part of more encompassing projects seeking to steer the leadership of the ruling bloc, generating consent amongst 'kindred and allied groups' (Gramsci in Hoare and Nowell Smith, 2005: 57–8). In the United States not entirely dissimilar shifts are detectable with the emergence of what Fraser ironically terms 'progressive' neoliberalism 'celebrating "diversity", meritocracy and "emancipation" while dismantling social protections and re-externalizing social reproduction. The result is not only to abandon defenceless populations to capital's predations, but also to redefine emancipation in market terms' (Fraser, 2016: 113). At the level of electoral politics, this form of neoliberalism was embodied, during the 2016 presidential election campaign, by the defeated Hillary Clinton: economically business-as-usual, hawkish overseas, but keen to pursue a liberal social agenda particularly in terms of issues pertaining to gender and sexuality.

Others, however, suggest that neoliberalism is being recalibrated in rather different ways, with Davies (2016), for example, arguing that neoliberalism has passed through three stages. A form of 'combative' or insurgent neoliberalism (1979–1989), followed by the 'normative' neoliberalism which began with the fall of the Berlin Wall in 1989 and culminated in the 'crash' of 2008. Since then, neoliberalism can be perceived as entering an unfinished 'punitive' phase in which debt and punishment becomes more prominent. Perhaps anticipating something of the 'spirit' of the rebarbative and erratic Trump administration, Davies (2016: 130) interprets this development as related to the evolution of a 'melancholic condition in which governments and societies unleash hatred and violence'. Moreover, integral to 'punitive' neoliberalism is the decline in mental health, and a public vocabulary inculcating self-blaming.

WELFARE WORDS AND DISRUPTIVE THINKING

This book has explored a cluster of words which are, to varying degrees, omnipresent during this period when the trajectory of the neoliberal project is more edgily uncertain. These words, along with others not explored, condense various ideological and hegemonic themes at this particular historical conjuncture, amplifying the 'state of play' in particular fields of operation such as social work and social policy. Attentiveness to such words is of the utmost importance because they can reflect how the dominant order is assembled; they contribute to its constitution and consolidation but, on occasions, they can also become the focus of challenges to the status quo.

Initially inspired by Raymond Williams, this approach to analysing the changes under way has recognised and acknowledged the importance of 'keyword-anchored theorising' (Wilson, 2016: 4). Indeed, there may be something of a resurgence of interest in this form of inquiry within social work, social policy and sociology (Eagleton-Pierce, 2016; Fritsch et al., 2016a; Moran, 2015; Wilson, 2016). According to Williams, it is informative to focus on how significant 'social and historical processes occur *within* language ... New kinds of relationship, but also new ways of seeing existing relationships, appear in language in a variety of ways' (Williams, 1983: 22, original emphasis). It is possible to observe, therefore, the 'invention of new terms' and the adaptation, alteration, extension and transfer of 'older terms' (1983: 22) Hence, particular words and related concepts, as the Soviet linguist Valentin Voloshinov (1895–1936) suggested, exhibit an 'extraordinary sensitivity to ... fluctuations in the social atmosphere' (Voloshinov, 1973: 20). Following this same line of analysis, many of the selected words examined in the book have evolved into 'fully fledged ideological products' with layer upon layer of meaning accumulated over time (Voloshinov, 1973: 20).

As Marx and Engels maintained, the class which is 'the ruling *material* force of society is at the same time its ruling *intellectual* force' (in Easthope and McGowan, 2004: 39, original emphases). Given it has the means of material production at its disposal, it consequently controls the 'means of mental production ... [The ruling class] among other things rule as thinkers, as producers of ideas, and regulate the production and distribution of the ideas of their age' (2004: 39). That capitalism organises 'matter and perception' (Fritsch et al., 2016b: 7) is reflected, for example, in the eagerness with which the concept of underclass was embraced and amplified by reputed media outlets such as *The Sunday Times* (see also Chapter 4). Yet, when critical and sceptical voices challenged Murray's promulgation of this degrading label, the word became central to the struggle to define the purpose and boundaries of welfare provision.

Partly in tune with Gramsci's and Bourdieu's approach, Fraser and Gordon (1997: 122) stress the need to construct and promote a 'critical political semantics' to better discern how neoliberalism seeks to maintain domination across societies and within particular institutions and bureaucratic fields. Such critical vigilance is imperative, since 'unreflective' use of welfare words might 'serve to enshrine certain interpretations of social life as authoritative and ... obscure others', generally to the advantage of powerful groups in society and to the disadvantage of subordinate ones (Fraser and Gordon, 1997: 123).

Language does not 'produce the world as various strands of idealist philosophy have maintained; however, it does organise and delimit its objects' (Fritsch et al., 2016b: 12). In this context, Safri and Ruccio (2013: 8) argue that the exploration of particular words can potentially provide a 'specific "interventionist" scholarship' exposing the political, ethical, and class stakes inherent to particular words or phrases. This book has tried to *pull* and *stretch* a series of welfare words, to view them from different angles and places, to *defamiliarise* and *disrupt* their taken-for-granted meanings. This is vital because the words and phrases we have explored constitute the 'linguistic habitus' (Hayward, 2003) of social workers and aid, what we have seen Bourdieu (1994: 9) refers to as, the attainment of the 'feel for the game'.

Words are notably unstable and can always have their meanings overturned. However, as Voloshinov (1973: 23) argued in the 1920s, the ruling class strive to impart a dominant, hegemonic 'supraclass, eternal character' to particular words. Relatedly, Sanford Schram, whose *Words of Welfare* (1995) influenced the writing of this book, argues that attempts to 'rename' can serve to progressively 'destabilize prevailing institutional practices' which may be harmful or damaging (Schram, 1995: 21). Renaming can help 'denaturalize and delegitimate ascendant categories and constraints they place on political possibility' (1995: 22), yet Schram is also alert to how labels and keywords, even those aiming at a progressive re-framing, are constantly shifting and in flux because all 'terms are partial and incomplete characterizations' with every new term failing to capture 'all that needs to be said about any topic' (1995: 24). Similar points have more recently been made by Fritsch et al. who argue that 'purely nominal shifts are never enough' to resolve political problems (2016b: 3). Nevertheless, projects of re-signification and attempts to 'change the valuations assigned to particular terms' have progressive utility (2016b: 14).

Given that 'no particular list of words ... should be considered fixed or final' (Durant, 2008, p. 126), it may be useful to think and speak against the grain of current and dominant forms of, for example, resilience talk: could it be possible to re-orientate this welfare word so as to interrogate the resilience, solidity and durability of structures of privilege nurtured by elite networks (Rivera, 2015). Moreover, can a progressive agenda within social work and social policy strive to revive and foreground alternative and more oppositional keywords, such as 'solidarity' and 'resistance' (Caygill, 2013; see also Scottish Unemployed Workers Network, 2016)?

Clearly, a range of entirely different words and phrases could have been selected for the purposes of this book. For example, increasingly to the fore in what Bourdieu and Wacquant (2001: 2) term the neoliberal 'vulgate', are words such as therapy, happiness and mindfulness. It is also clear that some words, such as 'prevention', are being subjected to transfer or extension. In the area of social work with children and families, this word is increasingly harnessed to 'radicalisation' and is reflected in worries about a conflationary rhetorical logic linking, for example, the Troubled Families Programme with notions of 'terror' and 'radicalisation' (Stanley and Guru, 2015; McKendrick and Finch, 2016: 1). The words 'entrepreneur' or 'social entrepreneur' are becoming omnipresent and crossing the traditional divide between political left and right. Symptomatic of this trend, John McDonnell (2016), as UK Labour Shadow Chancellor, has proclaimed the commitment of a future Labour government to 'create an entrepreneurial state that works with the wealth creators'. Conversely, traditionally progressive phrases such as 'social justice' have been incorporated within the political discourse of the ruling Conservative Party in the UK, being disassembled and reassembled in such a way as to eliminate all semblance of radical leftist intent.

In conclusion, the ubiquitous words and phrases explored in this book can be regarded as 'tips of the iceberg', hinting at the concealed contours of a much larger phenomenon (Stubbs in Holborow, 2015: 116). Looking beneath the surface of the water might, therefore, help to cultivate new habits of disruptive thinking, new modes of resistance and new political possibilities in and beyond social work and social policy.

NOTES

CHAPTER 1

1. For convenience sake, I will tend to avoid using quotation marks to highlight the welfare words and phrases discussed. However, readers are welcome to infer them given my quizzical explorations.
2. This reworked table initially appeared in Garrett (2014c). It mainly relates to the UK and it is recognised that even its broad brush validity is questionable in relation to other jurisdictions where readers may be located. In the Republic of Ireland, for example, the welfare state was never particularly 'embedded' even during the period loosely referred to as one of 'embedded neoliberalism'.
3. Financialization refers to a marked increase in the 'significance of financial markets and institutions in the economy and a dramatic increase in the volume, velocity, complexity, and connectedness of financial flows ... Financialization of the economy furnished the prerequisites for the dramatic growth of household debt and the connection between debt and discipline' (Mahmud, 2012: 474–5).
4. Examining the 'deep semiotic structure of deservedness' in the United States, Sanford F. Schram (2015: 85) makes a useful distinction between 'discourse' and 'narrative'. In his rendering:

> Narratives are the surface textual representations of actions and events, while discourse is the underlying interpretative context for making sense of those surface narratives. Consciously or not, we inevitably rely on the underlying discourse for interpreting the implicit understandings that are only suggested by the explicit surface narratives ... Narratives are potent with meaning in ways that only discourse can reveal. Just as we rely on implicit understandings to interpret nonverbal cues, we rely on the structure of intelligibility associated with any discourse to connect the dots in any narrative. To focus on the explicit narrative at the expense of the implicit discourse is, metaphorically speaking, to miss the forest for the trees. (Schram, 2015: 85)

5. Nancy Fraser (2013: 214) argues 'second-wave feminists expanded the number of axes that could harbour injustice. Rejecting the primacy of class, socialist-feminists, black-feminists, and anti-imperialist feminists also opposed radical feminist efforts to install gender in that same position of category privilege. Focusing not only on gender, but also on class, "race", sexuality, and nationality, they pioneered an "intersectionalist" alternative that is widely accepted today.'

CHAPTER 2

1. In Ireland, an interesting example of such an approach is provided by the Social Work Action Network and its bulletin *Frontline* https://socialworkactionnetworkireland.files.wordpress.com/2016/05/frontline-issue-2-june-20163.pdf.
2. I am very grateful to Michael Gorman and the publisher, the Lighthouse Press, for allowing me refer to his poem 'The People I Grew Up With Were Afraid'.
3. I am grateful to the poet Sarah Clancy for drawing Baldwin's book to my attention.
4. Wacquant also conceptualises 'advanced marginality' and, relatedly, 'territorial stigmatization'. Here the aim is to focus very briefly on 'neoliberal penality', but his other core thematic concerns will be examined in Chapter 4 in the discussion on the underclass.
5. The Health and Care Professions Council succeeded the GSCC in August 2012.

CHAPTER 3

1. An earlier version of this chapter, now radically revised, featured in *Critical and Radical Social Work*, 3 (3): 389–406. I am grateful to the Policy Press for allowing me to use part of my earlier published article.
2. Serving from 1969 to 1974, Richard Milhous Nixon (1913–1994) was the 37th President of the United States.
3. One respected US author has argued that it was a historical 'British preoccupation with welfare dependency' which was actually 'imported to the United States and came to be infused into the systems of social provision' (Schram, 2015: 93).
4. In 2013, for example, Michael Philpott was found guilty of the manslaughter of six of his children and the then Chancellor, George Osborne, linked the tragedy to the need to curtail 'excessive' child benefit and welfare payments (see also the Editorial 'From Death to Distortion', *The Guardian*, 6 April, 2013: 40). Osborne remarked: 'The courts are responsible for sentencing him, but I think there is a question for government and for society about the welfare state – and the tax-payers who pay for the welfare state – subsidizing lifestyles like that, and I think that debate needs to be had' ('Lib Dem anger at Osborne's Philpott speech', *The Guardian*, 6 April, 2013: 2).

CHAPTER 4

1. I take the phrase '*scum semiotics*' from Imogen Tyler.
2. Vulgate refers to an ancient Latin version of the Scriptures made by St Jerome and others in the fourth century.
3. A resident condemned the '*Shameless*-like portrayal' (Critchley, 2012: 34). Screened from January 2004 to May 2013, *Shameless* was a comedy-drama set on a fictional council estate in Manchester.
4. See also Keenan (2013) referring to an advertisement for *The Irish Examiner* which featured an image of the city of Limerick with police yellow criminal incident tape plastered over it.

CHAPTER 5

1. What follows is partly derived from Garrett (2015c). I am grateful to Taylor & Francis for permitting me to have recourse to this article again.
2. Stephen Lawrence (1974–1993) was a young, black Londoner murdered in a racially motivated attack on the evening of 22 April 1993. A public inquiry headed by Sir William Macpherson (1999) examined the original Metropolitan Police Service (MPS) investigation and concluded that the force was 'institutionally racist'.
3. Elsewhere, Fraser (2013: 193) has elaborated that according this 'radical-democratic interpretation of the principle of equal moral worth, justice requires social arrangements that permit all to participate as peers in social life. Overcoming injustice means dismantling institutionalised obstacles that prevent some people from participating on a par with others, as full partners in social interaction.'

CHAPTER 7

1. A different, but foundational version of this chapter was published by the *British Journal of Social Work*, 46 (4): 873–89. I am grateful to Cambridge University Press for allowing me refer to this earlier contribution.
2. This summation is derived from Howell (2015). However see also the US military website Comprehensive Soldier and Family Fitness: Building Resilience, Strengthening Performance. This includes an overview video http://csf2.army.mil/. In addition, the US Army now also has its own 'Resilience Directorate'.

CHAPTER 8

1. In England and Wales, under the auspices of the Children Act 1989, being 'in care' was discursively rebranded as being 'looked after'. This was partly because of the stigma associated with the former phrase, but the switch has not impacted on media reporting.
2. Tronto (2010) provides a similar attempt to identify what she terms 'warning signs'.

CHAPTER 9

1. The author of the article used a pseudonym. The words used in relation to adoption are points of political terminological tussle. In what follows, I will use the phrase 'birth mother' to refer to an adopted child's biological mother. However, some would challenge this phrase because it qualifies the term 'mother'.
2. International adoption *rates* in the United States are lower, in terms of population ratios, than several other countries, particularly Sweden and Norway (Bartholet, 2007).

REFERENCES

Abi-Rached, J. M. and Rose, N. (2010) 'The birth of the neuromolecular gaze', *History of the Human Sciences*, 23 (1): 11–36.

Abramovitz, M. (2006) 'Welfare reform in the United States', *Critical Social Policy*, 26 (2): 336–65.

Action for Children, National Children's Bureau and The Children's Society (2016) *Losing in the Long Run: Trends in Early Intervention Funding*. www.actionfor-children.org.uk/media/5826/losing_in_the_long_run.pdf.

Adams, A. (2015) 'Lessons in resilience from rural Greece', *The Washington Post*, 24 July. www.washingtonpost.com/opinions/greeces-invisible-economy/2015/07/24/cb166814-3161-11e5-8f36-18d1d501920d_story.html.

Adamson, C., Beddoe, L. and Danys, A. (2012) 'Building resilient practitioners', *British Journal of Social Work*, 44 (3): 522–41. First published online 10 October 2012. DOI: 10.1093/bjsw/bcs142.

Adamson, M. (2009) 'The human capital strategy', *ephemera*, 9 (4): 271–84.

Adcock, M. and White, R. (1985) *Good Enough Parenting*. London: BAAF.

Adger, W. N. (2000) 'Social and ecological resilience: are they related?', *Progress in Human Geography*, 24 (3): 347–64.

Alcock, P. (1998) 'Bringing Britain together?', *Community Care*, 26 November–2 December: 18–25.

Ali, S. (2014a) 'Governing multicultural populations and family life', *British Journal of Sociology*, 65 (1): 82–107.

Ali, S. (2014b) 'Multicultural families: Deracializing transracial adoption', *Critical Social Policy, Critical Social Policy*, 34 (1): 66–89.

All-Party Parliamentary Group on Social Mobility (2014) *Character and Resilience Manifesto*. www.educationengland.org.uk/documents/pdfs/2014-appg-social-mobility.pdf.

Allen, G. (2011a) *Early Intervention: Next Steps*. London: Cabinet Office.

Allen, G. (2011b) *Early Intervention: Smart Investment, Massive Savings*. London: Cabinet Office.

Allen, G. and Duncan Smith, I. (2008) *Early Intervention: Good Parents, Great Kids, Better Citizens*. London: Centre for Social Justice.

Allen, K. (2012) 'The model pupil who faked the test: Social policy in the Irish crisis', *Critical Social Policy*, 32 (3): 422–40.

American Psychological Association (APA) (2009) 'Staying resilient through tough economic times', 26 March. www.apapracticecentral.org/news/resilient.pdf.

Amnesty International (2013) *The State of the World's Human Rights*. http://files. amnesty.org/air13/AmnestyInternational_AnnualReport2013_complete_en.pdf.

Anderson, P. (1976) 'The antinomies of Antonio Gramsci', *New Left Review*, 100: 5–79.

Anderson, P. (2016) 'Heirs of Gramsci', *New Left Review*, 100: 71–99.

Anderson, S. G. and Gryzlak, B. M. (2002) 'Social work advocacy in the post-TANF environment', *Social Work*, 47 (3): 301–15.

Andersson, J. (2009) 'Nordic nostalgia and Nordic light: The Swedish model as Utopia 1930–2007', *Scandinavian Journal of History*, 34 (3): 229–45.

Andreou, A. (2015) 'Anti-homeless spikes: Sleeping rough opened my eyes to the city's barbed cruelty', *The Guardian*, G2, 19 February: 4–8.

Áras Attracta Swinford Review Group (2016) Key messages. www.hse.ie/eng/services/ publications/Disability/AASRGkeymessages.pdf.

Archer, V. (2009) 'Tax payers and the new right: Constructing discourses of welfare in 1970s Australia', *Labour History*, 96: 177–90.

Asen, R. (2003) 'Women, work, welfare', *Rhetoric and Public Affairs*, 6 (2): 285–312.

Ash, A. (2010) 'Ethics and the street-level bureaucrat: Implementing policy to protect elders from abuse', *Ethics and Social Welfare*, 4 (2): 201–9.

Atkinson, R. and Flint, J. (2004) 'Fortress UK? Gated communities, the spatial revolt of the elites and time-space trajectories of segregation', *Housing Studies*, 19 (6): 875–92.

Atkinson, W. (2014) 'A sketch of "family" as a field: From realized category to space of struggle', *Acta Sociologica*, 57 (3): 223–35.

Aviram, H. (2016) 'The Correctional Hunger Games: Understanding realignment in the context of the great recession', *Annals of the American Academy or Political and Social Science*, 664 (1): 260–80.

Bacchi, C. (1999) *Women, Policy and Politics*. London: Sage.

Badiou, A. (2002) *Ethics*. London: Verso.

Badiou, A. (2008) *The Meaning of Sarkozy*. London: Verso.

Badiou, A. (2012) *The Rebirth of History*. London: Verso.

Bagguley, P. and Mann, K. (1992) 'Idle thieving bastards? Scholarly representations of the "underclass"', *Work, Employment & Society*, 6: 113–26.

Bailey, A., Hannays-King, C., Clarke, J., Lester, E. and Velasco, D. (2013) 'Black mothers' cognitive process of finding meaning and building resilience after loss of a child to gun violence', *British Journal of Social Work*, 43: 336–54.

Bailey, N. (2016) 'Exclusionary employment in Britain's broken labour market', *Critical Social Policy*, 36 (1): 82–104.

Baines, D. (2004) 'Caring for nothing', *Work, Employment and Society*, 12 (2): 267–95.

Baines, D. (2013) 'Resistance in and outside the workplace', in M. Carey and L. Green (eds), *Practice Social Work Ethics*. Farnham: Ashgate, pp. 227–44.

Baines, D. and Van Den Broek, D. (2016) 'Coercive care: Control and coercion in the restructured care workplace', *British Journal of Social Work*, advance electronic access from 22 March. DOI: 10.1093/bjsw/bcw013.

Bakker, I. (2003) 'Neo-liberal governance and the reprivatization of social reproduction', in I. Bakker and S. Gil (eds), *Power, Production and Social Reproduction*. Houndsmill: Palgrave Macmillan, pp. 66–83.

Baldwin, J. (1993 [1963]) *The Fire Next Time*. New York: Vintage International.

Balibar, E. (2007) 'Uprisings in the *Banlieues*', *Constellations*, 14 (1): 47–72.

Ball, S. (2015) 'Accounting for a sociological life', *British Journal of Sociology of Education*, 36 (6): 817–31.

Baptist Union of Great Britain, Methodist Church, Church of Scotland and the United Reformed Church (2013) *The Lies We Tell Ourselves: Ending Comfortable Myths about Poverty*. www.jointpublicissues.org.uk/wp-content/uploads/2013/02/Truth-And-Lies-Report-smaller.pdf.

Barbier, J. C. (2014) 'Languages of "social policy" at the EU Level', in D. Béland and K. Petersen (eds), *Analysing Social Policy Concepts and Language*. Bristol: Policy Press, pp. 59–81.

Barnes, M. (2015) 'Beyond the dyad: Exploring the multidimensionality of care', in M. Barnes, M., Brannelly, T., Ward, L. and Ward, N. (eds), *Ethics of Care*. Bristol: Policy Press, pp. 31–44.

Barnes, M., Brannelly, T., Ward, L. and Ward, N. (2015) 'Introduction: The critical significance of care', in M. Barnes, T. Brannelly, L. Ward and N. Ward (eds), *Ethics of Care*. Bristol: Policy Press, pp. 3–21.

Barrett, M. (1992) 'Words and things', in M. Barrett and A. Phillips (eds), *Destabilizing Theory*. Cambridge: Polity Press, pp. 201–20.

Bartholet, E. (2007) 'International adoption: Thoughts on the human rights issues', *Buffalo Human Rights Law Review*, 13: 151–204.

BASW (British Association of Social Workers) (2016) Adoption: A BASW UK Social Work Enquiry. www.basw.co.uk/adoption-enquiry/.

Bauman, Z. (1989) *Modernity and the Holocaust*. Cambridge: Polity Press.

Baumann, N. (2013) 'Paul Ryan changes his story on "makers and takers"', Mother Jones, 22 January. www.motherjones.com/mojo/2013/01/paul-ryan-changes-his-story-makers-and-takers.

Baumberg, B. (2016) 'The stigma of claiming benefits', *Journal of Social Policy*, 45 (2): 181–201.

Bawden, A. (2015) 'Is success of government's troubled families scheme too good to be true?', *The Guardian, Society*, 11 November: 42.

Beasley, C. and Bacchi, C. (2007) 'Envisaging a new politics for an ethical future', *Feminist Theory*, 8 (3): 279–98.

Becker, J. (2016) 'Europe's other periphery', *New Left Review*, 66: 39–67.

Beckett, A. (2009) *When the Lights Went Out*. London: Faber and Faber.

Beckett, A. (2014) 'Battles over language', *The Guardian* Saturday Review, 15 February: 19.

Beckett, C. (2003) 'The language of siege', *British Journal of Social Work*, 33: 625–39.

Beddoe, L. (2014) 'Feral families, troubled families', *New Zealand Sociology*, 29 (3): 51–69.

Begley, S. (1996) 'Your child's brain', *Newsweek*, 127, 19 February: 55–61.

Béland, D. (2014) 'Social policy concepts and language in France', in D. Béland and K. Petersen (eds), *Analysing Social Policy Concepts and Language*. Bristol: Policy Press, pp. 243–57.

Béland, D. and Petersen, K. (2014) 'Introduction', in D. Béland and K. Petersen (eds), *Analysing Social Policy Concepts and Language*. Bristol: Policy Press, pp. 1–13.

Bellamy, R. (ed.) (1994) *Gramsci: Pre-Prison Writings*. Cambridge: Cambridge University Press.

Bellamy Foster, J. (1998) 'Introduction', in Harry Braverman, *Labour and Monopoly Capitalism: The Degradation of Work in the Twentieth Century*, 25th Anniversary Edition. New York: Monthly Review Press, pp. ix–xxv.

Bellow, S. (2008 [1982]) *The Dean's December*. London: Penguin.

Benjamin, M. (2010) '"War on terror" psychologist gets giant no-bid contract', *Salon*, 14 October. www.salon.com/2010/10/14/army_contract_seligman/.

Bennett, T., Grossberg, L. and Morris, M. (eds) (2005) *New Keywords*. Oxford: Blackwell.

Berardi, F. (2009) *Precarious Rhapsody*. London: Minor Compositions.

Bhattacharyya, G. (2015) *Crisis, Austerity, and Everyday Life*. Houndsmill: Palgrave Macmillan.

Biestek, F. P. (1975) 'Client self-determination', in F. E. McDermott (ed.), *Self Determination in Social Work*. London: Routledge & Kegan Paul, pp. 17–32.

Birns, B. (1999) 'Attachment theory revisited', *Feminism & Psychology*, 9 (1): 10–21.

Blacker, C. P. (ed.) (1952) *Problem Families*. London: Eugenics Society.

Blair, T. (2006a) 'Our nation's future – social exclusion', 5 September. http://web archive.nationalarchives.gov.uk/20040105034004/http:/number10.gov.uk/page10037.

Blair, T. (2006b) Interview with BBC on social exclusion, 31 August. http://webarchive.nationalarchives.gov.uk/20040105034004/http://number10.gov.uk/page10023.

Boffey, D. (2014) 'The care workers left behind as private equity targets NHS', *The Observer*, 10 August: 10–11.

Boltanski, L. and Chiapello, E. (2005) *The New Spirit of Capitalism*. London: Verso.

Bond-Taylor, S. (2015) 'Dimensions of family empowerment in work with so-called "troubled" families', *Social Policy and Society*, 14 (3): 371–85.

Bosanquet, B. (ed.) (1895a) *Aspects of the Social Problem*. London: Macmillan.

Bosanquet, B. (1895b) 'Character in its bearing on social causation', in B. Bosanquet (ed.), *Aspects of the Social Problem*. London: Macmillan, pp. 103–18.

Bottrell, D. (2009) 'Understanding "marginal" perspectives', *Qualitative Social Work*, 8 (3): 321–39.

Bourdieu, P. (1991) *Language and Symbolic Power*. Cambridge: Polity Press.

Bourdieu, P. (1994) *In Other Words*. Cambridge: Polity Press.

Bourdieu, P. (1996) 'On the family as a realized category', *Theory, Culture & Society*, 13 (3): 19–26.

Bourdieu, P. (1998) *On Television and Journalism*. London: Pluto.

Bourdieu, P. (2000) *Pascalian Meditations*. Cambridge: Polity Press.

Bourdieu, P. (2001) *Acts of Resistance*. Cambridge: Polity Press.

Bourdieu, P. (2002) 'Habitus', in J. Hillier and E. Rooksby (eds), *Habitus: A Sense of Place*. Aldershot: Ashgate, pp. 27–36.

Bourdieu, P. and Accardo, A., Balazas, G., Beaud, S., Bonvin, F., Bourdieu, E., Bourgois, P., Broccolichi, S., Champagne, P., Christin, R., Faguer, J. P., Garcia, S., Lenoir, R., Euvrard, F., Pialoux, M., Pinto, L., Podalydes, D., Sayad, A., Soulie, C. and Wacquant, J. D. (2002) *The Weight of the World: Social Suffering in Contemporary Society*. Cambridge: Polity Press.

Bourdieu, P. and Wacquant, L. (1999) 'On the cunning of imperialist reason', *Theory, Culture & Society*, 16 (1): 41–59.

Bourdieu, P. and Wacquant, L. (2001) 'NewLiberalSpeak', *Radical Philosophy*, Jan/Feb, 105: 2–6.

Bourdieu, P. and Wacquant, L. (2004) *An Invitation to Reflexive Sociology*. Cambridge: Polity Press.

Bowers, J. (2013) 'Blunkett's Roma rubbish', *The Guardian*, 14 November: 36.

Bowker, G. C. and Star, S. L. (1999) *Sorting Things Out*. Cambridge, MA: MIT.

Bowlby, J. (1990) *Child Care and the Growth of Love*, 3rd edn. Harmondsworth: Penguin.

Bowring, F. (2004) 'From the mass worker to the multitude', *Capital & Class*, 83: 101–33.

Boyden, J. and Cooper, E. (2007) *Questioning the Power of Resilience*. Oxford: CPRC Working Paper 73.

Boym, S. (2001) *The Future of Nostalgia*. New York: Basic Books.

Brading, F. (2012) 'Is the time ripe for a transatlantic response to the crisis in capitalism?, *Henry Jackson Society* http://henryjacksonsociety.org/2012/08/10/is-the-time-ripe-for-a-transatlantic-response-to-the-crisis-in-capitalism/.

Brandist, C. (1996) 'Gramsci, Bakhtin and the semiotics of hegemony', *New Left Review*, 216: 94–110.

Braverman, H. (1998) *Labour and Monopoly Capitalism: The Degradation of Work in the Twentieth Century*, 25th Anniversary Edition. New York: Monthly Review Press.

Brindle, D. (2014) 'Is this a good time to dilute care home rules', *The Guardian*, 22 October: 38.

Broadhurst, K., Shaw, M., Kershaw, S., Harwin, J., Alrouh, B., Mason, C. and Pilling, M. (2015) 'Vulnerable birth mothers and repeated losses of infants to public care', *Journal of Public Welfare and Family Law*, 37 (1): 84–98.

Broberg, G. and Roll-Hansen, N. (eds), (1996) *Eugenics and the Welfare State*. East Lansing, MI: Michigan State University.

Brooks, D., Barth, B. P., Bussiere, A. and Patterson, G. (1999) 'Adoption and race: Implementing the multi-ethnic placement act and interethnic adoption provisions', *Social Work*, 44 (2): 167–79.

Brooks, R. and Goldstein, S. (2006) *The Power of Resilience*. New York: McGraw-Hill.

Brown, J. (1968) 'Charles Booth and labour colonies, 1889–1905', *The Economic History Review*, 21: 349–61.

Brown, R. and Ward, H. (2012) *Decision-Making within a Child's Timeframe*. London: Childhood Wellbeing Research Centre.

Brown, W. (2015) *Undoing the Demos*. New York: Zone Books.

Bruer, J. T. (1997) 'Education and the brain', *Educational Researcher*, 26 (8): 4–16.

Bunting, M. (2005) 'Importing our carers adds up to emotional imperialism', *The Guardian*, 24 October: 27.

Bunting, M. (2016) 'Who will care for us in the future?', *The Guardian*, 7 March: 23.

Burdett, C. (2007) 'Eugenics old and new', *Soundings*, 60: 7–13.

Burling, S. (2010) 'The power of a positive thinker', *Philadelphia Inquirer*, 30 May. http://articles.philly.com/2010-05-30/news/24964448_1_positive-psychology-positive-thinker-soldiers.

Bush, G. (1990) Presidential Proclamation 6158, 17 June. www.loc.gov/loc/brain/proclaim.html.

Butler, I. (2014) 'New families, new governance and old habits', *Journal of Social Welfare and Family Law*, 36 (4): 415–25.

Byrne, D. (1999) *Social Exclusion*. Buckingham: Open University.

Byrne, D. (2017) 'Beyond mere equality – a politics of class analysis not "evidence"', *Soundings*, 64: 105–17.

Bywaters, P., Brady, G., Sparks, T., Bos, E., Bunting, L., Daniel, B., Featherstone, B., Morris, K. and Scourfield, J. (2015) 'Exploring inequities in child welfare and child protection services: Explaining the "inverse intervention law"', *Children and Youth Services Review*, 57: 98–105.

Bywaters, P., Brady, G., Sparks, T. and Bos, E. (2016a) 'Child welfare inequalities: New evidence, further questions', *Child & Family Social Work*, 21 (3): 369–80.

Bywaters, P., Brady, G., Sparks, T. and Bos, E. (2016b) 'Inequalities in child welfare rates: the intersection of deprivation and identity', *Child & Family Social Work*, 21 (4): 452–63.

Cabinet Office (2010) 'Prime Minister launches the Big Society Bank and announces the first four big society communities', Press Notice, 19 July. www.gov.uk/government/news/prime-minister-launches-the-big-society-bank.

Cacioppo, J. T., Reis, H. T. and Zautra, A. J. (2011) 'Social resilience: The value of social fitness with an application to the military', *American Psychologist*, 66 (1): 43–52.

Callinicos, A. (2010) *Bonfire of Illusions*. Cambridge: Polity Press.

Cameron, D. (1998) 'Dreaming the dictionary', *Key Words*, 1: 35–7.

Cameron, D. (2010) 'Together in the national interest': Speech to the Conservative Party Conference, 6 October. www.theguardian.com/politics/2010/oct/06/david-cameron-speech-tory-conference.

Cameron, D. (2011a) 'PM statement on violence in England', 10 August. www.number10.gov.uk/news/pm-statement-on-violence-in-england/.

Cameron, D. (2011b) 'PM's speech on the fightback after the riots', 15 August. www.number10.gov.uk/news/pms-speech-on-the-fightback-after-the-riots/.

Cameron, D. (2011c) 'Troubled families speech', 15 December www.gov.uk/government/speeches/troubled-families-speech.

Cameron. D. (2011d) 'PM's speech at Munich Security Conference', 5 February. www.number10.gov.uk/news/pms-speech-at-munich-security-conference/.

Cameron, N. and McDermott, F. (2007) *Social Work and the Body*. Houndsmill: Palgrave Macmillan.

Campbell, B. (1993) *Goliath*. London: Methuen.

Canvin, K., Marrtila, A., Burstrom, B. and Whitehead, M. (2009) 'Tales of the unexpected? Hidden resilience in poor households in Britain', *Social Science & Medicine*, 69: 238–45.

Carey, M. and Foster, V. (2011) 'Introducing "deviant" social work', *British Journal of Social Work*, 41 (3): 576–93.

Carney, M. (2014) 'Inclusive capitalism', speech at the Conference on Inclusive Capitalism, 27 May. www.bankofengland.co.uk/publications/Documents/speeches/2014/speech731.pdf.

Cartwright, L. (2003) 'Photographs of "Waiting Children": The transnational adoption market', *Social Text*, 21 (1): 83–110.

Carvel, J. (2007) 'Prospect of moving to a care home frightens two thirds of Britons', *The Guardian*, 3 December: 2.

Casey, L. (2012) *Listening to Troubled Families*. London: Department for Communities and Local Government. www.gov.uk/government/uploads/system/uploads/attachment_data/file/6151/2183663.pdf.

Casey, L. (2016) *The Casey Review: Executive Summary.* www.gov.uk/government/uploads/system/uploads/attachment_data/file/575975/The_Casey_Review_Executive_Summary.pdf.

Caygill, H. (2013) *On Resistance*. London: Bloomsbury.

Centre for Social Justice (2008) 'Early intervention: Good parents, great kids. better citizens'. http://www.centreforsocialjustice.org.uk/press-releases/early-intervention-good-parents-great-kids-better-citizens

Centre for Social Justice and the John Smith Institute (2008) *Breakthrough Britain: The Next Generation*. London: Centre for Social Justice.

Chadda, D. (1999) 'Disclose and protect', *Community Care*, 8–14 July: 13.

Chakrabortty, A. (2015) 'Corporate welfare: The £93bn handshake', *The Guardian*, 8 July: 1–2.

Chandler, D. and Reid, J. (2016) *The Neoliberal Subject*. London: Rowman & Littlefield.

Charlesworth, S. J. (2000) *A Phenomenology of Working Class Experience*. Cambridge: Cambridge University Press.

Chaskin, R. (2013) 'Integration and exclusion: Urban poverty, public housing reform, and the dynamics of neighborhood restructuring', *Annals of the American Academy of Political and Social Science*, 674: 237–68.

Chiapello, E. and Fairclough, N. (2002) 'Understanding the new management ideology', *Discourse & Society*, 13 (2): 185–208.

Christensen, K. and Guldvik, I. (2014) *Migrant Care Workers*. Farnham: Ashgate.

Christopher, J. C., Wendt, D. C., Marecek, J. and Goodman, D. M. (2014) 'Critical cultural awareness', *American Psychologist*, 69 (7): 645–56.

Clapton, G. (1997) 'Birth fathers, the adoption process and fatherhood', *Adoption & Fostering*, 21 (1): 29–37.

Clarke, A. M. and Clarke, A. D. B. (1976) *Early Experience: Myth and Evidence*. New York: The Free Press.

Clarke, J. (2004) *Changing Welfare, Changing States*. London: Sage.

Clarke, J. (2005) 'New Labour's citizens: Activated, empowered, responsibilized, abandoned', *Critical Social Policy*, 25 (4): 447–63.

Clarke, J. (2013) 'Rancière, politics and the social question', in O. Davis (ed.), *Rancière Now*. Cambridge: Polity Press, pp. 13–27.

Clarke, J. and Newman, J. (2012) 'The alchemy of austerity', *Critical Social Policy*, 32 (3): 299–319.

Clarke, J., Newman, J., Smith, N., Vidler, E. and Westmarland, L. (2007) *Creating Citizen-Consumers*. London: Sage.

Clayton, J., Donovan, C. and Merchant, J. (2015) 'Emotions of austerity', *Emotion, Space and Society*, 14: 24–32.

Cleaver, H. and Freeman, P. (1995) *Parental Perspectives in Cases of Suspected Child Abuse*. London: HMSO.

Clery, E. (2012) 'Are tough times affecting attitudes to welfare?', in A. Park, E. Clery, J. Curtice, M. Phillips and D. Utting (eds), *British Social Attitudes: The 29th Report*. London: NatCen Social Research. www.bsa-29.natcen.ac.uk/read-the-report/welfare/introduction.aspx.

Clifford, D. (2002) 'Resolving uncertainties? The contribution of some recent feminist ethical theory to the social professions', *European Journal of Social Work*, 5 (1): 31–41.

Coates, K. and Silburn, R (1970) *Poverty: The Forgotten Englishmen*. Harmonds worth: Penguin.

Coates, K. and Topham, T. (1972) *The New Unionism: The Case for Workers' Control*. Harmondsworth: Penguin.

Cockburn, T. (2005) 'Children and the feminist ethic of care', *Childhood*, 12 (1): 71–89.

Cohen, R. L. (2011) 'Time, space and touch at work: Body work and labour process (re) organisation', *Sociology of Health & Illness*, 33 (2): 189–205.

Cole, M. (2006) 'The role of the confession in reflective practice: Monitored continuing professional development (CPD) in health care and the paradox of professional autonomy', in D. Lyon (ed.) *Theorizing Surveillance*. Cullompton: Willan, pp. 206–30.

Colley, H. and Hodkinson, P. (2001) 'Problems with *Bridging the Gap*: The reversal of structure and agency in addressing social exclusion', *Critical Social Policy*, 21 (3): 335–59.

Collins, P. (2015) 'Australian parents who don't vaccinate children will lose childcare payments', *The Irish Times*, 13 April: 10.

Collinson, P. (2016) 'Bringing up a child costs more than an average house', *The Guardian*, 16 February: 2.

Commission on Social Justice (1994) *Social Justice: Strategies for National Renewal*. London: Vintage.

Commissioner for Human Rights (2013) 'Irresponsible media reporting on Roma propagates negative myths', Council of Europe Press Release, 24 October.

Connell, R. (2007) *Southern Theory*. Cambridge: Polity Press.

Connor, S. (2010) 'Promoting "employ ability": The changing subject of welfare reform in the UK', *Critical Discourse Studies*, 7 (1): 41–5.

Cooper, M. (2008) *Life as Surplus*. Seattle, WA: University of Washington.

Corbett, S. (2002) 'Where do babies come from?', *The New York Times Magazine*, 16 June. www.nytimes.com/2002/06/16/magazine/where-do-babies-come-from.html?pagewanted=all.

Couldry, N., Gilbert, J., Hesmondhalgh, D. and Nash, K. (2010) 'The new spirit of capitalism', *Soundings*, 45: 109–24.

Covey, S. (1989) *The Seven Habits of Highly Effective People*. London: Simon & Schuster.

Coward, R. (2011) 'Southern Cross wakes us up to the business of caring', *The Guardian*, 12 July: 28.

Cowen, D. (2008) *Military Workfare*. Toronto: University of Toronto.

Crehan, K. (2011) 'Gramsci's concept of common sense: A useful concept for anthropologists?', *Journal of Modern Italian Studies*, 16 (2): 273–87.

Crehan, K. (2016) *Gramsci's Common Sense*. Durham, NC: Duke University.

Critchley, A. (2012) 'Resident hits back over "blatantly prejudiced" portrayal of her estate', *The Guardian*, 3 October: 34.

Cross-Party Manifesto (2014) *The 1001 Critical Days: The Importance of the Conception to Age Two Period*. www.wavetrust.org/our-work/publications/reports/1001-critical-days-importance-conception-age-two-period.

Crossley, N. (2005) *Key Concepts in Critical Social Theory*. London: Sage.

Crossley, S. (2016) 'Realising the (troubled) family, crafting the neoliberal state', *Families, Relationships and Societies*, 5 (2): 263–73.

Cullen, P. (2006) 'Bookies criticised for giving odds on African adoptions', *The Irish Times*, 4 April: 10.

Cullen, P. (2014a) 'Mistreatment in home raises issues for HSE', *The Irish Times*, 9 December: 1.

Cullen, P. (2014b) 'Casual nature of Áras Attracta abuse most disturbing', *The Irish Times*, 9 December: 3.

Cullen, P. (2016) 'HSE urged to apologise over "trespassing" patients memo', *The Irish Times*, 10 November: 12.

D'Arcy, C. (2016) 'No social workers for 1,000 child cases', *The Irish Times*, 3 June: 2.

Darling, A. (1999) 'Work is the way off welfare', *The Guardian*, 16 June. www.theguardian.com/politics/1999/jun/16/welfarereform.society.

Davies, K. (ed.) (2015) *Social Work with Troubled Families*. London: Jessica Kingsley.

Davies, M. (ed.) (2000) *The Blackwell Encyclopaedia of Social Work*. Oxford: Blackwell.

Davies, W. (2016) 'Neoliberalism 3.0', *New Left Review*, 101: 121–37.

Davis, M. (1990) *City of Quartz*. London: Vintage.

Davis, O. (2010) *Jacques Rancière*. Cambridge: Polity Press.

De Benedictus, S. (2012) '"Feral" parents: Austerity parenting under neoliberalism', *Studies in the Maternal*, 4 (2). www.mamsie.bbk.ac.uk.

De Vos, J. and Pluth, E. (eds), (2016) *Neuroscience and Critique*. London: Routledge.

Deacon, A. (2000) 'Learning from the US? The influence of American ideas upon "new labour" thinking on welfare reform', *Policy & Politics*, 28 (1): 5–18.

Deacon, A. and Mann, K. (1999) 'Agency, modernity and social policy', *Journal of Social Policy*, 28: 413–35.

Dean, H. (1992) 'Poverty discourse and the disempowerment of the poor', *Critical Social Policy*, 35: 79–89.

Dean, M. (1999) *Governmentality*. London: Sage.

Deleuze, G. (1995) *Negotiations*. New York: Columbia University.

Dendy, H. (1895) 'The Industrial Residuum', in B. Bosanquet (ed.), *Aspects of the Social Problem*. London: Macmillan. pp. 82–103.

Denham, A. and Garnett, M. (2001) *Keith Joseph: The Mad Monk*. Durham: Acumen.

Department for Education (2011) 'Breaking down barriers to adoption', Press Release, 22 February. www.gov.uk/government/news/breaking-down-barriers-to-adoption.

Department for Education (2012a) 'Ex-military personnel to drive up standards among disengaged pupils', Press Notice, 7 December. www.education.gov.uk/inthenews/inthenews/a00218197/ex-military-standards-disengaged-pupils.

Department for Education (2012b) *An Action Plan for Adoption: Tackling Delay*. www.gov.uk/government/uploads/system/uploads/attachment_data/file/180250/action_plan_for_adoption.pdf.

Department for Education (2013) *Further Action on Adoption: Finding More Loving Homes*. www.gov.uk/government/uploads/system/uploads/attachment_data/file/219661/Further_20Action_20on_20Adoption.pdf.

Department for Education (2014) 'Adoption scorecards and thresholds published', Press Release, 14 January. www.gov.uk/government/news/adoption-scorecards-and-thresholds-published.

Department for Education (2016a) 'Education Secretary unveils a new blueprint for adoption', 27 March. www.gov.uk/government/news/education-secretary-unveils-a-new-blueprint-for-adoption.

Department for Education (2016b) *Adoption: A Vision for Change*. www.gov.uk/government/uploads/system/uploads/attachment_data/file/510924/Adoption-Policy-Paper.pdf.

Department of Children and Youth Affairs (2014) *Report of the Inter-departmental Group on Mother and Baby Homes*. www.dcya.gov.ie/documents/publications/20140716InterdepartReportMothBabyHomes.pdf.

Department of Health (1998) *Adoption – Achieving the Right Balance*. LAC (98) 20. London: HMSO.

Department of Health (1999) *Adoption Now: Messages from Research*. Chichester: Wiley.

Department of Health (2000) '150 teenage pregnancy co-ordinators appointed to drive campaign to cut teenage pregnancy', Press Release, 29 February.

Department of Health and Welsh Office (1992) *Review of Adoption Law*. London: HMSO.

Department of Justice (2011) Ireland's National Traveller/Roma Integration Strategy. http://ec.europa.eu/justice/discrimination/files/roma_ireland_strategy_en.pdf

Department of Social Protection (2015) 'New Intreo Centre in heart of Galway city opened by Tánaiste', Press Release, 11 November. https://www.welfare.ie/en/pressoffice/Pages/pr111115.aspx

Deranty, J-P. (2003) 'Jacques Rancière's contribution to the ethics of recognition', *Political Theory*, 31 (1): 136–56.

Deranty, J-P. (2010) 'Introduction', in *Jacques Rancière: Key Concepts*. Durham: Acumen, pp. 1–17.

Diprose, K. (2014–15) 'Resilience is futile', *Soundings*, 58: 44–57.

Dobbernack, J. (2014) *The Politics of Social Cohesion in Germany, France and the United Kingdom*. Houndsmill: Palgrave Macmillan.

Dodds, A. (2009) 'Families "at risk" and the family nurse partnership', *Journal of Social Policy*, 38 (3): 499–514.

Doughty, S. (2012) 'Naked racism in the apartheid-era adoption system has been tolerated for too long', *Mail Online*, 9 March. www.dailymail.co.uk/debate/article-2112654/Mixed-race-adoption-Racism-tolerated-long.html.

Dowling, E. and Harvie, D. (2014) 'Harnessing the social', *Sociology*, 48 (5): 869–886.

Drakeford, M. (2012) 'Wales in the age of austerity', *Critical Social Policy*, 32 (3): 454–66.

Dubinsky, K. (2008) 'The fantasy of the global cabbage patch: Making sense of transracial adoption', *Feminist Theory*, 9 (3): 339–45.

Duncan Smith, I. (2011) 'We cannot arrest our way out of these riots', *The Times*, 15 September. www.thetimes.co.uk/tto/opinion/columnists/article3164510.ece.

Duncan Smith, I. (2014) 'Speech to Conservative Party Conference'. http://press.conservatives.com/post/98728606860/iain-duncan-smith-speech-to-conservative-party.

Durant, A. (2006) 'Raymond Williams's *Keywords*', *Critical Quarterly*, 48 (4): 1–27.

Durant, A. (2008) '"The significance is in the selection": identifying contemporary keywords', *Critical Quarterly*, 50 (1–2): 122–42.

Dutt, R. and Sanyal, A. (1991) '"Openness" in adoption or open adoption – a Black perspective', *Adoption & Fostering*, 15 (4): 111–15.

Dwork, D. (1987) *War Is Good for Babies and Other Young Children*. London: Routledge & Kegan Paul.

Dyer-Witheford, N. (2015) *Cyber-Proletariat*. London: Pluto.

Eagleton, T. (1976) 'Criticism and politics: The work of Raymond Williams', *New Left Review*, 95: 3–23.

Eagleton, T. (1998) 'Raymond Williams, communities and universities', *Key Words*, 1: 28–35.

Eagleton-Pierce, M. (2016) *Neoliberalism: Key Concepts*. London: Routledge.

Easton, M. (2011) 'England riots: The return of the underclass', BBC News, 11 August. www.bbc.co.uk/news/uk-14488486.

Easthope, A. and McGowan, K. (eds), (2004) *A Critical and Cultural Theory Reader*. Maidenhead: Open University.

Ecclestone, K. and Lewis, L. (2014) 'Interventions for resilience in educational settings', *Journal of Education Policy*, 29 (2): 195–216.

Edwards, C. (2009) *Resilient Nation*. London: Demos.

Edwards, R., Gillies, V. and Horsley, N. (2015) 'Brain science and early years policy: Hopeful ethos or "cruel optimism"', *Critical Social Policy*, 35 (2): 167–88.

Ehrenreich, B. (2006) *Bait and Switch*. London: Granta.

Etzioni, A. (1995) *The Spirit of the Community*. London: Fontana.

European Commission (2013) *Investing in Children: Breaking the Cycle of Disadvantage*. http://ec.europa.eu/justice/fundamental-rights/files/c_2013_778_en.pdf.

European Union Agency for Fundamental Rights (2010) *Towards More Effective Policing: Understanding and Preventing Discriminatory Ethnic Profiling – A Guide*. www.paveepoint.ie/tempsite3/wp-content/uploads/2013/11/1133-Guide-ethnic-profiling_EN.pdf.

Expert Working Group on Adoption (2012) *Redesigning Adoption*. www.gov.uk/government/uploads/system/uploads/attachment_data/file/180251/working_groups_report_on_redesigning_adoption.pdf.

Fairclough, N. (2003) '"Political correctness": The politics of culture and language', *Discourse and Society*, 14 (1): 127–8.

Fairclough, N. and Graham, P. (2002) 'Marx as a critical discourse analyst', *Estudios de Sociolinguistica*, 3 (1): 185–229.

Falconer, C. (2006) 'Why did the Banlieues burn?', *Radical Philosophy*, March/April: 2–6.

Farnsworth, K. (2006) 'Capital to the rescue', *Critical Social Policy*, 26 (4): 817–43.

Farnsworth, K. and Holden, C. (2006) 'The business-social policy nexus', *Journal of Social Policy*, 35 (3): 473–95.

Farris, S. R. (2012) 'Femonationalism and the "regular" army of labor called migrant women', *History of the Present*, 2 (2): 184–99.

Feast, J. and Howe, D. (1997) 'Adopted adults who search for background information and contact with birth relatives', *Adoption & Fostering*, 21 (2): 8–16.

Featherstone, B., Morris, K. and White, B. (2014) 'A marriage made in hell: Early intervention meets child protection', *British Journal of Social Work*, 44, 1735–49.

Federal Interagency Forum on Child and Family Statistics (2015) *America's Children: Key National Indicators of Well-Being*. www.childstats.gov/pdf/ac2015/ac_15.pdf.

Federici, S. (2004) *Caliban and the Witch*. Brooklyn: NY: Autonomedia.

Feldman, L. C. (2002) 'Redistribution, recognition, and the state', *Political Theory*, 30 (3): 410–40.

Ferrara, F. (1989) 'Raymond Williams and the Italian left', in T. Eagleton (ed.), *Raymond Williams: Critical Perspectives*. Cambridge: Polity, pp. 95–108.

Field, F. (1989) *Losing Out*. Oxford: Blackwell.

Finch, J. and Groves, D. (eds) (1983) *A Labour of Love*. London: Routledge.

Fink, J. (2008) 'Inside a hall of mirrors: Residential care and the shifting constructions of childhood in mid-twentieth-century Britain', *Paedagogica Historica: International Journal of the History of Education*, 43 (3): 287–307.

Fitzpatrick, T. (2002) 'In search of welfare democracy', *Social Policy and Society*, 1 (1): 11–21.

Fleming, P. (2015) *The Mythology of Work*. London: Pluto.

Fletcher, D. R. (2015) 'Workfare – a blast from the past?', *Social Policy and Society*, 14 (3): 329–39.

Flynn, M. (2012) *Winterbourne View Hospital: A Serious Case Review*. www.south-glos.gov.uk/news/serious-case-review-winterbourne-view/.

Flynn, R. (2000) 'Black carers for white children', *Adoption & Fostering*, 24 (1): 47–53.

Forbat, L. (2004) 'The care and abuse of minoritized ethnic groups', *Critical Social Policy*, 24 (3): 312–31.

ForcesWatch (2015) 'Government funding for "military ethos" in schools', Press Notice. www.forceswatch.net/news/government-funding-military-ethos-schools.

Forgacs, D. (1988) *A Gramsci Reader*. London: Lawrence and Wishart.

Forkert, K. (2014) 'The new moralism: Austerity, silencing and debt morality', *Soundings*, 56: 41–54.

Forkert, K. (2016) 'Austere creativity and volunteer-run public services', *New Formations*, 87: 11–29.

Foucault, M. (1991 [1977]) *Discipline and Punish* (trans. Alan Sheridan). London: Penguin.

Foucault, M. (2008) *The Birth of Biopolitics* (trans. Graham Burchill). Houndsmill: Palgrave Macmillan.

Foucault. M. (2009) *Security, Territory, Population*. Houndsmill: Palgrave Macmillan.

Francis, R. (2013) *Report of the Mid Staffordshire NHS Foundation Trust Public Inquiry: Executive summary*. www.gov.uk/government/uploads/system/uploads/attachment_data/file/279124/0947.pdf

Frase, P. (2016) *Four Futures*. London: Verso.

Fraser, N. (2000) 'Rethinking recognition', *New Left Review*, 3: 107–20.

Fraser, N. (2003) 'Social justice in an age of identity politics: Redistribution, recognition and participation', in N. Fraser and A. Honneth, *Redistribution or Recognition?* London: Verso, pp. 7–110.

Fraser, N. (2013) *Fortunes of Feminism*. London: Verso.

Fraser, N. (2016) 'Capital and care', *New Left Review*, 100: 99–119.

Fraser, N. and Gordon, L. (1997) 'A genealogy of dependency', in N. Fraser, *Justice Interruptus*. London: Routledge, pp. 121–51.

Frayne, D. (2015) *The Refusal of Work*. London: Zed Books.

Freeman, R. (1999) 'Recursive politics: Prevention, modernity and social systems', *Children and Society*, 13: 232–41.

French, D. (2016) 'Working-class whites have moral responsibilities – in defense of Kevin Williamson', 14 March. www.nationalreview.com/corner/432796/working-class-whites-have-moral-responsibilities-defense-kevin-williamson.

Friedli, L. and Stearn, R. (2015) 'Positive affect a coercive strategy: Conditionality, activation and the role of psychology in UK government workfare programmes', *Medical Humanities*, 41: 40–7.

Fritsch, K., O'Connor, C. and Thompson, A. K. (eds) (2016a) *Keywords for Radicals*. Chico, CA/Edinburgh, Scotland: AK Press.

Fritsch, K., O'Connor, C. and Thompson, A. K. (2016b) 'Introduction', in K. Fritsch, C. O'Connor and A. K. Thompson (eds), *Keywords for Radicals*. Chico, CA/Edinburgh, Scotland: AK Press, pp. 1–23.

Fu Keung Wong, D. (2008) 'Differential impacts of stressful life events and social support on the mental health of mainland Chinese immigrant and local youth in Hong Kong: A resilience perspective', *British Journal of Social Work*, 38: 236–52.

Furman, R., Epps, D. and Lamphear, G. (eds) (2016) *Detaining the Immigrant Other*. New York: Oxford University.

Gallagher, A. (2014) 'The "caring entrepreneur"? Childcare policy and private provision in an enterprising age', *Environment and Planning A*, 46: 1108–23.

Gallagher, K. (2012) 'Scandal of the babies parents won't adopt because they're called Chrystal and Chardonnay … and the social workers who won't let them change their names', *Mail Online*, 7 May. www.dailymail.co.uk/news/article-2140586/Scandal-babies-parents-wont-adopt-theyre-called-Chrystal-Chardonnay.html.

Garland, D. (2001) *The Culture of Culture*. Oxford: Oxford University Press.

Garmezy, N. and Rutter, M. (1983) *Stress, Coping and Development in Children*. New York: McGraw–Hill.

Garrett, P. M. (2003) *Remaking Social Work with Children and Families: A Critical Discussion on the 'Modernisation' of Social Care*. London: Routledge.

Garrett, P. M. (2005) 'Social work's "Electronic Turn": notes on the deployment of information and communication technologies in social work with children and families', *Critical Social Policy*, 25 (4): 529–54.

Garrett, P. M. (2007a) '"Sinbin" Solutions: The "pioneer" projects for "problem families" and the forgetfulness of social policy research', *Critical Social Policy*, 27 (2): 203–30.

Garrett, P. M. (2007b) 'Making "anti-social behaviour": A fragment on the evolution of "ASBO politics" in Britain', *British Journal of Social Work*, 37 (5): 839–56.

Garrett, P. M. (2008) 'How to be modern: New Labour's neoliberal modernity and the *Change for Children* programme', *British Journal of Social Work*, 38 (2): 270–89.

Garrett, P. M. (2009) *'Transforming' Children's Services? Social Work, Neoliberalism and the 'Modern' World*. Maidenhead: McGraw–Hill/Open University.

Garrett, P. M. (2010) 'Creating happier children and more fulfilled social workers', *Journal of Progressive Human Services*, 21: 83–101.

Garrett, P. M. (2012a) 'Adjusting "our notions of the nature of the State": A political reading of Ireland's child protection crisis', *Capital & Class*, 36 (2): 263–81.

Garrett, P. M. (2012b) 'From "solid modernity" to "liquid modernity"? Zygmunt Bauman and social work', *British Journal of Social Work*, 42 (4): 634–51.

Garrett, P. M. (2013a) *Social Work and Social Theory*. Bristol: Policy Press.

Garrett, P. M. (2013b) 'Beyond the community of persons to be accorded "respect"? Messages from the past for social work in the Republic of Ireland', in M. Carey and L. Green (eds), *Practical Social Work Ethics*. Farnham: Ashgate, pp. 23–43.

Garrett, P. M. (2014a) 'Re-enchanting social work? The emerging "spirit" of social work in an age of economic crisis', *British Journal of Social Work*, 44 (3): 503–21.

Garrett, P. M. (2014b) 'The children not counted: Reports on the deaths of children in the Republic of Ireland', *Critical and Radical Social Work*, 2 (1): 23–43.

Garrett, P. M. (2014c) *Children and Families: Critical and Radical Debates in Social Work*. Bristol: Policy Press.

Garrett, P. M. (2015a) 'Active equality: Jacques Rancière's contribution to social work's "New Left"', *British Journal of Social Work*, 45 (4): 1207–23.

Garrett, P. M. (2015b) 'Disrupting, destabilising and declassifying: Jacques Rancière's potential contribution to social work', *International Social Work*, Online First from 27 November, DOI: 10.1177/0020872815603988.

Garrett, P. M. (2015c) 'Constraining and confining ethnic minorities: Impoverishment and the logics of control in neoliberal Ireland', *Patterns of Prejudice*, 49 (4): 414–34.

Garrett, P. M. (2016a) 'Unmarried mothers in the Republic of Ireland', *Journal of Social Work*, 16 (6): 708–725.

Garrett, P. M. (2016b) 'Introducing Michael Gove to Loïc Wacquant: Why social work needs critical sociology', *British Journal of Social Work*, 46 (4): 873–89.

Garrett, P. M. (2016c) 'Confronting neoliberal penality: Placing prison reform and critical criminology at the core of social work's social justice agenda', *Journal of Social Work*, 16 (1): 83–103.

Garrett, P. M. (2017) 'Excavating the past: Mother and Baby Homes in the Republic of Ireland', *British Journal of Social Work*, 47 (2): 358–374.

Garrett, P. M. and Bertotti, T. F. (2017) 'Social work and the politics of "austerity": Ireland and Italy', *European Journal of Social Work*, 20 (1): 29–41

Garside, J. (2016) 'Benefit fraud or tax evasion: Row over the Tories' targets', *The Guardian*, 14 April: 1–2.

Gartland, F. (2016) 'Children's foster care costs three times more when private companies are used', *The Irish Times*, 19 September: 2.

Gellately, R. and Stoltzfus, N. (ed.) (2001) *Social Outcasts in Nazi Germany*. Princeton, NJ: Princeton University.

Giddens, A. (1981) *The Class Structure of Advanced Societies*, 2nd edn. London: Hutchinson.

Giddens, A. (1998) *The Third Way*. Cambridge: Polity Press.

Giddens, A. (ed.) (2001) *The Global Third Way Debate*. Cambridge: Polity Press.

Gilbert, J. (2015) 'Disaffected consent: that post-democratic feeling', *Soundings*, 60: 29–42.

Gilgun, J. F. (2005) 'Evidence-based practice, descriptive research and the Resilience-Schema-Gender-Brain Functioning (RSGB) assessment', *British Journal of Social Work*, 35: 843–62.

Gill, R. and Pratt, A. (2008) 'Precarity and cultural work: In the social factory?', *Theory, Culture & Society*, 25 (7–8): 1–30.

Gillard, J. (2013) *National Apology for Forced Adoptions*. www.ag.gov.au/About/ForcedAdoptionsApology/Documents/Nationalapologyforforcedadoptions.PDF.

Gilligan, C. (1982) *In a Different Voice*. Cambridge, MA: Harvard University Press.

Gilligan, R. (1999) 'Enhancing the resilience of children and young people in public care by mentoring their talents and interests', *Child and Family Social Work*, 4: 187–96.

Giordano, C. (2014) *Migrants in Translation*. Oakland, CA: University of California.

Giridharadas, A. (2013) 'Silicon Valley roused by secession call', *The New York Times*, 28 October. www.nytimes.com/2013/10/29/us/silicon-valley-roused-by-secession-call.html.

Goffman, I. (1971 [1959]) *The Presentation of Self in Everyday Life*. Harmondsworth: Pelican.

Goldman, R. and Papson, S. (2011) *Landscapes of Capital*. Cambridge: Polity Press.

Goodin, R. E. (1996) 'Inclusion and exclusion', *Archives Européennes de Sociologie*, 34 (2): 343–71.

Goodstein, L. (2011) 'Bishops close adoption services over new rule on gay parents', *The Irish Times*, 30 December: 13.

Gorman, M. (1984) *Waiting for the Sky to Fall*. Galway: Lighthouse Press.

Gough, I. (2015) 'Climate change and sustainable welfare', *Cambridge Journal of Economics*, 39: 1191–214.

Gough, I. and Olofsson, G. (eds), (1999) *Capitalism and Social Cohesion*. London: Macmillan.

Gove, M. (2012a) 'Ministerial foreword', in Department for Education, *An Action Plan for Adoption: Tackling Delay*. www.gov.uk/government/uploads/system/uploads/attachment_data/file/180250/action_plan_for_adoption.pdf.

Gove, M. (2012b) 'The failure of child protection and the need for a fresh start', 16 November. www.gov.uk/government/speeches/the-failure-of-child-protection-and-the-need-for-a-fresh-start.

Gove, M. (2013) 'Getting it right for children in need: speech to the NSPCC', 12 November. www.gov.uk/government/speeches/getting-it-right-for-children-in-need-speech-to-the-nspcc.

Grandin, G. (2010) *Fordlandia*. London: Icon.

Grass, G. and Bourdieu, P. (2002) 'The "progressive" restoration', *New Left Review*, 14: 63-79.

Gravois, J. (2004) 'Bringing up babes: Why do adoptive parents prefer girls?', *Slate*, 16 January. www.slate.com/articles/news_and_politics/hey_wait_a_minute/2004/01/bringing_up_babes.html.

Gray, M. (2014) 'The swing to early intervention and prevention and its implications for social work', *British Journal of Social Work*, 44: 1750–69.

Green, S., Kelly, R., Nixon, E., Kelly, G., Borska, Z., Murphy, S., Daly, A., Whyte, J. and C. Murphy (2007) *A Study of Intercountry Adoption Outcomes in Ireland: Summary Report*. Dublin: TCD Children's Research Centre and The Adoption Board.

Gregg, M. (2011) *Work's Intimacy*. Cambridge: Polity Press.

Gregg, P. (2008) *Realising Potential: A Vision for Personalised Conditionality and Support*. London: Department for Work and Pensions.

Gregory, M. and Holloway, M. (2005) 'Language and the shaping of social work', *British Journal of Social Work*, 35: 37–53.

Greve, B. (2014) *Historical Dictionary of the Welfare State*, 3rd edn. Plymouth: Rowman & Littlefield.

Grimwood, T. (2016) *Key Debates in Social Work and Philosophy*. London: Routledge.

Grover, C. (2011) 'Social protest in 2011: Material and cultural aspects of economic inequalities', *Sociological Research Online*, 16 (4). www.socresonline.org.uk/16/4/18.html.

Guentner, S., Luke, S., Stanton, R., Vollmer, B. A. and Wilding, J. (2016) 'Bordering practices in the UK welfare system', *Critical Social Policy*, 36 (3): 391–411.

Guha, R. (1997) *Dominance without Hegemony*. Cambridge, MA: Harvard University Press.

Gurmu, S. and Smith, W. J. (2006) 'Recidivism among welfare recipients', *Atlantic Economic Journal*, 34: 405–19.

Gustafson, K. S. (2011) *Cheating Welfare*. New York: New York University Press.

Gustavsson, N. S. (1991) 'Pregnant chemically dependent women: The new criminals', *Affilia*, 6 (2): 61–73.

Hague Convention (1993) *Convention on Protection of Children and Co-operation in Respect of Intercountry Adoption*. https://assets.hcch.net/docs/77e12f23-d3dc-4851-8f0b-050f71a16947.pdf.

Hall, A. (2010) 'These people could be anyone: Fear, contempt (and empathy) in a British immigration removal centre', *Journal of Ethnic and Migration Studies*, 36 (6): 881–98.

Hall, P. (1960) *The Social Services of Modern England*. London: Routledge and Kegan Paul.

Hall, P. A. and Lamont, M. (eds), (2013) *Social Resilience in the Neoliberal Era*. Cambridge: Cambridge University Press.

Hall, S. (1989) 'Politics and letters', in T. Eagleton (ed.), *Raymond Williams: Critical Perspectives*. Cambridge: Polity Press, pp. 54–67.

Hall, S. (1996) 'The problem of ideology: Marxism without guarantees' in David Morley and Kuan-Hsing Chen (eds), *Stuart Hall: Critical Dialogues in Cultural Studies*. London: Routledge, pp. 24–46.

Hall, S. (2003) 'New Labour's double-shuffle', *Soundings*, 24: 10–25.

Hall, S. (2011) 'The neo-liberal revolution', *Cultural Studies*, 25 (6): 705–28.

Hall, S. and Jacques, M. (1989) *New Times*. London: Lawrence and Wishart.

Hall, S. and Massey, D. (2010) 'Interpreting the crisis', *Soundings*, 44: 57–72.

Hall, S. and O'Shea, A. (2015) 'Common-sense neoliberalism', in S. Hall, D. Massey and M. Rustin (eds), *After Neoliberalism*. London: Lawrence and Wishart, pp. 52–69.

Hall, S., Critcher, C., Jefferson, T., Clarke, J. and Roberts, B. (1978) *Policing the Crisis*. Houndsmill: Macmillan Education.

Hallward, P. (2005) 'Jacques Rancière and the subversion of mastery', *Paragraph*, 28 (1): 26–46.

Hammett, C. (2010) 'Moving the poor out of central London?', The implications of the Coalition cuts to Housing Benefits', *Environment and Planning A*, 42: 2809–19.

Hancock, L. and Mooney, G. (2013) 'Welfare ghettos' and the "broken society"', *Housing, Theory and Society*, 30 (1): 46–64.

Hanley, L. (2007) *Estates*. London: Granta.

Hanley, L. (2016) *Respectable*. London: Allen Lane.

Harkins, S. and Lugo-Ocando, J. (2016) 'How Malthusian ideology crept into the newsroom: British tabloids and the coverage of the "underclass"', *Critical Discourse Studies*, 13 (1): 78–93.

Harley, N. (2015) 'Adopted boy taken off white couple to grow up with black aunt he had never met', *Daily Telegraph*, 1 August. www.telegraph.co.uk/news/uknews/law-and-order/11777819/Adopted-boy-taken-off-white-couple-to-grow-up-with-black-aunt-he-had-never-met.html.

Harms, L. (2015) *Understanding Trauma and Resilience*. London: Palgrave.

Harrington, M. (1962) *The Other America*. New York: Macmillan.

Harris, J. (2002) 'Caring for citizenship', *British Journal of Social Work*, 32: 267–81.

Harris, J. (2003) *The Social Work Business*. London: Routledge.

Harris, J. (2012) 'Chav bashing – a bad joke turning into bilious policy', *The Guardian*, 7 January: 29.

Harrison, E. (2013) 'Bouncing back? Recession, resilience and everyday lives', *Critical Social Policy*, 33 (1): 97–114.

Harvey, D. (2005) *A Brief History of Neoliberalism*. Oxford: Oxford University Press.

Hastings, A. (2004) 'Stigma and social housing estates', *Journal of Housing and the Built Environment*, 19: 233–54.

Hastings. M. (2011) 'Years of liberal dogma have spawned a generation of amoral, un-educated, welfare dependent, brutalised youngsters', *Daily Mail*, 11 August. http://www.dailymail.co.uk/debate/article-2024284/UK-riots-2011-Liberal-dogma-spawned-generation-brutalised-youths.html.

Hatherley, O. (2016) *The Ministry of Nostalgia*. London: Verso.

Hauss, G. and Ziegler, B. (2008) 'City welfare in the sway of eugenics: A Swiss case study', *British Journal of Social Work*, 38 (4): 751–70.

Hayden, C. and Jenkins, C. (2014) '"Troubled families" programme in England', *Policy Studies*, 35 (6): 631–49.

Hayden, C. and Jenkins, C. (2015) 'Children taken into care and custody and the "troubled family" agenda in England', *Child & Family Social Work*, 20 (4): 459–69.

Haylett, C. (2000) 'This is about us: This is our film! Personal and popular discourses of underclass', in S. R. Munt (ed.), *Cultural Studies and the Working Class*. London: Cassell, pp. 69–82.

Hayward, C. (2003) 'Doxa and deliberation', *Critical Review of International Social and Political Philosophy*, 7 (1): 1–24.

Hayward, K. and Yar, M. (2006) 'The "chav" phenomenon: Consumption, media and the construction of a new underclass', *Crime, Media, Culture*, 2 (1): 9–28.

Healy, K. (2016) 'After the biomedical technology revolution: Where to now for a bio-psycho-social approach to social work?', *British Journal of Social Work*, 46 (5): 1446–62.

Heawood, S. (2008) 'The world around Baby P is wrong, Why are we afraid to say so', *The Independent on Sunday*, 16 November: 42–43.

Heffernan, K. (2006) 'Social work, New Public Management and the language of "service user"', *British Journal of Social Work*, 36: 139–47.

Helms, G, Vishmidt, M. and Berlant, L. (2010) 'Affect and the politics of austerity', *Variant*, 39/40. www.variant.org.uk/39_40texts/berlant39_40.html.

Henman, P. (2004) 'Targeted! Population segmentation, electronic surveillance and governing the unemployed in Australia', *International Sociology*, 19 (2): 173–91.

Hern, A. (2013) 'IDS cites "personal observations" to defend junk statistic', *New Statesman*, 13 April. www.newstatesman.com/economics/2013/04/ids-cites-personal-observations-defend-junk-statistic.

Hietala, M. (1996) 'From race hygiene to sterilisation: The eugenics movement in Finland', in G. Broberg and N. Roll-Hansen (eds), *Eugenics and the Welfare State*. East Lansing, MI: Michigan State University, pp. 195–258.

Higgs, E. (2010) 'Fingerprints and citizenship', *History Workshop Journal*, 69: 52–67.

Hill, A. (2009) 'Foster agency holds parties to adopt a child', *The Observer*, 30 September: 6.

Hill, A. (2012) 'Adoption process is being rushed by councils, says judges', *The Guardian*, 19 November: 10.

Hills, J. (2015) *Good Times, Bad Times*. Bristol: Policy Press.

Hilpern, K. (2008) 'Unfit to be a mother?', *The Guardian*, G2, 15 January: 6–12.

Himmelfarb, G. (1970) 'Bentham's Utopia' *Journal of British Studies*, 10 (1): 80–125.

Hine, J. (2005) 'Early multiple intervention', *Children & Society*, 19: 117–30.

Hinsliff, G. (2016) 'Could the care we need come from the internet of things?', *The Guardian*, 14 October: 29.

HM Government (2012) *Social Justice: Transforming Lives*, Cm 8314. London: TSO.

Hoare, Q. and Nowell Smith, G. (eds) (2005) *Antonio Gramsci: Selections from Prison Notebooks*. London: Lawrence and Wishart, 10th reprint.

Holborow, M. (2015) *Language and Neoliberalism*. London: Routledge.

Holland, S. (2010) 'Looked after children and the ethic of care', *British Journal of Social Work*, 40: 1664–80.

Hollings, C. S. (1973) 'Resilience and the stability of ecological systems', *Annual Review of Ecology and Systematics*, 4: 1–23.

Hollingworth, S. and Williams, K. (2009) 'Constructions of the working class "other" among urban white middle class youth', *Journal of Youth Affairs*, 12 (5): 467–8.

Home Office (2003) *Respect and Responsibility: Taking a Stand Against Anti-Social Behaviour*. London: Home Office.

Honneth, A. (1995) *The Struggle for Recognition*. Cambridge: Polity Press.

Hourigan, N. (ed.) (2011) *Understanding Limerick: Social Exclusion and Change*. Cork: Cork University.

Houston, S. (2016) 'Beyond individualism', *British Journal of Social Work*, 46 (2): 532–48.

Howe, D., Sawbridge P. and Hinings, D. (1992) *Half a Million Women*. Harmondsworth: Penguin.

Howell, A. (2015) 'Resilience, war and austerity: The ethics of military human enhancement and the politics of data', *Security Dialogue*, 46 (1): 15–31.

Hozić, A. A. and True, J. (eds), (2016) *Scandalous Economics*. New York: Oxford University Press.

Hughes, B., McKie, L., Hopkins, D. and Watson, N. (2005) 'Love's labours lost? Feminism, the Disabled People's Movement and an ethic of care', *Sociology*, 39 (2): 259–75.

Humber, L. (2016) 'The impact of neoliberal market relations of the production of care on the quantity and quality of support for people with learning disabilities', *Critical and Radical Social Work*, 4 (2): 149–67.

Hunter, B. and Jordan, K. (2010) 'Explaining social exclusion: Towards social inclusion for Indigenous Australians', *Australian Journal of Social Issues*, 45 (2): 243–66.

Hutton, W. (2007) 'Open the gates and free people from Britain's ghettos', *The Observer*, 18 February. www.theguardian.com/commentisfree/2007/feb/18/comment.homeaffairs.

Iglesias, P. (2015) 'Understanding Podemos', *New Left Review*, 93: 7–23.

Independent Age (2016) *Brexit and the Future of Migrants in the Social Care Workforce*. www.independentage.org/sites/default/files/2016-09/IA-Brexit-Migration-report.pdf.

Ingle, R. (2009) 'Getting to grips with life on the dole', *The Irish Times*, 23 January: 19.

IMF (International Monetary Fund) (2013) 'The IMF's Work Program: Invigorating a sustainable recovery and restoring resilience', Press Release, 6 June. www.imf.org/external/np/sec/pr/2013/pr13199.htm.

Institute for Employment Research/The Research Institute for Federal Employment Agency (2014) *Patterns of Resilience during Socioeconomic Crises among Households in Europe (RESCuE)*. http://doku.iab.de/forschungsbericht/2014/fb0514.pdf.

Institute for Fiscal Studies (2016) 'The big challenge of living standards is to boost incomes for those in work', Press Release, 19 July. www.ifs.org.uk/publications/8373.

Irish Statute Book (2011) *Code of Professional Conduct and Ethics for Social Workers Bye-Law 2011* http://www.irishstatutebook.ie/pdf/2011/en.si.2011.0143.pdf.

Ives, P (2004) *Language and Hegemony in Gramsci*. London: Pluto.

Jameson, F. (2002) 'The dialectics of disaster', *The South Atlantic Quarterly*, 101 (2): 197–305.

Jensen, T. (2013) 'A summer of television poverty porn', *The Sociological Imagination*, 9 September. http://sociologicalimagination.org/archives/14013/comment-page-1.

Jensen, T. (2014) 'Welfare commonsense, poverty porn and doxosophy', *Sociological Research Online*, 19 (3). www.socresonline.org.uk/19/3/3.html.

Jensen, T. and Tyler, I. (2015) 'Benefit broods', *Critical Social Policy*, 35 (4): 470–92.

Jenson, J. M., Alter, C. F., Nicotera, N., Anthony, E. K., and Forrest-Bank, S. S. (2013) *Risk, Resilience, and Positive Youth Development*. New York: Oxford University Press.

Johansson, A. and Vinthagen, S. (2015) 'Dimensions of everyday resistance: the Palestinian Sumud', *Journal of Political Power*, 8 (1): 109–39.

Jones, O. (2011) *Chav: The Demonization of the Working Class*. London: Verso.

Jones, R. (2014) *The Story of Baby P*. Bristol: Policy Press.

Jones, S. (2006) *Antonio Gramsci*. London: Routledge.

Jönsson, J. H. (2015) 'The contested field of social work in a retreating welfare state: the case of Sweden', *Critical and Radical Social Work*, 3 (3): 357–75.

Jørgensen, M. B. and Thomsen, T. L. (2016) 'Deservingness in the Danish context: Welfare chauvinism in times of crisis', *Critical Social Policy*, 36 (3): 330–51.

Joseph, J. (2006) *Marxism and Social Theory*. Houndsmill: Palgrave Macmillan.

Katz, M. D. (ed.) (1993) *The 'Underclass' Debate: Views from History*. Princeton, NJ: Princeton University.

Kaul, K. (2016) 'Experience', in K. Fritsch, C. O'Connor and A. K. Thompson (eds), *Keywords for Radicals*. Chico, CA/Edinburgh, Scotland: AK Press, pp. 151–8.

Keena, C. (2015) 'Development of nursing homes needs a helping hand as banks fail to fund sector', *The Irish Times, Business Section*, 26 June: 5.

Keenan, D. (2013) 'Limerick protests at newspaper advert which depicts city as a crime scene', *The Irish Times*, 6 June. www.irishtimes.com/news/crime-and-law/limerick-protests-at-newspaper-advert-which-depicts-city-as-a-crime-scene-1.1419857.

Keil, R. (2009) 'The urban politics of roll-with-it neoliberalization', *City*, 13 (2–3): 231–246.

Kelly, S. and Blythe, B. J. (2000) 'Family preservation: A potential not yet realized', *Child Welfare*, Jan/Feb: 29–43.

Keogh, P. and Byrne, C. (2016) *Crisis, Concern and Complacency*. www.socialcareireland.ie/wp-content/uploads/2016/09/Crisis-Concern-and-Complacency.compressed.pdf.

Keskinen, S., Norocel, O. C., Jørgensen, M. B. (2016) 'The politics and policies of welfare chauvinism under the economic crisis', *Critical Social Policy*, 36 (3): 321–9.

Kinman, G. and Grant, L. (2011) 'Exploring stress resilience in trainee social workers', *British Journal of Social Work*, 41: 261–75.

Kirton, D. (2000) *'Race', Ethnicity and Adoption*. Buckingham: Open University.

Kirton, D. (2013) '"Kinship by design" in England: Reconfiguring adoption from Blair to the Coalition', *Child and Family Social Work*, 18: 97–106.

Kirton, D. (2016) 'Neo-liberal racism: Excision, ethnicity and the Children Act 2014', *Critical Social Policy*, 36 (4): 1–20.

Kittay, E. F. (2014) 'The moral harm of migrant carework', in A. M. Jaggar (ed.), *Gender and Global Justice*. Cambridge: Polity Press, pp. 62–85.

Klein, J., Béland, D. and Petersen, K. (2014) 'Social policy language in the United States', in D. Béland and K. Petersen (eds), *Analysing Social Policy Concepts and Language*. Bristol: Policy Press, pp. 227–97.

Klein, N. (2007) *The Shock Doctrine*. London: Allen Lane.

Kundnani, A. (2012) 'Radicalisation: the journey of a concept', *Race & Class*, 54 (2): 3–25.

Kunstreich, T. (2003) 'Social welfare in Nazi Germany', *Journal of Progressive Human Services*, 14 (2): 23–53.

Lacey, M. (2006) 'Guatemala system is scrutinized as Americans rush in to adopt', *The New York Times*, 5 November. www.nytimes.com/2006/11/05/world/americas/05guatemala.html?fta=y&_r=0.

Laclau, E. and Mouffe, C. (1985) *Hegemony and Socialist Strategy*. London: Verso.

Lagan, B. (2015) '"Poverty porn" TV accused of mocking Sydney families', *The Times*, 7 May: 27.

Lagarde, C. (2014) 'Economic inclusion and financial integrity', speech at conference on Inclusive Capitalism, 27 May. www.imf.org/external/np/speeches/2014/052714.htm

Landy, M. (1994) *Film, Politics and Gramsci*. Minneapolis, MN: University of Minnesota.

Lane, T. (1987) *Liverpool: Gateway of Empire*. London: Lawrence and Wishart.

Lavinas, L. (2013) '21st century welfare', *New Left Review*, 84: 5–41.

Lawler, S. (2014) *Identity: Sociological Perspectives*. Cambridge: Polity Press.

Lawrence, J. and Stocks, J. (2011) 'Why we couldn't adopt in Britain', *Daily Mail*, 16 November. www.dailymail.co.uk/femail/article-2062031/Adoption-Couples-rejected-UK-agencies-white.html.

Lazzarato, M. (1996) 'Immaterial labor', in P. Virno and M. Hardt (eds), *Radical Thought in Italy*. Minneapolis, MN: University of Minneapolis, pp. 133–51.

Lee, E., Bristow, J., Faircloth, S. and Macvarish, J. (2014) *Parenting Culture Studies*. London: Palgrave Macmillan.

Legrain, P. (2016) *Refugees Work: A Humanitairian Investment that Yields Economic Dividends*. www.integrazionemigranti.gov.it/Documenti-e-ricerche/Tent-Open-Refugees+Work_VFINAL-singlepages.pdf.

Leiber, N. (2016) 'Europe bets on robots to help care for seniors', *Bloomberg Businessweek*, 17 March. www.bloomberg.com/news/articles/2016-03-17/europe-bets-on-robots-to-help-care-for-seniors.

Lens, V. and Cary, C. (2010) 'Negotiating the discourse of race within the United States welfare system', *Ethnic and Racial Studies*, 33 (6): 1032–1048.

Levitas, R. (1996) 'The concept of social exclusion and the new Durkheimian hegemony', *Critical Social Policy*, 16 (1): 5–20.

Levitas, R. (1998) *The Inclusive Society?* Houndsmill: Macmillan.

Levitas, R. (2012) There may be 'trouble' ahead: What we know about those 120,000 'troubled' families. www.poverty.ac.uk/system/files/WP%20Policy%20 Response%20No.3-%20%20'Trouble'%20ahead%20(Levitas%20Final%20 21April2012).pdf.

Levitas, R. (2014) 'Troubled Families' in a Spin'. www.poverty.ac.uk/sites/default/ files/attachments/Troubled%20Families%20in%20a%20Spin.pdf.

Lewis, J. and West, A. (2014) 'Re-shaping social care services for older people in England', *Journal of Social Policy*, 43 (1): 1–19.

Lewis, P., Taylor, M. and Ball, J. (2011) 'Kenneth Clarke blames English riots on a "broken penal system"', *The Guardian*, 5 September. www.theguardian.com/ uk/2011/sep/05/kenneth-clarke-riots-penal-system.

Lister, R. (2001) 'New Labour: A study in the ambiguity from a position of ambiva- lence', *Critical Social Policy* 21 (4): 425–48.

Littlejohn, R. (2014) 'Duggan was a gangster not Nelson Mandela', *Mail Online*, 10 January. www.dailymail.co.uk/debate/article-2536869/RICHARD-LITTLEJOHN- Duggan-gangster-not-Nelson-Mandela.html.

Littler, J. (2013) 'The rise of the "Yummy Mummy"', *Communication, Culture and Critique*, 6: 227–43.

Liverpool Mental Health Consortium (2014) *The Impact of Austerity on Women's Wellbeing.* www.liverpoolmentalhealth.org/_wp/wp-content/uploads/2012/11/ Impact-of-Austerity-on-Womens-Wellbeing-LMHC-Sept-2014.pdf.

Lloyd, L. (2006) 'Call us carers: Limitations and risks in campaigning for recogni- tion and exclusivity', *Critical Social Policy*, 26 (4): 945–60.

Lloyd, M. (2001) 'The politics of disability and feminism: Discord or synthesis?', *Sociology*, 35 (3): 715–28.

Logan, E. (2014) *Garda Síochána 2005 (Section 42) (Special Inquiries relating to Garda Síochána Order 2013).* www.irishstatutebook.ie/eli/2013/si/481/made/en/ print.

Lohr, S. (2014) 'Unthinking eyes track employees', *The New York Times*, 21 June. www.nytimes.com/2014/06/22/technology/workplace-surveillance-sees-good- and-bad.html?_r=0.

Loughton, T. (2010) 'Ethnicity shouldn't be a barrier to adoption', Press Release, 2 November. www.gov.uk/government/news/tim-loughton-ethnicity-shouldnt-be- a-barrier-to-adoption.

Loyal, S. (2003) 'Welcome to the Celtic Tiger: Racism, immigration and the state', in C. Coulter and S. Coleman (eds), *The End of Irish History?* Manchester: Manchester University, pp. 74–5.

Lundberg, M. and Wuermli, A. (eds) (2012a) *Child and Youth in Crisis.* Washington, DC: The World Bank.

Lundberg, A. and Wuermli, A. (2012b) 'Introduction' in M. Lundberg and A. Wuermli (eds), *Child and Youth in Crisis.* Washington DC: The World Bank, pp. 3–29.

Lynch, K. (2007) 'Love labour as a distinct and non-commodifiable form of care labour', *The Sociological Review*, 55 (3): 550–70.

Lynch, K. (2010) 'Carelessness: A hidden doxa of higher education', *Arts & Humanities in Higher Education*, 9 (1): 54–67.

Lynch, R. and Garrett, P. M. (2010) 'More than words': Touch practices in child and family social work', *Child & Family Social Work*, 15 (4): 389–398.

Lyon, D. (ed.) (2006) *Theorizing Surveillance*. Cullompton: Willan.

MacAlister, J. (ed.) (2012) *Frontline*. London: IPPR.

MacGregor, D. (1996) *Hegel, Marx, and the English State*. London: University of Toronto.

MacKinnon, D. and Driscoll Derickson, K. (2012) 'From resilience to resourcefulness', *Progress in Human Geography*, 37 (2): 253–70.

MacLeavy, J. and Peoples, C. (2009) 'Workfare-warfare: Neoliberalism, "active" welfare and the new American way of war', *Antipode*, 41 (5): 890–915.

Macnicol, J. (1987) 'In pursuit of the underclass', *Journal of Social Policy*, 16 (3): 293–318.

Macnicol, J. (2015) 'Reconstructing the underclass', London School of Economics & Social Policy Association Seminar, 9 April. www.social-policy.org.uk/wordpress/wp-content/uploads/2015/06/Macnicol-Reconstructing-the-underclass.pdf.

Macpherson, Sir William of Cluny (1999) *The Stephen Lawrence Inquiry*. London: The Stationery Office.

Macvarish, J., Lee, E. and Low, P. (2015) 'Neuroscience and family policy', *Critical Social Policy*, 35 (2): 167–88.

Mahmud, T. (2012) 'Debt and discipline', *American Quarterly*, 64 (3): 469–94.

Malabou, C. (2008) *What Shall We Do with Our Brains?* New York: Fordham University.

Mann, K. (1994) 'Watching the defectives: Observers of the underclass in the USA, Britain and Australia', *Critical Social Policy*, 41: 79–100.

Mann, K. and Roseneil, S. (1994) 'Some mothers do 'ave 'em: Backlash and gender politics of the underclass debate', *Journal of Gender Studies*, 3 (3): 317–32.

Marre, D. (2012) 'Gender, feminism and mothering in Spain', *Feminist Theory*, 13 (1): 89–91.

Martin, L. L. and Mitchelson, M. L. (2009) 'Geographies of detention and imprisonment', *Geography Compass*, 3 (1): 459–77.

Marx, K. (1990) *Capital, Volume 1*. London: Penguin.

Marx, K. (2000) 'The Eighteenth Brumaire of Louis Bonaparte', in D. McLellan (ed.), *Karl Marx: Selected Writings*. Oxford: Oxford University Press, pp. 329–56.

Massey, D. (2015) 'Vocabularies of the economy', in S. Hall, D. Massey and M. Rustin (eds), *After Neoliberalism*. London: Lawrence & Wishart, pp. 24–37.

Masten, A. S. (2001) 'Ordinary magic: Resilience processes in development', *American Psychologist*, 56 (3): 227–38.

Masten, A. S. (2014) 'Global perspectives on resilience in children and youth', *Child Development*, 85 (1): 6–20.

Matthews, M. D. (2014) *Head Strong: How Psychology is Revolutionizing War.* Oxford: Oxford University Press.

Matza, D. (1967) 'The disreputable poor', in R. Bendix and S. M. Lipset (eds), *Class, Status and Power.* London: Routledge and Kegan Paul.

May, T. (2016a) Statement from the new Prime Minister, 13 July. www.gov.uk/government/speeches/statement-from-the-new-prime-minister-theresa-may.

May, T. (2016b) 'The good that Government can do': Speech to the Conservative Party Conference, 5 October. http://press.conservatives.com/post/151378268295/prime-minister-the-good-that-government-can-do.

Mayes, R. and Horwitz, A. V. (2005) 'DSM-111 and the revolution in the classification of mental illness', *Journal of the History of the Behavioural Sciences*, 41 (3): 249–67.

McCann, E. (2014) 'Care "homes" where church destroyed lives of children', *The Irish Times*, 30 January: 16.

McDonald, C. and Chenoweth, L. (2006) 'Workfare Oz-style', *Journal of Policy Practice*, 5 (2–3): 109–28.

McDonald, C. and Chenoweth, L. (2009) '(Re) Shaping social work: An Australian case study', *British Journal of Social Work*, 39: 144–60.

McDonald, C. and Marston, G. (2005) 'Workfare as welfare', *Critical Social Policy*, 25 (3): 374–401.

McDonnell, J. (2016) 'Our economy is failing on productivity because the Tories are failing to deliver the investment it needs', Labour Party Conference Speech, 26 September. http://press.labour.org.uk/post/150957354109/our-economy-is-failing-on-productivity-because-the .

McDowell, L. (2004) 'Work, workfare, work/life balance and an ethic of care', *Progress in Human Geography*, 28 (2): 145–63.

McGarry, A. (2017) *Roma Phobia: The Last Acceptable form of Racism.* London: Zed.

McGuigan, J. and Moran, M. (2014) 'Raymond Williams and sociology', *The Sociological Review*, 62: 167–88.

McKendrick, D. and Finch, J. (2016) 'Under heavy manners? Social work, radicalisation, troubled families and non-linear war', *British Journal of Social Work*, Advance Access from 12 January, DOI:10.1093/bjsw/bcv141.

McKenzie, L. (2012) 'The stigmatised and de-valued working class: The state of a council estate', in W. Atkinson, S. Roberts and M. Savage (eds), *Class Inequality in Austerity Britain.* Houndsmill: Palgrave, pp. 128–45.

McKenzie, L. (2015) *Getting By.* Bristol: Policy Press.

McLaughlin, K. (2007) 'Regulation and risk in social work: The General Social Care Council and the Social Care Register in context', *British Journal of Social Work*, 37 (2): 1263–77.

McLaughlin, H. (2009) 'What's in a name: "Client", "patient", "customer", "consumer", "expert by experience", "service user" – what's next?', *British Journal of Social Work*, 39: 1101–17.

McLennan, G. (2004) 'Travelling with vehicular ideas: The case of the Third Way', *Economy and Society*, 33 (4): 484–99.

McMahon, A. (2016) 'More than 130 children missing from State care units in 2015', *The Irish Times*, 30 May: 2.

McMorrow, C. (2006) 'Notorious Limerick estate stranded in no-man's land', *The Sunday Tribune*, 17 September: 9.

McNay, L. (2008) *Against Recognition*. Cambridge: Polity Press.

McNay, L (2009) 'Self as enterprise: Dilemmas of control and resistance in Foucault's the Birth of Biopolitics', *Theory, Culture & Society*, 26 (6): 55–77.

McNay, L. (2014) *The Misguided Search for the Political*. Cambridge: Polity Press.

McRoy, R. G. (1991) 'American experience and research on openness', *Adoption & Fostering*, 15 (4): 99–111.

McVeigh, T. (2009) 'Take more babies away from bad parents, says Barnardo's chief', *The Guardian*, 6 September. www.theguardian.com/society/2009/sep/06/children-babies-parents-care-barnardos.

McVeigh, T. (2016) 'Deaths are not just happening in the US: why activists brought the Black Lives movement to the UK', *The Observer*, 7 August: 6.

Mead, L. W. (1992) *The New Politics of Poverty*. New York: Basic Books.

Meloni, M. (2016) *Political Biology*. Houndsmill: Palgrave.

Milner, J. (1993) 'A disappearing act: The differing career paths of fathers and mothers in child protection investigations', *Critical Social Policy*, 13 (2): 48–64.

Mincy, R. B., Sawhill, I. V. and Wolf, D. A. (1990) 'The underclass: Definition and measurement', *Science*, 248: 450–3.

Mirowski, P. and Plehwe, D. (ed.) (2009) *The Road from Mont Pèlerin*. Cambridge MA: Harvard University Press.

Mohaupt, S. (2009) 'Resilience and social exclusion', *Social Policy & Society*, 8 (1): 63–71.

Moi, T. (1991) 'Appropriating Bourdieu: Feminist theory and Pierre Bourdieu's sociology of culture' *New Literary History*, 22: 1017–49.

Mooney, G. and Scott, G. (2015) 'The 2014 Scottish independence debate: Questions of social welfare and social justice', *Journal of Poverty and Social Justice*, 23 (1): 5–16.

Moorhead, J. (2014) 'We knew he was special', *The Guardian, Family Supplement*, 11 January: 1–3.

Moran, M. (2006) 'Social inclusion and the limits of pragmatic liberalism: The Irish case', *Irish Political Studies*, 21 (2): 181–201.

Moran, M. (2015) *Identity and Capitalism*. London: Sage.

Morgan, P. (1998) *Adoption and the Care of Children*. London: IEA Health and Welfare Unit.

Morgen, S., Acker, J. and Weigt, J. (2010) *Stretched Thin*. Ithaca and London: Cornell University Press.

Morris, B. (2004) 'On ethnic cleansing', *New Left Review*, 26: 35–53.

Morris, K. (2013) 'Troubled families: Vulnerable families' experiences of multiple service use', *Child & Family Social Work*, 18: 189–206.

Morris, M. (1989) 'From the culture of poverty to the underclass', *The American Sociologist*, 20 (2): 123–33.

Moser, I. and Thygesan, H. (2015) 'Exploring the possibilities in telecare for ageing societies' in M. Barnes, T. Brannelly, L. Ward and N. Ward (eds), *Ethics of Care*. Bristol: Policy Press, pp. 111–25.

Mottier, V. and Gerodetti, N. (2007) 'Eugenics and social democracy', *Soundings*, 60: 35–50.

Mountz, A., Coddington, K., Catania, R. T. and Loyd, J. M. (2013) 'Conceptualizing detention', *Progress in Human Geography*, 37 (4): 522–41.

Movement for an Adoption Apology (2011) 'Mission statement for the Movement for an Adoption Apology', Adopted 3 October. http://movementforanadoptiona-pology.org/

Moxon, D. (2011) 'Consumer Culture and the 2011 "Riots"', *Sociological Research Online* http://www.socresonline.org.uk/16/4/19.html.

Muehlebach, A. (2012) *The Moral Neoliberal*. Chicago: University of Chicago Press.

Murphy, T. (2016) 'The Frontline programme: Conservative ideology and the creation of a social work officer class', *Critical and Radical Social Work*, 4 (2): 279–89.

Murray, C. (1990) *The Emerging British Underclass*. London: Institute of Economic Affairs.

Murray, C. (1994a) 'The new Victorians … and the new rabble', *The Sunday Times*, 29 May.

Murray, C. (1994b) *Underclass: The Crisis Deepens*. London, IEA.

Murray, C. (2010) 'Conceptualizing young people's strategies of resistance to offending as "active resilience"', *British Journal of Social Work*, 40: 115–32.

Myrdal, G. (1960) *Beyond the Welfare State*. London: Duckworth.

Myrdal, G. (1963) *Challenge to Affluence*. London: Gollancz.

Nadesan, M. H. (2002) 'Engineering the entrepreneurial infant', *Cultural Studies*, 16 (3): 401–32.

Narey, Sir M. (2014) *Making the Education of Social Workers Consistently Effective*. www.gov.uk/government/uploads/system/uploads/attachment_data/file/278741/Social_worker_education_report.PDF.

NASC (The Irish Immigrant Support Centre) (2013) *In from the Margins: Roma in Ireland*. www.nascireland.org/wp-content/uploads/2013/05/NASC-ROMA-REPORT.pdf.

National Center on Family Homelessness (2014) *America's Youngest Outcasts: A Report Card on Child Homelessness*. www.air.org/resource/americas-youngest-outcasts-report-card-child-homelessness.

National Institute of Economic and Social Research (2016) 'No evidence Troubled Familes Programme had significant impact on key objectives, NIESC evaluation finds', Press Release, 17 October. www.niesr.ac.uk/media/niesr-press-release-%E2%80%93-no-evidence-troubled-families-programme-had-any-significant-impact-key#.WAYIg_krLIU.

Nayak, A. (2003) 'Displaced masculinities: Chavs, youth and class in the post-industrial city', *Sociology*, 40 (5): 813–31.

Nayak, A. and Kehily, M. J. (2014) '"Chavs, chavettes and pramface girls"', *Journal of Youth Studies*, 17 (10): 1330–45.

Neale, A. and Lopez, N. (2017) *Suffer the Little Children & their Mothers*. London: Crossroad Books.

Negri, A. (2005) *The Politics of Subversion*. Cambridge: Polity Press.

Neocleous, M. (2008) *Critique of Security*. Edinburgh: Edinburgh University Press.

Neocleous, M. (2013) 'Resisting resilience', *Radical Philosophy*, 178: 2–8.

Neocleous, M. and Kastrinou, M. (2016) 'The EU hotspot: police war against the migrant', *Radical Philosophy*, 200: 3–11.

Newberry-Koroluk, A. M. (2014) 'Hitting the ground running: Neo-Conservatism and first-year Canadian social workers', *Critical Social Work*, 15 (1) www1.uwindsor.ca/criticalsocialwork/system/files/Newberry_Koroluk_2014.pdf.

Newman, J. and Clarke, J. (2015) 'States of imagination', in S. Hall, D. Massey and M. Rustin (eds), *After Neoliberalism*. London: Lawrence and Wishart, pp. 99–116.

Ngai, P. (2016) *Migrant Labor in China*. Cambridge: Polity Press.

Nichols, A. L. and Zeckhauser, R. J. (1982) 'Targeting transfers through restrictions on recipients', *American Economic Review*, 72 (2): 372–8.

Nicolson, E. (2004) 'Red light on human traffic', *The Guardian*, 1 July. www.the-guardian.com/society/2004/jul/01/adoptionandfostering.europeanunion.

Noddings, N. (1984) *Caring*. Berkeley, CA: University of California Press.

Norocel, O. C. (2016) 'Populist radical right protectors of the folkhem: Welfare chauvinism in Sweden', *Critical Social Policy*, 36 (3): 371–90.

O'Hagan, A. (2009) 'The age of indifference', *The Guardian Review*, 10 January: 1–4.

O'Malley, P. (2010) 'Resilient subjects: Uncertainty, warfare and liberalism', *Economy and Society*, 39 (4): 488–509.

O'Neale, V. (2000) *Excellence not Excuses*. London: Department of Health.

O'Toole, F. (2012) 'Blind search for profits behind care home abuse', *The Irish Times*, 14 August: 12.

Offe, C. (1984) *Contradictions of the Welfare State*. London: Hutchinson.

Oreskovic, J. and Maskew, T. (2008) 'Red thread or slender reed: Deconstructing Prof. Bartholet's mythology of international adoption', *Buffalo Human Rights Law Review*, 14: 71–129.

Ortiz, A. T. and Briggs, L. (2003) 'The culture of poverty, crack babies and welfare cheats', *Social Text*, 21 (3): 39–58.

Osborne, G. (2015) 'Calling all progressives: Help us reform the welfare state', *The Guardian*, 20 July: 27.

Osborne, H. (2016) 'Workers bear the brunt of system that won't pay for social care', *The Guardian*, 18 November: 8–9.

Oxfam (2017) An Economy for the 99%. www.oxfam.org/sites/www.oxfam.org/files/file_attachments/bp-economy-for-99-percent-160117-en.pdf.

Oxfam America (2016) *Broken at the Top*, Media Briefing, 14 April. www.oxfamamerica.org/static/media/files/Broken_at_the_Top_FINAL_EMBARGOED_4.12.2016.pdf.

Palmer, A. (2010) 'The only to stop youth crime is help parents', *The Telegraph*, 27 March. www.telegraph.co.uk/comment/7530902/The-only-way-to-stop-youth-crime-is-to-help-the-parents.html.

Pande, A. (2016) 'Global reproductive inequalities, neo-eugenics and commercial surrogacy in India', *Current Sociology Monograph*, 64 (2): 244-58.

Parker, A. (2003) 'Editor's introduction', in J. Rancière, *The Philosopher and His Poor*. Durham, NC and London: Duke University, pp. ix–xxv.

Parker, R., Ward, H., Jackson, S., Aldgate, J. and Wedge, P. (1991) *Looking After Children*. London: HMSO.

Pavee Point Traveller and Roma Centre (2013) 'Pavee Point response to child protection case in Tallaght', Press Release, 22 October. www.paveepoint.ie/pavee-point-response-to-child-protection-case-in-tallaght/.

Paxson, C. and Waldfogel, J. (2003) 'Welfare reforms, family resources, and child maltreatment', *Journal of Policy Analysis and Management*, 22 (1): 85–113.

Pearson, G. (1975) *The Deviant Imagination*. London: Macmillan.

Peck, J. (1998) 'Workfare: A geopolitical etymology', *Environment and Planning D: Society and Space*, 16: 133–61.

Peck, J, (2001) *Workfare States*. New York: Guilford Press.

Peck, J. (2010) *Constructions of Neoliberal Reason*. Oxford: Oxford University Press.

Peck, J. and Theodore, N. (2010a) 'Mobilizing policy: Models, methods, and mutations', *Geoforum*, 41: 169–74.

Peck, J. and Theodore, N. (2010b) 'Recombinant workfare, across the Americas: Transnationalizing "fast" social policy', *Geoforum*, 41: 195–208.

Pemberton, C. (2010) 'Sterilise parents who abuse children, top professor says', *Community Care*, 24 August. www.communitycare.co.uk/Articles/2010/08/24/115157/sterilise-parents-who-abuse-children-top-professor-says.htm.

Pemberton, S., Fahy, E., Sutton, E. and Bell, K. (2016) 'Navigating the stigmatised identities of poverty in austere times', *Critical Social Policy*, 36 (1): 21–38.

Pentaraki, M. (2013) 'If we do not cut spending, we will end up like Greece', *Critical Social Policy*, 33 (4): 700–12.

Pentaraki, M. (2016) 'I am in a constant state of insecurity trying to make ends meet, like our service users', *British Journal of Social Work*, advance access from 31 August, DOI: 10.1093/bjsw/bcw099.

Performance and Innovation Unit (2000) *The Prime Minister's Review of Adoption*. London: HMSO.

Perkins, A. (2016) *The Welfare Trait*. London: Palgrave Macmillan.

Peterson C., Park N. and Castro C. (2011) 'Assessment for the US Army Comprehensive Soldier Fitness Program: The Global Assessment Tool', *American Psychologist* 66 (1): 10–18.

Pfau-Effinger, B. (2005) 'Culture and welfare state policies', *Journal of Social Policy*, 34 (1): 3–20.

Phelan, S. (2007) 'The discourses of neoliberal hegemony: The case of the Irish Republic', *Critical Discourse Studies*, 4 (1): 29–48.

Phillips, J. (2007) *Care*. Cambridge: Polity Press.

Phillips, M. (2011) 'Britain's liberal intelligentsia has smashed virtually every social value', *Mail Online*, 11 August. www.dailymail.co.uk/debate/article-2024690/UK-riots-2011-Britains-liberal-intelligentsia-smashed-virtually-social-value.html.

Philp, A. F. and Timms, N. (1957) *The Problem of 'the Problem Family'*. London: Family Service Units.

Philpot, T. (ed.) (1999) *Political Correctness and Social Work*. London: IEA.

Piachaud, D. and Sutherland, H. (2001) 'Child poverty in Britain and the New Labour government', *Journal of Social Policy* 3 (1): 95–118.

Pickersgill, M. (2011) 'Ordering disorder: Knowledge production and uncertainty in neuroscience research', *Science as Culture*, 20 (1): 71–87.

Pine, L. (1995) 'Hasude: The imprisonment of "asocial" families in the Third Reich', *The Germany History Society*, 13 (2): 182–98.

Pine, L. (1997) *Nazi Family Policy, 1933–1945*. Oxford: Berg.

Pitcher, B. (2016) 'Race, debt and the welfare state', *New Formations*, 87: 47–64.

Pithouse, A. (2008) 'Early intervention in the round: A great idea but ...', *British Journal of Social Work*, 38 (8): 1536–52.

Powell, M. (2000) 'New Labour and the third way in the British welfare state', *Critical Social Policy*, 20 (1): 39–61.

Prideaux, S. J. (2010) 'The welfare politics of Charles Murray are alive and well in the UK', *International Journal of Social Welfare*, 19: 293–302.

Purnell, J. (2008) 'Ready to work, skilled for work: Unlocking Britain's talent' conference, 28 January, http://webarchive.nationalarchives.gov.uk/20100210151716/dwp.gov.uk/policy/welfare-reform/legislation-and-key-documents/ready-to-work-skilled-for-work/.

Raffass, T. (2016) 'Work enforcement in Liberal democracies', *Journal of Social Policy*, 45 (3): 417–35.

Raisborough, J. and Adams, M. (2008) 'Mockery and morality in popular cultural representations of the white working class', *Sociological Research Online*, 13 (6) www.socresonline.org.uk/13/6/2.html.

Rajan-Rankin, S. (2014) 'Self-identity, embodiment and the development of emotional resilience', *British Journal of Social Work*, 44 (8): 2426–42.

Ramani, D. (2009) 'The brain seduction: The public perception of neuroscience', *Journal of Science Communication*, 8 (4): 1–9.

Rancière, J. (1991) *The Ignorant Schoolmaster*. Stanford, CA: Stanford University. (First published in France in 1981.)

Rancière, J. (1999) *Dis-agreement*. Minneapolis, USA: University of Minnesota. (First published in France in 1995.)

Rancière, J. (2003) *The Philosopher and His Poor*. Durham, NC and London: Duke University. (First published in France in 1983.)

Rancière, J. (2007) 'What does it mean to be *Un*?', *Continuum*, 21 (4): 559–69.

Rancière, J. (2012) *Proletarian Nights*. London: Verso. (First published in France in 1981.)

Rancière, J. (2016) *The Method of Equality*. Cambridge: Polity Press.

Reed, A. (2016) 'The post-1965 trajectory of race, class, and urban politics in the United States reconsidered', *Labor Studies Journal*, 41 (3): 260–91.

Reid, J. (2016) 'Resilience', in D. Chandler and J. Reid (2016) *The Neoliberal Subject*. London: Rowman & Littlefield, pp. 51–73.

Reivich, K. and Shatte, A. (2002) *The Resilience Factor*. Chicago, IL: Broadway Books.

Richter-Devroe, S. (2011) 'Palestinian women's everyday resistance', *Journal of International Women's Studies*, 12 (2): 32–46.

Riddell, M. (2011) 'London riots: The underclass lashed out', *Daily Telegraph*, 12 June. www.telegraph.co.uk/news/uknews/law-and-order/8630533/Riots-the-underclass-lashes-out.html.

Riots Communities and Victims Panel (2012) *After the Riots*. http://webarchive.nationalarchives.gov.uk/20121003195935/http:/riotspanel.independent.gov.uk/wp-content/uploads/2012/03/Riots-Panel-Final-Report1.pdf.

Rivera, L. A. (2015) *Pedigree*. Princeton, NJ: Princeton University Press.

Roberts, D. E. (2012) 'Prison, foster care, and the systemic punishment of black mothers', *UCLA Law Review*, 59: 1474–501.

Roberts, D. E. (2014a) 'Child protection as surveillance of African American families', *Journal of Social Welfare and Family Law*, 36 (4): 426–37.

Roberts, D. (2014b) 'Complicating the triangle of race, class and state: the insights of black feminists', *Ethnic and Racial Studies*, 37 (10): 1776–82.

Robinson, F. (1999) *Globalizing Care*. Boulder, CO: Westview.

Robinson, F. (2006) 'Care, gender and global social justice', *Journal of Global Ethics*, 2 (1): 5–25.

Rodger, J. (1992) 'The welfare state and social closure: Social division and the "underclass"', *Critical Social Policy*, 35: 45–64.

Rose, G. (2016) *Visual Methodologies*, 4th edn. London: Sage.

Rose, H. and Rose, S. (2016) *Can Neuroscience Change Our Minds?* Cambridge: Polity Press.

Rose, N. (2000) 'Government and control', *British Journal of Criminology*, 40: 321–39.

Ross, K. (2002) *May '68 and Its Afterlives*. Chicago, IL and London: University of Chicago.

Rustin, M. (2009) 'Reflections on the present', *Soundings*, 43: 18–35.

Rustin, S. (2012) 'Andrea Leadsom: lobbying for more support for parents and children', *The Guardian*, 27 November. www.theguardian.com/society/2012/nov/27/andrea-leadsom-lobbying-parents-children.

Ryan, D. and Garrett, P. M. (2017) 'Social work "logged on": contemporary dilemmas in an evolving "techno-habitat"', *European Journal of Social Work*, 23 January, DOI: 10.1080/13691457.2016.1278520.

Safri, M. and Ruccio, D. F. (2013) 'Keywords: An introduction', *Rethinking Marxism*, 25 (1): 7–10.

Saville, J. (1957) 'The welfare state: An historical approach', *The New Reasoner*, 3: 5–25.

Schofield, G. and Beek, M. (2005) 'Risk and resilience in long-term foster-care', *British Journal of Social Work*, 35: 1283–301.

Schram, S. F. (1995) *Words of Welfare*. Minneapolis, MN: University of Minnesota.

Schram, S. F. (2015) *The Return of Ordinary Capitalism*. New York: Oxford University Press.

Schram, S. F., Soss, J., Houser, L. and Fording, R. C. (2010) 'The third level of US welfare reform: Governmentality under neoliberal paternalism', *Citizenship Studies*, 14 (6): 739–54.

Scottish Unemployed Workers' Network (2016) *Righting Welfare Wrongs: Dispatches from the Front Line of the Fight Against Austerity.* Glasgow: Common Print.

Scourfield, P. (2007) 'Are there reasons to be worried about the "caretelisation" of residential care', *Critical Social Policy*, 27 (2): 155–81.

Scourfield, P. (2012) 'Caretelization revisited and the lesson of Southern Cross', *Critical Social Policy*, 32 (1): 137–49.

Scourfield, P. (2013) 'Even further beyond street-level bureaucracy', *British Journal of Social Work*, 45: 914–31.

Seccombe, K. (2002) 'Beating the odds versus changing the odds: Poverty, resilience, and family policy', *Journal of Marriage and Family*, 64: 384–94.

Seccombe, K. (2007) *So You Think I Drive a Cadillac?* Boston, MA: Allyn and Bacon.

Seligman, M. E. P (2015) *Authentic Happiness.* London: Nicholas Brealey.

Seligman, M. E. P. and Fowler, R. D. (2011) 'Comprehensive soldier fitness and the future of psychology', *American Psychologist*, 66 (1): 82–7.

Selman, P. (2012) 'The global decline of intercountry adoption', *Social Policy and Society*, 11 (3): 381–99.

Sen, A. (2000) *Social Exclusion.* Manila, Philippines: Asian Development Bank.

Sevenhuijsen, S. (1998) *Citizenship and the Ethics of Care.* London: Routledge.

Shahid, M. and Jha, M. K. (2014) 'Revisiting the client–worker relationship: Biestek through a Gramscian gaze', *Journal of Progressive Services*, 25: 18–36.

Shakespeare, T. (1997) 'Cultural representation of disabled people', in L. Barton and M. Oliver (eds), *Disability Studies: Past, Present and Future.* Leeds: Disability Press, pp. 217–36.

Shakespeare, T. (2000) *Help.* Birmingham: British Association of Social Workers.

Shannon, G. and Gibbons, N. (2012) *Report of the Independent Child Death Review Group.* www.dcya.gov.ie/documents/publications/Report_ICDRG.pdf.

Sharry, J. (2011) 'The resilience of children can give us a reason to be hopeful about the future', *The Irish Times Weekend Review*, 1 January: 1.

Sherwood, H. (2016) 'Our babies were taken – not given away', *The Guardian*, 3 November: 3.

Shipman, T. (2012) ' "Criminal culture at the heart of feckless families": Shocking report lifts lid on incest, abuse and spiral of alcohol abuse', *Mail Online*, 17 July. www.dailymail.co.uk/news/article-2175094/Troubled-Families-report-lifts-lid-120-000-problem-households.html.

Shoesmith, S. (2016) *Learning from Baby P.* London: Jessica Kingsley.

Siebert, A. (2005) *The Resiliency Advantage: Master Change, Thrive Under Pressure and Bounce Back from Setbacks.* Portland, OR: Practical Psychology Press.

Silver, H. (1994) 'Social exclusion and social solidarity', *International Labour Review*, 133 (5/6): 531–79.

Silver, H. (2010) 'Understanding social inclusion and its meaning for Australia', *Australian Journal of Social Issues*, 45 (2): 183–212.

Sissay, L. (2012) 'On inter-racial adoption, Cameron is wrong. Colour blindness is a disability', *The Guardian*, 13 March. www.theguardian.com/commentisfree/2012/mar/13/inter-racial-adoption-cameron-wrong.

Skeggs, B. (2014) 'Values beyond value? Is anything beyond the logic of capital', *British Journal of Sociology*, 65 (1): 1–21.

Slater, T. (2012) 'The myth of "Broken Britain": Welfare reform and the production of ignorance', *Antipode*, 46 (4): 948–69.

Small, J. (1982) 'New black families', *Adoption & Fostering* 6 (3): 35–40.

Small, J. with Prevatt Goldstein, A. (2000) 'Ethnicity and placement: beginning the debate', *Adoption & Fostering* 24 (1): 9–15.

Smart, C. (ed.) (1992) *Regulating Womanhood*. London: Routledge.

Smith, A. M. (1998) *Laclau and Mouffe: The Radical Democratic Imaginary*. London: Routledge.

Smith, A. M. (2010) 'Neo-eugenics: A feminist critique of Agamben', *Occasion: Studies in the Humanities*, 2. http://arcade.stanford.edu/sites/default/files/article_pdfs/Occasion_v02_Smith_122010_0.pdf.

Smith, G. (2011) 'Selective hegemony and beyond-populations with "no productive function"', *Identities*, 18 (1): 2–38.

Smith, L. (2014) 'It's not true that growing up in poverty damages your brain', *The Guardian, Society*, 7 May: 36.

Smith, O. (2016) 'The kind of revolution I'll deliver', Knowledge Transfer Centre Advanced Manufacturing Park, Orgreave, 27 July. http://labourlist.org/2016/07/the-kind-of-revolution-ill-deliver-owen-smiths-speech-on-industry/.

Snir, I. (2016) '"Not just one common sense": Gramsci's common sense and Laclau and Mouffe's radical democratic politics', *Constellations*, 23 (2): 269–81.

Sommers, J. (2015) 'Labour's bizarre "Controls On Immigration" mug is perfect for the ardent Ukipper in your life', *The Huffington Post*, 28 March. www.huffingtonpost.co.uk/2015/03/28/labour-immigration-mug_n_6961756.html.

Spinley, B. M. (1953) *The Deprived and the Privileged*. London: Routledge & Kegan Paul.

Staffordshire County Council (1991) *The Pindown Experience and the Protection of Children*. Staffordshire: Staffordshire County Council.

Stamm, J. (2007) *Bright from the Start*. New York: Gotham Books.

Stanley, T. and Guru, S. (2015) 'Childhood radicalisation risk', *Practice*, 27 (3): 353–66.

Starkey, P. (2000) 'The feckless mother: Women, poverty and social workers in war-time and post-war England', *Women's History Review*, 9 (3): 539–59.

Stavrakakis, Y. (2013) 'Dispatches from the Greek lab: Metaphors, strategies and debt in the European crisis', *Psychoanalysis, Culture & Society*, 18 (3): 313–24.

Stehlik, D. (2001) 'A Brave New World? Neo-eugenics and its challenge to difference', *Violence Against Women*, 7 (4): 370–92.

Stein, M. (2011) 'The fixation on early years intervention is naïve', *The Guardian*, 11 January. www.theguardian.com/society/joepublic/2011/jan/11/fixation-early-years-intervention-flawed.

Stevenson, L. (2016) 'Record number of care applications in December figures show', *Community Care*, 13 January. www.communitycare.co.uk/2016/01/13/record-number-care-applications-december-figures-show/.

Stoddard, L. (1922) *The Revolt Against Civilization: The Menace of the Under Man*. New York: Charles Scribner's Sons.

Strangleman, T. (2008) 'Visual sociology and work', *Sociology Compass*, 2 (5): 1491–505.

Surowiecki, J. (2016) 'Trump sets private prisons free', *The New Yorker*, 5 December. www.newyorker.com/magazine/2016/12/05/trump-sets-private-prisons-free.

Sutton, L., Smith, N., Deardon, C. and Middleton, S. (2007) *A Child's-eye View of Social Difference*. York: Joseph Rowntree Foundation.

Swansen, G. (2007) 'Serenity, self-regard and the genetic sequence: Social psychiatry and preventive eugenics in Britain, 1930s–1950s', *Soundings*, 60: 50–66.

Tangenberg, K. M. and Kemp, K. (2002) 'Embodied practice', *Social Work*, 47 (1): 8–19.

Tapscott, D. (2013) 'World Economic Forum: Creating a dynamic, resilient world', *The Globe and Mail*, 21 January. www.theglobeandmail.com/report-on-business/international-business/world-economic-forum-creating-a-dynamic-resilient-world/article7564083/.

Tarnoff, B. (2016) 'Why tech now loves Trump', *The Guardian*, 14 December: 33.

Taylor, C. (2002) 'Modern social imaginaries', *Public Culture*, 17 (1): 91–124.

Taylor, D. (2014) 'Councils using online auctions to find carers for elderly people', *The Guardian*, 28 August: 10.

Taylor-Gooby, P. (2013) *The Double Crisis of the Welfare State and What We Can Do About It*. Houndsmill: Palgrave.

Tazzioli, M. (2015) *Spaces of Governmentality: Autonomous Migration and the Arab Uprising*. London: Rowman & Littlefield.

Teague, A. (1989) *Social Change, Social Work and the Adoption of Children*. Aldershot: Avebury/Gower.

Tepe-Belfrage, D. and Montgomerie, J. (2016) 'Broken Britain: Post-crisis austerity and the trouble with the troubled families programme', in A. A. Hozić and J. True (eds), *Scandalous Economics*. New York: Oxford University Press pp. 79–92.

Thornton, D. J. (2011) 'Neuroscience, affect, and the entrepreneurialization of motherhood', *Communication and Critical/Cultural Studies*, 8 (4): 399–424.

Thorpe, V. (2014) 'From Bullingdon boys to Chelsea ladies: Our new fascination with posh', *The Observer*, 25 May: 35.

Tickle, L. (2014) 'Adoption should be the last port of call – even in the storm of local authority funding', *The Guardian*, 25 September. www.theguardian.com/social-care-network/2014/sep/25/adoption-last-resort-local-authority.

Tickle, L. (2015) 'Is pressure to speed up adoptions leaving children out in the cold?', *The Guardian*, 15 July: 36.

Timms, N. and Timms, R. (1982) *Dictionary of Social Welfare*. London: Routledge & Kegan Paul.

Timpson, E. (2013) 'Foreword', in Department for Education, *Further Action on Adoption: Finding More Loving Homes*. www.gov.uk/government/uploads/system/uploads/attachment_data/file/219661/Further_20Action_20on_20 Adoption.pdf.

Timpson, E. (2015) 'I've seen babies addicted to heroin go into spasms', *Society Guardian: Fostering and Adoption* supplement, 4 March: 3.

Tomlinson, M. (2016) 'Risking peace in the "war against the poor"? Social exclusion and the legacies of the Northern Ireland conflict', *Critical Social Policy*, 36 (1): 104–24.

Townsend, P. (1979) *Poverty in the United Kingdom*. London: Allen Lane.

Toynbee, P. (2010) 'Loyal, public service merits more than this cold trashing', *The Guardian*, 24 August: 27.

Toynbee, P. (2011) 'Chav: the vile word at the heart of fractured Britain', *The Guardian*, 31 March: 29.

Triseliotis, J. (1973) *In Search of Origins*. London: Routledge & Kegan Paul.

Tronto, J. C. (1993) *Moral Boundaries*. London: Routledge.

Tronto, J. C. (2010) 'Creating caring institutions', *Ethics and Social Welfare*, 4 (2): 158–71.

Tronto, J. C. (2015) 'Democratic caring and global care responsibilities', in M. Barnes, T. Brannelly, L. Ward and N. Ward (eds), *Ethics of Care*. Bristol: Policy Press, pp. 21–31.

Tropp, E. (1974) 'Three problematic concepts: Client, help, worker', *Social Casework*, Jan: 19–30.

Trotter, J. (2000) 'Lesbian and gay issues in social work with young people: Resilience and success through confronting, conforming and escaping', *British Journal of Social Work*, 30, 115–23.

Turn2us (2012) *Benefits Stigma in Britain*. Elizabeth Finn Care/University of Kent. www.turn2us.org.uk/About-Us/Research-and-Insights/Benefits-Stigma-in-Britain.

Turner, A. (2017) 'Social workers transferred to Virgin Care under landmark deal', Community Care, 26 April http://www.communitycare.co.uk/2017/04/26/social-workers-transferred-virgin-care-landmark-deal/?cmpid=NLC|SCSC|SCNEW-2017-0425.

Twigg, J. (2000) 'Carework as a form of bodywork', *Ageing and Society*, 20 (4): 389–411.

Tyler, I. (2008) 'Chav mum chav scum: Class disgust in contemporary Britain', *Feminist Media Studies*, 8 (1): 17–35.

Tyler, I. (2013a) *Revolting Subjects: Social Abjection and Resistance in Neoliberal Britain*. London: Zed Books.

Tyler, I. (2013b) 'The riots of the underclass?: Stigmatisation, mediation and the government of poverty and disadvantage in neoliberal Britain', *Sociological Research Online*, 18 (4). www.socresonline.org.uk/18/4/6.html.

Tyler, I. and Bennett, B. (2010) 'Celebratory chav', *Feminist Media Studies*, 13 (3): 375–93.

Ungar, M. (2008) 'Resilience across cultures', *British Journal of Social Work*, 38: 218–35.

Ungar, M., Liebenberg, L. and Ikeda, J. (2012) 'Young people with complex needs: Designing coordinated interventions to promote resilience across child welfare, juvenile corrections, mental health and education services', *British Journal of Social Work*, advance access from 7 October.

United Nations (1948) The Universal Declaration of Human Rights. www.un.org/en/universal-declaration-human-rights/.

United Nations Development Programme (2005) *Human Development Report*. New York: Oxford University.

US State Department (2015) *Annual Report on Intercountry Adoption*, 31 March. https://travel.state.gov/content/dam/aa/pdfs/fy2014_annual_report.pdf.

Venugopal, R. (2015) 'Neoliberalism as concept', *Economy and Society*, 44 (2): 165–87.

Vickers, M. H. and Kouzmin, A. (2001) '"Resilience" in organizational actors and rearticulating "voice"', *Public Management Review*, 3 (1): 95–119.

Victor, P., Cooper G. and Taylor, D (1994) 'Fear rules in No-Go Britain', *The Independent on Sunday*, 17 April. www.independent.co.uk/news/uk/fear-rules-in-no-go-britain-a-report-on-the-parts-of-the-country-most-people-would-rather-not-think-1370747.html.

Virno, P. (1996) 'Virtuosity and the revolution', in P. Virno and M. Hardt (eds), *Radical Thought in Italy*. Minneapolis, MN: University of Minneapolis, pp. 189–213.

Voloshinov, V. (1973) *Marxism and the Philosophy of Language*. Cambridge, MA: Harvard University Press.

Von Gliszczynski, M. and Leisering, L. (2016) 'Constructing new global models of social security', *Journal of Social Policy*, 45 (2): 325–43.

Wacquant, L. (1998) 'Pierre Bourdieu', in R. Stones (ed.), *Key Sociological Thinkers*. Houndsmill: Palgrave, pp. 215–30.

Wacquant, L. (2007) 'Territorial stigmatization in the age of advanced marginality', *Thesis Eleven*, 91: 66–77.

Wacquant, L. (2008) *Urban Outcasts*. Cambridge: Polity Press.

Wacquant, L. (2009) *Punishing the Poor*. Durham & London: Duke University.

Wacquant, L. (2014) '*Homines in extremis*: What fighting scholars teach us about habitus', *Body & Society*, 20 (2): 3–17.

Walker, J. and Cooper, M. (2011) 'Genealogies of resilience', *Security Dialogue*, 42 (2): 143–60.

Walker, P. (2016) 'Poverty afflicting 7 million people in UK working families, study finds', *The Guardian*, 7 December: 4.

Walker, R. (ed.) (1999) *Ending Child Poverty*. Bristol: Policy Press.

Walsh, C. (2011) 'Youth justice and neuroscience', *British Journal of Criminology*, 51: 21–39.

Ward, H. (ed.) (1995) *Looking After Children*. London: HMSO.

Ward, L. (2015) 'Caring for ourselves? Self-care and neoliberalism', in M. Barnes, T. Brannelly, L. Ward and N. Ward (eds), *Ethics of Care*. Bristol: Policy Press, pp. 45–57.

Ward, N. (2009) 'Social exclusion, social identity and social work', *Social Work Education*, 28 (3): 237–52.

Ward, N. (2015) 'Reciprocity and mutuality: People with learning difficulties as carers', in M. Barnes, T. Brannelly, L. Ward and N. Ward (eds), *Ethics of Care*. Bristol: Policy Press, pp. 165–79.

Wardhaugh, J. and Wilding, P. (1993) 'Towards an explanation of the corruption of care', *Critical Social Policy*, 13 (1): 4–32.

Washington, J. and Paylor, I. (1998) 'Europe, social exclusion and the identity of social work', *European Journal of Social Work*, 1 (3): 327–38.

Wastell, D. and White, S. (2012) 'Blinded by neuroscience', *Families, Relationships and Societies*, 1 (3): 397–414.

Waters, S. (2015) 'Suicide as protest in the French workplace', *Modern & Contemporary France*, 24 (4): 491–510.

Watkins, S. (2016) 'Casting off?', *New Left Review*, 100: 5–33.

Watt, P. (2008) '"Underclass" and "ordinary people" discourses', *Critical Discourse Studies*, 5 (4): 345–57.

Wayman, S. (2016) 'How surrogacy works – or doesn't – in Ireland', *The Irish Times, Family Supplement*, 16 February: 8–10.

Weale, S. (2015) 'Ready for action: Veterans bringing "military ethos" to schools', *The Guardian*, 22 January: 10.

Webb, S. and Webb, B. (1968 [1932]) *Methods of Social Study*. New York: Kelley.

Webster-Stratton, C. and Herbert, M. (1994) *Troubled Families, Problem Children*. Chichester: Wiley.

Weeks, K. (2011) *The Problem of Work*. Durham, NC and London: Duke University.

Welshman, J. (1999) 'The social history of social work: The issue of the "problem family" 1940–70', *British Journal of Social Work*, 29: 457–76.

Welshman, J. (2013) *Underclass*. London: Bloomsbury.

Werner, E. and Smith, R. (1988) *Vulnerable but Invincible*. New York: Adams, Bannister & Cox.

Wiggan, J. (2012) 'Telling stories of 21st century welfare: The UK Coalition government and the neo-liberal discourse of worklessness and dependency', *Critical Social Policy*, 32 (3): 383–405.

Wilcock, S. (2014) 'Official discourses of the Australian "welfare cheat"', *Current Issues in Criminal Justice*, 26 (2): 177–95.

Williams, F. (2005) 'A good-enough life: Developing the grounds for a political ethic of care', *Soundings*, 30: 17–33.

Williams, R. (1973) 'Base and superstructure in Marxist cultural theory', *New Left Review*, Nov–Dec: 3–17.

Williams, R. (1977) *Marxism and Literature*. Oxford: Oxford University Press.

Williams, R. (1979) *Politics and Letters*. London: Verso.

Williams, R. (1983) *Keywords: A Vocabulary of Culture and Society*, 2nd edn. Norton: New York. (First published 1976.)

Williams, R. (2015) 'Gay, bisexual and transgender foster parents and adopters step forward', *Society Guardian: Fostering and Adoption* supplement, 4 March: 4.

Williams, R. and Eagleton, T. (1989) 'The politics of hope: An interview', in T. Eagleton (ed.), *Raymond Williams: Critical Perspectives*. Cambridge: Polity Press, pp. 176–84.

Williams, Z. (2013) 'Skivers v Strivers', *The Guardian*, G2, 10 January: 10–11.

Willis, P. (1977) *Learning to Labour*. Farnborough: Saxon House.

Wilson, T. E. (2016) 'Repairing what's left in social work, or, when knowledge no longer cuts', *British Journal of Social Work*, advance electronic access from 22 September. DOI: 10.1093/bjsw/bcw114.

Wilson, W. J. (1978) *The Declining Significance of Race*. Chicago, IL: University of Chicago.

Wilson, W. J. (1987) *The Truly Disadvantaged: The Inner City, the Underclass and Public Policy*. Chicago, IL: University of Chicago Press.

Wincott, D. (2014) 'Original and limited or elusive and limited? Towards a genealogy of the welfare state in Britain', in D. Béland and K. Petersen (eds), *Analysing Social Policy Concepts and Language*. Bristol: Policy Press, pp. 127–43.

Winslow, S. and Hall, S. (2012) 'A predictably obedient riot', *Cultural Politics*, 8 (3): 465–88.

Winslow, S. and Hall, S. (2013) *Rethinking Social Exclusion*. London: Sage.

Wintour, P. (1997) 'Ghetto busters tackle poverty', *The Observer*, 7 December.

Wintour, P. (2000) What the memo tells us about Tony Blair's style of leadership. www.theguardian.com/politics/2000/jul/18/labour.politicalnews.

Wintour, P. (2008) 'Timely interventions', *Society Guardian*, 30 April: 6.

Wintour, P. (2010) 'Iain Duncan Smith: It's a sin that people fail to take up work', *The Guardian*, 22 November. www.theguardian.com/politics/2010/nov/11/welfare-iain-duncan-smith.

Wintour, P. (2015) 'Harman struggles to hold Labour together over welfare changes', *The Guardian*, 14 July: 4.

Wolkowitz, C. (2002) 'The social relations of body work', *Work, Employment and Society*, 16 (3): 497–510.

Women's Group on Public Welfare (1943) *Our Towns*. London: Oxford University Press.

Wood, C. and Salter, J. (2013) *The Power of Prepaid*. www.demos.co.uk/files/Power_of_prepaid_-_web.pdf?1359476379.

Woodroofe, K. (1962) *From Charity to Social Work*. London: Routledge & Kegan Paul.

Woods, J. (2011) 'Adoption: "We don't need white couples"', *The Daily Telegraph*, 25 January. www.telegraph.co.uk/women/mother-tongue/8279525/Adoption-We-dont-need-white-couples.html.

Wooton, B. (1959) *Social Science and Social Pathology*. London: Allen and Unwin.

Wright, S. (2008) 'Mapping pathways within autonomist Marxism', *Historical Materialism*, 16: 111–40.

Wu, Q., Tsang, B. and Ming, H. (2012) 'Social capital, family support, resilience and educational outcomes of Chinese migrant children', *British Journal of Social Work*, advance access from 15 October.

Wuermli, A., Silbereisen, Lundberg, M., Lamont, M., Behrman, J. R. and Aber, L. (2012) 'A conceptual framework', in M. Lundberg and A. Wuermli (eds), *Child and Youth in Crisis*. Washington, DC: The World Bank, pp. 29–103.

Yaqub, S. (2002) '"Poor children grow into poor adults": Harmful mechanisms or over-deterministic theory', *Journal of International Development*, 14, 1081–93.

Žižek, S. (2004) 'The lesson of Rancière', in J. Rancière, *The Politics of Aesthetics*, London, Continuum, pp. 65–76.

Zuboff, S. (2015) 'Big other: Surveillance capitalism and the prospects of an information civilization', *Journal of Information Technology*, 30: 75–89.

INDEX

'Tab' denotes table